CAMBRIDGE READINGS IN
THE HISTORY OF POLITICAL THOUGHT

Cambridge Readings in the History of Political Thought is an authoritative new series of anthologies intended for students of politics, history and philosophy at all levels from introductory undergraduate upwards. Designed to cover major historical themes such as the Enlightenment, or the impact of the French Revolution, each volume of Cambridge Readings will contain extracts from the principal political texts of the period, together with substantial editorial commentary and apparatus. The textual extracts are extensive but manageable for the beginning student, and well-known canonical writings are complemented by less familiar texts. The texts themselves are generally taken from the acclaimed editions published in the series of Cambridge Texts in the History of Political Thought, with authoritative new translations where necessary. There is an accessible introduction to each volume, and further guidance is offered by biographies of each writer and carefully selected bibliographies. These volumes enable the student to engage in depth with the intellectual context of particular periods, and to encounter at first hand some of the most influential and profound political thinking in the western tradition.

Britannia between Scylla & Charybdis (James Gillray, 1793). In book twelve of Homer's Odyssey (which would have been known to all educated Englishmen), one of the perils encountered by Odysseus returning from the Trojan Wars was having to steer his ship between the tall rock of Scylla, a dreadful monster who plucks sailors from ships which pass too close, and another, Charybdis, who sucks the waters down in a whirlpool from which none can escape. Here, pursued by sharks in the shape of Fox and Sheridan, William Pitt helms the ship 'Constitution' containing an alarmed Britannia between the rock of democracy with the liberty cap on its summit and the whirlpool of arbitrary power (in the shape of an inverted crown) to the distant haven of liberty.

CAMBRIDGE READINGS IN
THE HISTORY OF POLITICAL THOUGHT

The Impact of the French Revolution

Texts from Britain in the 1790s

INTRODUCED AND EDITED BY

IAIN HAMPSHER-MONK

CAMBRIDGE UNIVERSITY PRESS
Cambridge, New York, Melbourne, Madrid, Cape Town, Singapore, São Paulo

Cambridge University Press
The Edinburgh Building, Cambridge CB2 2RU, UK

Published in the United States of America by Cambridge University Press, New York

www.cambridge.org
Information on this title: www.cambridge.org/9780521579117

© in the editorial matter and selection only Cambridge University Press 2005

First published 2005

Printed in the United Kingdom at the University Press, Cambridge

A catalogue record for this book is available from the British Library

ISBN-10 521-57005-0 hardback
ISBN-10 521-57911-2 paperback
ISBN-13 978-0-521-57005-3 hardback
ISBN-13 978-0-521-57911-7 paperback

CONTENTS

Contents

ILLUSTRATIONS

Cartoon prints were an important part of the increasingly popular political culture of the later eighteenth century. The cartoons reproduced here have been chosen to show how some of the more abstract ideas of political theorists, and the theorists themselves, were represented visually to contemporary audiences.

ACKNOWLEDGEMENTS

I should like to acknowledge the assistance of the British Academy and Leverhulme Trust for a senior research fellowship, a part of which was devoted to finishing this project. Over the years I have greatly benefited from conversations on the 1790s with Greg Claeys, the late John Dinwiddy, Gunther Lottes, Rhonda Lovell, John Hope Mason, John Morrow, Frank O'Gorman, Mark Philp, John Pocock, Fred Rosen and Bill Stafford. My thanks go to all of these, and to students who took 'Pigs, Porcupines and Poets'. Special thanks to Robert Lamb for discussions on this and other subjects and help in the preparation of the typescript and index. Huge thanks to my copy-editor, Sue Dickinson, to Alison Powell and her production team for their expertise and patience, and to Richard Fisher for encouragement (and for indulging me with the illustrations).

This book is dedicated to my students, past, present and not yet signed up.

INTRODUCTION

The French Revolution as the touchstone of modernity

The French Revolution has been regarded by subsequent generations as the emergence of the modern political world. It comprised a paradigm shift that irrevocably changed the way in which we think about, speak of and therefore conduct our politics. Notwithstanding attempts to find the roots of the revolution in the *ancien régime*, and to trace continuities across the revolutionary period,[1] conceptions of political legitimacy, human agency, historical process and even time itself were fundamentally restructured by this cataclysmic event.

Dramatic evidence of this was the fate of the historiography of Ancient Rome. Ever since antiquity, the rise and fall of Ancient Rome was the key historical phenomenon to be understood if political processes were ever to be brought within human understanding. Numerous writers, famously Machiavelli, Montesquieu and, most recently, Edward Gibbon, had devoted major works to the subject.[2] After the French Revolution, the rise and fall of Rome became an essentially antiquarian study. The French Revolution, whether good or bad, repeatable or unique, successful or disastrous, completed or not, a product of ideology or of essentially material forces, becomes the problematic political event and the focus of political enquiry and understanding. For Burke and Hegel; James and John Stuart Mill; Constant;

---

[1] Such attempts date from as early as Alexis de Tocqueville's *Ancient Regime and the French Revolution* (1856). Marxist historiography tended to emphasise discontinuities, but recent historiography has been re-exploring these issues. See the first two essays in Dale van Kley (ed.), *The French Idea of Freedom*, (Stanford: Stanford University Press, 1994): David B. Bien, 'Old Regime Origins of Democratic Liberty', in Dale van Kley (ed.), *The French Idea of Freedom: The Old Regime and the Declaration of Rights of 1789* (Stanford: Stanford University Press, 1994), pp. 23–71. Dale van Kley, 'Origins of an Anti-Historical Declaration', in van Kley (ed.), *The French Idea of Freedom*, pp. 72–113.

[2] For an overview of the historiography of the demise of the Roman Empire see J. G. A. Pocock, *Barbarism and Religion*, 3 vols. (Cambridge: Cambridge University Press, 1999–2003), vol. III: *The First Decline and Fall* (2003). Pocock identifies and discusses almost forty titles preceding the first volume of Gibbon's *Decline and Fall* (1776).

Tocqueville and the emerging science of sociology; Guizot and a whole line of eminent French historians; Karl Marx and his followers; and not excluding modern political scientists; an understanding of the Revolution was the key to understanding the processes and conditions of modern republican and nationalist politics and modern political action which the Revolution itself had ushered in. Nor was its importance confined to commentators and analysts. An understanding of class politics, the role of secular ideology and of revolutionary transformation drawn from the French Revolution inspired and made possible the nineteenth-century nationalist revolutions, the Russian Revolution, its twentieth-century communist and post-colonial imitators, and the whole world-wide communist experiment of the twentieth century.

The Revolution did not exert this influence through establishing any agreed truths about politics: on the contrary, it generated – and continues to generate – heated opposition and disagreement. But it did construct a field of controversy and placed at centre-stage certain issues and claims that have become the core of political argument. Some have become so much part of modern political thinking that we are hardly aware of them. We take them, almost unexamined, to be constitutive and irrefutable parts of political reality. One example is the central revolutionary claim that individuals possess natural rights which, when exercised collectively, give them the right – and the capacity – to shape their political world to their wills without regard to inherited institutions. Such beliefs inspired humans to free themselves from the injustices of the *ancien régime* but they contributed to a modern belief that social processes were more tractable than has in fact proved to be the case. Arguably too, such beliefs, together with the economic forces of modern markets, have fuelled processes hugely destructive of traditional societies. For good or ill the shadow of the Revolution has fallen heavily across the face of world politics.

In Britain this first modern revolution provoked the biggest public debate on political principles since the Civil War, a hundred and fifty years earlier. The unpacking of the implications of the languages of politics was crammed into a period of barely a decade, from the winter following the Revolution until 1799 when political debate and association was proscribed by law.[3] These texts and prints are chosen to illustrate

[3] A series of acts in the summer of 1799 suspended *Habeas Corpus*, proscribed the London Corresponding Society and others by name and made a 'combination' (i.e. association for political or economic purposes) illegal. Public meetings and discussion of politics had already been rendered illegal by the Treasonable and Seditious Practices, and Unlawful Assemblies Acts of 1795.

something of the range of responses. The rest of this introduction sets out the context from within which writers responded and indicates some features of these political languages.

France, America, England – Different Revolutions?

Between 1789 and the present, most European nations and many others underwent 'revolutions' modelled to some degree on that of the French. The significant feature of these revolutions was the attempted destruction of pre-existing political orders in which political authority was grounded; usually in a mixture of custom, heredity and in some cases theological endorsement, most obviously combined in the institution of Monarchy but including also the authority derived from an aristocratic or sometimes priestly elite.[4] This was replaced by a notion of political authority and legitimacy deriving from the will of a 'people' considered (at least rhetorically) as undifferentiated in status; claimed indeed to derive ultimately (if for a long time only in principle) from the supposed consent of each adult individual.[5] Such a political order we have come to call a democratic republic, or, where – as often in Europe – it was combined with a residual monarchical element, a constitutional monarchy. The United States, Britain and its 'white' settler colonies were the only major exceptions to this process.

The United States of America, of course, was also born from a revolution – that of 1776 – involving a war of independence from Britain, closely followed in 1787 by the creation of a federal republican constitution. Nevertheless important differences distinguish the American Revolution from the French and its imitators.[6] First the

---

[4] All early modern European monarchies and republics claimed a mythical 'Ancient Constitution' grounding their institutions. Beyond Europe many of these revolutionary movements were directed at colonial rule. But, with few exceptions, they persisted in the undermining of traditional forms of authority begun under the ruling powers.

[5] Of course these universalist proclamations almost automatically presupposed the exclusion of women, Jews, blacks and, for most politicians, the poor, leading one Jewish writer to wryly observe that in order to enjoy the proclaimed rights of humankind it was necessary to be the owner of a white foreskin! However, the universalism of these claims enabled those groups to demand – as most of them eventually did – their political inclusion.

[6] This, like almost all statements about the Revolution, is a contested claim with political overtones. Liberal historians, sympathetic to the Revolution (like contemporaries at the time), stressed its similarities to the American.

American Revolution was begun, and for long fought, as a claim by Englishmen to *traditional* English rights. 'No taxation without representation' was as much the catch-phrase of English colonists in America as of the English Parliamentarians against King Charles – from whom, along with their eighteenth-century 'commonwealthsmen' descendants, Americans had drawn inspiration.[7] Secondly the American 'revolutionary moment' – the Declaration of Independence – crucially involved a pre-existing, politically organised society (actually a group of such societies) *separating* from an imperial power. Moreover, the Americans constituted their state not on the basis of the individual, but on the basis of a federal union of already existing states. The definition of citizenship had already been defined independently by each state and they would continue to do this separately for some time. Despite the Declaration of Independence's claim to the self-evidence of human equality, no deductions were drawn from this about the status of individuals within the states. The Declaration was an act performed on a third party – Britain – by the politically constituted 'United Colonies'. Both the Articles of Confederation (1776), operating immediately following independence, and the American Constitution (1787) guaranteed to each colony the various customs, rights and laws there established. Neither the American Revolution nor the Constitution (and contrary to the beliefs of most Americans) *enshrined or claimed to regulate the political rights of individuals* within the separate states as the basis of its authority.[8] The franchise – then typically reserved to white male property-holders – remained essentially a state concern. Not until the middle of the nineteenth century did the United States seek to impose on individual states the full political implications of 'natural equality' and then it took a civil war to do it.

The American Revolution provoked a political reform debate in Britain, but it was a debate that, for the most part, focused on legislative, parliamentary and taxation reform.[9] Importantly it stimulated an emerging national political culture amongst what was then called the 'middling sort of people' – and it generated the beginnings of free-standing constituency-based and national political educational associations,

[7] The classic (and again disputed) case is Bernard Bailyn, *The Ideological Origins of the American Revolution* (Cambridge, Mass.: Harvard University Press, 1967).
[8] Art. I, 4 and Art. II, 1 specifically reserves these powers to the several state legislatures, requiring only that state constitutions be of 'republican form' (Art. IV 4), a phrase which at the time did not have specific implications for the extent of the franchise.
[9] Ian R. Christie, *Wilkes, Wyville and Reform: The Parliamentary Reform Movement in British Politics, 1760–1785* (London: Macmillan, 1962), and for a selection of texts see M. Beloff, *The Debate on the American Revolution 1761–1783* (London: Nicholas Kaye, 1960).

such as the Society for Constitutional Information. Some of these survived to the 1790s, becoming important in the reaction to the French Revolution.[10]

The French Revolution embodied drastically different constitutional principles to the American. It involved not the separation of already-constituted political societies from a geographically distant, if culturally proximate authority but a single *society seeking to reconstitute itself* on the basis of new norms and principles. The man who articulated this most clearly and did so much to bring the revolution about was the Abbé Sieyes (1748–1836). Trained as a priest, and a representative of the Clergy in the pre-revolutionary provincial government, Sieyes burst into print – and history – in the preparations for the meeting of the Estates General, the French Ancient Regime's equivalent of Parliament.

The Estates General had not met since 1614, the French Monarchy having achieved for a while what the Stuarts in England had failed to do, namely to rule and raise revenue without recourse to a parliament. But by 1786, France was in a deep and continuing fiscal crisis: interest payments on debt consumed almost half the annual revenue of the government. Already by 1786 Calonne, controller of the Royal Finances, told Louis XVI that piece-meal reform was impossible: 'The disparity, the dis-accord, the incoherence of the different parts of the body of the monarchy is the principle of the constitutional vices which enervate its strength and hamper all its organisation; . . . one cannot destroy any one of them without attacking them all in the principle which has produced and perpetuates them.'[11] In order to generate public confidence in the regime's credit the King had had to open the finances to inspection, and ultimately to convene the Estates General.

The 'Estates General' were representatives of the three legal orders of politically active Frenchmen – the Aristocracy, the Clergy and the property-owning Commoners – the last of which was known as 'Third Estate'. Inactive since 1614, even the rules of procedure had been forgotten, and so aware were participants of the impact of the franchise, number of seats, orders of voting, and so on that there was from the start intense debate about such matters.[12] Into this debate the Abbé Sieyes inserted his famous pamphlet *What is the third Estate?*

---

[10] Eugene C. Black. *The Association, British Extraparliamentary Political Organisation 1769–1793* (Cambridge, Mass.: Harvard University Press, 1963).

[11] Calonne, *Summary of a Plan for the Improvement of the Finances*, quoted in William Doyle, *Origins of the French Revolution* (Oxford: Oxford University Press, 1988), p. 52.

[12] Condorcet's reflections on the implications of different voting procedures are the source of much of that part of modern political science. Burke himself refers to the issue of Estates voting in *Reflections*, siding with those who wished to keep the integrity of the three estates voting separately

Sieyes – who had an ear for what we would now call the sound-bite – gave a notorious answer to this question. In contrast to the two other orders – the nobility and the priesthood – which, he claimed, were guardians of their own corporate privilege, the Third Estate had 'no corporate interest to defend . . . it demands nothing less than to make the totality of citizens a *single* social body'.[13] It was, he claimed, not one order amongst others, but itself, alone, 'the nation': it was 'everything'. Sieyes's radical claim was that all other institutions and corporations of the *ancien régime* were indefensible privileges and so must be done away with. Moreover, if – as seemed vital – a new constitution were to be constructed, it would have to be done by some pre-political entity, for all existing political entities were partial – were selfishly constituted. For Sieyes that entity was 'the nation'. The nation was made up of *natural* individuals who logically preceded any conventional distinctions (such as status, education, profession, etc.) for these could only arise from within political associations. Being pre-social and undifferentiated these individuals must be equal. In a distinctly Rousseauvian fashion Sieyes saw the nation as a union of equal individuals bound to the common will of the whole as expressed by their majority. Only such an entity could exercise constitutive power, i.e. the power of constituting, or setting up, the institutions comprising a state – a political and social order. Moreover the resulting constitutional order could not itself constrain the nation that had created it. The nation's will was, he thought, 'free and independent of civil forms . . . its will is always the supreme law' and in this sense 'a nation never leaves the state of nature'.[14] It followed from Sieyes's logic that the Third Estate – which lacked the privileged corporate status of the nobility or the clergy – composed the representatives of the nation, who alone were competent to undertake the work of constitution-making. Hence his epochal claim that the Third Estate should either declare itself a constituent assembly empowered to create a new constitution in the name of the nation or (preferably) get the nation to create an assembly with this competence. In a momentous vote on 17 June 1789 the Third Estate declared itself a 'National Assembly' and the work of constructing the new constitution began. Astonished Britons looked across the channel and began to consider the implications.

(p. 72; not fully included in this selection). These controversies may have informed his observation that once we lose the conventions of our political institutions we have no way even of deciding how to agree collectively on a course of action, since even majority decision-making is a convention.

[13] Abbé Sieyes, *Déliberations . . . prendre dans les assemblées* (1789), cited in Murray Forsyth, *Reason and Revolution: The Political Thought of the Abbé Sieyes* (Leicester: Leicester University Press, 1987) See *ibid.*, p. 1 for his persuasive reasons for using the unaccented form of the name.

[14] Sieyes, *What is the Third Estate?*, cited in Forsyth, *Sieyes*, p. 78.

The 'Ancient Regime' in Britain

Britain itself had undergone two political upheavals in the seventeenth century, each of which are sometimes called 'revolutions'. The first – the Civil War between Parliament and the King (1642–9) – had indeed overthrown existing political forms – abolishing the Monarchy, the Lords and the established Church – and it had generated some very radical ideas and theories about the rights of individuals and the limitations of institutional power – of both the Monarchy and Parliament.[15] Many of these theoretical positions were to re-emerge in the 1790s. But the seventeenth-century Commonwealth failed to produce a lasting political constitution, revealing how difficult early modern societies found it to escape the power of traditional forms of rule. Exhausted by civil war, constitutional experimentation and instability, the welcome restoration of the Monarchy, Lords and traditional institutions had left many Englishmen with a profound fear of civil unrest.[16] Despite this, fears of a Catholic and autocratic monarch seeking to rule and impose taxation without parliamentary consent led to a second political upheaval in 1688–9, the so-called Glorious Revolution. This was effectively an aristocratic Protestant coup against a would-be absolutist Catholic monarch – James II. The great eighteenth-century political groupings, Whigs and Tories, derive ultimately from their support or rejection of the principle of resistance articulated at this time. The Glorious Revolution was seen by some as re-establishing the principle of co-ordination, or England's 'Balanced Constitution' – a balance of King, Lords and Commons in which no one branch could act unilaterally without the co-operation of the others. The nation here was identified with its corporate orders not, as did Sieyes, with its undifferentiated individuals. Another, more radical interpretation of the event, enshrined in the second of Locke's *Two Treatises of Government* (1690), could be claimed to show the people's right to intervene to determine to whom the powers of government should be entrusted.[17] Even though this left open to dispute the identity of 'the people', the centrality of this 'right of resistance' was an ambiguous legacy on which to build a regime, and an

[15] For a good selection of such texts see the anthology by David Wootton, *Divine Right and Democracy* (Harmondsworth: Penguin Books, 1986).

[16] This was not unjustifiable. In proportionate terms The Civil War was one of the most destructive in which Britain has ever been involved.

[17] Locke's political theory was notoriously ambiguous in the degree of its radicalism. Although a whig 'hero' some of his views licensed conclusions far more radical and disturbing than respectable whigs were willing to countenance. See Richard Ashcraft, *Revolutionary Politics and John Locke's Two Treatises of Government* (Princeton: Princeton University Press, 1986).

increasingly embarrassing one through which the Whigs were forced to protest their loyalty to the monarch. These issues were played out in the famous trial of the High Tory priest, Dr Sacheverell, where the Whigs gave a very conservative account of the ideological significance of 1688.[18] (See Burke, *Appeal*, pp. 183–4.)

Britain had maintained a monarchy whilst curbing its power, and had made constitutional liberty a principle of its political order. As Montesquieu had famously put it, England was a 'republic disguised as a monarchy',[19] whilst in virtually the whole of the rest of Europe royal power was being increased and concentrated.[20]

Yet, though anomalous, Britain was regarded by significant observers – including Montesquieu before, and Hegel after the French Revolution – as something of a model to be emulated, combining the liberty associated with a republic and the stability associated with monarchy. Secondly, although this is clear to historians, it is less often noted by historians of political thought, although the *monarch's* powers were constitutionally limited, that the emergent British *state* was more powerful and effective than any other at the time.[21] A crucial feature of any state's power is its capacity to wage war (as Britain and France did – often mutually – throughout much of the eighteenth century): military power was dependent on the state's ability to raise the necessary manpower and material resources through taxation. Through the early development of modern fiscal institutions the British state succeeded in raising money through un-coerced borrowing from its citizens, establishing a national debt, the security of which was the lenders' confidence in its ability to extract taxation to pay interest and, perhaps ultimately, the principal.[22] This confidence in turn was grounded in the state's political stability – which, as political commentators increasingly recognised, was based on 'public opinion'. 'Credit' was thus at once a feature of

[18] See Geoffrey Holmes, *The Trial of Dr Sacheverell* (London: Methuen, 1973); transcript of the trial, *Sources of English Constitutional History*, http://www.constitution.org/sech/sech_124.html. The Sacheverell Trial records are used by Burke in his *Appeal . . .* in an attempt to show that the 'Old' whigs of the Revolution generation would not have supported those whigs of his generation, such as Charles James Fox, Lord Richmond and others who flirted with radicalism.

[19] Charles de Secondat, Baron de Montesquieu, *The Spirit of the Laws*, bk 5, §19.

[20] The other important exceptions were the federal republican cultures of the Netherlands and Switzerland, although the Netherlands too, experienced a relative concentration of the power of the sovereign during the eighteenth century.

[21] On the power of the state see John Brewer, *The Sinews of Power – War Money and the English State 1688–1783* (London: Unwin, 1985). From the Union of the (English and Scottish) Crowns in 1707, it becomes legitimate to talk about Britain as a political entity.

[22] See P. G. M. Dickson, *The Financial Revolution in England . . . 1688–1756* (London: Macmillan, 1967), and Peter Mathias and Patrick O'Brien, 'Taxation in England and France 1715–1810 . . .' *Journal of European Economic History* 5 (1976), 601–50.

fiscal and of political legitimacy, and Britain enjoyed both because decision-makers in Parliament, having property of their own to protect, had personal interests in maintaining both the security of property-rights and the solvency and political stability of the regime. Whilst Britain had managed to sustain a symmetry between fiscal confidence and political support, France by contrast was caught in a vicious spiral in which it used up political credit to support its finances, endangering both in the process.

Despite Britain's advantage, this symmetry was always recognised to be precarious.[23] There were huge ideological battles over the growing role of the state and over the tensions between the landed gentry whose land tax originally paid the interest on the national debt, the poorer consumers who paid excise tax on certain items and the 'monied men' who received as interest the taxes of the others but risked their capital on the stability of the regime. But the British state was able to raise money far more readily and at a lower rate of interest than could the French monarch. British 'liberty' in all three senses of the independence of the state from foreign control, the representation of the propertied elite in the state's decision-making and (and as a result) the guarantees that the state would respect individuals' property rights, paradoxically resulted in a state that was economically stronger than one claiming 'absolute' powers – and for that very reason. An absolute monarch might at any time default on his own debts, or impose tax burdens which rendered others liable to do so – the former a policy under active consideration by Louis from early on in the crisis. A constitutionally limited, parliamentary-based regime would not do this as long as those with the power to default were broadly the same as those who would suffer from doing so.[24]

It is only the last generation of scholars that has recovered credit as a major context for an understanding of the French Revolution.[25] Yet it was the burden of debt and the collapse of credit that forced the calling of the Estates General and structured the

[23] See David Hume's essay 'Of Public Credit', and J. G. A. Pocock, 'Hume on the American Revolution, Dying Thoughts of a North Briton', in Pocock (ed.), *Virtue Commerce and History* (Cambridge University Press, 1985).

[24] For a brilliant synoptic outline of the case see the essay by David D. Bien, 'Old Regime Origins of Democratic Liberty', in Dale van Kley (ed.), *The French Idea of Freedom: The Old Regime and the Declaration of Rights of 1789* (Stanford: Stanford University Press, 1994).

[25] Florin Aftalion, *The French Revolution: An Economic Interpretation* (Cambridge: Cambridge University Press, 1990) and Michael Sonenscher, 'Republicanism, State Finances and the Emergence of Commercial Society in Eighteenth-Century France', in Martin van Gelderen and Quentin Skinner (eds.), *Republicanism: A Shared European Heritage*, 2 vols. (Cambridge: Cambridge University Press, 2002), vol. II.

whole of the early revolutionary debate in France. Reading Burke's *Reflections* in the light of this shows how his thinking about political stability is influenced either by explicitly financial issues or by political issues relating to the likely creditworthiness of the resulting regime.

The account given above suggests the British eighteenth-century constitution, in contrast to the French, was a successfully modernising one, and that the Revolution was an attempt to overcome a 'modernisation deficit'. Early on some British supporters indeed saw it in that way – in fact there are elements of this in James Mackintosh's analysis (see pp. 169–70). However, more characteristic of the Radicals was the view that the French Revolution, far from seeking to imitate Britain's constitution, sought to initiate a new and different political order which Britain should copy. For radicals of the day then, both pre-revolutionary France *and* contemporary Britain fell on the far side of the line dividing the reformed present from what increasingly came to be regarded as 'Feudal' and 'Gothic'. Burke's defence of the existing 'customary' constitution and the radicals' denunciation of it as Feudal mutually assisted in the emergence of a peculiar political Englishness in which economic and institutional modernity was combined with an ideological defence which, in its identification with the past, was distinctly un-modern.[26]

Radicals too were caught between defending an idealised economic simplicity and trying to think through the ways in which political and economic modernisation could be bought at a price which bore less heavily on the poor. The loss of smallholders' access to land owing to enclosure and increasingly commercial farming increased the numbers of urban landless labourers, and, in times of dearth such as the winter of 1795, fears of starvation. Some (Spence, p. 278) responded by claiming Lockean natural rights to the land as subsistence farmers and proposing similarly simplistic political institutions. These were essentially nostalgic models that were nevertheless to persist for some time.[27] Others such as Thelwall (see pp. 340–1), recognising the potential benefits of the sophisticated exchange economy, sought to apply such theories to justify redistributive rights *within*, rather than in a way destructive of, the modern economy. These moral, social and economic oppositions were argued out in terms of a polarity between 'Feudal' and 'natural' which often

---

[26] The characterisation of pre-1832 political orthodoxy as an *ideological* ancient regime is most famously argued by J. C. D. Clark, *English Society 1688–1832* (Cambridge: Cambridge University Press, 1985).
[27] M. Chase, *The People's Farm: English Agrarian Radicalism 1775–1840* (Oxford: Oxford University Press, 1988).

cuts across modern categories of analysis and of the temporal processes in which they are now thought to be embedded, both of which were in process of being forged at the time.

The Language of British Reform

As Linda Colley has emphasised, British identity was forged in the eighteenth century very much around Protestantism and around specific (English) libert*ies* (rather than an abstract liberty), both of which were characteristically opposed to the arbitrary powers of absolute continental monarchs whose absolutism was believed to be intimately related to their Catholicism.[28] Limited, Protestant, government guaranteed the liberties and rights – particularly of property – which stimulated trade and the economy. Even modestly well-off Englishmen, it was claimed, notoriously ate better – symbolically of beef – than their impoverished neighbours.[29]

The liberties and prosperity that Englishmen enjoyed were believed to derive from their famous mixed constitution. King, Lords and Commons formed three independent powers that could nevertheless only act in concert. Thus the Commons was able to prevent the monarchy from becoming arbitrary and the King and Lords to prevent the popular part of the constitution from descending into anarchy (Plate 5) thus preserving the liberties of the subject. To guarantee this happy state of affairs each constitutional power had to be independent of the other. Independence was seen as a pervasive political virtue, applicable to both individuals and corporate elements of the constitution, its absence – dependence – leading to or identified with corruption. Corruption too was thus both a systemic property – of constitutions in decline – and a personal quality of individuals who, through personal circumstance or disposition, lacked what was necessary for political virtue. Burke and the Radicals disputed the identity, nature and location of independence – and of the virtue it was supposed to foster – in the debate on France. Maintaining the independence of the Commons was a persistent preoccupation, and the Crown – whether the Monarch personally or, as later, his administration – was persistently seen as a threat to such independence. 'Corruption' in eighteenth-century British politics commonly

[28] Linda Colley, *Britons: Forging the Nation, 1701–1837* (New Haven, Conn.: Yale University Press, 1992).
[29] Ben Rogers, *Beef and Liberty: Roast Beef, John Bull and the English Nation* (London: Vintage, 2003).

referred to attempts to control or influence the independence of MPs or their constituents, in the former case usually through the strategic location of government
expenditure and placing of contracts – itself derived from taxation. The ultimate
guarantee of the independence of the House was the independence of its MPs and in
turn of the electors – each of whose independence was guaranteed by their ownership
of property. How large this property had to be to guarantee independence became
increasingly a subject of debate. In the eighteenth century the franchise in the County
seats required ownership of property to the value of forty shillings; in the Borough
seats it varied according to the Royal Charter which incorporated the Borough. Some
were closed, self-perpetuating elites of a few wealthy aldermen; at the other extreme
were the 'potwalloper' boroughs whose charters gave the vote to all with their own
hearth – or 'pot'.[30]

Although the 'true' Whigs liked to think of themselves as ideological descendants
of the parliamentarians who had successfully ejected James II for his Catholic and
autocratic pretensions, it was Robert Walpole's modernising Whigs after the fall of
the Tories in the early eighteenth century who had developed the art of 'managing'
the House of Commons so as to generate majorities consistently enough to be able
to conduct coherent policy. The identification of this as 'corruption' was essentially
part of Tory ideology, although any group finding themselves in opposition invariably
used such arguments.[31]

Radical critics of the 'corruption' of the government could, in this sense, be seen,
ideologically speaking, as Tories.[32] Concerned at the increase in taxation and at what
they saw as the pliability of parliaments, they typically argued for increasing parliamentary independence through more stringent controls on government spending
and (here departing from traditional, though not all, Toryism) increasing the size of
the electorate to make bribery or influence prohibitively expensive. Although such
arguments might be used alongside radical claims about voting being a fundamental, or even natural, universal (male) right, they were conceptually quite distinct in
seeing the extent of the franchise as a matter not of individual right, but as instrumental in 'restoring' the independence of Parliament and hence the balance of the

---

[30] Eighteenth-century franchises varied enormously. For a survey see John Brooke, *The House of
Commons 1754–1790* (Oxford: Oxford University Press, 1964), part 1, 'The Constituencies'.
[31] Burke's famous attempt in his *Thoughts on the cause of the Present Discontents* (1770) and
elsewhere to defend the idea of a 'party' as a loyal opposition involved, as did other of his writings,
an attempt to move out of this rather sterile polarity.
[32] As evidenced by the political careers of a number of them. Thelwall and Cobbett both started
out as Tory critics of Whigs.

constitution.[33] During the course of the French Revolution radicals' concerns about the cause of poverty moved from a concern with the corrupt political appropriation of public revenues ('Old Corruption') to a perception that the emergent economic relations themselves might engender, or at least inhibit the alleviation of poverty (Godwin and Thelwall, pp. 249–50 and 338–9).

This notion of reform as 'restoration' is also ideologically important. Unlike today, the eighteenth century attached no great value to political innovation: rather the presumption was quite the other way. Reform was almost always presented as (and mostly believed to be) an attempt to *restore* a constitution which had become disordered or corrupted to an earlier state of integrity. The most fanciful versions of this identified the perfection of the constitution in its Anglo-Saxon origins. Historically naive radical belief held that this constitution had involved an elective kingship, or at least the endorsement by acclamation of monarchs at their succession, and the close involvement of the 'Wittemagote' or popular assembly in all major political decision-making. A few – notoriously the indefatigable reformer Major Cartwright – insisted that this assembly had been elected annually by manhood suffrage and that restoring this right was essential to the full recovery of the ancient constitution. Many believed that various tyrants – William the Conqueror or Charles I – had imposed a 'yoke' of slavery on the free constitution, or that corruptors – such as James II or the Whig 'managers' of the Commons – had obscured its original purity. The constitution thus required some 'reformation' to restore it.[34] Like the aspiration to 'independence', the idea of the free ancient Anglo-Saxon constitution and the Norman or other 'yokes' was politically ambiguous. Inasmuch as it was essentially backward-looking it might now be called conservative, yet it was used by radicals to criticise the existing order and yet again was to be adapted by conservatives to defend it.[35] James Cheetham, an English émigré to America, criticised Paine because he 'ignorantly refers to the Norman Conquest [as the basis of the constitution], he either knows nothing of the Saxon Principles which form the basis of it . . . or in

---

[33] Most eighteenth-century radicals regarded universal manhood suffrage as something to be considered on its merits, in terms of its likelihood of delivering good government. Only a few of these claimed that it was derivable from a universal natural right, and amongst these even fewer claimed it was irresistibly so derived. One of the most famous of these was Major John Cartwright. See John Osborne, *John Cartwright* (Cambridge: Cambridge University Press, 1972).

[34] A good start and overview is ch. 1 of Glen Burgess's, *The Politics of the Ancient Constitution* (London: Macmillan, 1992).

[35] Janice Lee, 'Political antiquarianism unmasked, the conservative attack on the Ancient Constitution', *Institute of Historical Research Bulletin* 60 (November 1982), 166–79.

order to excite the people to tumult and devote the government to subversion, he chose falsely to represent it as one of conquest only'.[36] The appeal to the past, the 'predisposition to antiquity' as Burke called it, was a deeply embedded and widespread feature of the political culture. The Glorious Revolution of 1688 for example was a revolution, not in the yet-to-be-invented sense of being a thorough-going innovative secular transformation, but in the then-established, and more literal sense of being a re-volution, a turning back of the inevitable processes of corruption which affect all human contrivances.[37] Even Paine, who rejected the authority of 1688 or any past constitutional settlement, nevertheless used the past – in the sense of the beginning of society – as a source of legitimacy for the present. In a society so drenched in history it was difficult for natural rights not to mean *aboriginal* rights, and for those claiming them to avoid a return to an economic or constitutional past. One of the effects of the French Revolution would be to relocate the temporal source of our values from the past to something that had yet to be achieved in the future.[38] 'Radical' could then take on its modern meaning of pursuing progressive but fundamental change, and gradually lose its original and etymological meaning of returning to the root. Before this could happen the past had to be thoroughly delegitimised, and replaced by abstract principles.

Something which prepared the way for this was a critical unpicking of the historical process by which the constitution had come into existence. Burke, strangely close to the radical William Blake in his unwillingness to analyse, nevertheless recognised that modern institutions may rely on older (chivalric) values in order to function properly. This opened up a wide debate about the status and value of chivalry and 'Gothic' institutions – of which the mixed constitution was clearly one example. The analysis and de-mystification of these much lauded historical survivals were crucial radical ploys 3 (Wollstonecraft, Paine, Thelwall).

Political Theology and Religious Dissent

A certain way of thinking, however, had managed to escape the pervasive historicity in which both defenders and critics of the existing constitution were implicated. This is

---

[36] James Cheetham, *Life of Thomas Paine* (New York, 1808), p. 140.
[37] Reinhart Koselleck, 'Historical Criteria of the Modern Concept of Revolution', in *Futures Past: On the Semantics of Historical Time*, trans. Keith Tribe (Cambridge, Mass.: MIT Press, 1985).
[38] *Ibid.*

the thought most characteristic of rational dissent and it brings us to a further feature of the British political thinking which was challenged by the French Revolution, and that is the role accorded to religion. Let us start with Rational Dissent before returning to the broader themes of religion, the Church and the State.

Dissenters were defined as those who, for whatever reason, refused communion with the Anglican Church.[39] Eighteenth-century England was a confessional state in the sense that being prepared to take Anglican communion was a condition of full civil membership. Both Catholics and Protestant dissenters were thus politically disfranchised – they could not legally hold even relatively minor offices, nor could they vote, attend university or be admitted to a profession. However, this condition was not always rigorously imposed, nor did all dissent preclude Anglican communication. Doctrinally, dissenters were a very mixed bunch – some dissented on grounds of church organisation, rejecting the authority of bishops, or the subordination of the Church to the monarch for example, some rejected the Anglican forms of worship, rejecting infant baptism and disliking the imposition of the Anglican prayer-book. Where dissent was not based on disagreement about central matters of faith, dissenters sometimes felt able to take Anglican communion without contravening their religious principles, thus qualifying themselves for political office. But the role of the state in tempting individuals to compromise their belief for earthly gain was resented by many. Moreover such 'occasional conformity' was not possible for those who dissented from the Anglican Church on grounds of doctrine, holding a different view about the nature of God – or more usually the status of Christ – and the central tenets of belief, since these were affirmed during the communion service.[40]

The most politically influential element of dissent at this time were those, such as Richard Price, Joseph Priestley and William Godwin (whilst he remained a believer), who rejected trinitarianism – the belief, common to Catholic and Anglican Churches, that the Godhead is three beings in one: Father, Son and Holy Spirit. Philosophical difficulties surrounding the convincing articulation of this belief which, in England, go back at least as far as John Locke and Sir Isaac Newton, had led rational dissenters to abandon it and they were joined in the 1770s by exiles from Anglicanism. These 'Unitarians' rejected trinitarianism as irrational, and rejected too, the related idea

[39] Another important group of non-communicants were the Catholics, but 'Dissent' generally referred to Protestant non-conformists.
[40] An excellent account of the varieties and development of dissent is to be found in M. Watts, *The Dissenters, from the Reformation to the French Revolution* (Oxford: Oxford University Press, 1978).

that Christ existed eternally. In the minds of some (almost certainly Burke included) unitarianism, in denying the co-substantiality of God and Christ, denied Christ's divinity and was thus indistinguishable from the Deism of earlier in the century, or of the pantheism or irreligion so prevalent in France. A number of rational dissenters indeed seem to have become deists of a kind or to have lost their faith altogether, William Godwin – for whom political and moral authority derives entirely from the individual – being a prime example (see pp. 220–1).

Two social and political issues hinged on these theological differences[41]: first the existence or otherwise of original sin, and secondly the role of religion in re-enforcing morality. As suggested at the start, a major feature of modern politics is to ascribe to individuals the capacity to shape their political world. This in turn presupposes an ability to know what is politically right and wrong. For believers in original sin, human beings' capacities for moral knowing were irrevocably damaged by the Fall, and attempts to exercise such choice without the guidance of institutions such as the Church liable to disaster. Secondly, for virtually all Christians except the most radical rationalists, morality required a sanction in order for people to be motivated to adhere to it. That motivation was provided by the fear of divine punishment – Hell Fire. Consequently, any system of moral thought which attempted to identify the content of morality and give a convincing account of the motivation to adhere to it (and these were distinct enterprises) without God was bound to fail. God had told us *what morality was* through His word, and *provided a motive to obey it* through His promise of eternal reward and punishment (Burke, *Reflections*, p. 85) Attempts to show that the standards of morality could be derived from and motivated by the human mind – in which rational dissenters were at the forefront – were thus seen as misguided at best and at worst subversive and a front for, or indistinguishable from, atheism.

Theology also had more direct political implications. For orthodox monarchists, one of the sources of the authority of the state was the claim that the monarch was 'God's anointed'. This was not just a poetic phrase. Certain institutions lent historical

---

[41] There is an excellent overview of politico-theological issues in J. C. D. Clark, *English Society 1660–1832, Religion, Ideology and Politics during the Ancient Regime* (Cambridge: Cambridge University Press, 2000). For an extremely analytical presentation see A. M. C. Waterman, 'The Nexus between Theology and Political Doctrine in Church and Dissent', in Knud Haakonssen (ed.), *Enlightenment and Religion: Rational Dissent in Eighteenth-Century Britain* (Cambridge: Cambridge University Press, 1996).

authenticity to the claim: the monarch was anointed by the archbishop at his coronation. For Anglicans it was important that the archbishop himself – even though appointed by the monarch – was consecrated by a bishop, and bishops claimed to have been consecrated in a continuous line back to Christ's entrusting of his earthly church to Peter, the first Bishop of Rome. Denying either the bishops' line of 'apostolic succession' – as did Presbyterians and Congregationalists, who dissented mainly on grounds of church organisation – or rejecting Christ's outright divinity, – as did those doctrinal dissenters who rejected the Trinity – by severing the monarch's historical link to the divine, undermined his or her historically derived religious authority for ruling. There was a more indirect, but increasingly important link too. The theology of the dissenters, much more than Anglicans, placed overwhelming importance on individual assent to matters of belief and to the authority. This psychological link, which made consent a condition for the full acceptance of (though not a grounds for) authority was easily applied to political authority too. This intimate link between consent and authority in religion and in politics was further re-enforced by the political exclusion of dissenters, who were thus led to see their disability deriving from their failure to consent – i.e. to exercise the franchise. Given the political exclusion from which they suffered, gaining political rights was seen by them to be an important instrumental means of defending the somewhat precarious toleration they enjoyed. Unitarian theology thus both undermined the theologically based respect for monarchy, and at the same time promoted individual consent as an alternative designation of legitimate authority (Price, pp. 46, 49).

A historical worry about dissent was the dangerous 'enthusiasm' it was seen to generate. Religiously inspired political disobedience was seen to have fuelled not only the parliamentary revolt against the King in the 1640s, but the even more subversive movements of groups such as the Quakers, the Ranters and the Diggers. These had receded as religion became more 'polite' in the eighteenth century and a dominant state religion was felt by the orthodox to be a way of containing the volatile emotions which religion was capable of generating. Most politically threatening had been millenarians who prophesied the end of the world and the resulting irrelevance of political authority. These ideas resurfaced most dramatically with the prophecies of Richard Brothers (p. 295 ff). However, chiliastic elements occur in thinkers who were not obviously 'enthusiasts' in the traditional sense of giving preeminence to the spirit over reason. One perhaps surprising feature of rational dissent is its capacity to harbour such ideas. Both Price and Priestley exhibit millennial expectations. Burke insightfully observed that one new feature of the Revolution was its revelation that rational theories could themselves become objects of 'enthusiasm'.

Rational dissenters enjoyed a prominence far in excess of their numbers. They were firm believers in education, and the dissenting academies, to which Burke deprecatingly refers, were some of the best institutions of higher education in the country at the time. The movement produced one of the most famous scientists – Joseph Priestley – and some of the most forward-looking industrialists and manufacturers – such as the ceramic manufacturer Josiah Wedgwood – of the generation. They were disproportionately represented in the new groups and classes emerging from the processes of urbanisation and incipient industrialisation taking place in Britain at the time, and their increasing prominence, combined with their doctrines, seemed to many to pose a threat to the delicate balance of legitimacy which the Anglican state had achieved.[42]

A concern with this balance is recounted in *Reflections*, more by implication, as so often with Burke, than systematically. His opponents by contrast demonstrate the strident confidence in reason and the importance of generating individuals' consent to the rule exercised over them.

Another political language with roots in the controversies of the 1640s was patriarchalism. The analogy between the state and the family, and between the Monarch and the Father, had been used notoriously by Filmer's supporters in the 1680s, and it was of course against him that Locke wrote his *Two Treatises of Government*. By the late eighteenth century the move to a less authoritarian and more companionate view of the family made the deployment of such arguments awkward. But gendered patriarchy could still be used to denounce not so much disobedience as lack of emotional feeling in Burke's image of the constitution as a father – being dismembered and boiled up in some ghastly experiment by the revolutionaries. These insinuations of familial relations into politics are taken up by Paine and deeply analysed by Mary Wollstonecraft (pp. 113–14, 124–6). Three important clusters of ideas behind the French Revolution therefore conflicted violently with those informing mainstream (and sometimes even radical) British political thinking. They can be summed up in three catchwords: innovation, individualism and secularism.

---

[42] John Seed, "A set of men powerful enough in many things": Rational Dissent and Political Opposition in England, 1770–1790', in Haakonssen (ed.), *Enlightenment and Religion*.

Language and Hegemony

Up to now we have been considering the theoretical content of the arguments, but a crucial feature of the debate in the 1790s was the question of who it was that was making them, and how. In a landmark trial in 1960, Penguin Books were charged with obscenity for publishing D. H. Lawrence's *Lady Chatterley's Lover*. The judge achieved notoriety by directing the jury to ask themselves whether this was the sort of book they would want their wives and servants to be reading: the implication being that it was not merely the publishing of *Lady Chatterley* that was offensive, but its being made available to those who ought not be allowed to read it – wives, and the *lower classes*. This was perhaps the last gasp of a culture in which a paternalist elite could hope to socially quarantine texts and knowledge.

This dimension of political discussion was a vital part of the 1790s, a period in which a popular political public was largely brought into existence by pamphleteers on both sides. The most famous exemplar of this, although apocryphal, is nevertheless plausible. It has often been said that when Godwin's *Political Justice* was brought to the attention of Pitt with a view to prosecution for sedition, he had rejected this on the grounds that a book costing three guineas (£3.15p) could not possibly be subversive.[43] A similar, though far less well-known story, is told of Paine's *Rights of Man*, Part One. The Attorney General was said not to have prosecuted this on the grounds that its price – even at 3/6d (17½ p) – would confine its sale to 'judicious readers', whereas Part Two had 'been ushered into the world in all shapes and sizes and thrust into the *hands of subjects of every description*'.[44] By contrast when the Rev. William Ogilvie, Professor of Philosophy at the University of Aberdeen, published his *Essay on the right of property in Land* in which he argued, on the authority of Locke, that even within society, natural right demanded that all have an equal share to the land, his publication – although asserting the same subversive propositions as Spence's (p. 280) – attracted no government attention. It was, as the author said 'a free and speculative disquisition' aimed at a readership comprising the 'learned, the ingenious

---

[43] 'A three guinea book could never do much harm amongst those who had not three shillings to spare.' The story is retold by Don Locke, who also points out that the price of the first edition was in fact £1.16s (£1.80). *A Fantasy of Reason: The Life and Thought of William Godwin* (London: Routledge & Kegan Paul, 1980), p. 60. The truth is cleared up in Mark Philp, *Godwin's Political Justice* (Oxford and Ithaca: Duckworth and Cornell University Press, 1986), p. 105.
[44] M. A. Best, *Thomas Paine* (New York: Harcourt Brace, 1927), pp. 265–6.

and the friends of all mankind'.[45] Conversely even very respectable authors, read in the wrong context, could seem subversive. When Henry Redhead Yorke – evidently a black radical – was arrested in Sheffield on a charge of making a seditious speech, his (successful) defence was that he had been reading from the second of John Locke's *Two Treatises of Government*! The cheap radical periodicals published by the likes of Spence, Pigott and Daniel Isaac Eaton delighted in the tendentious recycling of selected quotations from the gallery of Whig and classical heroes who were made to appear to support their radical egalitarian stance. In the highly politically charged atmosphere generated by the Revolution, similar arguments, similar – even identical – words, in the mouths of different social actors or reaching the ears and eyes of different classes, took on enormously different political implications.

These social divisions were revealed, and sometimes policed within speech and writing itself by stylistic markers. One reply to Paine dismissed his argument on the basis of his style: the author declared that he (Paine) 'writes in defiance of grammar, as if syntax were an aristocratical invention'.[46] The supposition was not as far-fetched as the author seemed to imagine. Radicals, impressed by the demotic political culture of the French revolutionaries, were deeply aware of the way language codes imposed barriers to political intervention. They tried to confront and overcome this in different ways. Wollstonecraft apologised (ironically) to Burke for her plain prose (implying the artificiality of his); Paine promoted plain-speaking as a way of unmasking imposture. Priestley wrote a grammar; Spence invented a phonetic alphabet to help working people read; Charles Pigott published a ribald *Political Dictionary*; Thelwall lectured on 'Oratory'; Horne Tooke defended the Anglo-Saxon vocabulary against the excluding preciousness of borrowed classical words and in the next generation William Cobbett famously – and for explicitly political purposes – wrote to teach the ploughboy how to read and to write with accuracy and conviction.[47] Nor was this all one-way traffic, in which the radicals sought access to an already formed language of public politics. It has been remarked that Paine not only created a language of

---

[45] Wm. Ogilvie, *An Essay on the right of property in Land* (1784?). This is most easily available in M. Beer, *Pioneers of Land Reform* (London, 1920), p. 30. And ch. 5 in William Stafford, *Socialism, Radicalism and Nostalgia: Social Criticism in Britain, 1775–1830* (Cambridge: Cambridge University Press, 1987). Although Ogilvie's publication was not 'political' the tract was taken up by radicals, being quoted by Thomas Cooper of the London Corresponding Society. See Albert Goodwin, *The Friends of Liberty* (London: Hutchinson, 1979), p. 262.

[46] Sir Brooke Boothby, *Observations . . . on Mr Paine's Rights of Man* (London, 1792), p. 106n.

[47] On this and much else see the still excellent Olivia Smith, *The Politics of Language 1791–1819* (Oxford University Press, 1984).

popular politics but an audience as well. In very much the way that feminists have argued the importance of role-models in enabling other women to emerge into the public political world, Paine too, as an ordinary working man, showed that – and how – they could use words to exercise huge influence over their political world. His demonstrative ability to write clearly and accessibly about politics to the disenfranchised populace was part of the process of creating a public political world in which they could claim a space.

But this process went beyond language. Even the formal record-keeping of societies could be deployed for political purposes. When the London Corresponding Society (p. 266) ostentatiously published its records – which included intentionally provocative correspondence both with British societies and their French peers – it doubtless did so partly as a way of educating potential supporters. But it was surely also a deliberate act of political insubordination designed to show the ruling elite and its supporters that the lower orders were capable of organising themselves, conducting themselves with dignity and ordering their affairs in a way that was quite as impressive as their supposed betters. The formal properties of these works are at least as important as their content and this enabled writers to insinuate all sorts of claims which they did not dare to make directly – such as the title and address, 'Citizen!', with its anti-monarchical association, and the use of the term 'convention' with its ambiguous reference to the French Constitutional Convention.

By radically extending the power and status of, for example the 'convention', and in exploiting its French constitutive status, it could be given an undoubtedly subversive thrust, yet in fact the convention had a long history and many associations within British politics, and this means that its use was highly ambiguous. Like the imitation of their superiors' organisational models, it had both a subversive and a conservative facet. 'Citizen', for example, was a perfectly well recognised status within the urban communities of Britain – but it could be used in critical opposition to the royalist term 'subject', just as it could be used with reference to a universal community of radical democrats rather than with reference to a particular nation state – both politically momentous polarities.[48] Were radicals *invading* the political space hitherto held by their superiors? Or, in appropriating existing forms and imitating established practices, were radicals themselves being co-opted or socialising themselves into the hegemony of an existing political culture? Just which of these

[48] James A. Epstein, *Radical Expression: Political Language, Ritual, and Symbol in England, 1790–1850* (Oxford University Press, 1994), pp. 7–8.

gained predominance seemed to many to be in the balance in the 1790s. In the end the 'powerful prepossession to antiquity', which Burke famously asserted to be such a feature of British political culture, won out, assisted by the judicious application of state violence and repression. But radicalism too had by then established itself, and would re-emerge in the nineteenth century as an enduring and important strand in the rich complexity of British political culture.

The French Revolution and English Politics

The French Revolution reconstituted English politics. It famously split the Whig party: the more conservative Whigs joined Pitt's government, whilst Charles James Fox and his followers continued to support the reformist, although not the revolutionary, stimulus of the French Revolution.[49] The Whig party which emerged at the end of the Revolutionary era was a more radical one with a considerably wider social appeal. The Tories too were transformed by the experience. They redefined themselves against the rationalist reformist individualism of the French Revolution.[50] Pitt's style was famously pragmatic – indeed he was a populist with a reformist past – and that populism was a recurrent feature of conservatism through Disraeli down to Margaret Thatcher. The defenders of the constitution also saw the need to engage in popular politics and in popular language (More, p. 196). But in terms of ideas it was Edmund Burke who made the lasting impact. His distinctive account of an adaptive, procedural conservatism, has often led to him being called the founder of modern conservatism, by which is meant, at least in part, that it is a conservatism which, rather than identifying a specific socio-political order which must be retained (or recovered), provides a way of proceeding with respect to innovation which enabled English conservatives to continually adapt to changing social circumstance. Moreover it can do this because, rather than claiming (as do many other versions of conservatism, such as those identified with a particular religious truth) certain knowledge about society, it relies on a sophisticated and sceptical understanding of human knowledge and insists on the importance of the way it is socially transmitted.

[49] F. O'Gorman, *The Whig Party and the French Revolution* (London: Macmillan, 1967), and L. G. Mitchell, *Charles James Fox and the Disintegration of the Whig Party 1782–1794* (Oxford: Oxford University Press, 1971).
[50] J. Ehrman, *The Reluctant Transition* (London: Constable, 1985), Jennifer Mori, *William Pitt and the French Revolution 1785–1795* (Edinburgh: Keele University Press, 1999).

Radicalism too was to re-emerge from repression after Waterloo, in some cases carried forward by the same individuals, such as Francis Place and the reformed William Cobbett.[51] The venerable Major Cartwright, who had defended American Independence in 1776, testified on behalf of the radicals at the treason trials of 1794, and was still, in his eighties, indefatigably campaigning for universal manhood suffrage when he died in 1823.[52] More darkly, the 'Spencean philanthropists', self-styled followers of Thomas Spence, formed an insurrectionist plot – the Cato Street Conspiracy – and were convicted of High Treason. Some individuals changed sides: most notoriously the poets Wordsworth, Coleridge and Southey rejected their radical pasts to defend, in Coleridge's case, a recognisably Burkean conservatism. James Mackintosh, author of the *Vindiciae Gallicae* (Vindication of the French) written against Burke's *Reflections*, came to agree with many of this old rival's views. But not all the changes were in that direction. William Cobbett had written conservative tracts during the early revolutionary years but subsequently converted to radicalism in America and famously returned to England with the bones of Tom Paine to symbolically re-enthuse postwar reformers with the ideas of the 1790s.[53] A new generation of republican radicals emerged such as Richard Carlisle (who himself as a youthful Tory had burnt Paine's effigy), T. J. Wooler and W. T. Sherwin. They were every bit as abrasive and assertive as Paine himself, to whom they professed their indebtedness. They reprinted his works, sold statues of him and generally celebrated him as the founder of 'the rising principles of the age'.[54] As late as the middle of the nineteenth century Paine's birthday was still being celebrated by working-class communities in industrial England.[55] English radicalism of the nineteenth century was true to its origins in the 1790s. However brash and outspoken, it was rarely revolutionary in its aims or, certainly, in its methods. To this extent it was different from the events in France to which it had responded.

The rise of socialism – some themes of which were indeed broached by radicals like Thelwall and Spence – comprised a turn to different and more potentially revolutionary preoccupations and to different intellectual sources. These came to dominate

[51] See 'The Tradition Preserved', ch. 6 in Edward Royle and James Walvin, *English Radicals and Reformers 1760–1848* (Brighton: Harvester Press, 1982).
[52] John Osborne, *John Cartwright* (Cambridge University Press, 1972).
[53] James Sambrook, *William Cobbett* (London: Routledge & Kegan Paul 1973).
[54] Richard Carlisle, cited in James A. Epstein, *Radical Expression Political Language, Ritual, and Symbol in England, 1790–1850* (Oxford: Oxford University Press, 1994) p. 123.
[55] Gregory Claeys, *Thomas Paine, Social and Political Thought* (London and New York: Unwin, 1989), p. 213.

radical discourse for one hundred and fifty years. But the renewed importance of democracy and natural and human rights in the last half-century along with the collapse of 'really existing socialism' has re-emphasised the importance of the language of the politics which Paine and Wollstonecraft sought to oppose to that of Burke.[56]

In terms not only of British politics, but also, as suggested in the opening remarks, of the wider world, the legacy of the French Revolution is the political language it inspired, and that language, the language of natural rights and a secular, democratic Republicanism, is today no more escapable than the language which was opposed to it – the cautiously religious procedural conservatism of Edmund Burke.

[56] *Ibid.*, pp. 215–16.

FURTHER READING

For a recent survey of interpretations of the Revolution see Bailey Stone, *Reinterpreting the French Revolution: A Global-Historical Perspective* (Cambridge University Press, 2002). A more focused and now classic work is François Furet, *Interpreting the French Revolution* (Cambridge: Cambridge University Press, 1981). On the idea of the French Revolution and its role in subsequent history see Geoffrey Best, *The Permanent Revolution: The French Revolution and its Legacy, 1789–1989* (London: Fontana, 1988). The idea of tracing continuities across the Revolution is as old as Alexis de Tocqueville, *The Ancien Régime and the French Revolution* (1856). It is found in many of the essays in Dale van Kley (ed.), *The French Idea of Freedom: The Old Regime and the Declaration of Rights of 1789* (Stanford University Press, 1994) and Colin Lucas (ed.), *The Political Culture of the French Revolution* (1988) below. On the Revolution as generating a new political vocabulary and discourse see Keith Michael Baker, *Inventing the French Revolution* (Cambridge: Cambridge University Press, 1990), esp. chs. 10 and 11; *The French Revolution and the Creation of Modern Political Culture*, 4 vols. (Oxford: Pergamon, 1987–94), vol. II, *The Political Culture of the French Revolution*, ed. Colin Lucas (1988); and François Furet and Mona Ozuf, *Critical Dictionary of the French Revolution* (Cambridge, Mass.: Bellknap Press, 1989). R. R. R. Palmer, *The Age of The Democratic Revolution: A Political History of Europe and America, 1760–1800* (Oxford: Oxford University Press, 1959) viewed the American and French revolutions as essentially similar. For a developed account of the differences hinted at here see my 'Founding and Federation in the Early Modern Republic' in Ivo Comparato, Hans Bödecker and Catherine Larrere (eds.) *Republican Founding* (Florence: Olski, forthcoming); for the revolution as betrayal of the Enlightenment see R. Wokler, 'The Enlightenment Project as Betrayed by Modernity', *History of European Ideas* 24 (4–5) (1998), pp. 301–13; and on Abbé Sieyes, see M. Forsyth, *Reason and Revolution: The Political Thought of the Abbé Sieyes* (Leicester: Leicester University Press, 1987). For a modern analysis of the economic background to the revolution see Florin Aftalion, *The French Revolution: An Economic Interpretation* (Cambridge: Cambridge University Press, 1990), and Michael Sonenscher, 'Republicanism, State Finances and the Emergence of Commercial Society in Eighteenth-Century France', in Martin van Gelderen and Quentin Skinner (eds.), *Republicanism: A Shared European Heritage*, 2 vols. (Cambridge: Cambridge University Press, 2002), vol. II.

On the British background to the American Revolution and constitution see Bernard Bailyn, *The Ideological Origins of the American Revolution* (Cambridge, Mass.: Harvard University Press, 1967), and Donald S. Lutz, *The Origins of American Constitutionalism* (Baton Rouge: Louisiana State University Press, 1988). On the debate on America in Britain see Ian R. Christie, *Wilkes, Wyville and Reform: The Parliamentary Reform Movement in British Politics, 1760–1785* (London: Macmillan, 1962), on the constitutional societies see my own 'Civic Humanism and Parliamentary Reform, the Case of the Society of the Friends of the People', *Journal of British Studies* 18 (spring, 1979); and Mary Thale (ed.), *Selections from the Papers of the London Corresponding Society* (Cambridge University Press, 1983).

On the English 'Revolutions' see Lawrence Stone, 'The Results of the English Revolutions of the Seventeenth Century' and other essays in J. G. A. Pocock (ed.), *Three British Revolutions: 1641, 1688, 1776* (Princeton: Princeton University Press, 1980). On co-ordination see C. C. Weston and J. R. Greenberg, *Subjects and Sovereigns: The Grand Controversy over Legal Sovereignty in Stuart England* (Cambridge: Cambridge University Press, 1981); on Sacheverell see Geoffrey Holmes, *The Trial of Doctor Sacheverell* (London: Methuen, 1973). On Montesquieu's views on England see C. P. Courtney, 'Montesquieu and English Liberty', in David W. Carrithers, Michael A. Mosher and Paul A. Rahe (eds.), *Montesquieu's Science of Politics* (Lanham, Md. and Oxford: Rowman and Littlefield, 2001), and work cited there. On the growing power of the British state and its reliance on modern fiscal administration see P. G. M. Dickson, *The Financial Revolution in England . . . 1688–1756* (London: Macmillan, 1967), John Brewer, *The Sinews of Power: War Money and the English State 1688–1783* (London and Winchester, Mass.: Unwin, 1989), and Betty Behrens, 'Nobles, Privileges and Taxes in France at the end of the Ancient Regime' *Economic History Review*, 15 (1963), 451–75; there is a good comparison of England and France in Peter Mathias and Patrick O'Brien, 'Taxation in England and France 1715–1810 . . .' *Journal of European Economic History*, 5 (1976), 601–50.

On ideologies of corruption and independence in eighteenth-century England the best introduction is still J. G. A. Pocock's 'Machiavelli, Harrington and English Eighteenth-Century Ideologies', in his *Politics, Language and Time: Essays on Political Thought and History* (London and New York: Methuen and Atheneum, 1971; 1972); see also M. M. Goldsmith, 'Liberty, Virtue and the Rule of Law, 1689–1770', in David Wootton (ed.), *Republicanism, Liberty and Commercial Society 1649–1776* (Stanford: Stanford University Press, 1994). For a more detailed view see Pocock's 'Neo-Machiavellian Political Economy', ch. xiii of his *The Machiavellian Moment* (Princeton: Princeton University Press, 1975). On electoral conventions and practices of the time see John Brooke, *The House of Commons 1754–1790* (Oxford: Oxford University Press, 1964). On John Wilkes, liberty and the parties in the mid-century see John Brewer, *Party Ideology and Popular Politics at the Accession of George III* (Cambridge: Cambridge University Press, 1976). On the power and authority of the past the best original treatment in relation to England is Pocock, *The Ancient Constitution and the Feudal Law* (Cambridge: Cambridge University Press, 1957, reissued with a retrospective essay 1987). The notion of ideals becoming temporally translocated to be forward- rather than backward-looking is a feature of this period identified by the German conceptual historian Reinhard Koselleck in his *Futures Past*, trans. Keith Tribe (Cambridge, Mass.: MIT Press, 1985).

For the most pointed account of relations between political legitimacy and religious belief in the period see J. C. D. Clark, *English Society 1688–1832* (Cambridge: Cambridge University Press, 1985). More focused on this period, and with a good introductory chapter, 'Christian Political Theory', is Robert Hole, *Pulpits, Politics, and Public Order in England 1760–1832* (Cambridge: Cambridge University Press, 1989); see also F. C. Mather, *High Church Prophet: Bishop Samuel Horsley (1733–1806) and the Caroline Tradition in the Later Georgian Church* (Oxford: Clarendon Press, 1992). For a survey of eighteenth-century dissent see Michael Watts, *The Dissenters from Reformation to the French Revolution* (Oxford: Oxford University Press, 1978). Martin FitzPatrick, 'Heretical Religion and Radical Political Ideas in Late Eighteenth Century England', in Eckhart Helmuth (ed.), *The Transformation of Political Culture, England and Germany in the Late Eighteenth Century* (Oxford: Oxford University Press, 1990). On specifically rational dissent see Knud Haakonssen (ed.), *Enlightenment and Religion: Rational Dissent in Eighteenth-Century Britain*, especially ch. 6, 'Rational Dissent and Political Opposition in England 1770–1790' by John Seed, and ch. 8, 'The Nexus between Theology and Political Doctrine in Church and Dissent', by A. M. C. Waterman. On rational dissent's social standing see John Seed, 'Gentlemen Dissenters: The Social and Political Meanings of Rational Dissent in the 1770s and 1780s', *Historical Journal* 28 (2) (1985), pp. 299–325.

On Pocock's notion of language see 'Languages and their Implications', in *Politics, Language and Time*, 'The Concept of a Language and the *métier d'historien*: Some Considerations on Practice' in A. Pagden (ed.), *The Languages of Political Theory in Early-Modern Europe* (Cambridge: Cambridge University Press, 1987), and his 'The State of the Art', in his *Virtue, Commerce and History* (Cambridge: Cambridge University Press, 1985). On speech acts see Quentin Skinner, 'Interpretation and the Understanding of Speech Acts', in *Visions of Politics*, vol. 1: *Regarding Method* (Cambridge University Press, 2002). Exemplifying this conception of language in the history of early modern thought see various essays in Pagden (ed.), *Languages of Political Theory*, particularly Richard Tuck, 'The "Modern" Theory of Natural Law' and Istvan Hont, 'The Language of Sociability and Commerce . . .'. For the technique applied to the subject of this book see Pocock's essay 'Burke and the Ancient Constitution: A Problem in the History of Ideas', in *Politics, Language and Time*.

On political actions as speech acts see Keith Baker, 'Inventing the French Revolution', in his *Inventing the French Revolution*, and Bonnie Honig 'Declarations of Independence: Arendt and Derrida on the Problem of Founding a Republic', *American Political Science Review* 85 (1) (March 1991), pp. 17–114.

On Ancient Constitutionalism see Pocock's work cited above and Glenn Burgess, *The Politics of the Ancient Constitution* (Pennsylvania State University, 1992). The classic account of the 'Norman yoke' imposed on Saxon freedoms is Christopher Hill, 'The Norman Yoke', in his *Puritanism and Revolution: Studies in the Interpretation of the English Revolution of the 17th Century* (Harmondsworth: Penguin, 1986). On conservatives' use of the language see Janice Lee, 'Political Antiquarianism Unmasked: The Conservative Attack on the Ancient Constitution', *Institute of Historical Research Bulletin* 60 (November 1982), pp. 166–79. On the tendency of English radicals to look back to the past rather than forward see William Stafford, *Socialism, Radicalism and Nostalgia: Social Criticism in Britain, 1775–1830* (Cambridge: Cambridge University Press, 1987), and on the inhibiting features of historical mindedness see my 'On Not Inventing the British Revolution', forthcoming in Matthew Festenstein and Glenn Burgess (eds.), *English Radicalism 1550–1850* (Cambridge University Press, 2005).

On Patriarchy the classic seventeenth-century study is still Gordon Schochet's *Patriarchalism in Political Thought* (Oxford: Oxford University Press, 1975) and more briefly but acutely on the political theory implications: R. W. K. Hinton, 'Husbands, Fathers and Conquerors', *Political Studies*, 15 (1967), 291–300. There is no treatment of the subject in political theory for the period under discussion, although there are judicious observations as well as other good things in Robert Hole's work cited above. On issues of gender there is a good selection of texts: Vivien Jones (ed.), *Women in the Eighteenth Century: Constructions of Femininity* (London: Routledge,

1990); a range of issues are canvassed in Hilda Smith, *Women Writers and the Early Modern British Political Tradition* (Cambridge: Cambridge University Press, 1998); whilst on Wollstonecraft herself by far the best treatment from a political theory perspective is Virginia Sapiro, *A Vindication of Political Virtue: The Political Theory of Mary Wollstonecraft* (University of Chicago Press, 1992).

On natural jurisprudence see the essays cited above by Pocock, Skinner, Tuck, Hont and Pagden, exemplifying languages, and also Duncan Forbes, 'Natural Law and the Scottish Enlightenment', in R. H. Campbell and A. S. Skinner (eds.), *The Origins and Nature of the Scottish Enlightenment* (Edinburgh: John Donald, 1982). The origins of radical natural rights theories in the seventeenth century is explored in R. Tuck, *Natural Rights Theories* (Cambridge: Cambridge University Press, 1979); thereafter see Knud Haakonssen, *Natural Law and Moral Philosophy from Grotius to the Enlightenment* (Cambridge: Cambridge University Press, 1996). A good survey of issues raised in the Scottish enlightenment discussions about the development of society is C. Berry, *Social Theory and the Scottish Enlightenment* (Edinburgh University Press, 1997).

On political economy see Istvan Hont and Michael Ignatieff (eds.), *Wealth and Virtue* (Cambridge University Press, 1983); Istvan Hont: 'The Rhapsody of Public Debt: David Hume on Voluntary State Bankruptcy', in *Political Discourse in Early Modern Britain*; and T. A. Horne, *Property Rights and Poverty: Political Argument in Britain 1605–1834* (Chapel Hill: University of North Carolina Press, 1990). On issues of language (in the conventional, not Pocockian, sense) within the debate see J. T. Boulton, *The Language of Politics in the Age of Wilkes and Burke* (London: Routledge and Kegan Paul, 1975); Olivia Smith, *The Politics of Language, 1791–1819* (Oxford: Oxford University Press, 1984); Stephen Blakemore, *Burke and the Fall of Language: The French Revolution as Linguistic Event* (Hanover, N.H.: published for Brown University Press by University Press of New England, 1988).

On Royalism see J. C. D. Clark, *English Society . . .*; R. R. Dozier, *For King, Constitution and Country: The English Loyalists and the French Revolution* (Lexington, Ky.: University Press of Kentucky, 1983); Marilyn Morris, *The British Monarchy and the French Revolution* (New Haven, Conn.: Yale University Press, 1998); James J. Sack, *From Jacobite to Conservative: Reaction and Orthodoxy in Britain, c. 1760–1832* (Cambridge: Cambridge University Press, 1993); Harry Dickinson, 'Popular Loyalism in Britain in the 1790s', in Eckhart Hellmuth (ed.), *The Transformation of Political Culture: England and Germany in the Late Eighteenth Century* (Oxford University Press, 1990); David Eastwood, 'Patriotism and the English State in the 1790s', in

Mark Philp (ed.), *The French Revolution and British Popular Politics* (Cambridge: Cambridge University Press, 1991).

On the radicalism of the time the most recent comprehensive study is Albert Goodwin, *The Friends of Liberty* (London: Hutchinson, 1979). Earlier and still useful works include: Carl B. Cone, *The English Jacobins* (New York: Scribners, 1968); Eugene Black, *The Association 1769–1793* (Cambridge, Mass.: Harvard University Press, 1963); and the early part of E. P. Thompson's *The Making of the English Working Class* (London/Harmondsworth: Penguin Press, 1963). Recent works which, like Thompson's, carry the story through to the nineteenth century are Iain McCalman's *Radical Underworld: Prophets, Revolutionaries and Pornographers in London, 1795– 1840* (Cambridge: Cambridge University Press, 1988) and James Epstein, *Radical Expression: Political Language, Ritual, and Symbol in England, 1790–1850* (Oxford: Oxford University Press, 1994). Good collections include Mark Philp, *The French Revolution and British Popular Politics* (Cambridge: Cambridge University Press, 1991), and H. T. Dickinson (ed.), *Britain and the French Revolution 1789–1815* (Basingstoke: Macmillan, 1989). Important essays in other collections and journals include John Dinwiddy, 'Conceptions of Revolution in the English Radicalism of the 1790s', in Hellmuth (ed.), *The Transformation of Political Culture*; Gregory Claeys, 'The French Revolution Debate and British Political Thought', *History of Political Thought* 11 (1990), pp. 59–80; T. M. Parssinen, 'Association, Convention and Anti-Parliament in British Radical Politics, 1771–1848', *English Historical Review* 88 (1973), 504–33.

EDITORIAL PRINCIPLES

This selection of works seeks to present the major theoretical works of the British controversy over the French Revolution as it unfolded, together with some minor but representative writings that together illustrate the idioms of political argument deployed by contemporaries.

The editorial principle used in abbreviating the major works has been to try and retain the overall coherence of a thinker's argument. In some cases it has been possible to achieve this by selecting a more or less continuous section from within a work. In most cases it has involved the editing out of detail whilst leaving the general structure of the argument in place. Where it is not obvious from the numbering of chapters or sections, ellipses [. . .] have been used to indicate that omissions. Where these represent parts of a paragraph they remain on the same line as the retained text. Where they have a line to themselves they indicate that one or more (sometimes many more) paragraphs have been removed. Square brackets indicate new material supplied by the editor for information or to indicate continuity or the relation of one excerpt to another. In the most wordy authors (such as Godwin) individual sentences and paragraphs have had to be stripped of detail and flourish. The use of ellipses here is most intrusive, but still it was thought better to indicate where words or phrases had been deleted, even if at the cost of making the resulting prose appear fragmented.

Authors' footnotes have largely, although not completely, been retained and are identified at the start of footnote text. Editor's footnotes have been largely restricted to explaining the meaning of archaic words and indicating the identity and significance of individuals and issues mentioned in the text, which might not be familiar to modern student readers.

Readers should be aware that although the intention has been to try to present the texts as coherent entities, in the cases of long works, not only the detail of arguments and the illustrations but sometimes whole topics have had to be sacrificed to the limitations of space. Those interested in taking their studies of a work further will of course need to consult a full text of the work. Details of these and, where possible, modern editions have been given in each introduction.

THE DECLARATION OF THE
RIGHTS OF MAN AND OF CITIZENS

HISTORICAL NOTE

The *Declaration of the Rights of Man* is one of the seminal writings of western politics. It has inspired numerous subsequent national and international declarations.[1] Like these the original Declaration was not merely a statement, it invoked and set standards for action. Both this declaration and the American Declaration of Independence have often been accorded almost scriptural status in their respective countries and, particularly in the French case, beyond.[2] However, the text did not spring fully formed into existence as the result of inspiration. The actual circumstances of its composition both drew on historical exemplars – particularly those of the American States which, unlike the original version of the Federal Constitution, had declarations of rights attached – and was subject to the contingencies of revolutionary debate, during which the very emergence of a Declaration was several times in doubt.[3] More than thirty 'declarations of rights' jostled for immortality during the first year of the revolution alone.

What was distinctive, exciting and was to prove hugely contentious to conservative English readers was the claim not to be encapsulating historically held rights, but to be declaring – as a political programme – Natural Rights. It was one of the clear *foci* of an otherwise often confused British debate about the Revolution.

EDITORIAL NOTE

The text here is included in full in the translation which would have been familiar to many English readers, published in Paine's *Rights of Man*. Amongst

---

[1] Amos J. Peaslee and Dorothy X. Peaslee, *Constitutions of Nations*, 4 vols. (The Hague: Martinas Nighoff, 1965).
[2] Jacques Godechot, 'L'Expansion de la Déclaration des Droits de l'homme de 1789 dans le monde', *Annales Historiques de la Révolution Française* 232 (1978). For a brilliant and compelling study of the American case see Pauline Maier, *American Scripture* (New York: Vintage Books, 1997).
[3] Keith Michael Baker, in Dale van Kley (ed.), *The French Idea of Freedom* (Stanford University Press, 1994), p. 190.

modern collections which include the work in translation (Stewart) or in the original French (Fauré) in a wider context of documents from the period are:

Stewart, John Hall *A Documentary Survey of the French Revolution* (London and New York: Macmillan, 1951).

Fauré, Christine *Les Déclarations des Droits de L'Homme de 1789* (Paris: Editions Payot, 1988).

FURTHER READING

Baker, Keith Michael *Inventing the French Revolution* (Cambridge: Cambridge University Press, 1990).

   'The Idea of a Declaration of Rights', in Dale van Kley (ed.), *The French Idea of Freedom.*

Furet, François and Ozuf, Mona (eds.) *Critical Dictionary of the French Revolution* (Cambridge, Mass.: Pergamon, 1989).

van Kley, Dale (ed.) *The French Idea of Freedom: The Old Regime and the Declaration of Rights of 1789* (Stanford University Press, 1994).

Raynaud, Philippe 'La Déclaration des Droits de l'homme', in Colin Lucas (ed.), *The French Revolution and the Creation of Modern Political Culture*, 3 vols. (Oxford and New York: Pergamon Press, 1988), vol. II: *The Political Culture of the French Revolution.*

Declaration of the Rights of Man and of Citizens (1789)

By The National Assembly Of France

The representatives of the people of FRANCE, formed into a NATIONAL ASSEMBLY, considering that ignorance, neglect, or contempt of human rights, are the sole causes of public misfortunes and corruptions of Government, have resolved to set forth in a solemn declaration, these natural, imprescriptible, and inalienable rights: that this declaration being constantly present to the minds of the members of the body social, they may be forever kept attentive to their rights and their duties: that the acts of the legislative and executive powers of Government, being capable of being every moment compared with the end of political institutions, may be more respected: and also, that the future claims of the citizens, being directed by simple and incontestable principles, may always tend to the maintenance of the Constitution, and the general happiness.

For these reasons the NATIONAL ASSEMBLY doth recognize and declare, in the presence of the Supreme Being, and with the hope of his blessing and favour, the following sacred rights of men and of citizens:

I: *Men are born, and always continue, free and equal in respect of their rights. Civil distinctions, therefore, can be founded only on public utility.*

II: *The end of all political associations is the preservation of the natural and imprescriptible rights of man; and these rights are liberty, property, security, and resistance of oppression.*

III: *The nation is essentially the source of all sovereignty; nor can any* INDIVIDUAL, *or* ANY BODY *of* MEN, *be entitled to any authority which is not expressly derived from it.*

IV: Political liberty consists in the power of doing whatever does not injure another. The exercise of the natural rights of every man, has no other limits than those which are necessary to secure to every *other* man the free exercise of the same rights; and these limits are determinable only by the law.

V: The law ought to prohibit only actions hurtful to society. What is not prohibited by the law should not be hindered; nor should anyone be compelled to that which the law does not require.

VI: The law is an expression of the will of the community. All citizens have a right to concur, either personally or by their representatives, in its formation. It should be the same to all, whether it protects or punishes; and *all being equal in its sight, are equally eligible to all honours, places, and employments, according to their different abilities, without any other distinction than that created by their virtues and talents.*

VII: No man should be accused, arrested, or held in confinement, except in cases determined by the law, and according to the forms which it has prescribed. All who promote, solicit, execute, or cause to be executed, arbitrary orders, ought to be punished, and every citizen called upon, or apprehended by virtue of the law, ought immediately to obey, and renders himself culpable by resistance.

VIII: The law ought to impose no other penalties but such as are absolutely and evidently necessary; and no one ought to be punished, but in virtue of a law promulgated before the offence, and legally applied.

IX: Every man being presumed innocent till he has been convicted, whenever his detention becomes indispensable, all rigour to him, more than is necessary to secure his person, ought to be provided against by the law.

X: No man ought to be molested on account of his opinions, not even on account of his *religious* opinions, provided his avowal of them does not disturb the public order established by the law.

XI: The unrestrained communication of thoughts and opinions being one of the most precious rights of man, every citizen may speak, write, and publish freely, provided he is responsible for the abuse of this liberty, in cases determined by the law.

XII: A public force being necessary to give security to the rights of men and of citizens, that force is instituted for the benefit of the community and not for the particular benefit of the persons to whom it is intrusted.

XIII: A common contribution being necessary for the support of the public force, and for defraying the other expenses of government, it ought to be divided equally among the members of the community, according to their abilities.

XIV: Every citizen has a right, either by himself or his representative, to a free voice in determining the necessity of public contributions, the appropriation of them, and their amount, mode of assessment, and duration.

XV: Every community has a right to demand of all its agents an account of their conduct.

XVI: Every community in which a separation of powers and a security of rights is not provided for, wants a constitution.

XVII: The right to property being inviolable and sacred, no one ought to be deprived of it, except in cases of evident public necessity, legally ascertained, and on condition of a previous just indemnity.

RICHARD PRICE

Richard Price was born the son of a dissenting minister in rural Glamorganshire on 23 February 1723. Price rejected his father's strict Calvinist predestinarianism and adopted the increasingly rationalist non-conformity of many of his generation. He studied under John Eames, a friend of Newton, at the dissenting Academy in Moorfields, London, renowned for its mathematics and natural science. In 1758 Price became preacher to the famous dissenting community at Newington Green north of the City of London. This group included many political radicals, notably at this time James Burgh, author of *Political Disquisitions*, which became known as 'The Reformer's Bible'. Price also joined the 'Honest Whigs', a fortnightly discussion club whose membership included Burgh, Benjamin Franklin, Thomas Hollis who kept Civil War republicanism alive, Andrew Kippis another famous dissenting minister, Theophilus Lindsey, who would lead a Unitarian breakaway from the Church of England, and Joseph Priestley. Price was a member of the Royal Society, and associated with a group of radical thinkers surrounding the Earl of Shelburne.

His political writing career took off in 1776 with the publication of *Observations on the Nature of Civil Liberty*, a tract provoked by the emerging war against the American Colonists, and arguing, on general and abstract grounds, their – and indeed any people's – right to govern themselves. Price grounded his case for civil liberty on a comprehensive discussion of freedom of the will, of moral judgement and religious worship. The tract was widely read and extremely influential. Price developed and elaborated the arguments, sometimes in the light of changing events. A second discourse – *Additional Observations on the Nature and Value of Civil Liberty and the War with America* – appeared in 1777, and the two thereafter appeared together as *Two Tracts on Civil Liberty*, and went through numerous editions in Britain and America. One important consequence of the American Independence movement had been the emergence of demands for political reform in Britain. This had taken the innovative – and to some, threatening – form of extra-parliamentary associations, the Societies for

Promoting Constitutional Information, and of Supporters of the Bill of Rights, county, provincial and metropolitan constituency-based associations, notably those in Ulster, Yorkshire, Westminster, and Middlesex, and The Revolution Society which sought to commemorate and promote a radical interpretation of Britain's 1688 Revolution. Although Price's sermon of 1790 provoked Burke's response, and the spate of pamphlets which followed, Price himself died the following year.

EDITORIAL NOTE

A Discourse on the Love of our Country (1790) was a sermon preached to the annual dinner of the Revolution Society held at Old Jewry in the City of London on 4 November 1789. Price had already written excitedly to Jefferson of hope that what the French were doing would 'astonish Europe' and 'be the commencement of a general reformation in the governments of the world'. In contrast, he thought, the British were 'Duped by the forms of liberty'.[1] The hopes for France, together with the long-standing aims of the Revolution Society for reform in Britain, established the strategy of the piece. Praise for the 'principles of 1688' was a well-established way for British reformers to insinuate the need for further political change whilst appearing to support the constitution, based as it was on the 'Revolution Settlement' (of 1688). France added another, and objective, dimension to this by displaying a constitutional reform which was going further, and certainly propounding principles far more radical than had been claimed as the basis for 1688 – as Burke was to point out in his *Appeal*. By projecting French principles back onto 1688 and implicitly comparing them with contemporary politics, Price was able to suggest that Britain's politics fell short of its own principles, and that the Glorious Revolution needed 'perfecting'.

The peroration of the sermon adds another dimension as Price's language (like that of a number of other radical dissenters at the time) becomes apocalyptic in tone, adding to the general mood of expectation. At the dinner which followed the sermon a congratulatory address was passed which was sent to the National Assembly in Paris, the establishment of a national network of reform societies was projected, and the following 'fundamental principles' of the Society were voted:

1. That all Civil and Political authority is derived from the People.
2. That abuse of Power justifies Resistance.

[1] Price to Jefferson, 3 August, 1789, *Correspondence of Richard Price*, ed. W. Bernard Peach and D. O. Thomas (Durham, N.C. and Cardiff: Duke University Press and University of Wales Press, 1994).

3. That the Right of Private Judgement, Liberty of Conscience, Trial by Jury, the Freedom of the Press, and the Freedom of Election ought ever to be held sacred and inviolable.

Although Price asserted a very clear principle of natural right, he did not think that universal manhood suffrage could be immediately derived from these without taking other considerations into account, denying, for example that he was either a republican or a democrat.

The text reproduced here is that of the 6th edition (1790) as used in *Political Writings*, ed. D. O. Thomas (Cambridge: Cambridge University Press, 1991).

Modern editions are:
Political Writings, ed. D. O. Thomas (Cambridge: Cambridge University Press, 1991), contains the *Two Tracts*, and the *Discourse on the Love of our Country*.
Richard Price and the Ethical Foundations of the American Revolution (Durham, N.C.: North Carolina University Press, 1979), contains the *Two Tracts* and other material relating to the American Revolution.

FURTHER READING

Fruchtman, J., 'The Apocalyptic Politics of Richard Price and Joseph Priestley', *Transactions of the American Philosophical Society* 73 (4) (1983), pp. 1–125.
Haakonssen, K. (ed.), *Enlightenment and Religion: Rational Dissent in Eighteenth-Century Britain* (Cambridge: Cambridge University Press, 1996).
Laboucheix, H., *Richard Price as Moral Philosopher and Political Theorist*, trans. S. and D. D. Raphael (Oxford: Oxford University Press, 1982).
Thomas, D. O., *The Honest Mind: The Thought and Work of Richard Price* (Oxford: Oxford University Press, 1977).

A Discourse on the Love of our Country (1790)

Psalm cxxii. verses 2 and 4–9

Our feet shall stand within thy gates, O Jerusalem, whither the tribes go up, the tribes of the Lord unto the testimony of Israel. To give thanks to the name of the Lord, for there sit the thrones of judgment, the throne of the House of David. Pray for the peace of Jerusalem. They shall prosper that love thee. Peace be within thy walls, and prosperity within thy palaces. For my brethren and companions sake I will now say peace be within thee. Because of the House of the Lord our God, I will seek thy good.

In these words the Psalmist expresses, in strong and beautiful language, his love of his country and the reasons on which he founded it; and my present design is to take occasion from them to explain the duty we owe to our country, and the nature, foundation, and proper expressions of that love to it which we ought to cultivate. I reckon this a subject particularly suitable to the services of this day, and to the anniversary of our deliverance at the Revolution from the dangers of Popery and arbitrary power, and should I, on such an occasion, be led to touch more on political subjects than would at any other time be proper in the pulpit, you will, I doubt not, excuse me.[1]

The love of our country has in all times been a subject of warm commendations and it is certainly a noble passion, but, like all other passions, it requires regulation and direction. There are mistakes and prejudices by which, in this instance, we are in particular danger of being misled. I will briefly mention some of these to you and observe.

First, that by our country is meant, in this case, not the soil or the spot of earth on which we happen to have been born, not the forests and fields, but that community of which we are members, or that body of companions and friends and kindred who are associated with us under the same constitution of government, protected by the same laws, and bound together by the same civil polity.

Secondly, it is proper to observe that even in this sense of our country, that love of it which is our duty does not imply any conviction of the superior value of it to other countries, or any particular preference of its laws and constitution of government. Were this implied, the love of their country would be the duty of only a very small part of mankind, for there are few countries that enjoy the advantage of laws and governments which deserve to be preferred. To found, therefore, this duty on such a preference would be to found it on error and delusion. It is, however, a common delusion. There is the same partiality in countries to themselves that there is in individuals. All our attachments should be accompanied, as far as possible, with right opinions. We are too apt to confine wisdom and virtue within the circle of our own acquaintance and party. Our friends, our country, and, in short, every thing related to us we are disposed to overvalue. A wise man will guard himself against this delusion . . . but, notwithstanding this, our obligation to love our own

---

[1] The revolution of 1688/9 was celebrated for having overthrown what was perceived as the absolutist rule of James II, who was regarded as seeking to introduce Catholicism as the state religion and, like Charles II, to rule and raise revenues without the consent of Parliament.

families, friends, and country, and to seek, in the first place, their good, will remain the same.

Thirdly, it is proper I should desire you particularly to distinguish between the love of our country and that spirit of rivalship and ambition which has been common among nations. What has the love of their country hitherto been among mankind? What has it been but a love of domination, a desire of conquest, and a thirst for grandeur and glory, by extending territory and enslaving surrounding countries? What has it been but a blind and narrow principle, producing in every country a contempt of other countries, and forming men into combinations and factions against their common rights and liberties? This is the principle that has been too often cried up as a virtue of the first rank: a principle of the same kind with that which governs clans of Indians or tribes of Arabs, and leads them to plunder and massacre. As most of the evils which have taken place in private life, and among individuals, have been occasioned by the desire of private interest overcoming the public affections, so most of the evils which have taken place among bodies of men have been occasioned by the desire of their own interest overcoming the principle of universal benevolence and leading them to attack one another's territories, to encroach on one another's rights, and to endeavour to build their own advancement on the degradation of all within the reach of their power . . . What is now the love of his country in a Spaniard, a Turk, or a Russian? Can it be considered as any thing better than a passion for slavery, or a blind attachment to a spot where he enjoys no rights and is disposed of as if he was a beast?

Let us learn by such reflexions to correct and purify this passion, and to make it a just and rational principle of action.

It is very remarkable that the founder of our religion has not once mentioned this duty or given us any recommendation of it, and this has, by unbelievers, been made an objection to Christianity. What I have said will entirely remove this objection. Certain it is, that by inculcating on men an attachment to their country, Christianity would at the time it was propagated have done unspeakably more harm than good. . . . Our Lord and his apostles have done better. They have recommended that Universal Benevolence which is an unspeakably nobler principle than any partial affections. They have laid such stress on loving all men, even our enemies, and made an ardent and extensive charity so essential a part of virtue, that the religion they have preached may, by way of distinction from all other religions, be called the Religion of

Benevolence . . . If you want any proof of this, think of our Saviour's parable of the good Samaritan . . . The design of this parable was to shew a Jew that even a Samaritan and consequently all men of all nations and religions were included in the precept, *Thou shalt love thy neighbour as thyself.*

But I am digressing from what I had chiefly in view, which was, after noticing that love of our country which is false and spurious, to explain the nature and effects of that which is just and reasonable. With this view I must desire you to recollect that we are so constituted that our affections are more drawn, to some among mankind than to others, in proportion to their degrees of nearness to us, and our power of being useful to them . . . Our regards, according to the order of nature, begin with ourselves, and every man is charged primarily with the care of himself. Next come our families, and benefactors, and friends, and after them our country. We can do little for the interest of mankind at large. To this interest, however, all other interests are subordinate . . . yet we must remember that a narrower interest ought always to give way, to a more extensive interest. In pursuing particularly the interest of our country we ought to carry our views beyond it. We should love it ardently but not exclusively. We ought to seek its good, by all the means that our different circumstances and abilities will allow, but at the same time we ought to consider ourselves as citizens of the world, and take care to maintain a just regard to the rights of other countries.

The enquiry by what means (subject to this limitation) we may best promote the interest of our country is very important, and all that remains of this discourse shall be employed in answering it and in exhorting you to manifest your love to your country by the means I shall mention.

The chief blessings of human nature are the three following: truth, virtue, and liberty. These are, therefore, the blessings in the possession of which the interest of our country lies, and to the attainment of which our love of it ought to direct our endeavours. By the diffusion of knowledge it must be distinguished from a country of barbarians: by the practice of religious virtue, it must be distinguished from a country of gamblers, atheists, and libertines: and by the possession of liberty, it must be distinguished from a country of slaves. I will dwell for a few moments on each of these heads.

Our first concern as lovers of our country must be to enlighten it. Why are the nations of the world so patient under despotism? Why do they crouch to tyrants, or submit to be treated as if they were a herd of cattle? Enlighten them and you will elevate them. Shew them they are *men* and they will act like *men*. Give them just

ideas of civil government and let them know that it is an expedient for gaining protection against injury and defending their rights, and it will be impossible for them
to submit to governments which, like most of those now in the world, are usurpations on the rights of men and little better than contrivances for enabling the, *few* to
oppress, the *many*. Convince them that the Deity is a righteous and benevolent as well
as omnipotent being, who regards with equal eye all his creatures and connects his
favour with nothing but an honest desire to know and to do his will, and that zeal for
mystical doctrines which has led men to hate and harass one another will be extermi-
nated. Set religion before them as a rational service consisting not in any rites and ceremonies, but in worshipping God with a pure heart and practising righteousness from
the fear of his displeasure and the apprehension of a future righteous judgment and
that gloomy and cruel superstition will be abolished which has hitherto gone under
the name of religion, and to the support of which civil government has been perverted.
Ignorance is the parent of bigotry, intolerance, persecution and slavery . . . Inform and
instruct mankind, and these evils will be excluded . . . In short, we may, in this instance,
learn our duty from the conduct of the oppressors of the world. They know that light
is hostile to them, and therefore they labour to keep men in the dark. With this intention they have appointed licensers of the press, and, in Popish countries, prohibited
the reading of the Bible.[2] Remove the darkness in which they envelope the world
and their usurpations will be exposed, their power will be subverted, and the world
emancipated.

The next great blessing of human nature which I have mentioned is virtue. This
ought to follow knowledge and to be directed by it. Virtue without knowledge makes
enthusiasts and knowledge without virtue makes devils, but both united elevates to
the top of human dignity and perfection. We must, therefore, if we would serve our
country, make both these the objects of our zeal. We must discourage vice in all its
forms, and our endeavours to enlighten must have ultimately in view a reformation
of manners, and virtuous practice.

I must add here that in the practice of virtue I include the discharge of the public duties of religion. By neglecting these we may injure our country essentially.
But it is melancholy to observe that it is a common neglect among us and in a
great measure owing to a cause which is not likely to be soon removed: I mean,
the defects (may I not say, the absurdities?) in our established codes of faith and

[2] Catholic countries retained the Latin version of the Bible, which the common people could not
read.

worship. In foreign countries, the higher ranks of men, not distinguishing between the religion they see established and the Christian religion, are generally driven to irreligion and infidelity. The like evil is produced by the like cause in this country, and if no reformation of our established formularies can be brought about, it must be expected that religion will go on to lose its credit, and that little of it will be left except among the lower orders of people, many of whom, while their superiors give up all religion, are sinking into an enthusiasm in religion lately revived,[3] and mistaking, as the world has generally done, the service acceptable to God for a system of faith souring the temper, and a service of forms; supplanting morality.

I hope you will not mistake what I am now saying, or consider it as the effect of my prejudices as a Dissenter from the established church. The complaint I am making, is the complaint of many of the wisest and best men in the established church itself, who have long been urging the necessity of a revival of its Liturgy and Articles. These were framed above two centuries ago when Christendom was just emerging from the ignorance and barbarity of the dark ages. They remain now much the same as they were then and, therefore, cannot be properly adapted to the good sense and liberality of the present times. This imperfection, however, in our public forms of worship, affords no excuse to any person for neglecting public worship. All communities will have some religion, and it is of infinite consequence that they should be led to that which, by enforcing the obligations of virtue and putting men upon loving instead of damning one another, is most favourable to the interest of society.

If there is a Governor of the world who directs all events, he ought to be invoked and worshipped, and those who dislike that mode of worship which is prescribed by public authority ought (if they can find no worship out of the church which they approve) to set up a separate worship for themselves and by doing this and giving an example of a rational and manly worship, men of weight, from their rank or literature, may do the greatest service to society in the world.[4] They may bear a testimony against that

[3] A probable reference to the ministry of Charles and John Wesley – founders, with John Whitfield, of Methodism – who offended the rationalism of Price by preaching in the open air a doctrine of salvation by faith through the intervention of the holy spirit. The emotional displays of converts at such gatherings were far from the cool rational religion recommended by Unitarians and evoked the much feared 'enthusiastic' religion of the seventeenth century. See H. Davies, *Worship and Theology in England from Watts and Wesley to Maurice, 1690–1850* (Princeton: Erdmans, 1961), p. 143 ff.
[4] Burke was to denounce this endorsement of religious diversity which he called a 'zeal for difference'.

application of civil power to the support of particular modes of faith which obstructs human improvement and perpetuates error, and they may hold out an instruction which will discountenance superstition, and at the same time recommend religion by making it appear to be (what it certainly is when rightly understood) the strongest incentive to all that is generous and worthy, and, consequently, the best friend to public order and happiness.

Liberty is the next great blessing which I have mentioned as the object of patriotic zeal. It is inseparable from knowledge and virtue and together with them completes the glory of a community. An enlightened and virtuous country must be a free country. It cannot suffer invasions of its rights, or bend to tyrants. I need not, on this occasion, take any pains to shew you how great a blessing liberty is. The smallest attention to the history of past ages and the present state of mankind, will make you sensible of its importance. Look round the world and you will find almost every country, respectable or contemptible, happy or miserable, a fruitful field or a frightful waste, according as it possesses or wants this blessing . . .

The observations I have made include our whole duty to our country, for by endeavouring to liberalize and enlighten it, to discourage vice and to promote virtue in it, and to assert and support its liberties, we shall endeavour to do all that is necessary to make it great and happy. But it is proper that, on this occasion, I should be more explicit and exemplify our duty to our country by observing farther that it requires us to obey its laws and to respect its magistrates.

Civil government (as I have before observed) is an institution of human prudence for guarding our persons, our property, and our good name, against invasion, and for securing to the members of a community that liberty to which all have an equal right, as far as they do not, by any overt act, use it to injure the liberty of others. Civil laws are regulations agreed upon by the community for gaining these ends, and civil magistrates are officers appointed by the community for executing these laws. Obedience, therefore, to the laws and to magistrates is a necessary expression of our regard to the community. Without it a community must fall into a state of anarchy that will destroy those rights and subvert that liberty which it is the end of government to protect.

I wish it was in my power to give you a just account of the importance of this observation. It shews the ground on which the duty of obeying civil governors stands, and that there are two extremes in this case which ought to be avoided. These extremes are adulation and servility on one hand, and a proud and licentious contempt on the other. The former is the extreme to which mankind in general have been most prone, for it has oftener happened that men have been too passive than too unruly, and the rebellion of Kings against their people has been more common and done more mischief than the rebellion of people against their Kings.

Adulation is always odious and when offered to men in power it corrupts them by giving them improper ideas of their situation, and it debases those who offer it by manifesting an abjectness founded on improper ideas of themselves. I have lately observed in this kingdom too near approaches to this abjectness. In our late addresses to the King on his recovery from the severe illness with which God has been pleased to afflict him, we have appeared more like a herd crawling at the feet of a master than like enlightened and manly citizens rejoicing with a beloved sovereign, but at the same time conscious that he derives all his consequence from themselves. . . .

Civil governors are properly the servants of the public and a King is no more than the first servant of the public, created by it, maintained by it, and responsible to it; and all the homage paid him is due to him on no other account than his relation to the public. His sacredness is the sacredness of the community. His authority is the authority of the community, and the term *Majesty*, which it is usual to apply to him, is by no means his own majesty, but the majesty of the people. For this reason, whatever he may be in his private capacity and though, in respect of personal qualities, not equal to or even far below many among ourselves – for this reason I say (that is, as representing the community and its first magistrate) he is entitled to our reverence and obedience. The words *Most Excellent Majesty* are rightly applied to him and there is a respect which it would be criminal to withhold from him.

You cannot be too attentive to this observation. The improvement of the world depends on the attention to it: nor will mankind be ever as virtuous and happy as they are capable of being till the attention to it becomes universal and efficacious. If we forget it we shall be in danger of an idolatry as gross and stupid as that of the ancient heathens, who, after fabricating blocks of wood and stone, fell down and worshipped them. The disposition in mankind to this kind of idolatry is indeed a very mortifying subject of reflexion. In Turkey, millions of human beings adore a silly mortal and are ready to throw themselves at his feet and to submit their lives to his discretion.[5] In Russia, the common people are only a stock on the lands of grandees or appendages to their estates, which, like the fixtures in a house, are bought and

---

[5] The governments of Turkey and Russia were synonymous with absolutism in the eighteenth century; both gave sacral status to their rulers and lacked any representative or balancing institutions as restraints on the ruler.

sold with the estates. In Spain, in Germany, and under most of the governments of the world, mankind are in a similar state of humiliation. Who, that has a just sense of the dignity of his nature, can avoid execrating such a debasement of it?

Had I been to address the King on a late occasion, I should have been inclined to do it in a style very different from that of most of the addressers, and to use some such language as the following:

> I rejoice, Sir, in your recovery. I thank God for his goodness to you. I honour you not only as my King, but as almost the only lawful King in the world, because the only one who owes his crown to the choice of the people. May you enjoy all possible happiness. May God shew you the folly of those effusions of adulation which you are now receiving, and guard you against their effects. May you be led to such a sense of the nature of your situation and endowed with such wisdom as shall render your restoration to the government of these kingdoms a blessing to it, and engage you to consider yourself as more properly the *servant* than the sovereign of your people.

But I must not forget the opposite extreme to that now taken notice of, that is, a disdainful pride derived from a consciousness of equality, or, perhaps, superiority in respect of all that gives true dignity to men in power and producing a contempt of them, and a disposition to treat them with rudeness and insult. It is a trite observation, that extremes generally beget one another. This is particularly true in the present case. Persons justly informed on the subject of government, when they see men dazzled by looking up to high stations and observe loyalty carried to a length that implies ignorance and servility, such persons, in such circumstances, are in danger of spurning at all public authority and throwing off that respectful demeanour to persons invested with it which the order of society requires. There is undoubtedly a particular deference and homage, due to civil magistrates on account of their stations and offices; . . . *You must needs*, says St. Paul, *be subject to rulers, not only for wrath* (that is, from the fear of suffering the penalties annexed to the breach of the laws) *but for conscience sake. For rulers are ministers of God, and revengers for executing wrath on all that do evil.*

Another expression of our love to our country is defending it against enemies. These enemies are of two sorts; internal and external, or domestic and foreign. The former are the most dangerous, and they have generally been the most successful. I have just observed that there is a submission due to the executive officers of a government which is our duty, but you must not forget what I have also observed that it must not be a blind and slavish submission. Men in power (unless better disposed than is common) are always endeavouring to extend their power. They hate the doctrine that it is a trust derived from the people and not a right vested in themselves. For this reason the tendency of every government is to despotism, and in this the best constituted governments must end, if the people are not vigilant, ready to take alarms, and determined to resist abuses as soon as they begin. This vigilance, therefore, it is our duty to maintain. Whenever it is withdrawn and a people cease to reason about their rights and to be awake to encroachments, they are in danger of being enslaved and their servants will soon become their masters.

I need not say how much it is our duty to defend our country against foreign enemies. When a country is attacked in any of its rights by another country, or when any attempts are made by ambitious foreign powers to injure it, a war in its defence becomes necessary: and, in such circumstances, to die for our country is meritorious and noble. These defensive wars are, in my opinion, the only just wars. Offensive wars are always unlawful and to seek the aggrandizement of our country by them, that is, by attacking other countries in order to extend dominion, or to gratify avarice, is wicked and detestable . . .

Among the particulars included in that duty to our country by discharging which we should shew our love to it, I will only further mention praying for it and offering up thanksgivings to God for every event favourable to it. At the present season we are called upon to express in this way our love to our country. It is the business of this day and of the present service, and, therefore, it is necessary that I should now direct your attention to it particularly.

We are met to thank God for that event in this country to which the name of *The Revolution* has been given, and which, for more than a century, it has been usual for the friends of freedom and more especially Protestant Dissenters to celebrate with expressions of joy and exultation. My highly valued and excellent friend [Andrew Kippis], who addressed you on this occasion last year,[6] has given you an interesting account of the principal circumstances that attended this event and of the reasons we have for rejoicing in it. By a bloodless victory the fetters which despotism had long been preparing for us were broken, the rights of the people were asserted, a tyrant expelled, and a sovereign of our own choice appointed in his room. Security was given to our property, and our consciences were emancipated. The bounds of

---

[6] Andrew Kippis (d. 1795), a leading dissenter, lecturer at the Dissenting Hackney College and Fellow of the Royal Society.

free enquiry were enlarged, the volume in which are the words of eternal life was laid more open to our examination, and that aera of light and liberty was introduced among us, by which we have been made an example to other kingdoms and become the instructors of the world. Had it not been for this deliverance, the probability is that, instead of being thus distinguished, we should now have been a base people, groaning under the infamy and misery of popery and slavery. Let us, therefore, offer thanksgivings to God, the author of all our blessings. *Had he not been on our side, we should have been swallowed up quick, and the proud waters would have gone over our souls. But our souls are escaped, and the snare has been broken. Blessed then be the name of the Lord, who made heaven and earth.*

. . . We have particular reason, as Protestant Dissenters, to rejoice on this occasion. It was at this time we were rescued from persecution, and obtained the liberty of worshipping God in the manner we think most acceptable to him. It was then our meeting-houses were opened, our worship was taken under the protection of the law, and the principles of toleration gained a triumph . . . But let us remember that we ought not to satisfy ourselves with thanksgivings. Our gratitude, if genuine, will be accompanied with endeavours to give stability to the deliverance our country has obtained, and to extend and improve the happiness with which the Revolution has blest us. Let us, in particular, take care not to forget the principles of the Revolution. This Society has, very properly, in its reports, held out these principles, as an instruction to the public. I will only take notice of the three following:

> First, the right to liberty of conscience in religious matters. Secondly, the right to resist power when abused. And Thirdly, the right to chuse our own governors, to cashier them for misconduct, and to frame a government for ourselves.[7]

---

[7] [Price's footnote in the fourth edition] 'Mr. Burke in his *Reflections on the Revolution in France* [1790], denies several of the principles which in these pages are said to be the principles of the Revolution. He asserts that our Kings do not derive their right to the crown from the choice of their people, and that they are not responsible to them. And yet, with wonderful inconsistency, he indicates (p. 123) that a wicked king may be punished, provided it is done with dignity and he is under the necessity of granting that King James was justly deprived of his crown for misconduct. In p. 19, he mentions the legal conditions of the compact of sovereignty by which our kings are bound. The succession of the crown he calls a succession by law (p. 28) and the law, he calls an "emanation from the common agreement and original compact of the State", and the constitution also he calls the "engagement and pact of society". In p. 26 he cites, as an authority against the right of the people to chuse their own governors, the very act for settling the crown on William and Mary which was an exercise of that right and the words of which are:

On these three principles, and more especially the last, was the Revolution founded. Were it not true that liberty of conscience is a sacred right, that power abused justifies resistance, and that civil authority is a delegation from the people. Were not, I say, all this true, the Revolution would have been not an assertion, but an invasion of rights, not a revolution, but a rebellion. . . .

I would farther direct you to remember that, though the Revolution [of 1688] was a great work, it was by no means a perfect work, and that all was not then gained which was necessary to put the kingdom in the secure and complete possession of the blessings of liberty. In particular, you should recollect that the toleration then obtained was imperfect. It included only those who could declare their faith in the doctrinal articles of the church of England. It has, indeed, been since extended, but not sufficiently, for there still exist penal laws on account of religious opinions which (were they carried into execution) would shut up many of our places of worship, and silence and imprison some of the ablest and best men. The Test Laws are also still in force and deprive of eligibility to civil and military offices all who cannot conform to the established worship. It is with great pleasure I find that the body of Protestant Dissenters, though defeated in their attempts to deliver their country from this disgrace to it, have determined to persevere. Should they at last succeed, they will have the satisfaction, not only of removing from themselves a proscription they do not deserve, but of contributing to lessen the number of our public iniquities. For I cannot call by a gentler name, laws which

"The Lords and Commons do in the name of all the people submit themselves, their heirs and posterities for ever", etc.

This act having been passed on purpose to establish a change in the succession for misconduct, it cannot be supposed that it was intended to deprive the nation for ever of the power of making again any such change, whatever reasons appearing to the nation sufficient might occur. That is, it cannot be supposed that it was the intention of the act to subject the nation for ever to any tyrants that might happen to arise in the new line of succession. And yet this is the sense in which Mr. Burke seems to understand it, and he grounds upon it his assertion in p. 27, "that so far was the nation from acquiring by the Revolution a right to elect our kings, that, if we had possessed it before, the English nation did then most solemnly renounce and abdicate it for themselves and their posterity for ever". Mr. Burke, before he published this assertion, should have attended to a subsequent act which has been recommended to my notice by the truly patriotic Earl Stanhope [Charles Stanhope, third Earl Stanhope (1753–1816)]. I mean the act of the 6th of Anne, chap 7th, by which it is enacted that, "if any person shall by writing or printing maintain and affirm that the Kings or Queens of this realm, with and by the 'authority of Parliament, are not able to make laws and statutes of sufficient validity to limit the Crown, and the descent, inheritance and government thereof, every such person shall be guilty of high treason, etc".

convert an ordinance appointed by our Saviour to commemorate his death into an instrument of oppressive policy, and a qualification of rakes and atheists for civil posts.[8] . . .

But the most important instance of the imperfect state in which the Revolution left our constitution, is the inequality of our representation. I think, indeed, this defect in our constitution so gross and so palpable, as to make it excellent chiefly in form and theory. You should remember that a representation in the legislature of a kingdom is the basis of constitutional liberty in it, and of all legitimate government, and that without it a government is nothing but an usurpation. When the representation is fair and equal, and at the same time vested with such powers as our House of Commons possesses, a kingdom may be said to govern itself, and consequently to possess true liberty. When the representation is partial, a kingdom possesses liberty only partially, and if extremely partial, it only gives a semblance of liberty; but if not only extremely partial but corruptly chosen, and under corrupt influence after being chosen, it becomes a nuisance and produces the worst of all forms of government: a government by corruption – a government carried on and supported by spreading venality and profligacy through a kingdom. May heaven preserve this kingdom from a calamity so dreadful! It is the point of depravity to which abuses under such a government as ours naturally tend, and the last stage of national unhappiness. We are, at present, I hope, at a great distance from it. But it cannot be pretended that there are no advances towards it or that there is no reason for apprehension and alarm.

The inadequateness of our representation has been long a subject of complaint. This is, in truth, our fundamental grievance, and I do not think that any thing is much more our duty, as men who love their country, and are grateful for the Revolution, than to unite our zeal in endeavouring to get it redressed.[9] At the

---

[8] Under the so-called 'Toleration Act' of 1689, voting rights, membership of the legal professions, and the holding of public office was conditional on being a communicant of the Church of England. The use of this 'sacramental test' was controversial, not only as excluding Catholics and non-conformists from political office, but because it did so through using a religious service with completely different intentions, and thereby providing men with an incentive to compromise their religious convictions for the sake of secular advancement. See Thomas Paine on this: p. 149.

[9] The 'us' here is the Dissenting Community. Movements for the enlargement of the franchise, in which Dissenters were disproportionately prominent, had been active since the outbreak of the American War, the agitation surrounding John Wilkes and the Association movement of the 1780s.

time of the American war, associations were formed for this purpose in London and other parts of the kingdom, and our present Minister himself has since that war directed to it an effort which made him a favourite with many of us.[10] But all attention to it seems now lost, and the probability is that this inattention will continue and that nothing will be done towards gaining for us this essential blessing till some great calamity again alarms our fears, or till some great abuse of power again provokes our resentment or, perhaps, till the acquisition of a pure and equal representation by other countries (while we are mocked with the shadow) kindles our shame.

Such is the conduct by which we ought to express our gratitude for the Revolution. We should always bear in mind the principles that justify it. We should contribute all we can towards supplying what is left deficient, and shew ourselves anxious about transmitting the blessings obtained by it to our posterity, unimpaired and improved. But, brethren, while we thus shew our patriotic zeal, let us take care not to disgrace the cause of patriotism by any licentiousness or immoral conduct. Oh! how earnestly do I wish that all who profess zeal in this cause were as distinguished by the purity of their morals as some of them are by their abilities, and that I could make them sensible of the advantages they would derive from a virtuous character, and of the suspicions they incur and the loss of consequence they suffer by wanting it. Oh! that I could see in men who oppose tyranny in the state a disdain of the tyranny of low passions in themselves, or, at least, such a sense of shame and regard to public order and decency as would induce them to hide their irregularities and to avoid insulting the virtuous part of the community by an open exhibition of vice! I cannot reconcile myself to the idea of an immoral patriot, or to that separation of private from public virtue, which some think to be possible.[11] Is it to be expected that – but I must forbear. I am afraid of applications

---

[10] The 'associations' here were the constitutional associations, in particular the Society for Constitutional Information which had a continuing existence down to the 1790s. 'The Minister' here referred to is the then Prime Minister, William Pitt, who had brought a resolution before the Commons (7 May 1783) to increase the numbers of county MPs and disenfranchise borough constituencies with proven records of bribery. Pitt there had explicitly repudiated the principle of a right of manhood suffrage – which Price endorsed. See E. N. Williams, *The Eighteenth Century Constitution* (Cambridge: Cambridge University Press, 1970), pp. 218–21; and *Parliamentary History* xxiii, 829.
[11] A reference to the notoriously profligate lifestyle of Charles James Fox, the most prominent populist and reformist Whig leader.

which many are too ready to make and for which I should be sorry to give any just occasion.

I have been explaining to you the nature and expressions of a just regard to our country. Give me leave to exhort you to examine your conduct by what I have been saying. You love your country and desire its happiness, and, without doubt, you have the greatest reason for loving it. It has been long a very distinguished and favoured country. Often has God appeared for it and delivered it. Let us study to shew ourselves worthy of the favour shewn us. Do you practise virtue yourselves, and study to promote it in others? Do you obey the laws of your country, and aim at doing your part towards maintaining and perpetuating its privileges? Do you always give your vote on the side of public liberty and are you ready to pour out your blood in its defence? Do you look up to God for the continuance of his favour to your country and pray for its prosperity, preserving, at the same time, a strict regard to the rights of other countries, and always considering yourselves more as citizens of the world than as members of any particular community? If this is your temper and conduct you are blessings to your country, and were all like you this world would soon be a heaven.

I am addressing myself to Christians. Let me, therefore, mention to you the example of our blessed Saviour . . . We read in Luke [xi]x.42, that when, upon approaching Jerusalem, in one of his last journeys to it, he beheld it, he wept over it and said, *Oh! that thou hadst known (even thou, at least in this thy day) the things that belong to thy peace.* What a tender solicitude about his country does the lamentation over Jerusalem imply, which is recorded in the same gospel, chap. xiii and 34. *Oh! Jerusalem, Jerusalem, thou that killest the prophets, and stonest them who are sent to thee, how often would I have gathered thy children together, as a hen gathereth her brood under her wings, but ye would not.*

. . .

It is too evident that the state of this country is such as renders it an object of concern and anxiety. It wants (I have shewn you) the grand security of public liberty. Increasing luxury has multiplied abuses in it. A monstrous weight of debt is crippling it. Vice and venality are bringing down upon it God's displeasure. That spirit to which it owes its distinction is declining, and some late events seem to prove that it is becoming every day more reconcileable to encroachments on the securities of its liberties. It wants, therefore, your patriotic services and, for the sake of the distinctions it has so long enjoyed, for the sake of our brethren and companions and all that should be dear to a free people, we ought to do our utmost to save it from the dangers that threaten it, remembering that by acting thus we shall promote, in the best manner, our own private interest as well as the interest of our country, for when the community prospers the individuals that compose it must prosper with it. But, should that not happen, or should we even suffer in our secular interest by our endeavours to promote the interest of our country, we shall feel a satisfaction in our own breasts which is preferable to all this world can give, and we shall enjoy the transporting hope of soon becoming members of a perfect community in the heavens, and *having an entrance ministered to us, abundantly into the everlasting kingdom of our Lord and Saviour Jesus Christ.*

You may reasonably expect that I should now close this address to you. But I cannot yet dismiss you. I must not conclude without recalling particularly to our recollection . . . the favourableness of the present times to all exertions in the cause of public liberty.

What an eventful period is this! I am thankful that I have lived to see it, and I could almost say, *Lord, now lettest thou thy servant depart in peace, for mine eyes have seen thy salvation.*[12] I have lived to see a diffusion of knowledge which has undermined superstition and error. I have lived to see the rights of men better understood than ever, and nations panting for liberty, which seemed to have lost the idea of it. I have lived to see thirty millions of people, indignant and resolute, spurning at slavery, and demanding liberty with an irresistible voice, their king led in triumph, and an arbitrary monarch surrendering himself to his subjects. After sharing in the benefits of one Revolution, I have been spared to be a witness to two other Revolutions, both glorious. And now, methinks, I see the ardor for liberty catching and spreading, a general amendment beginning in human affairs, the dominion of kings changed for the dominion of laws, and the dominion of priests giving way to the dominion of reason and conscience.

Be encouraged, all ye friends of freedom and writers in its defence! The times are auspicious. Your labours have not been in vain. Behold kingdoms, admonished by you, starting from sleep, breaking their fetters, and claiming justice from their oppressors! Behold, the light you have struck out, after setting America free, reflected to France and there kindled into a blaze that lays despotism in ashes and warms and illuminates Europe!

---

[12] Luke, 2, 29: the words of the aged and devout Simeon on seeing the infant Christ. Simeon had been promised he should not die before seeing the Messiah.

Tremble all ye oppressors of the world! Take warning all ye supporters of slavish governments and slavish hierarchies! Call no more (absurdly and wickedly) reformation, innovation. You cannot now hold the world in darkness. Struggle no longer against increasing light and liberality. Restore to mankind their rights and consent to the correction of abuses, before they and you are destroyed together.

Plate 1. *Smelling out a Rat, or The Atheistical Revolutionist disturbed in his Midnight Calculations* (James Gillray, December 1790). Burke, with *Reflections* in his head, a crucifix in one
hand and crown in the other, symbolising Church and State, is seen surprising Dr Price at
work on a piece entitled: 'On the benefits of Anarchy, Regicide, Atheism'. At his feet is his
sermon, and another 'Treatise on the ill effects of Order & Government in Society and the
absurdity of serving GOD & honouring the KING'. On the wall is a picture of the execution of
Charles I, subtitled 'the glory of Britain'.

EDMUND BURKE

BIOGRAPHICAL NOTE

Edmund Burke was born in Dublin in 1729 and attended Trinity College, Dublin before studying law in London. He moved in literary circles and produced an important work on aesthetics – the *Philosophical Enquiry into the Origin of our Ideas of the Sublime and Beautiful* (1757), before becoming secretary to the Whig leader Lord Rockingham and twice briefly holding political office. He was successively MP for Wendover, Bristol and Malton. His political career was distinguished by a series of reforming campaigns – in parliamentary politics, in opposing the attempts to impose taxation on the American Colonies against their will, in seeking to regulate state finances and so diminish the influence of the Crown. He had been concerned since the 1770s with the failure of Parliament to impose some kind of control over the British administration in India – then in the hands of a private commercial entity, the British East India Company. This was to culminate in his management of the impeachment of Warren Hastings, the returned Governor-General. The trial occupied him throughout the first six years of the French Revolution. More cautiously – for his Catholic background and prevailing anti-Catholic sentiments made this difficult – Burke sought to alleviate the condition of Ireland, then run effectively as an English colony, and in particular the treatment of Irish Catholics.

Burke's last great cause confused many who identified him as a reformer: it was his implacable opposition to the French Revolution and the influence of its ideas. In the course of this he formulated what have come to be seen by many as the doctrines distinctive of modern conservatism.

EDITORIAL NOTE

Reflections on the Revolution in France (1790) was written by Burke in the winter of 1789 and summer of 1790. A young French acquaintance, Charles Depont, had written asking Burke to comment on the extraordinary French political events in November 1789, which Burke had done in a private letter.[1] It was his reading

---

[1] *The Correspondence of Edmund Burke*, ed. T. Copeland and others, 10 vols. (Cambridge: Cambridge University Press, 1958–78), VI, p. 32.

of Price's sermon in January 1790 which precipitated his determination to go into print on the subject. Published in November, *Reflections* went through nine editions in the seven remaining years of Burke's life. He continued to revise the text throughout the first year of publication, with the third edition incorporating major revisions. The Seventh Edition (December 1790) was the last edition corrected by Burke himself and is regarded as definitive by most modern editors. *Reflections . . .* sold 13,000 copies in the first two weeks and a similar number in the French translation published a month later. By Burke's death in 1797, 30,000 copies had been sold.[2] The work provoked widely divergent responses: the King had copies of the first edition specially bound for presentation, the Convocation of the University of Oxford petitioned the Vice Chancellor to grant Burke an honorary degree,[3] and it generated a huge pamphlet debate.[4]

Reflections . . . is aptly named for the multiple ambiguities about its identity, what it is that it is supposed to shed light on and for whom. Even its literary form is extraordinary; it has been claimed to be the longest English work in epistolatory form.[5] Although *reflecting on* France, it is at least as much *about* England; Burke's intention, as he later explained, being to 'convey to a foreign people . . . the prevalent opinions and sentiments of a nation [England] renowned for wisdom, and celebrated in all ages for a well understood and well-regulated love of freedom'.[6] Furthermore, although the work *purports* to have been written as a private letter, and to a *Frenchman*, by publishing it, and doing so in England and in English, Burke shows (despite his claim above) that his intended *audience* was his own countrymen.

Structurally, the opening of the work is dominated by a discussion of the claims made in Richard Price's *Sermon* (p. 49), which Burke saw as an attempt to misrepresent the English Constitution, exemplified in the Glorious Revolution of 1688 as consistent with the principles of Revolutionary France, with the clear intention of stimulating further constitutional reform in England.[7] From the

[2] William B. Todd, *A Bibliography of Edmund Burke* (London: Hart-Davis, 1964), pp. 145, 150.
[3] The university's governing body refused on the grounds that Burke's well-known defence of his Catholic countrymen rendered equivocal his defence of the Church of England.
[4] See Gayle Trusdel Pendleton, 'Towards a Bibliography of the *Reflections* and *Rights of Man* Controversy', *Bulletin of Research in the Humanities* 85 (1982), pp. 65–103.
[5] *Reflections . . .* in *Writings and Speeches of Edmund Burke*, ed. L. G. Mitchell, vol. VIII (Oxford: Clarendon Press, 1989).
[6] *An Appeal from the New to the Old Whigs*, see below, p. 180.
[7] 'Extraordinary things have happened in France; extraordinary things have been said and done here, and published with great ostentation, in order to draw us into a connexion and concurrence with that nation upon principle of its proceedings, and to lead us into an imitation of them. I think such designs, as far as they go, highly dangerous to the constitution and property of this Country.' To Richard Bright, 8 May 1790, *Corr.*, VI, p. 82.

first then, the response to the French Revolution was inseparable from issues of domestic political identity and reform.

Reflections . . . is acknowledged to be an unsystematic work at both the strategic and immediate levels. Claims and ideas are often advanced without the grounds for them being fully stated; arguments and principles recur sporadically rather than being developed logically. However, there are a number of themes which run persistently throughout the work. At the most general level Burke opposes abstract theorising in politics to a reliance on custom and inherited institutions. He grounds this on a sceptical assessment of individual reasoning and knowledge, together with an assumption that historical processes (when not distorted by atheistical enthusiasts) are providentially guided. From this view certain institutions – the family, private property, a natural aristocracy, a state religion, and what he calls 'corporations', that is organised bodies capable of perpetuating themselves independently of the state or any individual, all follow. They are all vehicles for the trans-historical accumulation and perpetuation of human knowledge.

The radical claims of natural right he shows to be a claim to overturn this inherited experience and to restart our institutional history with a clean slate. Indeed with thinkers such as Paine this is made quite explicit. For Burke such a claim not only vastly overestimates the capacity of human reasoning but presupposes a universal *individual* right to judge and act on these matters. Taken together, these could be seen to constitute an act of epistemological and volitional original sin – pride. Since today we take for granted the rights of individuals to accept or reject their cultural and political inheritance it's worth underscoring that this in a sense was the core issue of the time. Burke's understanding of political societies and the practices and dispositions that comprise them is of something infinitely complex and nuanced. They comprise incredibly subtly enmeshed institutions, beliefs and practices. These historically produced 'gifts of time and chance' must be cared for; they cannot be recreated once lost. Once such social complexes are broken up, human beings revert to a 'natural state' which is at once Hobbesian (in the sense that each can do what violence is needed to survive) and Rousseavian (in the sense that it is culturally primitive). Civilisation is fragile: our primitive natures for Burke lie easily exposed below the veneer of civility.

At a less abstract level Burke's writing addresses long-standing eighteenth-century themes concerning the relationship between social institutions, public opinion, private property, government and religion, in which government was seen to rest on the people's opinion of its legitimacy; an opinion which in turn rested both on moral sentiments (supported by religion) and the securing of our personal interests and expectations through the property system. The French Revolutionary regime incurred huge financial problems from the virtually bankrupt *ancien régime*. Their attempts to solve this through the dis-establishment of the Church and the appropriation of its land to pay off the national debt were, for Burke, not only criminal – state-sanctioned robbery – and impious – because it destroyed respect for the Church – but foolish, because they destroyed the institutions which sustained the delicate balance by which moral opinions consistent with civilised society were perpetuated from generation to generation.

The text used here is that identified by William Todd as the fifth impression of the third edition, calling itself the seventh edition, and the last to be revised by Burke himself, C. C. O'Brien, J. G. A. Pocock and L. G. Mitchell all use this edition. J. C. D. Clark, however, uses the text of the first edition, that to which Paine, Wollstonecraft and Mackintosh all responded, with the later passages in an appendix.

Modern editions:

Writings and Speeches of Edmund Burke, vol. VIII: *The French Revolution 1790–1794*, ed. L. G. Mitchell (Oxford: Clarendon Press, 1989) (this is the relevant volume in the modern scholarly edition of Burke's works).

Reflections on the Revolution in France, ed. and intr. William Todd (New York: Holt, Reinhart and Wilson, 1959).

Reflections on the Revolution in France, ed. and intr. Conor Cruise O'Brien, (Harmondsworth: Penguin Books, 1969).

Reflections on the Revolution in France: A Critical Edition, ed. J. C. D. Clark (Stanford: Stanford University Press, 2001) (contains an excellent introduction and a detailed and wide-ranging bibliographical essay).

Reflections on the Revolution in France, ed. and intr. J. G. A. Pocock (Indianapolis: Hackett, 1987).

Reflections on the Revolution in France, vol. II of *Select Works of Edmund Burke*, with foreword and notes by Frances Canovan (Indianapolis: Liberty Fund, 1999).

FURTHER READING

Chapman, Gerald W. *Edmund Burke: The Practical Imagination* (Cambridge, Mass.: Harvard University Press, 1967).

Cobban, A. *Edmund Burke and the Revolt against the Eighteenth Century* (London, 1929).

Lock, F. P. *Burke's Reflections on the Revolution in France* (London: Unwin, 1985).

Lock, F. P. *Edmund Burke*, vol. I: *1730–1784* (Oxford: Clarendon Press, 1998).

Macpherson, C. B. *Burke* (Oxford: Oxford University Press, 1981).

O'Brien, Conor Cruise *The Great Melody* (London: Minerva, 1992).

O'Gorman, F. *Edmund Burke: His Political Philosophy* (London: Unwin, 1973).

Pocock, J. G. A. 'Burke and the Ancient Constitution: A Problem in the History of Ideas', *Historical Journal* 3 (2) (1960), pp. 125–43 and in his *Politics, Language and Time* (London: Methuen, 1971), pp. 202–32.

Parkin, C. *The Moral Basis of Burke's Political Thought* (Cambridge: Cambridge University Press, 1956).

Whale, J. (ed.) *Edmund Burke's Reflections on the Revolution in France: New Interdisciplinary Essays* (Manchester University Press, 2000).

Wilkins, B. T. *The Problem of Burke's Political Philosophy* (Oxford: Oxford University Press, 1967).

Reflections on the Revolution in France and on the proceedings in certain societies in London relative to that event in a letter intended to have been sent to a gentleman in Paris by the right honourable Edmund Burke[1] (1790)

. . .

You imagined, when you wrote last, that I might possibly be reckoned among the approvers of certain proceedings in France, from the solemn public seal of sanction they have received from two clubs of gentlemen in London, called the Constitutional Society and the Revolution Society.[2]

I certainly have the honour to belong to more clubs than one, in which the constitution of this kingdom and the principles of the glorious Revolution, are held in high reverence: and I reckon myself among the most forward in my zeal

[1] The Gentleman was Charles Jean-François Depont, a career politician who had both visited Burke in England and hosted him in France. Depont was an enthusiastic reformer and represented Metz in the National Assembly. Depont had written to Burke asking whether 'the French are worthy of being free, that they know how to distinguish liberty from licence, and legitimate government from despotic power' and whether he thought the revolution could succeed. *Correspondence*, vi, Depont to Burke, 4 Nov. 1789, p. 31.

[2] The Society for Constitutional Information, founded by John Cartwright, John Jebb and Brand Hollis in 1780, printed and distributed reformist Tracts. The Revolution Society was a Dissenters association which celebrated the protestant values of 1688. It appears to have become more political as the centenary approached. On both see Eugene Black, *The Association: British Extra-Parliamentary Political Organisation 1769–1793* (Cambridge, Mass.: Harvard University Press, 1963), and Albert Goodwin, *The Friends of Liberty: The English Democratic Movement in the Age of the French Revolution* (London: Hutchinson, 1979).

for maintaining that constitution and those principles in their utmost purity and vigour. . . .

. . .

I flatter myself that I love a manly, moral, regulated liberty as well as any gentleman of that society, be he who he will; and perhaps I have given as good proofs of my attachment to that cause, in the whole course of my public conduct. I think I envy liberty as little as they do, to any other nation. But I cannot stand forward, and give praise or blame to any thing which relates to human actions, and human concerns, on a simple view of the object as it stands stripped of every relation, in all the nakedness and solitude of metaphysical abstraction. Circumstances (which with some gentlemen pass for nothing) give in reality to every political principle its distinguishing colour, and discriminating effect. The circumstances are what render every civil and political scheme beneficial or noxious to mankind. Abstractedly speaking, government, as well as liberty, is good; . . . Am I to congratulate an highwayman and murderer, who has broke prison, upon the recovery of his natural rights? This would be to act over again the scene of the criminals condemned to the galleys, and their heroic deliverer, the metaphysic Knight of the Sorrowful Countenance.[3]

When I see the spirit of liberty in action, I see a strong principle at work; and this, for a while, is all I can possibly know of it. The wild *gas*, the fixed air, is plainly broke loose: but we ought to suspend our judgment until the first effervescence is a little subsided, till the liquor is cleared, and until we see something deeper than the agitation of a troubled and frothy surface. I must be tolerably sure, before I venture publicly to congratulate men upon a blessing, that they have really received one. Flattery corrupts both the receiver and the giver; and adulation is not of more service to the people than to kings. I should therefore suspend my congratulations on the new liberty of France, until I was informed how it had been combined with government; with public force; with the discipline and obedience of armies; with the collection of an effective and well-distributed revenue; with morality and religion; with the solidity of property; with peace and order; with civil and social manners. All these (in their way) are good things too; and, without them, liberty is not a benefit whilst it lasts, and is not likely to continue long. The effect of liberty to individuals

---

[3] A reference to *Don Quixote*, who, having freed a gang of convicted prisoners, is then attacked and robbed by them. Burke was often subsequently caricatured as Don Quixote (see Plate 2).

is that they may do what they please: we ought to see what it will please them to do, before we risk congratulations, which may be soon turned into complaints. Prudence would dictate this in the case of separate insulated private men; but liberty, when men act in bodies, is *power*. Considerate people, before they declare themselves, will observe the use which is made of *power*, and particularly of so trying a thing as *new* power in *new* persons, of whose principles, tempers, and dispositions, they have little or no experience, and in situations where those who appear the most stirring in the scene may possibly not be the real movers.

All these considerations however were below the transcendental dignity of the Revolution Society....

. . .

On the forenoon of the 4th of November last, Doctor Richard Price, a non-conforming minister of eminence, preached at the dissenting meeting-house of the Old Jewry, to his club or society . . .

. . .

That sermon is in a strain which I believe has not been heard in this kingdom, in any of the pulpits which are tolerated or encouraged in it, since the year 1648, when a predecessor of Dr. Price, the Reverend Hugh Peters,[4] made the vault of the king's own chapel at St. James's ring with the honour and privilege of the Saints, who, with the 'high praises of God in their mouths, and a *two*-edged sword in their hands, were to execute judgment on the heathen, and punishments upon the *people*, to bind their *kings* with chains, and their *nobles* with fetters of iron.' . . .

. . .

His doctrines affect our constitution in its vital parts. He tells the Revolution Society, in this political sermon, that his majesty 'is almost the *only* lawful king in the world, because the *only* one who owes his crown to the *choice of his people*;' . . .

This doctrine, as applied to the prince now on the British throne, either is nonsense, and therefore neither true nor false, or it affirms a most unfounded, dangerous, illegal, and unconstitutional position. According to this spiritual doctor of politics, if his majesty does not owe his crown to the choice of his people, he is no lawful king. Now nothing can be more untrue than that the crown of this kingdom is so held by his majesty. Therefore if you follow their rule, the king of Great Britain, who most certainly does not owe his high office to any form of popular election, is in no respect

---

[4] Hugh Peters: a famous Puritan preacher and chaplain to the Roundhead Army, executed for treason at the restoration.

better than the rest of the gang of usurpers, who reign, or rather rob, all over the face of this our miserable world, without any sort of right or title to the allegiance of their people . . . By this policy, whilst our government is soothed with a reservation in its favour, to which it has no claim, the security, which it has in common with all governments, so far as opinion is security, is taken away.

. . .

. . . Lest the foundation of the king's exclusive legal title should pass for a mere rant of adulatory freedom, the political Divine proceeds dogmatically to assert that by the principles of the Revolution the people of England have acquired three fundamental rights, all which, with him, compose one system, and lie together in one short sentence; namely, that we have acquired a right

1. 'To choose our own governors.'
2. 'To cashier them for misconduct.'
3. 'To frame a government for ourselves.'

This new, and hitherto unheard-of bill of rights, though made in the name of the whole people, belongs to those gentlemen and their faction only. The body of the people of England have no share in it. They utterly disclaim it. They will resist the practical assertion of it with their lives and fortunes. They are bound to do so by the laws of their country, made at the time of that very Revolution, which is appealed to in favour of the fictitious rights claimed by the society which abuses its name.

These gentlemen of the Old Jewry, in all their reasonings on the Revolution of 1688, have a revolution which happened in England about forty years before,[5] and the late French revolution, so much before their eyes, and in their hearts, that they are constantly confounding all the three together. It is necessary that we should separate what they confound. We must recall their erring fancies to the *acts* of the Revolution which we revere, for the discovery of its true *principles*. If the *principles* of the Revolution of 1688 are any where to be found, it is in the statute called the *Declaration of Right*. In that most wise, sober, and considerate declaration, drawn up by great lawyers and great statesmen, and not by warm and inexperienced enthusiasts, not one word is said, nor one suggestion made, of a general right 'to choose our own governors; to cashier them for misconduct; and to form a government for ourselves.'

[5] The English Civil War and the Interregnum, 1642–1660.

This Declaration of Right (the act of the 1st of William and Mary, sess. 2. ch. 2)[6] is the corner-stone of our constitution, as reinforced, explained, improved, and in its fundamental principles for ever settled. It is called 'An act for declaring the rights and liberties of the subject, and for *settling* the *succession* of the crown.' You will observe, that these rights and this succession are declared in one body, and bound indissolubly together.

A few years after this period, a second opportunity offered for asserting a right of election to the crown. On the prospect of a total failure of issue from King William, and from the Princess, afterwards Queen Anne, the consideration of the settlement of the crown, and of a further security for the liberties of the people, again came before the legislature. Did they this second time make any provision for legalizing the crown on the spurious Revolution principles of the Old Jewry? No. They followed the principles which prevailed in the Declaration of Right; indicating with more precision the persons who were to inherit in the Protestant line. This act also incorporated, by the same policy, our liberties, and an hereditary succession in the same act. Instead of a right to choose our own governors, they declared that the *succession* in that line (the protestant line drawn from James the First) was absolutely necessary 'for the peace, quiet, and security of the realm,' and that it was equally urgent on them 'to maintain a *certainty in the succession* thereof, to which the subjects may safely have recourse for their protection.'[7] . . .

Unquestionably there was at the Revolution, in the person of King William, a small and a temporary deviation from the strict order of regular hereditary succession; but it is against all genuine principles of jurisprudence to draw a principle from a law made in a special case, and regarding an individual person. *Privilegium non transit in exemplum.*[8] If ever there was a time favourable for establishing the principle, that

---

[6] The Bill of Rights passed by the Convention Parliament declared King James to have 'abdicated the government and the throne thereby being vacant . . . Resolve(d) that William and Mary . . . be, and be declared King and Queen'. But it also listed the offences of which James had been guilty, and took the opportunity to assert various ancient rights and liberties. The Royal succession, and the enjoyment of these rights and liberties, Burke suggests, are bound together in this 'settlement'. See E. N. Williams, *The Eighteenth Century Constitution* (Cambridge University Press, 1960) pp. 26ff.
[7] The Act referred to is the 'Act of Settlement' passed in 1701 which identified Sophia, Duchess of Hanover and grand-daughter of James I (and the 'heirs of her body') as next in line to the throne after Princess Anne of Denmark, (subsequently Queen Anne) daughter of James II, as the only surviving protestant discendants of the Stuart line, Williams, *Eighteenth Century Constitution*, p. 56 ff.
[8] 'Privilege does not constitute a rule.'

a king of popular choice was the only legal king, without all doubt it was at the Revolution. Its not being done at that time is a proof that the nation was of opinion it ought not to be done at any time. . . .

. . .

So far is it from being true, that we acquired a right by the Revolution to elect our kings, that if we had possessed it before, the English nation did at that time most solemnly renounce and abdicate it, for themselves and for all their posterity forever.

. . .

A state without the means of some change is without the means of its conservation. Without such means it might even risque the loss of that part of the constitution which it wished the most religiously to preserve. The two principles of conservation and correction operated strongly at the two critical periods of the Restoration and Revolution, when England found itself without a king. At both those periods the nation had lost the bond of union in their ancient edifice; they did not, however, dissolve the whole fabric. On the contrary, in both cases they regenerated the deficient part of the old constitution through the parts which were not impaired. They kept these old parts exactly as they were, that the part recovered might be suited to them. They acted by the ancient organized states in the shape of their old organization, and not by the organic *moleculae*[9] of a disbanded people. . . .

. . .

The gentlemen of the Society for Revolutions see nothing in that of 1688 but the deviation from the constitution; and they take the deviation from the principle for the principle. They have little regard to the obvious consequences of their doctrine, though they must see, that it leaves positive authority in very few of the positive institutions of this country. . . .

. . .

The second claim of the Revolution Society is 'a right of cashiering their governors for *misconduct.*' . . .

No government could stand a moment, if it could be blown down with anything so loose and indefinite as an opinion of '*misconduct.*' They who led at the Revolution, grounded the virtual abdication of King James upon no such light and uncertain principle. They charged him with nothing less than a design, confirmed by a multitude of illegal overt acts, to *subvert the Protestant church and state*, and their *fundamental,*

---

[9] I.e. molecules or atoms.

unquestionable laws and liberties: they charged him with having broken the *original contract* between king and people. This was more than *misconduct*. A grave and over-ruling necessity obliged them to take the step they took, and took with infinite reluctance, as under that most rigorous of all laws. . . .

. . .

. . . The question of dethroning, or, if these gentlemen like the phrase better, 'cashiering kings', will always be, as it has always been, an extraordinary question of state, and wholly out of the law; a question (like all other questions of state) of dispositions, and of means, and of probable consequences, rather than of positive rights. As it was not made for common abuses, so it is not to be agitated by common minds. The speculative line of demarcation, where obedience ought to end, and resistance must begin, is faint, obscure, and not easily definable. It is not a single act, or a single event, which determines it. Governments must be abused and deranged indeed, before it can be thought of; and the prospect of the future must be as bad as the experience of the past. . . .

The third head of right, asserted by the pulpit of the Old Jewry, namely, the 'right to form a government for ourselves,' has, at least, as little countenance from any thing done at the Revolution, either in precedent or principle, as the two first of their claims. The Revolution was made to preserve our *ancient* indisputable laws and liberties, and that *ancient* constitution of government which is our only security for law and liberty . . . Such a claim is as ill-suited to our temper and wishes as it is unsupported by any appearance of authority. The very idea of the fabrication of a new government is enough to fill us with disgust and horror. We wished at the period of the Revolution, and do now wish, to derive all we possess as *an inheritance from our forefathers*. Upon that body and stock of inheritance we have taken care not to inoculate any cyon alien to the nature of the original plant. All the reformations we have hitherto made, have proceeded upon the principle of reference to antiquity; and I hope, nay I am persuaded, that all those which possibly may be made hereafter, will be carefully formed upon analogical precedent, authority, and example.

Our oldest reformation is that of Magna Charta. You will see that Sir Edward Coke, that great oracle of our law, and indeed all the great men who follow him, to Blackstone, are industrious to prove the pedigree of our liberties. They endeavour to prove, that the ancient charter, the Magna Charta of King John, was connected with another positive charter from Henry I, and that both the one and the other were nothing more than a re-affirmance of the still more ancient standing law of the kingdom.[10] In the matter of fact, for the greater part, these authors appear to be in the right; perhaps not always: but if the lawyers mistake in some particulars, it proves my position still the more strongly; because it demonstrates the powerful prepossession towards antiquity, with which the minds of all our lawyers and legislators, and of all the people whom they wish to influence, have been always filled; and the stationary policy of this kingdom in considering their most sacred rights and franchises as an *inheritance.*

. . .

You will observe, that from Magna Charta to the Declaration of Right, it has been the uniform policy of our constitution to claim and assert our liberties, as an *entailed inheritance*[11] derived to us from our forefathers, and to be transmitted to our posterity; as an estate specially belonging to the people of this kingdom without any reference whatever to any other more general or prior right. By this means our constitution preserves an unity in so great a diversity of its parts. We have an inheritable crown; an inheritable peerage; and an house of commons and a people inheriting privileges, franchises, and liberties, from a long line of ancestors.

This policy appears to me to be the result of profound reflection; or rather the happy effect of following nature, which is wisdom without reflection, and above it. A spirit of innovation is generally the result of a selfish temper and confined views. People will not look forward to posterity, who never look backward to their ancestors. Besides, the people of England well know, that the idea of inheritance furnishes a sure principle of conservation, and a sure principle of transmission; without at all excluding a principle of improvement. It leaves acquisition free; but it secures what it acquires. Whatever advantages are obtained by a state proceeding on these maxims, are locked fast as in a sort of family settlement; grasped as in a kind of mortmain[12] for ever. By

[10] Sir Edward Coke, d. 1634, Lord Chief Justice, defended extension of the Royal prerogative by elaborating the doctrine of Common Law as immemorial tradition, an important argument in the conflict between Parliament and Charles I. Sir William Blackstone (d. 1780) was Solicitor General and a famous jurist and author of *Commentaries on the Laws of England* (1765), which was one of the first attempts to provide a systematic account of the laws and constitution of Great Britain.

[11] *Entailment* made the inheritance of an estate conditional upon passing it on intact to the succeeding generation. It was a way of ensuring that the King's nobles retained sufficient resources to discharge their military duties.

[12] *Mortmain*, literally (Norman French) 'dead hand', signified a feudal property right which could not be alienated at will (so related to the above). Also a way of establishing property right in a corporation or other legally fictive person, for the same purpose.

a constitutional policy, working after the pattern of nature, we receive, we hold, we transmit our government and our privileges, in the same manner in which we enjoy and transmit our property and our lives. The institutions of policy, the goods of fortune, the gifts of Providence, are handed down, to us and from us, in the same course and order. Our political system is placed in a just correspondence and symmetry with the order of the world, and with the mode of existence decreed to a permanent body composed of transitory parts; wherein, by the disposition of a stupendous wisdom, moulding together the great mysterious incorporation of the human race, the whole, at one time, is never old, or middle-aged, or young, but in a condition of unchangeable constancy, moves on through the varied tenor of perpetual decay, fall, renovation, and progression. Thus, by preserving the method of nature in the conduct of the state, in what we improve, we are never wholly new; in what we retain we are never wholly obsolete. By adhering in this manner and on those principles to our forefathers, we are guided not by the superstition of antiquarians, but by the spirit of philosophic analogy. In this choice of inheritance we have given to our frame of polity the image of a relation in blood; binding up the constitution of our country with our dearest domestic ties; adopting our fundamental laws into the bosom of our family affections; keeping inseparable, and cherishing with the warmth of all their combined and mutually reflected charities, our state, our hearths, our sepulchres, and our altars.

. . . By this means our liberty becomes a noble freedom. It carries an imposing and majestic aspect. It has a pedigree and illustrating ancestors. It has its bearings and its ensigns armorial. It has its gallery of portraits; its monumental inscriptions; its records, evidences, and titles. We procure reverence to our civil institutions on the principle upon which nature teaches us to revere individual men; on account of their age; and on account of those from whom they are descended. All your sophisters cannot produce any thing better adapted to preserve a rational and manly freedom than the course that we have pursued, who have chosen our nature rather than our speculations, our breasts rather than our inventions, for the great conservatories and magazines of our rights and privileges. You might, if you pleased, have profited of our example, and have given to your recovered freedom a correspondent dignity. Your privileges, though discontinued, were not lost to memory. Your constitution, it is true, whilst you were out of possession, suffered waste and dilapidation; but you possessed in some parts the walls, and in all the foundations, of a noble and venerable castle. You might have repaired those walls; you might have built on those old foundations. Your constitution was suspended before it was perfected; but you had the elements of a constitution very nearly as good as could be wished. . . .

. . .

Compute your gains: see what is got by those extravagant and presumptuous speculations which have taught your leaders to despise all their predecessors, and all their contemporaries, and even to despise themselves, until the moment in which they became truly despicable. By following those false lights, France has bought undisguised calamities at a higher price than any nation has purchased the most unequivocal blessings. France has bought poverty by crime! France has not sacrificed her virtue to her interest; but she has abandoned her interest, that she might prostitute her virtue. All other nations have begun the fabric of a new government, or the reformation of an old, by establishing originally, or by enforcing with greater exactness some rites or other of religion. All other peoples have laid the foundations of civil freedom in severer manners, and a system of more austere and masculine morality. France, when she let loose the reins of legal authority, doubled the licence of a ferocious dissoluteness in manners, and of an insolent religion in opinions and practices; . . .

. . .

This was unnatural. The rest is in order. They have found their punishment in their success. Laws overturned; tribunals subverted; industry without vigour; commerce expiring; the revenue unpaid, yet the people impoverished; a church pillaged, and a state not relieved; civil and military anarchy made the constitution of the kingdom; every thing human and divine sacrificed to the idol of public credit, and national bankruptcy the consequence; and to crown all, the paper securities[13] of new, precarious, tottering power, the discredited paper securities of impoverished fraud, and beggared rapine, held out as a currency for the support of an empire, in lieu of the two great recognized species[14] that represent the lasting conventional credit of mankind, which disappeared and hid themselves in the earth from whence they came, when the principle of property, whose creatures and representatives they are, was systematically subverted.

Were all these dreadful things necessary? Were they the inevitable results of the desperate struggle of determined patriots, compelled to wade through blood and tumult, to the quiet shore of a tranquil and prosperous liberty? No! nothing like it . . .

---

[13] Paper money, the *assignat*.   [14] Gold and silver, the normal basis of currency at the time.

This unforced choice, this fond election of evil, would appear perfectly unaccountable, if we did not consider the composition of the National Assembly; I do not mean its formal constitution, which, as it now stands, is exceptionable enough, but the materials of which in a great measure it is composed, which is of ten thousand times greater consequence than all the formalities in the world . . . No name, no power, no function, no artificial institution whatsoever, can make of the men of whom any system of authority is composed, any other than God, and nature, and education, and the habits of life have made them . . .

After I had read over the list of the persons and descriptions elected into the *Tiers Etat*, nothing which they afterwards did could appear astonishing. Among them, indeed, I saw some of known rank; some of shining talents; but of any practical experience in the state, not one man was to be found. The best were only men of theory. . . .

. . . Nothing can secure a steady and moderate conduct in such assemblies, but that the body of them should be respectably composed, in point of condition in life, of permanent property, of education, and of such habits as enlarge and liberalize the understanding.

. . .

Judge, Sir, of my surprize, when I found that a very great proportion of the Assembly (a majority, I believe, of the members who attended) was composed of practitioners in the law. It was composed not of distinguished magistrates, who had given pledges to their country of their science, prudence, and integrity; not of leading advocates, the glory of the bar; not of renowned professors in universities – but for the far greater part, as it must in such a number, of the inferior, unlearned, mechanical, merely instrumental members of the profession. There were distinguished exceptions; but the general composition was of obscure provincial advocates, of stewards of petty local jurisdictions, country attorneys, notaries, and the whole train of the ministers of municipal litigation, the fomenters and conductors of the petty war of village vexation. From the moment I read the list I saw distinctly, and very nearly as it has happened, all that was to follow.

. . .

. . . Who could flatter himself that these men, suddenly, and, as it were, by enchantment, snatched from the humblest rank of subordination, would not be intoxicated with their unprepared greatness? Who could conceive, that men who are habitually meddling, daring, subtle, active, of litigious dispositions and unquiet minds, would easily fall back into their old condition of obscure contention, and laborious, low, unprofitable chicane? Who could doubt but that, at any expense to the state, of which they understood nothing, they must pursue their private interests, which they understood but too well? It was not an event depending on chance or contingency. It was inevitable; it was necessary; it was planted in the nature of things. . . .

. . . To the faculty of law was joined a pretty considerable proportion of the faculty of medicine. This faculty had not, any more than that of the law, possessed in France its just estimation. Its professors therefore must have the qualities of men not habituated to sentiments of dignity. But supposing they had ranked as they ought to do, and as with us they do actually, the sides of sick beds are not the academies for forming statesmen and legislators. Then came the dealers in stocks and funds, who must be eager, at any expense, to change their ideal paper wealth for the more solid substance of land. To these were joined men of other descriptions, from whom as little knowledge of or attention to the interests of a great state was to be expected, and as little regard to the stability of any institution; men formed to be instruments, not controls. Such in general was the composition of the *Tiers Etat* in the National Assembly; in which was scarcely to be perceived the slightest traces of what we call the natural landed interest of the country.

. . .

. . . That Assembly, since the destruction of the orders, has no fundamental law, no strict convention, no respected usage to restrain it. Instead of finding themselves obliged to conform to a fixed constitution, they have a power to make a constitution which shall conform to their designs. Nothing in heaven or upon earth can serve as a control on them. . . .

Having considered the composition of the third estate as it stood in its original frame, I took a view of the representatives of the clergy. There too it appeared, that full as little regard was had to the general security of property, or to the aptitude of the deputies for their public purpose, in the principles of their election. That election was so contrived as to send a very large proportion of mere country curates[15] to the great and arduous work of new-modelling a state; men who never had seen the state so much as in a picture; men who knew nothing of the world beyond the bounds of an obscure village; who, immersed in hopeless poverty, could regard all property, whether secular or ecclesiastical, with no other eye than that of envy; among whom

[15] A curate was a clergyman hired to perform the duties of another who was the true holder of the living. It is used here to denote the lowest and least secure professional office.

must be many, who, for the smallest hope of the meanest dividend in plunder, would readily join in any attempts upon a body of wealth, in which they could hardly look to have any share, except in a general scramble . . .

To observing men it must have appeared from the beginning, that the majority of the Third Estate, in conjunction with such a deputation from the clergy as I have described, whilst it pursued the destruction of the nobility, would inevitably become subservient to the worst designs of individuals in that class. In the spoil and humiliation of their own order these individuals would possess a sure fund for the pay of their new followers. To squander away the objects which made the happiness of their fellows, would be to them no sacrifice at all . . . [Whereas] To be attached to the subdivision, to love the little platoon we belong to in society, is the first principle (the germ as it were) of public affections. It is the first link in the series by which we proceed towards a love to our country and to mankind. The interests of that portion of social arrangement is a trust in the hands of all those who compose it; and as none but bad men would justify it in abuse, none but traitors would barter it away for their own personal advantage.

. . .

. . . Other revolutions have been conducted by persons, who whilst they attempted or effected changes in the commonwealth, sanctified their ambition by advancing the dignity of the people whose peace they troubled. They had long views. They aimed at the rule, not at the destruction of their country. They were men of great civil, and great military talents, and if the terror, the ornament of their age . . .

These disturbers were not so much like men usurping power, as asserting their natural place in society. Their rising was to illuminate and beautify the world. Their conquest over their competitors was by outshining them . . . But your present confusion, like a palsy, has attacked the fountain of life itself. Every person in your country, in a situation to be actuated by a principle of honour, is disgraced and degraded, and can entertain no sensation of life, except in a mortified and humiliated indignation . . . The associations of tailors and carpenters, of which the republic (of Paris, for instance) is composed, cannot be equal to the situation, into which, by the worst of usurpations, an usurpation on the prerogatives of nature, you attempt to force them.

The chancellor of France at the opening of the states, said, in a tone of oratorical flourish, that all occupations were honourable. If he meant only, that no honest employment was disgraceful, he would not have gone beyond the truth. But in asserting, that any thing is honourable, we imply some distinction in its favour.

The occupation of an hair-dresser, or of a working tallow-chandler,[16] cannot be a matter of honour to any person – to say nothing of a number of other more servile employments. Such descriptions of men ought not to suffer oppression from the state; but the state suffers oppression, if such as they, either individually or collectively, are permitted to rule. In this you think you are combating prejudice, but you are at war with nature.

. . .

. . . There is no qualification for government, but virtue and wisdom, actual or presumptive. Wherever they are actually found, they have, in whatever state, condition, profession or trade, the passport of Heaven to human place and honour. Woe to the country which would madly and impiously reject the service of the talents and virtues, civil, military, or religious, that are given to grace and to serve it; and would condemn to obscurity every thing formed to diffuse lustre and glory around a state. Woe to that country too, that passing into the opposite extreme, considers a low education, a mean contracted view of things, a sordid mercenary occupation, as a preferable title to command. Every thing ought to be open; but not indifferently to every man . . . I do not hesitate to say, that the road to eminence and power, from obscure condition, ought not to be made too easy, nor a thing too much of course. If rare merit be the rarest of all rare things, it ought to pass through some sort of probation. The temple of honour ought to be seated on an eminence. If it be open through virtue, let it be remembered too, that virtue is never tried but by some difficulty, and some struggle.

Nothing is a due and adequate representation of a state, that does not represent its ability, as well as its property. But as ability is a vigorous and active principle, and as property is sluggish, inert, and timid, it never can be safe from the invasions of ability, unless it be, out of all proportion, predominant in the representation. It must be represented too in great masses of accumulation, or it is not rightly protected. The characteristic essence of property, formed out of the combined principles of its acquisition and conservation, is to be *unequal*. The great masses therefore which excite envy, and tempt rapacity, must be put out of the possibility of danger. Then they form a natural rampart about the lesser properties in all their gradations. . . .

The power of perpetuating our property in our families is one of the most valuable and interesting circumstances belonging to it, and that which tends the most to the perpetuation of society itself. It makes our weakness subservient to our virtue;

---

[16] Tallow (animal fat) was used in the preparation of candles and soap and in treating leather.

it grafts benevolence even upon avarice. The possessors of family wealth, and of the distinction which attends hereditary possession (as most concerned in it) are the natural securities for this transmission. With us, the house of peers is formed upon this principle. It is wholly composed of hereditary property and hereditary distinction; and made therefore the third of the legislature; and in the last event, the sole judge of all property in all its subdivisions. The house of commons too, though not necessarily, yet in fact, is always so composed in the far greater part. Let those large proprietors be what they will, and they have their chance of being amongst the best, they are at the very worst, the ballast in the vessel of the commonwealth. . . .

. . .

. . . Whilst they [the French revolutionaries] are possessed by these notions [of natural rights], it is vain to talk to them of the practice of their ancestors, the fundamental laws of their country, the fixed form of a constitution, whose merits are confirmed by the solid test of long experience, and an increasing public strength and national prosperity. They despise experience as the wisdom of unlettered men; and as for the rest, they have wrought under-ground a mine that will blow up at one grand explosion all examples of antiquity, all precedents, charters, and acts of parliament. They have 'the rights of men.' Against these there can be no prescription; against these no agreement is binding: these admit no temperament, and no compromise: any thing withheld from their full demand is so much of fraud and injustice. Against these their rights of men let no government look for security in the length of its continuance, or in the justice and lenity of its administration . . . They are always at issue with governments, not on a question of abuse, but a question of competency, and a question of title. I have nothing to say to the clumsy subtlety of their political metaphysics. . . .

Far am I from denying in theory; full as far is my heart from withholding in practice (if I were of power to give or to withhold) the *real* rights of men. In denying their false claims of right, I do not mean to injure those which are real, and are such as their pretended rights would totally destroy. If civil society be made for the advantage of man, all the advantages for which it is made become his right. It is an institution of beneficence; and law itself is only beneficence acting by a rule. Men have a right to live by that rule; they have a right to justice; as between their fellows, whether their fellows are in politic function or in ordinary occupation. They have a right to the fruits of their industry; and to the means of making their industry fruitful. They have a right to the acquisitions of their parents; to the nourishment and improvement of their offspring; to instruction in life, and to consolation in death. Whatever each man can separately do, without trespassing upon others, he has a right to do for himself; and he has a right to a fair portion of all which society, with all its combinations of skill and force, can do in his favour. In this partnership all men have equal rights; but not to equal things. He that has but five shillings in the partnership, has as good a right to it, as he that has five hundred pound has to his larger proportion. But he has not a right to an equal dividend in the product of the joint stock; and as to the share of power, authority, and direction which each individual ought to have in the management of the state, that I must deny to be amongst the direct original rights of man in civil society; for I have in my contemplation the civil social man, and no other. It is a thing to be settled by convention.

If civil society be the offspring of convention, that convention must be its law. That convention must limit and modify all the descriptions of constitution which are formed under it. Every sort of legislative, judicial, or executory power are its creatures. They can have no being in any other state of things; and how can any man claim, under the conventions of civil society, rights which do not so much as suppose its existence? Rights which are absolutely repugnant to it? One of the first motives to civil society, and which becomes one of its fundamental rules, is, *that no man should be judge in his own cause.* By this each person has at once divested himself of the first fundamental right of uncovenanted man, that is, to judge for himself, and to assert his own cause.[17] He abdicates all right to be his own governor. He inclusively, in a great measure, abandons the right of self-defence, the first law of nature. Men cannot enjoy the rights of an uncivil and of a civil state together. That he may obtain justice he gives up his right of determining what it is in points the most essential to him. That he may secure some liberty, he makes a surrender in trust of the whole of it.

Government is not made in virtue of natural rights, which may and do exist in total independence of it; and exist in much greater clearness, and in a much greater degree of abstract perfection: but their abstract perfection is their practical defect. By having a right to every thing they want every thing. Government is a contrivance of human wisdom to provide for human *wants.* Men have a right that these wants should be provided for by this wisdom. Among these wants is to be reckoned the want, out of civil society, of a sufficient restraint upon their passions. Society requires not only that the passions of individuals should be subjected, but that even in the mass and body as well as in the individuals, the inclinations of men should frequently be thwarted,

---

[17] Burke may have Hobbes in mind here: *Leviathan* xiv, but the point was common to modern natural law theorists (such as Selden, whom Burke also read) who followed Grotius in deriving sovereignty from the yielding up of the individual's right of self-protection.

their will controlled, and their passions brought into subjection. This can only be done *by a power out of themselves*; and not, in the exercise of its function, subject to that will and to those passions which it is its office to bridle and subdue.[18] In this sense the restraints on men, as well as their liberties, are to be reckoned among their rights. But as the liberties and the restrictions vary with times and circumstances, and admit of infinite modifications, they cannot be settled upon any abstract rule; and nothing is so foolish as to discuss them upon that principle.

The moment you abate any thing from the full rights of men, each to govern himself, and suffer any artificial positive limitation upon those rights, from that moment the whole organization of government becomes a consideration of convenience. This it is which makes the constitution of a state, and the due distribution of its powers, a matter of the most delicate and complicated skill. It requires a deep knowledge of human nature and human necessities, and of the things which facilitate or obstruct the various ends which are to be pursued by the mechanism of civil institutions. The state is to have recruits to its strength, and remedies to its distempers. What is the use of discussing a man's abstract right to food or to medicine? The question is upon the method of procuring and administering them. In that deliberation I shall always advise to call in the aid of the farmer and the physician, rather than the professor of metaphysics.

The science of constructing a commonwealth, or renovating it, or reforming it, is, like every other experimental science, not to be taught *a priori*. Nor is it a short experience that can instruct us in that practical science; because the real effects of moral causes are not always immediate; but that which in the first instance is prejudicial may be excellent in its remoter operation; and its excellence may arise even from the ill effects it produces in the beginning. The reverse also happens; and very plausible schemes, with very pleasing commencements, have often shameful and lamentable conclusions . . . it is with infinite caution that any man ought to venture upon pulling down an edifice which has answered in any tolerable degree for ages the common purposes of society, or on building it up again, without having models and patterns of approved utility before his eyes.

These metaphysic rights entering into common life, like rays of light which pierce into a dense medium, are, by the laws of nature, refracted from their straight line.

---

[18] Burke is here very close to Hobbes, who also regards the possibility of society as dependent on some power to 'awe' men into obedience, and who, like Burke, regards the claim to natural right as a threat to, and not the basis of political society. Hobbes, of course, would never have regarded such restraint as itself a right.

Indeed in the gross and complicated mass of human passions and concerns, the primitive rights of men undergo such a variety of refractions and reflections, that it becomes absurd to talk of them as if they continued in the simplicity of their original direction. The nature of man is intricate; the objects of society are of the greatest possible complexity; and therefore no simple disposition or direction of power can be suitable either to man's nature, or to the quality of his affairs. When I hear the simplicity of contrivance aimed at and boasted of in any new political constitutions, I am at no loss to decide that the artificers are grossly ignorant of their trade, or totally negligent of their duty. . . .

The pretended rights of these theorists are all extremes; and in proportion as they are metaphysically true, they are morally and politically false. The rights of men are in a sort of *middle*, incapable of definition, but not impossible to be discerned. The rights of men in governments are their advantages; and these are often in balances between differences of good; in compromises sometimes between good and evil, and sometimes, between evil and evil. Political reason is a computing principle; adding, subtracting, multiplying, and dividing, morally and not metaphysically or mathematically, true moral denominations.

By these theorists the right of the people is almost always sophistically confounded with their power. The body of the community, whenever it can come to act, can meet with no effectual resistance; but till power and right are the same, the whole body of them has no right inconsistent with virtue, and the first of all virtues, prudence. Men have no right to what is not reasonable, and to what is not for their benefit; . . .

. . .

. . . History will record, that on the morning of the 6th of October 1789, the king and queen of France, after a day of confusion, alarm, dismay, and slaughter, lay down, under the pledged security of public faith, to indulge nature in a few hours of respite, and troubled melancholy repose. From this sleep the queen was first startled by the voice of the sentinel at her door, who cried out to her, to save herself by flight – that this was the last proof of fidelity he could give – that they were upon him, and he was dead. Instantly he was cut down. A band of cruel ruffians and assassins, reeking with his blood, rushed into the chamber of the queen, and pierced with an hundred strokes of bayonets and poniards the bed, from whence this persecuted woman had but just had time to fly almost naked, and through ways unknown to the murderers had escaped to seek refuge at the feet of a king and husband, not secure of his own life for a moment.

. . .

[They] were then forced to abandon the sanctuary of the most splendid palace in the world which they left swimming in blood, polluted by massacre, and strewn with scattered limbs and mutilated carcases. Thence they were conducted into the capital of their kingdom. Two had been selected from the unprovoked unresisted promiscuous slaughter which was made of the gentlemen of birth and family who composed the king's body guard . . . Their heads were stuck on spears, and led the procession, whilst the royal captives . . . After they had been made to taste, drop by drop, more than the bitterness of death, in the slow torture of a journey of twelve miles, protracted to six hours, they were, under a guard, composed of those very soldiers who had thus conducted them through this famous triumph,[19] lodged in one of the old palaces of Paris, now converted into a Bastile for kings.

. . .

Is this a triumph to be consecrated at altars? . . .

. . .

It is now sixteen or seventeen years since I saw the queen of France, then the dauphiness, at Versailles; and surely never lighted on this orb, which she hardly seemed to touch, a more delightful vision. I saw her just above the horizon, decorating and cheering the elevated sphere she just began to move in; glittering like the morning star, full of life, and splendour, and joy. Oh! what a revolution! and what an heart must I have, to contemplate without emotion that elevation and that fall! Little did I dream when she added titles of veneration to those of enthusiastic, distant, respectful love, that she should ever be obliged to carry the sharp antidote against disgrace concealed in that bosom; little did I dream that I should have lived to see such disasters fallen upon her in a nation of gallant men, in a nation of men of honour and of cavaliers. I thought ten thousand swords must have leaped from their scabbards to avenge even a look that threatened her with insult. But the age of chivalry is gone. That of sophisters, economists, and calculators, has succeeded; and the glory of Europe is extinguished for ever. Never, never more, shall we behold that generous loyalty to rank and sex, that proud submission, that dignified obedience, that subordination of the heart, which kept alive, even in servitude itself, the spirit of an exalted freedom. The unbought grace of life, the cheap defence of nations, the nurse of manly sentiment and heroic enterprise, is gone! It is gone, that sensibility of principle, that chastity of honour, which felt a stain like a wound, which inspired courage whilst it mitigated ferocity,

[19] Burke is likening the treatment of the King and Queen of France to the Roman 'Triumph' granted after a successful campaign to a returning general who would parade his most important captives through the streets of the capital.

which ennobled whatever it touched, and under which vice itself lost half its evil, by losing all its grossness.

This mixed system of opinion and sentiment had its origin in the ancient chivalry; and the principle, though varied in its appearance by the varying state of human affairs, subsisted and influenced through a long succession of generations, even to the time we live in. If it should ever be totally extinguished, the loss I fear will be great. It is this which has given its character to modern Europe. It is this which has distinguished it under all its forms of government, and distinguished it to its advantage, from the states of Asia, and possibly from those states which flourished in the most brilliant periods of the antique world. It was this, which, without confounding ranks, had produced a noble equality, and handed it down through all the gradations of social life. It was this opinion which mitigated kings into companions, and raised private men to be fellows with kings. Without force, or opposition, it subdued the fierceness of pride and power; it obliged sovereigns to submit to the soft collar of social esteem, compelled stern authority to submit to elegance, and gave a domination vanquisher of laws, to be subdued by manners.

But now all is to be changed. All the pleasing illusions, which made power gentle, and obedience liberal, which harmonized the different shades of life, and which, by a bland assimilation, incorporated into politics the sentiments which beautify and soften private society, are to be dissolved by this new conquering empire of light and reason. All the decent drapery of life is to be rudely torn off. All the superadded ideas, furnished from the wardrobe of a moral imagination, which the heart owns, and the understanding ratifies, as necessary to cover the defects of our naked shivering nature, and to raise it to dignity in our own estimation, are to be exploded as a ridiculous, absurd, and antiquated fashion.

On this scheme of things, a king is but a man; a queen is but a woman; a woman is but an animal; and an animal not of the highest order. All homage paid to the sex in general as such, and without distinct views, is to be regarded as romance and folly. Regicide, and parricide, and sacrilege, are but fictions of superstition, corrupting jurisprudence by destroying its simplicity. The murder of a king, or a queen, or a bishop, or a father, are only common homicide; and if the people are by any chance, or in any way gainers by it, a sort of homicide much the most pardonable, and into which we ought not to make too severe a scrutiny.

On the scheme of this barbarous philosophy, which is the offspring of cold hearts and muddy understandings, and which is as void of solid wisdom, as it is destitute of all taste and elegance, laws are to be supported only by their own terrors, and by the concern which each individual may find in them from his own private speculations, or can spare to them from his own private interests. In the groves of *their* academy, at the end of every vista, you see nothing but the gallows. Nothing is left which engages the affections on the part of the commonwealth. On the principles of this mechanic philosophy, our institutions can never be embodied, if I may use the expression, in persons; so as to create in us love, veneration, admiration, or attachment. But that sort of reason which banishes the affections is incapable of filling their place. These public affections, combined with manners, are required sometimes as supplements, sometimes as correctives, always as aids to law. The precept given by a wise man, as well as a great critic, for the construction of poems, is equally true as to states. *Non satis est pulchra esse poemata, dulcia sunto.*[20] There ought to be a system of manners in every nation which a well-formed mind would be disposed to relish. To make us love our country, our country ought to be lovely.

. . .

When ancient opinions and rules of life are taken away, the loss cannot possibly be estimated. From that moment we have no compass to govern us; nor can we know distinctly to what port we steer. Europe undoubtedly, taken in a mass, was in a flourishing condition the day on which your Revolution was completed. How much of that prosperous state was owing to the spirit of our old manners and opinions is not easy to say; but as such causes cannot be indifferent in their operation, we must presume, that, on the whole, their operation was beneficial.

We are but too apt to consider things in the state in which we find them, without sufficiently adverting to the causes by which they have been produced, and possibly may be upheld. Nothing is more certain, than that our manners, our civilization, and all the good things which are connected with manners, and with civilization, have, in this European world of ours, depended for ages upon two principles; and were indeed the result of both combined; I mean the spirit of a gentleman, and the spirit of religion. The nobility and the clergy, the one by profession, the other by patronage, kept learning in existence, even in the midst of arms and confusions, and whilst governments were rather in their causes than formed. Learning paid back what it received to nobility and to priesthood; and paid it with usury, by enlarging their ideas, and by furnishing their minds. Happy if they had all continued to know their indissoluble union, and their proper place! Happy if learning, not debauched

[20] 'It is not enough for poems to be beautiful . . . they must be charming', Horace, *The Art of Poetry*, in *Classical Literary Criticism*, trans. and intr. T. S. Dorsch (Harmondsworth: Penguin, 1965), p. 82.

by ambition, had been satisfied to continue the instructor, and not aspired to be the master! Along with its natural protectors and guardians, learning will be cast into the mire, and trodden down under the hoofs of a swinish multitude.

If, as I suspect, modern letters owe more than they are always willing to own to ancient manners, so do other interests which we value full as much as they are worth. Even commerce, and trade, and manufacture, the gods of our economical politicians, are themselves perhaps but creatures; are themselves but effects, which, as first causes, we choose to worship. They certainly grew under the same shade in which learning flourished. They too may decay with their natural protecting principles. With you, for the present at least, they all threaten to disappear together. Where trade and manufactures are wanting to a people, and the spirit of nobility and religion remains, sentiment supplies, and not always ill supplies their place; but if commerce and the arts should be lost in an experiment to try how well a state may stand without these old fundamental principles, what sort of a thing must be a nation of gross, stupid, ferocious, and at the same time, poor and sordid barbarians, destitute of religion, honour, or manly pride, possessing nothing at present, and hoping for nothing hereafter?

. . .

Why do I feel so differently from the Reverend Dr. Price, and those of his lay flock, who will choose to adopt the sentiments of his discourse? For this plain reason – because it is *natural* I should; because we are so made as to be affected at such spectacles with melancholy sentiments upon the unstable condition of mortal prosperity, and the tremendous uncertainty of human greatness; because in those natural feelings we learn great lessons; because in events like these our passions instruct our reason; because when kings are hurled from their thrones by the Supreme Director of this great drama, and become the objects of insult to the base, and of pity to the good, we behold such disasters in the moral, as we should behold a miracle in the physical order of things. We are alarmed into reflection; our minds (as it has long since been observed) are purified by terror and pity[21]; our weak unthinking pride is humbled, under the dispensations of a mysterious wisdom. . . .

. . .

To tell you the truth, my dear Sir, I think the honour of our nation to be somewhat concerned in the disclaimer of the proceedings of this society of the Old Jewry and

---

[21] Aristotle observed that the effect of tragedy was to purge the mind. Aristotle, *The Art of Poetry*, in *Classical . . . Criticism*, ed. Dorsch, p. 39.

the London Tavern . . . Because half a dozen grasshoppers under a fern make the field ring with their importunate chink, whilst thousands of great cattle, reposed beneath the shadow of the British oak, chew the cud and are silent, pray do not imagine, that those who make the noise are the only inhabitants of the field; that, of course, they are many in number; or that, after all, they are other than the little shrivelled, meagre, hopping, though loud and troublesome insects of the hour.

. . . Thanks to our sullen resistance to innovation, thanks to the cold sluggishness of our national character, we still bear the stamp of our forefathers. We have not, as I conceive, lost the generosity and dignity of thinking of the fourteenth century; nor as yet have we subtilized ourselves into savages. We are not the converts of Rousseau; we are not the disciples of Voltaire; Helvetius has made no progress amongst us. Atheists are not our preachers; madmen are not our lawgivers. We know that *we* have made no discoveries, and we think that no discoveries are to be made, in morality; nor many in the great principles of government, nor in the ideas of liberty, which were understood long before we were born, altogether as well as they will be after the grave has heaped its mould upon our presumption, and the silent tomb shall have imposed its law on our pert loquacity. In England we have not yet been completely embowelled of our natural entrails; we still feel within us, and we cherish and cultivate, those inbred sentiments which are the faithful guardians, the active monitors of our duty, the true supporters of all liberal and manly morals . . . We fear God; we look up with awe to kings; with affection to parliaments; with duty to magistrates; with reverence to priests; and with respect to nobility. Why? Because when such ideas are brought before our minds, it is *natural* to be so affected; because all other feelings are false and spurious, and tend to corrupt our minds, to vitiate our primary morals, to render us unfit for rational liberty; and by teaching us a servile, licentious, and abandoned insolence, to be our low sport for a few holidays, to make us perfectly fit for, and justly deserving of slavery, through the whole course of our lives.

You see, Sir, that in this enlightened age I am bold enough to confess, that we are generally men of untaught feelings; that instead of casting away all our old prejudices, we cherish them to a very considerable degree, and, to take more shame to ourselves, we cherish them because they are prejudices; and the longer they have lasted, and the more generally they have prevailed, the more we cherish them. We are afraid to put men to live and trade each on his own private stock of reason; because we suspect that this stock in each man is small, and that the individuals would do better to avail themselves of the general bank and capital of nations, and of ages. Many of our men of speculation, instead of exploding general prejudices, employ their sagacity to discover the latent wisdom which prevails in them. If they find what they seek, (and they seldom fail) they think it more wise to continue the prejudice, with the reason involved, than to cast away the coat of prejudice, and to leave nothing but the naked reason; because prejudice, with its reason, has a motive to give action to that reason, and an affection which will give it permanence. Prejudice is of ready application in the emergency; it previously engages the mind in a steady course of wisdom and virtue, and does not leave the man hesitating in the moment of decision, sceptical, puzzled, and unresolved. Prejudice renders a man's virtue his habit; and not a series of unconnected acts. Through just prejudice, his duty becomes a part of his nature.

. . .

I hear on all hands that a cabal, calling itself philosophic, receives the glory of many of the late proceedings; and that their opinions and systems are the true actuating spirit of the whole of them. I have heard of no party in England, literary or political, at any time known by such a description. It is not with you composed of those men is it? Whom the vulgar, in their blunt, homely style, commonly call Atheists and Infidels? If it be I admit that we too have had writers of that description, who made some noise in their day. At present they repose in lasting oblivion. Who, born within the last forty years, has read one word of Collins, and Toland, and Tindal and Chubb, and Morgan, and that whole race who called themselves Freethinkers. Who now reads Bolingbroke? Who ever read him through?[22]

We know, and what is better, we feel inwardly, that religion is the basis of civil society, and the source of all good and of all comfort. In England we are so convinced of this, that there is no rust of superstition, with which the accumulated absurdity of the human mind might have crusted it over in the course of ages, that ninety-nine in an hundred of the people of England would not prefer to impiety . . .

We know, and it is our pride to know, that man is by his constitution a religious animal; that atheism is against, not only our reason, but our instincts; and that it cannot prevail long. But if, in the moment of riot, and in a drunken delirium from the hot spirit drawn out of the alembick[23] of hell, which in France is now so furiously

[22] All these writers were Deists who subjected religious dogma or history to critical, rationalist standards. This provoked a series of controversies in the early part of the century. Burke's own first work, the *Vindication of Natural Society*, had been an ironic attack on Bolingbroke. Justin Champion's *Pillar's of Priestcraft Shaken* (Cambridge: Cambridge University Press, 1992) unfortunately only covers the earlier of these thinkers. See also John Redwood, *Reason, Ridicule and Religion* (London: Thames & Hudson, 1976).
[23] Alembic: a very early form of distillation vessel. The association Burke insinuates is with alchemy and the occult – and unchristian – sciences.

boiling, we should uncover our nakedness by throwing off that Christian religion which has hitherto been our boast and comfort, and one great source of civilization amongst us, and among many other nations, we are apprehensive (being well aware that the mind will not endure a void) that some uncouth, pernicious, and degrading superstition, might take place of it.

. . .

On these ideas, instead of quarrelling with establishments, as some do, who have made a philosophy and a religion of their hostility to such institutions, we cleave closely to them. We are resolved to keep an established church, an established monarchy, an established aristocracy, and an established democracy, each in the degree it exists, and in no greater. I shall shew you presently how much of each of these we possess.

. . .

First, I beg leave to speak of our church establishment, which is the first of our prejudices; not a prejudice destitute of reason, but involving in it profound and extensive wisdom. . . .

. . .

The consecration of the state, by a state religious establishment, is necessary also to operate with an wholesome awe upon free citizens; because, in order to secure their freedom, they must enjoy some determinate portion of power . . . All persons possessing any portion of power ought to be strongly and awefully impressed with an idea that they act in trust; and that they are to account for their conduct in that trust to the one great master, author and founder of society.

This principle ought even to be more strongly impressed upon the minds of those who compose the collective sovereignty than upon those of single princes . . . , they are less under responsibility to one of the greatest controlling powers on earth, the sense of fame and estimation. The share of infamy that is likely to fall to the lot of each individual in public acts, is small indeed; the operation of opinion being in the inverse ratio to the number of those who abuse power. Their own approbation of their own acts has to them the appearance of a public judgment in their favour. A perfect democracy is therefore the most shameless thing in the world. As it is the most shameless, it is also the most fearless. No man apprehends in his person he can be made subject to punishment. Certainly the people at large never ought: for as all punishments are for example towards the conservation of the people at large, the people at large can never become the subject of punishment by any human hand. It is therefore of infinite importance that they should not be suffered

to imagine that their will, any more than that of kings, is the standard of right and
wrong. . . .

. . .

But one of the first and most leading principles on which the commonwealth
and the laws are consecrated, is lest the temporary possessors and life-renters in it,
unmindful of what they have received from their ancestors, or of what is due to their
posterity, should act as if they were the entire masters; that they should not think
it amongst their rights to cut off the entail, or commit waste on the inheritance, by
destroying at their pleasure the whole original fabric of their society; hazarding to
leave to those who come after them, a ruin instead of an habitation, and teaching these
successors as little to respect their contrivances, as they had themselves respected the
institutions of their forefathers. By this unprincipled facility of changing the state as
often, and as much, and in as many ways, as there are floating fancies or fashions,
the whole chain and continuity of the commonwealth would be broken. No one
generation could link with the other. Men would become little better than the flies
of a summer.

And first of all, the science of jurisprudence, the pride of the human intellect,
which, with all its defects, redundancies, and errors, is the collected reason of ages,
combining the principles of original justice with the infinite variety of human concerns, as a heap of old exploded errors, would be no longer studied. Personal self-
sufficiency and arrogance, the certain attendants upon all those who have never
experienced a wisdom greater than their own, would usurp the tribunal. Of course,
no certain laws, establishing invariable grounds of hope and fear, would keep the
actions of men in a certain course, or direct them to a certain end. Nothing stable
in the modes of holding property, or exercising function, could form a solid ground
on which any parent could speculate in the education of his offspring, or in a choice
for their future establishment in the world. No principles would be early worked
into the habits. As soon as the most able instructor had completed his laborious
course of institution, instead of sending forth his pupil, accomplished in a virtuous discipline, fitted to procure him attention and respect, in his place in society,
he would find everything altered; and that he had turned out a poor creature to
the contempt and derision of the world, ignorant of the true grounds of estimation . . . No part of life would retain its acquisitions. Barbarism with regard to science
and literature, unskilfulness with regard to arts and manufactures, would infallibly
succeed to the want of a steady education and settled principle; and thus the commonwealth itself would, in a few generations, crumble away, be disconnected into

the dust and powder of individuality, and at length dispersed to all the winds of heaven.

. . .

Society is indeed a contract. Subordinate contracts, for objects of mere occasional interest, may be dissolved at pleasure; but the state ought not to be considered as nothing better than a partnership agreement in a trade of pepper and coffee, callico[24] or tobacco, or some other such low concern, to be taken up for a little temporary interest, and to be dissolved by the fancy of the parties. It is to be looked on with other reverence; because it is not a partnership in things subservient only to the gross animal existence of a temporary and perishable nature. It is a partnership in all science; a partnership in all art; a partnership in every virtue, and in all perfection. As the ends of such a partnership cannot be obtained in many generations, it becomes a partnership not only between those who are living, but between those who are living, those who are dead, and those who are to be born. Each contract of each particular state is but a clause in the great primaeval contract of eternal society, linking the lower with the higher natures, connecting the visible and invisible world, according to a fixed compact sanctioned by the inviolable oath which holds all physical and all moral natures, each in their appointed place. This law is not subject to the will of those, who by an obligation above them, and infinitely superior, are bound to submit their will to that law. The municipal corporations of that universal kingdom are not morally at liberty at their pleasure, and on their speculations of a contingent improvement, wholly to separate and tear asunder the bands of their subordinate community, and to dissolve it into an unsocial, uncivil, unconnected chaos of elementary principles. . . .

These, my dear Sir, are, were, and I think long will be the sentiments of not the least learned and reflecting part of this kingdom. They who are included in this description form their opinions on such grounds as such persons ought to form them. The less enquiring receive them from an authority which those whom Providence dooms to live on trust need not be ashamed to rely on. These two sorts of men move in the same direction, tho' in a different place. They both move with the order of the universe. . . .

I assure you I do not aim at singularity. I give you opinions which have been accepted amongst us, from very early times to this moment, with a continued and general approbation; and which indeed are so worked into my mind, that I am unable to distinguish what I have learned from others from the results of my own meditation.

[24] A cotton cloth imported from India.

[Burke then, via a denunciation of the appropriation of Church lands to fund the national debt, turns his attention to a socio-economic analysis of the causes of the Revolution in France.]

. . .

By the vast debt of France a great monied interest had insensibly grown up, and with it a great power . . . ancient usages . . . had kept the landed and monied interests more separate in France, less miscible, and the owners of the two distinct species of property not so well disposed to each other as they are in this country.

The monied property was long looked on with rather an evil eye by the people. They saw it connected with their distresses, and aggravating them. It was no less envied by the old landed interests, partly for the same reasons that rendered it obnoxious to the people, but much more so as it eclipsed, by the splendour of an ostentatious luxury, the unendowed pedigrees and naked titles of several among the nobility. Even when the nobility, which represented the more permanent landed interest, united themselves by marriage (which sometimes was the case) with the other description, the wealth which saved the family from ruin, was supposed to contaminate and degrade it. In the mean time, the pride of the wealthy men, not noble or newly noble, increased with its cause. They felt with resentment an inferiority, the grounds of which they did not acknowledge . . .

. . .

Along with the monied interest, a new description of men had grown up, with whom that interest soon formed a close and marked union; I mean the political Men of Letters. Men of Letters, fond of distinguishing themselves, are rarely averse to innovation. Since the decline of the life and greatness of Lewis the XIVth, they were not so much cultivated either by him, or by the regent, or the successors to the crown; nor were they engaged to the court by favours and emoluments so systematically as during the splendid period of that ostentatious and not impolitic reign. What they lost in the old court protection, they endeavoured to make up by joining in a sort of incorporation of their own; to which the two academies of France, and afterwards the vast undertaking of the Encyclopaedia, carried on by a society of these gentlemen, did not a little contribute.

The literary cabal had some years ago formed something like a regular plan for the destruction of the Christian religion. This object they pursued with a degree of zeal which hitherto had been discovered only in the propagators of some system of piety. They were possessed with a spirit of proselytism in the most fanatical degree; and from thence by an easy progress, with the spirit of persecution according to their means . . .

. . . For the same purpose for which they intrigued with princes, they cultivated, in a distinguished manner, the monied interest of France; and partly through the means furnished by those whose peculiar offices gave them the most extensive and certain means of communication, they carefully occupied all the avenues to opinion.

Writers, especially when they act in a body, and with one direction, have great influence on the public mind; the alliance therefore of these writers with the monied interest had no small effect in removing the popular odium and envy which attended that species of wealth. These writers, like the propagators of all novelties, pretended to a great zeal for the poor, and the lower orders, whilst in their satires they rendered hateful, by every exaggeration, the faults of courts, of nobility, and of priesthood. They became a sort of demagogues. They served as a link to unite, in favour of one object, obnoxious wealth to restless and desperate poverty.

. . .

The spoil of the church was now become the only resource of all their operations in finance; the vital principle of all their politics; the sole security for the existence of their power. It was necessary by all, even the most violent means to put every individual on the same bottom, and to bind the nation in one guilty interest to uphold this act, and the authority of those by whom it was done. In order to force the most reluctant into a participation in their pillage, they rendered the paper circulation compulsory in all payments. . . .

. . .

[Burke next considers what kind of government the revolutionary regime might be.]

I do not know under what description to class the present ruling authority in France. It affects to be a pure democracy, though I think it in a direct train of becoming shortly a mischievous and ignoble oligarchy . . . Until now, we have seen no examples of considerable democracies. The ancients were better acquainted with them. Not being wholly unread in the authors, who had seen the most of those constitutions, and who best understood them, I cannot help concurring with their opinion, that an absolute democracy, no more than absolute monarchy, is to be reckoned among the legitimate forms of government. They think it rather the corruption and degeneracy, than the sound constitution of a republic. If I recollect rightly, Aristotle observes, that a democracy has many striking points of resemblance with a tyranny. Of this I am certain, that in a democracy, the majority of the citizens is capable of exercising the most cruel oppressions upon the minority, whenever strong divisions prevail in that kind of polity, as they often must; and that oppression of the minority will extend to far greater numbers, and will be carried on with much greater fury, than can almost ever be apprehended from the dominion of a single sceptre . . . They seem deserted by mankind; overpowered by a conspiracy of their whole species.

. . .

All this violent cry against the nobility I take to be a mere work of art. To be honoured and even privileged by the laws, opinions, and inveterate usages of our country, growing out of the prejudices of ages, has nothing to provoke horror and indignation in any man. Even to be too tenacious of those privileges is not absolutely a crime . . . your noblesse did not deserve punishment, but to degrade is to punish.

It was with the same satisfaction I found the result of my enquiry concerning your clergy was not dissimilar . . . Vices and abuses there were undoubtedly in that order, and must be. But I saw no crimes in the individuals that merited confiscation of their substance, nor those cruel insults and degradations, and that unnatural persecutions which have been substituted in the place of meliorating regulation . . .

. . . It is not very just to chastise men for the offences of their natural ancestors; but to take the fiction of ancestry in a corporate succession, as a ground for punishing men who have no relation to guilty acts, except in names and general descriptions, is a sort of refinement in injustice belonging to the philosophy of this enlightened age. The assembly punishes men, many, if not most, of whom abhor the violent conduct of ecclesiastics in former times as much as their present persecutors can do, and who would be as loud and as strong in the expression of that sense, if they were not well aware of the purposes for which all this declamation is employed.

Corporate bodies are immortal for the good of the members, but not for their punishment. Nations themselves are such corporations. As well might we in England think of waging inexpiable war upon all Frenchmen for the evils which they have brought upon us in the several periods of our mutual hostilities. You might, on your part, think yourselves justified in falling upon all Englishmen on account of the unparalleled calamities brought upon the people of France by the unjust invasions of our Henries and our Edwards. . . .

We do not draw the moral lessons we might from history. On the contrary, without care it may be used to vitiate our minds and to destroy our happiness. In history a great volume is unrolled for our instruction, drawing the materials of future wisdom from the past errors and infirmities of mankind. It may, in the perversion, serve for a magazine, furnishing offensive and defensive weapons for parties in church and state, and supply the means of keeping alive, or reviving dissensions and animosities, and adding fuel to civil fury. History consists, for the greater part, of the miseries brought upon the world by pride, ambition, avarice, revenge, lust, sedition, hypocrisy, ungoverned zeal, and all the train of disorderly appetites, which shake the public with the same troublous storms that toss the private state, and render life unsweet.[25]

These vices are the *causes* of those storms. Religion, morals, laws, prerogatives, privileges, liberties, rights of men, are the *pretexts*. The pretexts are always found in some specious appearance of a real good . . . Wickedness is a little more inventive.

. . .

. . . I cannot conceive how any man can have brought himself to that pitch of presumption, to consider his country as nothing but *carte blanche*, upon which he may scribble whatever he pleases. A man full of warm speculative benevolence may wish his society otherwise constituted than he finds it; but a good patriot, and a true politician, always considers how he shall make the most of the existing materials of his country. A disposition to preserve, and an ability to improve, taken together, would be my standard of a statesman. Every thing else is vulgar in the conception, perilous in the execution.

. . . A politician, to do great things, looks for a *power*, what our workmen call a *purchase*; and if he finds that power, in politics as in mechanics he cannot be at a loss to apply it. In the monastic institutions, in my opinion, was found a great *power* for the mechanism of politic benevolence. There were revenues with a public direction; there were men wholly set apart and dedicated to public purposes, without any other than public ties and public principles; men without the possibility of converting the estate of the community into a private fortune; men denied to self-interests, whose avarice is for some community; men to whom personal poverty is honour, and implicit obedience stands in the place of freedom. In vain shall a man look to the possibility of making such things when he wants them. The winds blow as they list. These institutions are the products of enthusiasm; they are the instruments of wisdom. Wisdom cannot create materials; they are the gifts of nature or of chance; her pride is in the use . . . On the view of this subject a thousand uses suggest themselves to a contriving mind. To destroy any power, growing wild from the rank productive force of the human mind, is almost tantamount, in the moral world, to the destruction of the apparently active properties of bodies in the material. It would be like the attempt to destroy (if it were in our competence to destroy) the expansive force of fixed air in nitre, or the power of steam, or of electricity, or of magnetism. These energies always existed in nature, and they were always discernible. They seemed, some of them unserviceable, some noxious, some no better than a sport to

[25] From Edmund Spenser, *The Faerie Queen*, Bk II, c. vii, xiv.

children; until contemplative ability, combining with practical skill, tamed their wild nature, subdued them to use, and rendered them at once the most powerful and the most tractable agents, in subservience to the great views and designs of men. Did fifty thousand persons, whose mental and whose bodily labour you might direct, and so many hundred thousand a year of a revenue, which was neither lazy nor superstitious, appear too big for your abilities to wield? Had you no way of using the men but by converting monks into pensioners? Had you no way of turning the revenue to account, but through the improvident resource of a spendthrift sale? If you were thus destitute of mental funds, the proceeding is in its natural course. Your politicians do not understand their trade; and therefore they sell their tools.

But the institutions savour of superstition in their very principle; and they nourish it by a permanent and standing influence. This I do not mean to dispute; but this ought not to hinder you from deriving from superstition itself any resources which may thence be furnished for the public advantage. You derive benefits from many dispositions and many passions of the human mind, which are of as doubtful a colour in the moral eye, as superstition itself . . . Superstition is the religion of feeble minds; and they must be tolerated in an intermixture of it, in some trifling or some enthusiastic shape or other, else you will deprive weak minds of a resource found necessary to the strongest. The body of all true religion consists, to be sure, in obedience to the will of the sovereign of the world; in a confidence in his declarations; and an imitation of his perfections. The rest is our own. It may be prejudicial to the great end; it may be auxiliary. Wise men, who as such are not *admirers* (not admirers at least of the *Munera Terrae*[26]) are not violently attached to these things, nor do they violently hate them . . .

. . .

. . . Why should the expenditure of a great landed property, which is a dispersion of the surplus product of the soil, appear intolerable to you or to me, when it takes its course through the accumulation of vast libraries, which are the history of the force and weakness of the human mind; through great collections of ancient records, medals, and coins, which attest and explain laws and customs; through paintings and statues, that, by imitating nature, seem to extend the limits of creation; through grand monuments of the dead, which continue the regards and connexions of life beyond the grave; through collections of the specimens of nature, which become a representative assembly of all the classes and families of the world, that by

[26] 'Those things the earth provides.'

disposition facilitate, and, by exciting curiosity, open the avenues to science? If, by great permanent establishments, all these objects of expense are better secured from the inconstant sport of personal caprice and personal extravagance, are they worse than if the same tastes prevailed in scattered individuals? Does not the sweat of the mason and carpenter, who toil in order to partake the sweat of the peasant, flow as pleasantly and as salubriously, in the construction and repair of the majestic edifices of religion, as in the painted booths and sordid sties of vice and luxury; as honourably and as profitably in repairing those sacred works, which grow hoary with innumerable years, as on the momentary receptacles of transient voluptuousness; in opera-houses, and brothels; and gaming-houses, and club-houses, and obelisks in the Champ de Mars? . . .

. . .

It is this inability to wrestle with difficulty which has obliged the arbitrary assembly of France to commence their schemes of reform with abolition and total destruction. But is it in destroying and pulling down that skill is displayed? Your mob can do this at least as well as your assemblies. . . .

At once to preserve and to reform is quite another thing. When the useful parts of an old establishment are kept, and what is superadded is to be fitted to what is retained, a vigorous mind, steady persevering attention, various powers of comparison and combination, and the resources of an understanding fruitful in expedients are to be exercised; they are to be exercised in a continued conflict with the combined force of opposite vices; with the obstinacy that rejects all improvement, and the levity that is fatigued and disgusted with every thing of which it is in possession. But you may object – 'A process of this kind is slow. It is not fit for an assembly, which glories in performing in a few months the work of ages. Such a mode of reforming, possibly might take up many years.' Without question it might; and it ought. It is one of the excellencies of a method in which time is amongst the assistants, that its operation is slow, and in some cases almost imperceptible. If circumspection and caution are a part of wisdom, when we work only upon inanimate matter, surely they become a part of duty too, when the subject of our demolition and construction is not brick and timber, but sentient beings, by the sudden alteration of whose state, condition, and habits, multitudes may be rendered miserable . . . The true lawgiver ought to have an heart full of sensibility. He ought to love and respect his kind, and to fear himself. It may be allowed to his temperament to catch his ultimate object with an intuitive glance; but his movements towards it ought to be deliberate. Political arrangement, as it is a work for social ends, is to be only wrought by social means. There mind must conspire with mind. Time is required to produce that union of minds which alone can produce all the good we aim at. Our patience will achieve more than our force . . . By a slow but well-sustained progress, the effect of each step is watched; the good or ill success of the first, gives light to us in the second; and so, from light to light, we are conducted with safety through the whole series. We see, that the parts of the system do not clash. The evils latent in the most promising contrivances are provided for as they arise. One advantage is as little as possible sacrificed to another. We compensate, we reconcile, we balance. We are enabled to unite into a consistent whole the various anomalies and contending principles that are found in the minds and affairs of men. . . .

. . .

Old establishments are tried by their effects. If the people are happy, united, wealthy, and powerful, we presume the rest. We conclude that to be good from whence good is derived. In old establishments various correctives have been found for their aberrations from theory. Indeed they are the results of various necessities and expediences. They are not often constructed after any theory; theories are rather drawn from them. In them we often see the end best obtained, where the means seem not perfectly reconcileable to what we may fancy was the original scheme. The means taught by experience may be better suited to political ends than those contrived in the original project. They again re-act upon the primitive constitution, and sometimes improve the design itself from which they seem to have departed. I think all this might be curiously exemplified in the British constitution. At worst, the errors and deviations of every kind in reckoning are found and computed, and the ship proceeds in her course. This is the case of old establishments; but in a new and merely theoretic system, it is expected that every contrivance shall appear, on the face of it, to answer its end; especially where the projectors are no way embarrassed with an endeavour to accommodate the new building to an old one, either in the walls or on the foundations.

. . .

Your legislators, in every thing new, are the very first who have founded a commonwealth upon gaming,[27] and infused this spirit into it as its vital breath. The great object in these politics is to metamorphose France from a great kingdom into one great play-table; to turn its inhabitants into a nation of gamesters; to make

---

[27] Gambling. Burke makes much play on the fact that the unit of currency, the paper assignat, is effectively a share, the value of which is dependent on speculation in the market.

speculations as extensive as life; to mix it with all its concerns; and to divert the whole of the hopes and fears of the people from their useful channels, into the impulses, passions, and superstitions of those who live on chances. They loudly proclaim their opinion, that this their present system of a republic cannot possibly exist without this kind of gaming fund; and that the very thread of its life is spun out of the staple of these speculations. The old gaming in funds was mischievious enough undoubtedly; but it was so only to individuals . . . But . . . by bringing the currency of gaming into the minutest matters and engaging everybody in it and in everything, a more dreadful epidemic distemper of that kind is spread than has yet appeared in the world. . . .

The truly melancholy part of the policy of systematically making a nation of gamesters is this; that tho' all are forced to play, few can understand the game; and fewer still are in a condition to avail themselves of the knowledge. The many must be the dupes of the few who conduct the machine of these speculations. What effect it must have on the country-people is visible. The townsman can calculate from day to day: not so the inhabitant of the country. When the peasant first brings his corn to market, the magistrate in the town obliges him to take the assignat at par; when he goes to the shop with this money, he finds it seven per cent. the worse for crossing the way. This market he will not readily resort to again. The townspeople will be inflamed! they will force the country-people to bring their corn. Resistance will begin, and the murders of Paris and St. Dennis may be renewed through all France.

. . . The landed gentlemen, the yeoman, and the peasant have, none of them, habits, or inclinations, or experience, which can lead them to any share in this the sole source of power and influence now left in France. The very nature of a country life, the very nature of landed property, in all the occupations, and all the pleasures they afford, render combination and arrangement (the sole way of procuring and exerting influence) in a manner impossible amongst country-people. Combine them by all the art you can, and all the industry, they are always dissolving into individuality. Any thing in the nature of incorporation is almost impracticable amongst them . . . The country gentleman therefore, the officer by sea and land, the man of liberal views and habits, attached to no profession, will be as completely excluded from the government of his country as if he were legislatively proscribed. . . .

All these considerations leave no doubt on my mind, that if this monster of a constitution can continue, France will be wholly governed by the agitators in corporations, by societies in the towns formed of directors of assignats, and trustees for the sale of church lands, attornies, agents, money-jobbers, speculators, and adventurers, composing an ignoble oligarchy founded on the destruction of the crown, the church, the nobility, and the people.

. . .

Passing . . . to the national assembly which is to appear and act as sovereign, we see a body in its constitution with every possible power, and no possible external controul. We see a body without fundamental laws, without established maxims, without respected rules of proceeding, which nothing can keep firm to any system whatsoever. . . .

Your all-sufficient legislators, in their hurry to do everything at once, have forgot one thing that seems essential, and which, I believe, never has been, in theory or the practice, omitted by any projector of a republic. They have forgotten to constitute a *Senate*, or something of that character. Never before this time, was heard of a body politic composed of one legislative and active assembly, and its executive officers, without such a council; without something to which foreign states might connect themselves; something to which, in the ordinary detail of government, the people could look up; something which might give bias and steadiness, and preserve something like consistency in the proceedings of state . . . A monarchy might exist without it; but it seems to be in the very essence of a republican government. . . .

Let us now turn our eyes to what they have done towards the formation of an executive power. For this they have chosen a degraded king. This their first executive officer is to be a machine, without any sort of deliberative discretion in any one act of his function. At best he is but a channel to convey to the national assembly such matter as may import that body to know . . .

. . . The king of France is not the fountain of justice. The judges, neither the original nor the appellate, are of his nomination. He neither proposes the candidates, nor has a negative on the choice. He is not even the public prosecutor. He serves only as a notary to authenticate the choice made of the judges in the several districts. By his officers he is to execute their sentence. When we look into the true nature of his authority, he appears to be nothing more than a chief of bumbailiffs, serjeants at mace, catchpoles, jailers, and hangmen.[28] It is impossible to place any thing called royalty in a more degrading point of view. . . .

. . .

---

[28] 'Bumbailiff', a collector of small debts, and 'catchpole', a minor revenue officer; both are derogatory terms.

A king circumstanced as the present, if he is totally stupified by his misfortunes, so as to think it not the necessity, but the premium and privilege of life, to eat and sleep, without any regard to glory, never can be fit for the office ... To inferior people such an office might be matter of honour. But to be raised to it, and to descend to it, are different things, and suggest different sentiments. Does he *really* name the ministers? They will have a sympathy with him. Are they forced upon him? The whole business between them and the nominal king will be mutual counteraction. In all other countries, the office of ministers of state is of the highest dignity. In France it is full of peril and incapable of glory. . . .

. . .

As little genius and talent am I able to perceive in the plan of judicature formed by the national assembly. According to their invariable course, the framers of your constitution have begun with the utter abolition of the parliaments. These venerable bodies, like the rest of the old government, stood in need of reform, even though there should be no change made in the monarchy. They required several more alterations to adapt them to the system of a free constitution. But they had particulars in their constitution, and those not a few, which deserved approbation from the wise. They possessed one fundamental excellence; they were independent. The most doubtful circumstance attendant on their office, that of its being vendible, contributed however to this independency of character . . . Whatever is supreme in a state, ought to have, as much as possible, its judicial authority so constituted as not only to depend upon it, but in some sort to balance it. It ought to give a security to its justice against its power. It ought to make its judicature, as it were, something exterior to the state.

. . . Such an independent judicature was ten times more necessary when a democracy became the absolute power of the country. In that constitution, elective, temporary, local judges, such as you have contrived, exercising their dependent functions in a narrow society, must be the worst of all tribunals. In them it will be vain to look for any appearance of justice towards strangers, towards the obnoxious rich, towards the minority of routed parties, towards all those who in the election have supported unsuccessful candidates. It will be impossible to keep the new tribunals clear of the worst spirit of faction. All contrivances by ballot, we know experimentally, to be vain and childish to prevent a discovery of inclinations. . . .

. . .

It is besides to be considered, whether an assembly like yours, even supposing that it was in possession of another sort of organ through which its orders were to pass, is fit for promoting the obedience and discipline of an army . . . In the weakness of one kind of authority, and in the fluctuation of all, the officers of an army will remain for some time mutinous and full of faction, until some popular general, who understands the art of conciliating soldiery, and who possesses the true spirit of command shall draw the eyes of all men upon himself . . . [then] the person who really commands the army is your master; the master (that is little) of your king, the master of your assembly, the master of your whole republic.

. . .

Every thing depends upon the army in such a government as yours; for you have industriously destroyed all the opinions, and prejudices, and, as far as in you lay, all the instincts which support government. Therefore the moment any difference arises between your national assembly and any part of the nation, you must have recourse to force. Nothing else is left to you; or rather you have left nothing else to yourselves. You see by the report of your war minister, that the distribution of the army is in a great measure made with a view of internal coercion. You must rule by an army; and you have infused into that army by which you rule, as well as into the whole body of the nation, principles which after a time must disable you in the use you resolve to make of it. The king is to call out troops to act against his people, when the world has been told, and the assertion is still ringing in our ears, that troops ought not to fire on citizens. The colonies assert to themselves an independent constitution and a free trade. They must be constrained by troops. In what chapter of your code of the rights of men are they able to read, that it is a part of the rights of men to have their commerce monopolized and restrained for the benefit of others? As the colonists rise on you, the negroes rise on them. Troops again – Massacre, torture, hanging![29] These are your rights of men! These are the fruits of metaphysic declarations wantonly made, and shamefully retracted! . . . You lay down metaphysic propositions which infer universal consequences, and then you attempt to limit logic by despotism. The leaders of the present system tell them of their rights, as men, to take fortresses, to murder guards, to seize on kings without the least appearance of authority even from the assembly, whilst, as the sovereign legislative body, that assembly was sitting in the name of the nation; and yet these leaders presume to order out the

---

[29] The French West Indian colonies took the *Declaration of the Rights of Man* at face value and established their own assemblies which were put down by force. A slave rebellion followed. Slaves were excluded from the rights accorded by the 1791 Constitution. See John Hall Stewart, *A Documentary Survey of the French Revolution* (New York: Macmillan, 1951), p. 262.

troops, which have acted in these very disorders, to coerce those who shall judge on the principles, and follow the examples, which have been guarantied by their own approbation.

. . .

Having concluded my few remarks on the constitution of the supreme power, the executive, the judicature, the military, and on the reciprocal relation of all these establishments, I shall say something of the ability shewed by your legislators with regard to the revenue.

. . .

The objects of a financier are, then, to secure an ample revenue; to impose it with judgment and equality; to employ it economically; and when necessity obliges him to make use of credit, to secure its foundations in that instance, and for ever, by the clearness and candour of his proceedings, the exactness of his calculations, and the solidity of his funds. On these heads we may take a short and distinct view of the merits and abilities of those in the national assembly . . . the amount of the national revenue, as compared with its produce before the revolution, was diminished by the sum of two hundred millions, or *eight millions sterling* of the annual income – considerably more than one third of the whole!

If this be the result of great ability, never surely was ability displayed in a more distinguished manner, or with so powerful an effect. No common folly, no vulgar incapacity, no ordinary official negligence, even no official crime, no corruption, no peculation, hardly any direct hostility which we have seen in the modern world, could in so short a time have made so complete an overthrow of the finances, and with them, of the strength, of a great kingdom . . .

The sophisers and declaimers . . . began with decrying the ancient constitution of its revenue – such as the public monopoly of salt. They charged it, as truly as unwisely, with being ill-contrived, oppressive and partial . . . At the same time as they passed the decree, with the same gravity they ordered this same absurd, oppressive, and partial tax to be paid, until they could find a revenue to replace it. The consequence was inevitable. . . .

The people of the salt provinces, impatient under taxes damned by the authority which had directed their payment . . . relieved themselves by throwing off the whole burden. Animated by this example, each district, or part of a district, judging of its own grievance by its own feeling, and of its remedy by its own opinion, did as it pleased with other taxes.

. . .

As to their other schemes of taxation, it is impossible to say any thing of them with certainty; because they have not yet had their operation; but nobody is so sanguine as to imagine they will fill up any perceptible part of the wide gaping breach which their incapacity has made in their revenues. At present the state of their treasury sinks every day more and more in cash, and swells more and more in fictitious representation. When so little within or without is now found but paper, the representative not of opulence but of want, the creature not of credit but of power, they imagine that our flourishing state in England is owing to that bank-paper, and not the bank-paper to the flourishing condition of our commerce, to the solidity of our credit, and to the total exclusion of all idea of power from any part of the transaction. They forget that, in England, not one shilling of paper-money of any description is received but of choice; that the whole has had its origin in cash actually deposited; and that it is convertible, at pleasure, in an instant, and without the smallest loss, into cash again. Our paper is of value in commerce, because in law it is of none. It is powerful on Change, because in Westminster-hall[30] it is impotent. In payment of a debt of twenty shillings, a creditor may refuse all the paper of the bank of England . . . it is the symbol of prosperity, and not the badge of distress. Never was a scarcity of cash, and an exuberance of paper, a subject of complaint in this nation.

. . .

It remains only to consider the proofs of financial ability furnished by the present French managers when they are to raise supplies on credit. Here I am a little at a stand; for credit, properly speaking, they have none . . . What offers has their government of pretended liberty had from Holland, from Hamburgh, from Switzerland, from Genoa, from England, for a dealing in their paper? Why should these nations of commerce and economy enter into any pecuniary dealings with a people who attempt to reverse the very nature of things; amongst whom they see the debtor prescribing, at the point of the bayonet, the medium of his solvency to the creditor; discharging one of his engagements with another; turning his very penury into his resource; and paying his interest with his rags?

Their fanatical confidence in the omnipotence of church plunder, has induced these philosophers to overlook all care of the public estate just as the dream of a philosopher's stone induces dupes, under the more plausible delusion of the

---

[30] 'Change': the Stock Exchange or Change Alley; 'Westminster Hall': the high court. That is to say, English paper currency has value precisely because it is not legally enforcible as a means of payment, by contrast the French has less in proportion as it is imposed on people.

hermetic[31] art to neglect all rational means of their fortunes . . . These gentlemen perhaps do not believe a great deal in the miracles of piety; but it cannot be questioned, that they have an undoubted faith in the prodigies of sacrilege. Is there a debt which presses them – Issue *assignats*.[32] Are compensations to be made, or a maintenance decreed to those whom they have robbed of their freehold in their office, or expelled from their profession – *Assignats*. Is a Fleet to be fitted out – *Assignats* . . . All experience of their inefficacy does not in the least discourage them. Are the old *assignats* depreciated at the market? What is the remedy? Issue new *assignats* . . .

. . .

Who but the most desperate adventurers in philosophy and finance could at all have thought of destroying the settled revenue of the state, the sole security for the public credit, in the hope of rebuilding it with the materials of confiscated property?

. . .

. . .

On recollection, I have said nothing of a scheme of finance which may be urged in favour of the abilities of these gentlemen, and which has been introduced with great pomp, though not yet finally adopted in the national assembly. It comes with something solid in aid of the credit of the paper circulation; and much has been said of its utility and its elegance. I mean the project for coining into money the bells of the suppressed churches. This is their alchemy.[33] There are some follies which baffle argument; which go beyond ridicule; and which excite no feeling in us but disgust; and therefore I say no more upon it.

. . .

But am I so unreasonable as to see nothing at all that deserves commendation in the indefatigable labours of this assembly? I do not deny that among an infinite number of acts of violence and folly, some good may have been done. They who destroy every thing certainly will remove some grievance. They who make every thing new, have

---

[31] 'Philosopher's stone' and 'Hermetic' are references to a tradition of occult sciences deriving from the figure of Hermes Trismegistus.

[32] The *assignat* was a unit of paper currency backed by the value, as yet unrealised, of the confiscated church lands. Since it was unknown what these lands would realise, and their purchasers would pay in *assignats*, the number of which in circulation was entirely at the discretion of the Revolutionary government and governed by their increasing revenue needs, the system was viciously circular and highly inflationary, quite apart, as Burke points out, from being founded on the violation of property rights.

[33] Alchemists pursued, amongst other things, the supposed secret of turning base metals into gold. Burke's epithet for those seeking to coin money from the melted-down bells of the churches is hardly even a metaphor.

a chance that they may establish something beneficial . . . The improvements of the national assembly are superficial; their errors, fundamental.

Whatever they are, I wish my countrymen rather to recommend to our neighbours the example of the British constitution, than to take models from them for the improvement of our own. In the former they have got an invaluable treasure. They are not, I think, without some causes of apprehension and complaint; but these they do not owe to their constitution, but to their own conduct . . . I would not exclude alteration neither; but even when I changed, it should be to preserve. I should be led to my remedy by a great grievance. In what I did, I should follow the example of our ancestors. I would make the reparation as nearly as possible in the style of the building. A politic caution, a guarded circumspection, a moral rather than a complexional timidity, were among the ruling principles of our forefathers in their most decided conduct . . . Let us imitate their caution, if we wish to deserve their fortune, or to retain their bequests. Let us add, if we please; but let us preserve what they have left; and, standing on the firm ground of the British constitution, let us be satisfied to admire rather than attempt to follow in their desperate flights the aëronauts of France.

I have told you candidly my sentiments. I think they are not likely to alter yours. I do not know that they ought. You are young; you cannot guide, but must follow the fortune of your country. But hereafter they may be of some use to you, in some future form which your commonwealth may take. In the present it can hardly remain; but before its final settlement it may be obliged to pass, as one of our poets says, 'through great varieties of untried being,' and in all its transmigrations to be purified by fire and blood.

I have little to recommend my opinions, but long observation and much impartiality. They come from one who has been no tool of power, no flatterer of greatness; and who in his last acts does not wish to belye the tenour of his life. They come from one, almost the whole of whose public exertion has been a struggle for the liberty of others; from one in whose breast no anger durable or vehement has ever been kindled, but by what he considered as tyranny . . . They come from one who desires honours, distinctions, and emoluments, but little, and who expects them not at all; who has no contempt for fame, and no fear of obloquy; who shuns contention, though he will hazard an opinion: from one who wishes to preserve consistency; but who would preserve consistency by varying his means to secure the unity of his end; and, when the equipoise of the vessel in which he sails may be endangered by overloading it upon one side, is desirous of carrying the small weight of his reasons to that which may preserve its equipoise.

Plate 2. *The Knight of the Woeful Countenance* (attr. to Frederick George Byron, 15 November 1790). Burke is depicted as Don Quixote (a self-reference in *Reflections* subsequently widely used by cartoonists to ridicule his championship of outdated chivalric values) riding out on a donkey or an ass which is wearing a Papal crown. He is leaving the shop of Dodsley, his publisher, to do battle with the national assembly. His spear is a quill pen and his shield symbolises his defence of 'Aristocracy and Despotism'. Around his neck he wears a picture of Marie Antoinette and on his head the black biretta of a Catholic priest on which sits, ironically, an owl of Minerva, symbol of wisdom.

MARY WOLLSTONECRAFT

BIOGRAPHICAL NOTE

Mary Wollstonecraft was born in 1759 into a genteel but declining (and some-times domestically violent) East London family who subsequently moved to var-ious parts of the country. Largely self-taught, she became a ladies' companion, then a governess and ultimately established her own school at Newington Green (1784) where she also became a member of Price's dissenting intellectual circle, and met the radical publisher Joseph Johnson who encouraged and supported her work. She wrote at this time, amongst other things, *Thoughts on the Education of Daughters* (1786) and articles for Johnson's liberal periodical the *Analytical Review*, a novel, *Mary, Original Stories* (1788), and several translations from French and German.

In 1792 she travelled to France, joining Tom Paine and the small community of English radicals in Paris. When war with England began in 1793 Mary escaped arrest by registering as the wife of her lover Gilbert Imlay, an American Citizen. In 1794 she bore their child, Fanny. Incredibly, in the midst of all this, and the first executions, she managed to write her *Historical and Moral view of the Origin and Progress of the French Revolution and the effect it has Produced on Europe* (1794). Deserted by Imlay, she travelled in Scandinavia and produced an original, popular and well-regarded travel memoir, *Letters written in . . . Sweden, Norway and Denmark.*

Returning to London she established a happy relationship with the philoso-pher William Godwin. After much deliberation – for they had both written against the institution – they married in 1797. Tragically Wollstonecraft died in 1797 from infection following the birth of their daughter Mary, the future author of *Frankenstein*. Her last novel, *The Wrongs of Woman, or Maria*, lay unfinished on her desk.

A Vindication of the Rights of Men (1790) was the first major response to Burke's *Reflections . . .* , published anonymously – and almost incredibly – within a month of that work on 29 November. It proved highly controversial, especially when (as was made clear in the second edition) the author of a book on politics was known to be a woman, provoking Horace Walpole's infamous description of her as 'a hyena in petticoats'. It introduces a range of themes that were to become crucial elements of the debate, the defence of natural rights, the rejection of 'gothic' social and aesthetic standards and beyond that the very identity of 'nature' and 'artifice', the defence of rationalist methods applied to moral and political thought, as well as some that were more specifically her own, namely the role of gender assumptions in political argument.

Little over a year later, in January 1792, Wollstonecraft completed *A Vindication of the Rights of Woman* which argued for the social and educational emancipation of women, issues then being discussed in Revolutionary France. That work, like Burke's, is presented as being written to a French recipient – Talleyrand-Perigord the revolutionary educationalist – and so, like Price's and Burke's though to a lesser degree, addresses English affairs obliquely, through the French. The book did not claim political rights for women (although a projected second volume may have done) but, more insidiously and subversively, stressed the political character of the private sphere in which women so often found themselves – sexual relations, child-rearing and education being of the utmost importance in shaping and sustaining virtuous citizens. That the book was broadly well received at the time suggests the political thrust of it was not perceived.

EDITORIAL NOTE

There were two original editions of *A Vindication of the Rights of Men*, 1790 and 1791. The first was anonymous. The second (used here) contained minor corrections and is used in most reprints.

Modern editions:

The Works of Mary Wollstonecraft, ed. Janet Todd and Marilyn Butler (London: Pickering, 1989).

A Vindication of the Rights of Men and A Vindication of the Rights of Woman, ed. Sylvana Tomaselli (Cambridge: Cambridge University Press, 1995).

A Vindication of the Rights of Men, ed. Eleanor Nicholes (Gainesville, Fl.: Scholars' Facsimiles and Reprints, 1960).

FURTHER READING

Flexner, E. *Mary Wollstonecraft: A Biography* (N.Y.: Coward, McCann and Geoghegan, 1972).

Godwin, W. *Memoirs of the Author of a 'Vindication of the Rights of Woman'* (London, 1798).

Kelly, G. *Revolutionary Feminist: The Mind and Career of Mary Wollstonecraft* (London: Macmillan, 1992).

Sapiro, V. *A Vindication of Political Virtue: The Political Theory of Mary Woll-stonecraft* (Chicago: University of Chicago Press, 1992).

Todd, J. *Mary Wollstonecraft: A Revolutionary Life* (London: Weidenfeld and Nicolson, 2001).

Tomalin, C. *The Life and Death of Mary Wollstonecraft* (Harmondsworth: Penguin, 1974).

A Vindication of the Rights of Men, in a letter to the right honourable Edmund Burke occasioned by his Reflections on the Revolution in France (1790)

Sir,

It is not necessary, with courtly insincerity, to apologise to you for thus intruding on your precious time, nor to profess that I think it an honour to discuss an important subject with a man whose literary abilities have raised him to notice in the state. I have not yet learned to twist my periods, nor, in the equivocal idiom of politeness, to disguise my sentiments, and imply what I should be afraid to utter: if, therefore, in the course of this epistle, I chance to express contempt, and even indignation, with some emphasis, I beseech you to believe that it is not a flight of fancy; for truth, in morals, has ever appeared to me the essence of the sublime; and, in taste, simplicity the only criterion of the beautiful. But I war not with an individual when I contend for the rights *of men* and the liberty of reason. You see I do not condescend to cull my words to avoid the invidious phrase, nor shall I be prevented from giving a manly definition of it, by the flimsy ridicule which a lively fancy has interwoven with the present acceptation of the term. Reverencing the rights of humanity, I shall dare to assert them; not intimidated by the horse laugh that you have raised, or waiting till time has wiped away the compassionate tears which you have elaborately laboured to excite.

. . .

The birthright of man, to give you, Sir, a short definition of this disputed right, is such a degree of liberty, civil and religious, as is compatible with the liberty of every other individual with whom he is united in a social compact, and the continued existence of that compact.

Liberty, in this simple, unsophisticated sense, I acknowledge, is a fair idea that has never yet received a form in the various governments that have been established on our beauteous globe; the demon of property has ever been at hand to encroach on the sacred rights of men, and to fence round with awful pomp laws that war with justice. But that it results from the eternal foundation of right – from immutable truth – who will presume to deny, that pretends to rationality – if reason has led them to build their morality and religion on an everlasting foundation – the attributes of God?

. . .

I perceive, from the whole tenor of your Reflections, that you have a mortal antipathy to reason; but, if there is any thing like argument, or first principles, in your wild declamation, behold the result: – that we are to reverence the rust of antiquity, and term the unnatural customs, which ignorance and mistaken self-interest have consolidated, the sage fruit of experience: nay, that, if we do discover some errors, our *feelings* should lead us to excuse, with blind love, or unprincipled filial affection, the venerable vestiges of ancient days. These are gothic notions of beauty – the ivy is beautiful, but, when it insidiously destroys the trunk from which it receives support, who would not grub it up?

Further, that we ought cautiously to remain for ever in frozen inactivity, because a thaw, whilst it nourishes the soil, spreads a temporary inundation; and the fear of risking any personal present convenience should prevent a struggle for the most estimable advantages. This is sound reasoning, I grant, in the mouth of the rich and short-sighted.

Yes, Sir, the strong gained riches, the few have sacrificed the many to their vices; and, to be able to pamper their appetites, and supinely exist without exercising mind or body, they have ceased to be men. – Lost to the relish of true pleasure, such beings would, indeed, deserve compassion, if injustice was not softened by the tyrant's plea – necessity; if prescription was not raised as an immortal boundary against innovation. Their minds, in fact, instead of being cultivated, have been so warped by education, that it may require some ages to bring them back to nature, and enable them to see their true interest, with that degree of conviction which is necessary to influence their conduct.

The civilization which has taken place in Europe has been very partial, and, like every custom that an arbitrary point of honour has established, refines the manners at the expence of morals, by making sentiments and opinions current in conversation that have no root in the heart, or weight in the cooler resolves of the mind. – And what has stopped its progress? – hereditary property – hereditary honours. The man has been changed into an artificial monster by the station in which he was born, and the consequent homage that benumbed his faculties like the torpedo's touch[1]; – or a being, with a capacity of reasoning, would not have failed to discover, as his faculties unfolded, that true happiness arose from the friendship and intimacy which can only be enjoyed by equals; and that charity is not a condescending distribution of alms, but an intercourse of good offices and mutual benefits, founded on respect for justice and humanity.

Governed by these principles, the poor wretch, whose *inelegant* distress extorted from a mixed feeling of disgust and animal sympathy present relief, would have been considered as a man, whose misery demanded a part of his birthright, supposing him to be industrious; but should his vices have reduced him to poverty, he could only have addressed his fellow-men as weak beings, subject to like passions, who ought to forgive, because they expect to be forgiven, for suffering the impulse of the moment to silence the suggestions of conscience, or reason, which you will; for, in my view of things, they are synonymous terms.

Will Mr. Burke be at the trouble to inform us, how far we are to go back to discover the rights of men, since the light of reason is such a fallacious guide that none but fools trust to its cold investigation?

In the infancy of society, confining our view to our own country, customs were established by the lawless power of an ambitious individual; or a weak prince was obliged to comply with every demand of the licentious barbarous insurgents, who disputed his authority with irrefragable arguments at the point of their swords; or the more specious requests of the Parliament, who only allowed him conditional supplies.

Are these the venerable pillars of our constitution? And is Magna Charta to rest for its chief support on a former grant, which reverts to another, till chaos becomes the base of the mighty structure – or we cannot tell what? – for coherence, without some pervading principle of order, is a solecism.

. . .

The imperfection of all modern governments must, without waiting to repeat the trite remark, that all human institutions are unavoidably imperfect, in a great measure have arisen from this simple circumstance, that the constitution, if such an heterogeneous mass deserve that name, was settled in the dark days of ignorance, when the minds of men were shackled by the grossest prejudices and most immoral

---

[1] Torpedo: not the modern weapon but the fish, the electric ray.

superstition. And do you, Sir, a sagacious philosopher, recommend night as the fittest time to analyze a ray of light?

Are we to seek for the rights of men in the ages when a few marks were the only penalty imposed for the life of a man, and death for death when the property of the rich was touched? when – I blush to discover the depravity of our nature – when a deer was killed?[2] Are these the laws that it is natural to love, and sacrilegious to invade? Were the rights of men understood when the law authorised or tolerated murder? – or is power and right the same in your creed?

. . .

It is necessary emphatically to repeat, that there are rights which men inherit at their birth, as rational creatures, who were raised above the brute creation by their improvable faculties; and that, in receiving these, not from their forefathers but, from God, prescription can never undermine natural rights.

A father may dissipate his property without his child having any right to complain; – but should he attempt to sell him for a slave, or fetter him with laws contrary to reason; nature, in enabling him to discern good from evil, teaches him to break the ignoble chain, and not to believe that bread becomes flesh, and wine blood, because his parents swallowed the Eucharist with this blind persuasion.[3]

There is no end to this implicit submission to authority – some where it must stop, or we return to barbarism; and the capacity of improvement, which gives us a natural sceptre on earth, is a cheat, an ignis-fatuus,[4] that leads us from inviting meadows into bogs and dung-hills. And if it be allowed that many of the precautions, with which any alteration was made, in our government, were prudent, it rather proves its weakness than substantiates an opinion of the soundness of the stamina, or the excellence of the constitution.

But on what principle Mr. Burke could defend American independence, I cannot conceive; for the whole tenor of his plausible arguments settles slavery on an everlasting foundation. Allowing his servile reverence for antiquity, and prudent attention to self-interest, to have the force which he insists on, the slave trade ought

---

[2] Marks: the unit of currency. Feudal Law Codes often allowed violent crimes to be recompensed by a money payment. Taking royal game such as deer or swan could attract the death penalty.
[3] A reference to the Catholic doctrine of transubstantiation – that during the communion service the bread and wine actually become the flesh and blood of Christ – which radical Protestants took as symptomatic of the superstitious character of Catholicism.
[4] Literally 'Fools' Fire'. The flames sometimes caused by marsh gas igniting over boggy ground, said to deceive unwary travellers: hence anything which deludes one into thinking something safe or useful which is in fact dangerous.

never to be abolished; and, because our ignorant forefathers, not understanding the native dignity of man, sanctioned a traffic that outrages every suggestion of reason and religion, we are to submit to the inhuman custom, and term an atrocious insult to humanity the love of our country, and a proper submission to the laws by which our property is secured. – Security of property! Behold, in a few words, the definition of English liberty . . . But softly – it is only the property of the rich that is secure; the man who lives by the sweat of his brow has no asylum from oppression; the strong man may enter – when was the castle of the poor sacred? and the base informer steal him from the family that depend on his industry for subsistence.

Fully sensible as you must be of the baneful consequences that inevitably follow this notorious infringement on the dearest rights of men, and that it is an infernal blot on the very face of our immaculate constitution, I cannot avoid expressing my surprise that when you recommended our form of government as a model, you did not caution the French against the arbitrary custom of pressing men for the sea service.[5] You should have hinted to them, that property in England is much more secure than liberty, and not have concealed that the liberty of an honest mechanic – his all – is often sacrificed to secure the property of the rich. For it is a farce to pretend that a man fights for *his country, his hearth, or his altars*, when he has neither liberty nor property. – His property is in his nervous arms – and they are compelled to pull a strange rope at the surly command of a tyrannic boy,[6] who probably obtained his rank on account of his family connections, or the prostituted vote of his father, whose interest in a borough, or voice as a senator, was acceptable to the minister.

. . .

You have shewn, Sir, by your silence on these subjects, that your respect for rank has swallowed up the common feelings of humanity; you seem to consider the poor as only the live stock of an estate, the feather of hereditary nobility. When you had so little respect for the silent majesty of misery, I am not surprised at your manner of treating an individual whose brow a mitre will never grace [Richard Price], and whose popularity may have wounded your vanity – for vanity is ever sore. Even in France, Sir, before the revolution, literary celebrity procured a man the treatment of

[5] 'Pressing' or 'impressment': the practice of kidnapping working men for service in the Navy.
[6] The officers commanding the men might be very young, having bought their commission or obtained it through family influence.

a gentleman; but you are going back for your credentials of politeness to more distant times. – Gothic affability is the mode you think proper to adopt, the condescension of a Baron, not the civility of a liberal man. Politeness is, indeed, the only substitute for humanity; or what distinguishes the civilised man from the unlettered savage? and he who is not governed by reason should square his behaviour by an arbitrary standard; but by what rule your attack on Dr. Price was regulated we have yet to learn.

. . .

. . . Granting, for a moment, that Dr. Price's political opinions are Utopian reveries, and that the world is not yet sufficiently civilized to adopt such a sublime system of morality; they could, however, only be the reveries of a benevolent mind . . .

. . .

Dr. Price, when he reasons on the necessity of men attending some place of public worship, concisely obviates an objection that has been made in the form of an apology, by advising those, who do not approve of our Liturgy, and cannot find any mode of worship out of the church, in which they can conscientiously join, to establish one for themselves. This plain advice you have tortured into a very different meaning, and represented the preacher as actuated by a dissenting frenzy, recommending dissensions, 'not to diffuse truth, but to spread contradictions.' A simple question will silence this impertinent declamation. – What is truth? A few fundamental truths meet the first enquiry of reason, and appear as clear to an unwarped mind, as that air and bread are necessary to enable the body to fulfil its vital functions; but the opinions which men discuss with so much heat must be simplified and brought back to first principles; or who can discriminate the vagaries of the imagination, or scrupulosity of weakness, from the verdict of reason? Let all these points be demonstrated, and not determined by arbitrary authority and dark traditions, lest a dangerous supineness should take place; for probably, in ceasing to enquire, our reason would remain dormant, and delivered up, without a curb, to every impulse of passion, we might soon lose sight of the clear light which the exercise of our understanding no longer kept alive. To argue from experience, it should seem as if the human mind, averse to thought, could only be opened by necessity; for, when it can take opinions on trust, it gladly lets the spirit lie quiet in its gross tenement. Perhaps the most improving exercise of the mind, confining the argument to the enlargement of the understanding, is the restless enquiries that hover on the boundary, or stretch over the dark abyss of uncertainty. These lively conjectures are the breezes that preserve the still lake from stagnating. We should be aware of confining all moral excellence to one channel, however capacious; or, if we are so narrow-minded, we should not forget how much we owe to chance that our inheritance was not Mahometism; and that the iron hand of destiny, in the shape of deeply rooted authority, has not suspended the sword of destruction over our heads. But to return to the misrepresentation.

Blackstone[7] to whom Mr. Burke pays great deference, seems to agree with Dr. Price, that the succession of the King of Great Britain depends on the choice of the people, or that they have a power to cut it off; but this power, as you have fully proved, has been cautiously exerted, and might with more propriety be termed a *right* than a power. Be it so! . . .

. . .

You further sarcastically animadvert on the consistency of the democratists, by wresting the obvious meaning of a common phrase, *the dregs of the people;* or your contempt for poverty may have led you into an error. Be that as it may, an unprejudiced man would have directly perceived the single sense of the word, and an old Member of Parliament could scarcely have missed it. He who had so often felt the pulse of the electors needed not have gone beyond his own experience to discover that the dregs alluded to were the vicious, and not the lower class of the community.

Again, Sir, I must doubt your sincerity or your discernment. – You have been behind the curtain; . . . you must have seen the clogged wheels of corruption continually oiled by the sweat of the laborious poor, squeezed out of them by unceasing taxation. You must have discovered that the majority in the House of Commons was often

---

[7] [Wollstonecraft's footnote:] The doctrine of *hereditary* right does by no means imply an *indefeasible* right to the throne. No man will, I think, assert this, that has considered our laws, constitution, and history, without prejudice, and with any degree of attention. It is unquestionably in the breast of the supreme legislative authority of this kingdom, the King and both Houses of Parliament, to defeat this hereditary right; and, by particular entails, limitations, and provisions, to exclude the immediate heir, and vest the inheritance in any one else. This is strictly consonant to our laws and constitution; as may be gathered from the expression so frequently used in our statute books, of "the King's Majesty, his heirs, and successors." In which we may observe that, as the word 'heirs' necessarily implies an inheritance, or hereditary right, generally subsisting in "the royal person"; so the word successors, distinctly taken, must imply that this inheritance may sometimes be broken through; or, that there may be a successor, without being the heir of the king. (Blackstone, *Commentaries on the Laws of England* [1765], 1, iii, p. 188.1) I shall not, however, rest in something like a subterfuge, and quote, as partially as you have done, from Aristotle. Blackstone has so cautiously fenced round his opinion with provisos, that it is obvious he thought the letter of the law leaned towards your side of the question – but a blind respect for the law is not a part of my creed.'

purchased by the crown, and that the people were oppressed by the influence of their own money, extorted by the venal voice of a packed[8] representation.

. . . that a man of merit cannot rise in the church, the army, or navy, unless he has some interest in a borough; and that even a paltry exciseman's place can only be secured by electioneering interest . . . that few Bishops, though there have been learned and good Bishops, have gained the mitre without submitting to a servility of dependence that degrades the man. – All these circumstances you must have known, yet you talk of virtue and liberty, as the vulgar talk of the letter of the law; and the polite of propriety. It is true that these ceremonial observances produce decorum; the sepulchres are white-washed, and do not offend the squeamish eyes of high rank; but virtue is out of the question when you only worship a shadow, and worship it to secure your property.

Man has been termed, with strict propriety, a microcosm, a little world in himself. – He is so; – yet must, however, be reckoned an ephemera, or, to adopt your figure of rhetoric, a summer's fly. The perpetuation of property in our families is one of the privileges you most warmly contend for; yet it would not be very difficult to prove that the mind must have a very limited range that thus confines its benevolence to such a narrow circle, which, with great propriety, may be included in the sordid calculations of blind self-love.

A brutal attachment to children has appeared most conspicuous in parents who have treated them like slaves, and demanded due homage for all the property they transferred to them, during their lives. It has led them to force their children to break the most sacred ties; . . . and that the barbarous cruelty of allowing parents to imprison their children, to prevent their contaminating their noble blood by following the dictates of nature when they chose to marry, or for any misdemeanour that does not come under the cognizance of public justice, is one of the most arbitrary violations of liberty.

Who can recount all the unnatural crimes which the *laudable, interesting* desire of perpetuating a name has produced? The younger children have been sacrificed to the eldest son; sent into exile, or confined in convents, that they might not encroach on what was called, with shameful falsehood, the *family* estate. Will Mr. Burke call this parental affection reasonable or virtuous? – No; it is the spurious offspring of over-weening, mistaken pride – and not that first source of civilization, natural parental

[8] Packed: as in a packed jury, i.e. filled with bribed or prejudiced members.

affection, that makes no difference between child and child, but what reason justifies by pointing out superior merit.

Another pernicious consequence which unavoidably arises from this artificial affection is, the insuperable bar which it puts in the way of early marriages. It would be difficult to determine whether the minds or bodies of our youth are most injured by this impediment. Our young men become selfish coxcombs, and gallantry with modest women, and intrigues with those of another description, weaken both mind and body, before either has arrived at maturity. The character of a master of a family, a husband, and a father, forms the citizen imperceptibly, by producing a sober manliness of thought, and orderly behaviour; but, from the lax morals and depraved affections of the libertine, what results? – a finical[9] man of taste, who is only anxious to secure his own private gratifications, and to maintain his rank in society.

The same system has an equally pernicious effect on female morals. – Girls are sacrificed to family convenience, or else marry to settle themselves in a superior rank, and coquet, without restraint, with the fine gentleman whom I have already described. And to such lengths has this vanity, this desire of shining, carried them, that it is not now necessary to guard girls against imprudent love matches; for if some widows did not now and then *fall* in love, Love and Hymen[10] would seldom meet, unless at a village church.

. . .

It would be an arduous task to trace all the vice and misery that arise in society from the middle class of people apeing the manners of the great . . . The grand concern of three parts out of four is to contrive to live above their equals, and to appear to be richer than they are. How much domestic comfort and private satisfaction is sacrificed to this irrational ambition! It is a destructive mildew that blights the fairest virtues; benevolence, friendship, generosity, and all those endearing charities which bind human hearts together, and the pursuits which raise the mind to higher contemplations, all that were not cankered in the bud by the false notions that 'grew with its growth and strengthened with its strength', are crushed by the iron hand of property![11]

Property, I do not scruple to aver it, should be fluctuating, which would be the case, if it were more equally divided amongst all the children of a family; else it is an

---

[9] Finical: over-concerned with trivial details of taste, finicky.
[10] Hymen: the Greek and Roman god of marriage.
[11] Alexander Pope, *An Essay on Man* (1733–4), lines, 135–6.

everlasting rampart, in consequence of a barbarous feudal institution, that enables the elder son to overpower talents and depress virtue.

Besides, an unmanly servility, most inimical to true dignity of character is, by this means, fostered in society. Men of some abilities play on the follies of the rich, and mounting to fortune as they degrade themselves, they stand in the way of men of superior talents, who cannot advance in such crooked paths, or wade through the filth which *parasites* never boggle at . . .

The only security of property that nature authorises and reason sanctions is, the right a man has to enjoy the acquisitions which his talents and industry have acquired; and to bequeath them to whom he chooses. Happy would it be for the world if there were no other road to wealth or honour; if pride, in the shape of parental affection, did not absorb the man, and prevent friendship from having the same weight as relationship. Luxury and effeminacy would not then introduce so much idiotism into the noble families which form one of the pillars of our state: the ground would not lie fallow, nor would undirected activity of mind spread the contagion of restless idleness, and its concomitant, vice, through the whole mass of society.

Instead of gaming they might nourish a virtuous ambition, and love might take place of the gallantry which you, with knightly fealty, venerate. Women would probably then act like mothers, and the fine lady, become a rational woman, might think it necessary to superintend her family and suckle her children, in order to fulfil her part of the social compact. But vain is the hope, whilst great masses of property are hedged round by hereditary honours; for numberless vices, forced in the hot-bed of wealth, assume a sightly form to dazzle the senses and cloud the understanding. The respect paid to rank and fortune damps every generous purpose of our soul and stifles the natural affections on which human contentment ought to be built. . . .

. . .

Of your partial feelings I shall take another view, and shew that 'following nature, which is', you say, 'wisdom without reflection, and *above it*' – has led you into great inconsistencies, to use the softest phrase . . . When you descanted on the horrors of the 6th of October,[12] and gave a glowing, and, in some instances, a most exaggerated description of that infernal night, without having troubled yourself to clean your palette, you might have returned home and indulged us with a sketch of the misery you personally aggravated.

. . .

[12] The night when the King and Queen were taken from Versailles to Paris. See *Reflections*, p. 78 ff in this collection.

In this state was the King, when you, with unfeeling disrespect, and indecent haste, wished to strip him of all his hereditary honours.[13] – You were so eager to taste the sweets of power, that you could not wait till time had determined, whether a dreadful delirium would settle into a confirmed madness; but, prying into the secrets of Omnipotence, you thundered out that God had *hurled him from his throne*, and that it was the most insulting mockery to recollect that he had been a king, or to treat him with any particular respect on account of his former dignity . . .

Where then was the infallibility of that extolled instinct which rises above reason? was it warped by vanity, or *hurled* from its throne by self-interest? To your own heart answer these questions in the sober hours of reflection – and, after reviewing this gust of passion, learn to respect the sovereignty of reason.

. . .

Whether the glory of Europe is set, I shall not now enquire; but probably the spirit of romance and chivalry is in the wane; and reason will gain by its extinction.

From observing several cold romantic characters I have been led to confine the term romantic to one definition – false, or rather artificial, feelings. Works of genius are read with a prepossession in their favour, and sentiments imitated, because they were fashionable and pretty, and not because they were forcibly felt.

In modern poetry the understanding and memory often fabricate the pretended effusions of the heart, and romance destroys all simplicity; which, in works of taste, is but a synonymous word for truth. This romantic spirit has extended to our prose, and scattered artificial flowers over the most barren heath; or a mixture of verse and prose producing the strangest incongruities. The turgid bombast of some of your periods fully proves these assertions; for when the heart speaks we are seldom shocked by hyperbole, or dry raptures.

. . .

A sentiment of this kind glanced across my mind when I read the following exclamation. 'Whilst the royal captives, who followed in the train, were slowly moved along, amidst the horrid yells, and shrilling screams, and frantic dances, and infamous contumelies, and all the unutterable abominations of the furies of hell, in the abused

---

[13] During George III's temporary madness Burke's party supported the regency of the Prince of Wales.

shape of the vilest of women.' Probably you mean women who gained a livelihood by selling vegetables or fish, who never had had any advantages of education; or their vices might have lost part of their abominable deformity, by losing part of their grossness. The queen of France – the great and small vulgar, claim our pity; they have almost insuperable obstacles to surmount in their progress towards true dignity of character; still I have such a plain downright understanding that I do not like to make a distinction without a difference. But it is not very extraordinary that *you* should, for throughout your letter you frequently advert to a sentimental jargon, which has long been current in conversation, and even in books of morals, though it never received the *regal* stamp of reason. A kind of mysterious instinct is *supposed* to reside in the soul, that instantaneously discerns truth, without the tedious labour of ratiocination. This instinct, for I know not what other name to give it, has been termed *common sense*, and more frequently *sensibility*; and, by a kind of *indefeasible* right, it has been *supposed*, for rights of this kind are not easily proved, to reign paramount over the other faculties of the mind, and to be an authority from which there is no appeal.

This subtle magnetic fluid, that runs round the whole circle of society, is not subject to any known rule, or, to use an obnoxious phrase, in spite of the sneers of mock humility, or the timid fears of some well-meaning Christians, who shrink from any freedom of thought, lest they should rouse the old serpent, to the *eternal fitness of things*.[14] It dips, we know not why, granting it to be an infallible instinct, and, though supposed always to point to truth, its pole-star, the point is always shifting, and seldom stands due north.

It is to this instinct, without doubt, that you allude, when you talk of the 'moral constitution of the heart.' To it, I allow, for I consider it as a congregate of sensations and passions, *Poets* must apply, 'who have to deal with an audience not yet graduated in the school of the rights of men.' They must, it is clear, often cloud the understanding, whilst they move the heart by a kind of mechanical spring; but that 'in the theatre the first intuitive glance' of feeling should discriminate the form of truth, and see her fair proportion, I must beg leave to doubt. Sacred be the feelings of the heart! concentred in a glowing flame, they become the sun of life; and, without his invigorating impregnation, reason would probably lie in

---

[14] A reference to debates provoked by Shaftesbury as to whether morality could be grounded in nature. 'Free thinkers' rejected, or at least questioned, a theological basis for morality.

helpless inactivity, and never bring forth her only legitimate offspring – virtue. But to prove that virtue is really an acquisition of the individual, and not the blind impulse of unerring instinct, the bastard vice has often been begotten by the same father.

. . .

But the cultivation of reason is an arduous task, and men of lively fancy, finding it easier to follow the impulse of passion, endeavour to persuade themselves and others that it is most *natural.* And happy is it for those, who indolently let that heaven-lighted spark rest like the ancient lamps in sepulchres, that some virtuous habits, with which the reason of others shackled them, supplies its place. – Affection for parents, reverence for superiors or antiquity, notions of honour, or that worldly self-interest that shrewdly shews them that honesty is the best policy? all proceed from the reason for which they serve as substitutes; – but it is reason at second-hand.

Children are born ignorant, consequently innocent; the passions, are neither good nor evil dispositions, till they receive a direction, and either bound over the feeble barrier raised by a faint glimmering of unexercised reason, called conscience, or strengthen her wavering dictates till sound principles are deeply rooted, and able to cope with the headstrong passions that often assume her awful form. What moral purpose can be answered by extolling good dispositions, as they are called, when these good dispositions are described as instincts: for instinct moves in a direct line to its ultimate end, and asks not for guide or support. But if virtue is to be acquired by experience, or taught by example, reason, perfected by reflection, must be the director of the whole host of passions, which produce a fructifying heat, but no light, that you would exalt into her place. – She must hold the rudder, or, let the wind blow which way it list, the vessel will never advance smoothly to its destined port; for the time lost in tacking about would dreadfully impede its progress.

In the name of the people of England, you say, 'that we know we have made no discoveries; and we think that no discoveries are to be made in morality; nor many in the great principles of government, nor in the ideas of liberty, which were understood long before we were born . . .; we still feel within us, and we cherish and cultivate those inbred sentiments which are the faithful guardians, the active monitors of our duty, the true supporters of all liberal and manly morals.' – What do you mean by inbred sentiments? From whence do they come? How were they bred? . . . The appetites are the only perfect inbred powers that I can discern; and they like instincts have a certain aim, they can be satisfied – but improveable reason has not yet discovered the perfection it may arrive at – God forbid!

First, however, it is necessary to make what we know practical. Who can deny, that has marked the slow progress of civilization, that men may become more virtuous and happy without any new discovery in morals? Who will venture to assert that virtue would not be promoted by the more extensive cultivation of reason? If nothing more is to be done, let us eat and drink, for to-morrow we die – and die for ever! . . . The power of exercising our understanding raises us above the brutes; and this exercise produces that 'primary morality,' which you term 'untaught feelings.'

If virtue be an instinct, I renounce all hope of immortality; and with it all the sublime reveries and dignified sentiments that have smoothed the rugged path of life: it is all a cheat, a lying vision; I have disquieted myself in vain; for in my eye all feelings are false and spurious, that do not rest on justice as their foundation, and are not concentred by universal love.

I reverence the rights of men. – Sacred rights! for which I acquire a more profound respect, the more I look into my own mind; and, professing these heterodox opinions, I still preserve my bowels; my heart is human, beats quick with human sympathies – and I FEAR God!

I bend with awful reverence when I enquire on what my fear is built. – I fear that sublime power, whose motive for creating me must have been wise and good; and I submit to the moral laws which my reason deduces from this view of my dependence on him. – It is not his power that I fear – it is not to an arbitrary will, but to unerring *reason* I submit . . .

This fear of God makes me reverence myself. – Yes, Sir, the regard I have for honest fame, and the friendship of the virtuous, falls far short of the respect which I have for myself. And this, enlightened self-love, if an epithet the meaning of which has been grossly perverted will convey my idea, forces me to see; and, if I may venture to borrow a prostituted term, to *feel*, that happiness is reflected, and that, in communicating good, my soul receives its noble ailment. – I do not trouble myself, therefore, to enquire whether this is the fear the *people* of England feel: – and, if it be *natural* to include all the modifications which you have annexed – it is not.

Besides, I cannot help suspecting that, if you had the *enlightened* respect for your-self, which you affect to despise, you would not have said that the constitution of our church and state, formed, like most other modern ones, by degrees, as Europe was emerging out of barbarism, was formed 'under the auspices, and was confirmed by the sanctions, of religion and piety.' You have turned over the historic page; have been hackneyed in the ways of men, and must know that private cabals and public feuds, private virtues and vices, religion and superstition, have all concurred to foment the mass and swell it to its present form; nay more, that it in part owes its sightly appearance to bold rebellion and insidious innovation. Factions, Sir, have been the leaven, and private interest has produced public good.

. . .

The people of England, Sir, in the thirteenth and fourteenth centuries, I will not go any further back to insult the ashes of departed popery, did not settle the establishment, and endow it with princely revenues, to make it proudly rear its head, as a part of the constitutional body, to guard the liberties of the community; but, like some of the laborious commentators on Shakespeare, you have affixed a meaning to laws that chance, or, to speak more philosophically, the interested views of men, settled, not dreaming of your ingenious elucidations.

What, but the rapacity of the only men who exercised their reason, the priests, secured such vast property to the church, when a man gave his perishable substance to save himself from the dark torments of purgatory; and found it more convenient to indulge his depraved appetites, and pay an exorbitant price for absolution, than listen to the suggestions of reason, and work out his own salvation: in a word, was not the separation of religion from morality the work of the priests, and partly achieved in those *honourable* days which you so piously deplore?

That civilization, that the cultivation of the understanding, and refinement of the affections, naturally make a man religious, I am proud to acknowledge. – What else can fill the aching void in the heart, that human pleasures, human friendships can never fill? What else can render us resigned to live, though condemned to ignorance? – What but a profound reverence for the model of all perfection, and the mysterious tie which arises from a love of goodness? What can make us reverence ourselves, but a reverence for that Being, of whom we are a faint image? . . . These are human feelings; but I know not of any common nature or common relation amongst men but what results from reason. The common affections and passions equally bind brutes together; and it is only the continuity of those relations that entitles us to the denomination of rational creatures; and this continuity arises from reflection – from the operations of that reason which you contemn with flippant disrespect.

If then it appears, arguing from analogy, that reflection must be the natural foundation of *rational* affections, and of that experience which enables one man to rise above another, a phenomenon that has never been seen in the brute creation, it may not be stretching the argument further than it will go to suppose, that those men who are obliged to exercise their reason have the most reason, and are the persons pointed out by Nature to direct the society of which they make a part, on any extraordinary emergency.

. . .

If you had given the same advice to a young history painter of abilities, I should have admired your judgment, and re-echoed your sentiments.[15] Study, you might have said, the noble models of antiquity, till your imagination is inflamed; and, rising above the vulgar practice of the hour, you may imitate without copying those great originals. A glowing picture, of some interesting moment, would probably have been produced by these natural means; particularly if one little circumstance is not overlooked, that the painter had noble models to revert to, calculated to excite admiration and stimulate exertion.

But, in settling a constitution that involved the happiness of millions, that stretch beyond the computation of science, it was, perhaps, necessary for the Assembly to have a higher model in view than the *imagined* virtues of their forefathers; and wise to deduce their respect for themselves from the only legitimate source, respect for justice. Why was it a duty to repair an ancient castle, built in barbarous ages, of Gothic materials? Why were the legislators obliged to rake amongst heterogeneous ruins; to rebuild old walls, whose foundations could scarcely be explored, when a simple structure might be raised on the foundation of experience, the only valuable inheritance our forefathers could bequeath? Yet of this bequest we can make little use till we have gained a stock of our own; and even then, their inherited experience would rather serve as lighthouses, to warn us against dangerous rocks or sand-banks, than as finger-posts that stand at every turning to point out the right road.

Nor was it absolutely necessary that they should be diffident of themselves when they were dissatisfied with, or could not discern the *almost obliterated* constitution of their ancestors.[16] They should first have been convinced that our constitution was not only the best modern, but the best possible one; and that our social compact was the

---

[15] 'History Painting': the genre had taken on the classical rhetorical role of history itself – to provide morally inspiring or instructive images from the past.

[16] Burke, *Reflections . . .* , this edition, p. 69.

surest foundation of all the *possible* liberty a mass of men could enjoy, that the human understanding could form. They should have been certain that our representation answered all the purposes of representation; and that an established inequality of rank and property secured the liberty of the whole community, instead of rendering it a sounding epithet of subjection, when applied to the nation at large. They should have had the same respect for our House of Commons that you, vauntingly, intrude on us, though your conduct throughout life has spoken a very different language; before they made a point of not deviating from the model which first engaged their attention.

That the British House of Commons is filled with every thing illustrious in rank, in descent, in hereditary, and acquired opulence, may be true, – but that it contains every thing respectable in talents, in military, civil, naval, and political distinction, is very problematical. Arguing from natural causes, the very contrary would appear to the speculatist to be the fact; and let experience say whether these speculations are built on sure ground.

. . .

But to examine the subject more closely. Is it among the list of possibilities that a man of rank and fortune *can* have received a good education? How can he discover that he is a man, when all his wants are instantly supplied, and invention is never sharpened by necessity? Will he labour, for every thing valuable must be the fruit of laborious exertions, to attain knowledge and virtue, in order to merit the affection of his equals, when the flattering attention of sycophants is a more luscious cordial?

. . . No; it is well known that talents are only to be unfolded by industry, and that we must have made some advances, led by an inferior motive, before we discover that they are their own reward.

But *full blown* talents *may*, according to your system, be hereditary, and as independent of ripening judgment, as the inbred feelings that, rising above reason, naturally guard Englishmen from error. Noble franchises! what a grovelling mind must that man have, who can pardon his step-dame Nature for not having made him at least a lord?

And who will, after your description of senatorial virtues, dare to say that our House of Commons has often resembled a beargarden; and appeared rather like a committee of *ways and means* than a dignified legislative body, though the concentrated wisdom and virtue of the whole nation blazed in one superb constellation? That it contains a dead weight of benumbing opulence I readily allow, and of ignoble ambition; nor is there any thing surpassing belief in a supposition that the raw recruits, when properly drilled by the minister, would gladly march to the Upper House to unite hereditary honours to fortune. But talents, knowledge, and virtue, must be a part of the man, and cannot be put, as robes of state often are, on a servant or a block, to render a pageant more magnificent.

. . .

There appears to be such a mixture of real sensibility and fondly cherished romance in your composition, that the present crisis carries you out of yourself; and since you could not be one of the grand movers, the next *best* thing that dazzled your imagination was to be a conspicuous opposer. Full of yourself, you make as much noise to convince the world that you despise the revolution, as Rousseau did to persuade his contemporaries to let him live in obscurity.

Reading your Reflections warily over, it has continually and forcibly struck me, that had you been a Frenchman, you would have been, in spite of your respect for rank and antiquity, a violent revolutionist; and deceived, as you now probably are, by the passions that cloud your reason, have termed your romantic enthusiasm an enlightened love of your country, a benevolent respect for the rights of men. Your imagination would have taken fire, and have found arguments, full as ingenious as those you now offer, to prove that the constitution, of which so few pillars remained, that constitution which time had almost obliterated, was not a model sufficiently noble to deserve close adherence. And, for the English constitution, you might not have had such a profound veneration as you have lately acquired; nay, it is not impossible that you might have entertained the same opinion of the English Parliament, that you professed to have during the American war.

. . .

But without fixed principles even goodness of heart is no security from inconsistency, and mild affectionate sensibility only renders a man more ingeniously cruel, when the pangs of hurt vanity are mistaken for virtuous indignation, and the gall of bitterness for the milk of Christian charity.

Where is the dignity, the infallibility of sensibility, in the fair ladies, whom, if the voice of rumour is to be credited, the captive negroes curse in all the agony of bodily pain, for the unheard of tortures they invent?[17] It is probable that some

---

[17] A reference to the sadistic taste ascribed to colonial wives.

of them, after the sight of a flagellation, compose their ruffled spirits and exercise their tender feelings by the perusal of the last imported novel. – How true these tears are to nature, I leave you to determine. But these ladies may have read your Enquiry concerning the origin of our ideas of the Sublime and Beautiful, and, convinced by your arguments, may have laboured to be pretty, by counterfeiting weakness.[18]

You may have convinced them that *littleness* and *weakness* are the very essence of beauty; and that the Supreme Being, in giving women beauty in the most supereminent degree, seemed to command them, by the powerful voice of Nature, not to cultivate the moral virtues that might chance to excite respect, and interfere with the pleasing sensations they were created to inspire. Thus confining truth, fortitude, and humanity, within the rigid pale of manly morals, they might justly argue, that to be loved, woman's high end and great distinction! they should 'learn to lisp, to totter in their walk, and nick-name God's creatures.' Never, they might repeat after you, was any man, much less a woman, rendered amiable by the force of those exalted qualities, fortitude, justice, wisdom, and truth; and thus forewarned of the sacrifice they must make to those austere, unnatural virtues, they would be authorized to turn all their attention to their persons, systematically neglecting morals to secure beauty. – Some rational old woman indeed might chance to stumble at this doctrine, and hint, that in avoiding atheism you had not steered clear of the mussulman's creed; but you could readily exculpate yourself by turning the charge on Nature, who made our idea of beauty independent of reason.[19] Nor would it be necessary for you to recollect, that if virtue has any other foundation than worldly utility, you have clearly proved that one half of the human species, at least, have not souls; and that Nature, by making women *little, smooth, delicate, fair* creatures, never designed that they should exercise their reason to acquire the virtues that produce opposite, if not contradictory, feelings.[20] The affection they excite, to be uniform and perfect, should not be tinctured with the respect which moral virtues inspire, lest pain should be blended with pleasure, and admiration disturb the soft intimacy of love. This laxity

[18] In Burke's *Philosophical enquiry in the Origin of our Ideas of the Sublime and the Beautiful* (1757) he argued that the idea of Beauty was associated with delicacy and weakness, the Sublime with vastness and power.
[19] 'Mussulman': muslim. Muslims granted the historical existence of Christ but denied his divinity.
[20] Wollstonecraft sets up a polarity between naturalistic and rationalist morality. If morality is not naturalistic (an atheist or Muslim position) it must be grounded in reason – but then women, on Burke's account, being devoted to beauty, which is opposed to austere morality, are incapable of virtue.

of morals in the female world is certainly more captivating to a libertine imagination than the cold arguments of reason, that give no sex to virtue. If beautiful weakness be interwoven in a woman's frame, if the chief business of her life be (as you insinuate) to inspire love, and Nature has made an eternal distinction between the qualities that dignify a rational being and this animal perfection, her duty and happiness in this life must clash with any preparation for a more exalted state. So that Plato and Milton were grossly mistaken in asserting that human love led to heavenly, and was only an exaltation of the same affection; for the love of the Deity, which is mixed with the most profound reverence, must be love of perfection, and not compassion for weakness.

To say the truth, I not only tremble for the souls of women, but for the good natured man, whom every one loves. The *amiable* weakness of his mind is a strong argument against its immateriality, and seems to prove that beauty relaxes the *solids* of the soul as well as the body.

It follows then immediately, from your own reasoning, that respect and love are antagonist principles; and that, if we really wish to render men more virtuous, we must endeavour to banish all enervating modifications of beauty from civil society. We must, to carry your argument a little further, return to the Spartan regulations, and settle the virtues of men on the stern foundation of mortification and self-denial; for any attempt to civilize the heart, to make it humane by implanting reasonable principles, is a mere philosophic dream. If refinement inevitably lessens respect for virtue, by rendering beauty, the grand tempter, more seductive; if these relaxing feelings are incompatible with the nervous exertions of morality, the sun of Europe is not set; it begins to dawn, when cold metaphysicians try to make the head give laws to the heart.

But should experience prove that there is a beauty in virtue, a charm in order, which necessarily implies exertion, a depraved sensual taste may give way to a more manly one – and *melting* feelings to rational satisfactions. Both may be equally natural to man; the test is their moral difference, and that point reason alone can decide.

Such a glorious change can only be produced by liberty. Inequality of rank must ever impede the growth of virtue, by vitiating the mind that submits or domineers; that is ever employed to procure nourishment for the body, or amusement for the mind. And if this grand example be set by an assembly of unlettered clowns, if they can produce a crisis that may involve the fate of Europe, and 'more than Europe,'[21] you

---

[21] [Wollstonecraft's footnote] *Reflections*, p. 11 [not in this edition].

must allow us to respect unsophisticated reason, and reverence the active exertions that were not relaxed by a fastidious respect for the beauty of rank, or a dread of the deformity produced by any *void* in the social structure.

. . .

Is hereditary weakness necessary to render religion lovely? and will her form have lost the smooth delicacy that inspires love, when stripped of its Gothic drapery? Must every grand model be placed on the pedestal of property? and is there no beauteous proportion in virtue, when not clothed in a sensual garb?

. . .

. . . You love the church, your country, and its laws, you repeatedly tell us, because they deserve to be loved; but from you this is not a panegyric: weakness and indulgence are the only incitements to love and confidence that you can discern, and it cannot be denied that the tender mother you venerate deserves, on this score, all your affection.

It would be as vain a task to attempt to obviate all your passionate objections, as to unravel all your plausible arguments, often illustrated by known truths, and rendered forcible by pointed invectives. I only attack the foundation. On the natural principles of justice I build my plea for disseminating the property artfully said to be appropriated to religious purposes, but, in reality, to support idle tyrants, amongst the society whose ancestors were cheated or forced into illegal grants. Can there be an opinion more subversive of morality, than that time sanctifies crimes, and silences the blood that calls out for retribution, if not for vengeance? If the revenue annexed to the Gallic church was greater than the most bigoted protestant would now allow to be its reasonable share, would it not have been trampling on the rights of men to perpetuate such an arbitrary appropriation of the common stock, because time had rendered the fraudulent seizure venerable? Besides, if Reason had suggested, as surely she must, if the imagination had not been allowed to dwell on the fascinating pomp of ceremonial grandeur, that the clergy would be rendered both more virtuous and useful by being put more on a par with each other, and the mass of the people it was their duty to instruct; – where was there room for hesitation? The charge of presumption, thrown by you on the most reasonable innovations, may, without any violence to truth, be retorted on every reformation that has meliorated our condition, and even on the improvable faculty that gives us a claim to the pre-eminence of intelligent beings.

. . .

It may be confidently asserted that no man chooses evil, because it is evil; he only mistakes it for happiness, the good he seeks. And the desire of rectifying these mistakes, is the noble ambition of an enlightened understanding, the impulse of feelings that Philosophy invigorates. To endeavour to make unhappy men resigned to their fate, is the tender endeavour of short-sighted benevolence, of transient yearnings of humanity; but to labour to increase human happiness by extirpating error, is a masculine godlike affection. This remark may be carried still further. Men who possess uncommon sensibility, whose quick emotions show how closely the eye and heart are connected, soon forget the most forcible sensations. Not tarrying long enough in the brain to be subject to reflection, the next sensations, of course, obliterate them. Memory, however, treasures up these proofs of native goodness; and the being who is not spurred on to any virtuous act, still thinks itself of consequence, and boasts of its feelings. Why? Because the sight of distress, or an affecting narrative, made its blood flow with more velocity, and the heart, literally speaking, beat with sympathetic emotion. We ought to beware of confounding mechanical instinctive sensations with emotions that reason deepens, and justly terms the feelings of *humanity*. This word discriminates the active exertions of virtue from the vague declamation of sensibility.

. . .

When we read a book that supports our favourite opinions, how eagerly do we suck in the doctrines, and suffer our minds placidly to reflect the images that illustrate the tenets we have previously embraced. We indolently acquiesce in the conclusion, and our spirit animates and corrects the various subjects. But when, on the contrary, we peruse a skilful writer, with whom we do not coincide in opinion, how attentive is the mind to detect fallacy. And this suspicious coolness often prevents our being carried away by a stream of natural eloquence, which the prejudiced mind terms declamation – a pomp of words! We never allow ourselves to be warmed; and, after contending with the writer, are more confirmed in our opinion; as much, perhaps, from a spirit of contradiction as from reason. A lively imagination is ever in danger of being betrayed into error by favourite opinions, which it almost personifies, the more effectually to intoxicate the understanding. Always tending to extremes, truth is left behind in the heat of the chace, and things are viewed as positively good, or bad, though they wear an equivocal face.

Some celebrated writers have supposed that wit and judgment were incompatible; opposite qualities, that, in a kind of elementary strife, destroyed each other: and many men of wit have endeavoured to prove that they were mistaken. Much may be adduced by wits and metaphysicians on both sides of the question. But, from experience, I am apt to believe that they do weaken each other, and that great quickness of comprehension, and facile association of ideas, naturally preclude profundity of research . . . Judgment is sublime, wit beautiful; and, according to your own theory, they cannot exist together without impairing each other's power. The predominancy of the latter, in your endless Reflections, should lead hasty readers to suspect that it may, in a great degree, exclude the former.

But, among all your plausible arguments, and witty illustrations, your contempt for the poor always appears conspicuous, and rouses my indignation. . . .

. . .

This is contemptible hard-hearted sophistry, in the specious form of humility, and submission to the will of Heaven. – It is, Sir, *possible* to render the poor happier in this world, without depriving them of the consolation which you gratuitously grant them in the next. They have a right to more comfort than they at present enjoy; and more comfort might be afforded them, without encroaching on the pleasures of the rich: not now waiting to enquire whether the rich have any right to exclusive pleasures. What do I say? – encroaching! No; if an intercourse were established between them, it would impart the only true pleasure that can be snatched in this land of shadows, this hard school of moral discipline.

I know, indeed, that there is often something disgusting in the distresses of poverty, at which the imagination revolts, and starts back to exercise itself in the more attractive Arcadia of fiction. The rich man builds a house, art and taste give it the highest finish. His gardens are planted, and the trees grow to recreate the fancy of the planter, though the temperature of the climate may rather force him to avoid the dangerous damps they exhale, than seek the umbrageous retreat. Every thing on the estate is cherished but man; – yet, to contribute to the happiness of man, is the most sublime of all enjoyments. But if, instead of sweeping pleasure-grounds, obelisks, temples, and elegant cottages, as *objects* for the eye, the heart was allowed to beat true to nature, decent farms would be scattered over the estate, and plenty smile around. Instead of the poor being subject to the griping hand of an avaricious steward, they would be watched over with fatherly solicitude, by the man whose duty and pleasure it was to guard their happiness, and shield from rapacity the beings who, by the sweat of their brow, exalted him above his fellows.

. . .

Why cannot large estates be divided into small farms? these dwellings would indeed grace our land. Why are huge forests still allowed to stretch out with idle pomp and all the indolence of Eastern grandeur? Why does the brown waste meet the traveller's view, when men want work? But commons cannot be enclosed without *acts of parliament* to increase the property of the rich![22] ...

...

Surveying civilized life, and seeing, with undazzled eye, the polished vices of the rich, their insincerity, want of natural affections, with all the specious train that luxury introduces, I have turned impatiently to the poor, to look for man undebauched by riches or power – but, alas! what did I see? a being scarcely above the brutes, over which he tyrannized; a broken spirit, worn-out body, and all those gross vices which the example of the rich, rudely copied, could produce. Envy built a wall of separation, that made the poor hate, whilst they bent to their superiors; who, on their part, stepped aside to avoid the loathsome sight of human misery.

What were the outrages of a day to these continual miseries? Let those sorrows hide their diminished head before the tremendous mountain of woe that thus defaces our globe? Man preys on man; and you mourn for the idle tapestry that decorated a gothic pile, and the dronish bell that summoned the fat priest to prayer. You mourn for the empty pageant of a name, when slavery flaps her wing, and the sick heart retires to die in lonely wilds, far from the abodes of men. Did the pangs you felt for insulted nobility, the anguish that rent your heart when the gorgeous robes were torn off the idol human weakness had set up, deserve to be compared with the long-drawn sigh of melancholy reflection, when misery and vice are thus seen to haunt our steps, and swim on the top of every cheering prospect? Why is our fancy to be appalled by terrific perspectives of a hell beyond the grave? – Hell stalks abroad; – the lash resounds on the slave's naked sides; and the sick wretch, who can no longer earn the sour bread of unremitting labour, steals to a ditch to bid the world a long good night – or, neglected in some ostentatious hospital, breathes his last amidst the laugh of mercenary attendants.

---

[22] The enclosure – in effect the privatisation – of common land enabled it to be farmed by the proprietor more intensely and productively but robbed the small farmer of pasture for his stock. The pace of enclosure had increased over the previous two centuries and it provoked agrarian opposition. Burke drew attention to it as an index of the health and productivity of the English economy in his *Third Letter on a Regicide Peace* (1797).

Such misery demands more than tears – I pause to recollect myself; and smother the contempt I feel rising for your rhetorical flourishes and infantine sensibility.

. . .

I have before animadverted on our method of electing representatives, convinced that it debauches both the morals of the people and the candidates, without rendering the member really responsible, or attached to his constituents; but, amongst your other contradictions, you blame the National Assembly for expecting any exertions from the servile principle of responsibility,[23] and afterwards insult them for not rendering themselves responsible. Whether the one the French have adopted will answer the purpose better, and be more than a shadow of representation, time only can shew. In theory it appears more promising.

Your real or artificial affection for the English constitution seems to me to resemble the brutal affection of some weak characters. They think it a duty to love their relations with a blind, indolent tenderness, that will *not* see the faults it might assist to correct, if their affection had been built on rational grounds. They love they know not why, and they will love to the end of the chapter.

Is it absolute blasphemy to doubt of the omnipotence of the law, or to suppose that religion might be more pure if there were fewer baits for hypocrites in the church? But our manners, you tell us, are drawn from the French, though you had before celebrated our native plainness. If they were, it is time we broke loose from dependance – Time that Englishmen drew water from their own springs; for, if manners are not a painted substitute for morals, we have only to cultivate our reason, and we shall not feel the want of an arbitrary model. Nature will suffice; but I forget myself – Nature and Reason, according to your system, are all to give place to authority; and the gods, as Shakespeare makes a frantic wretch exclaim, seem to kill us for their sport, as men do flies.[24]

Before I conclude my cursory remarks, it is but just to acknowledge that I coincide with you in your opinion respecting the *sincerity* of many modern philosophers. Your consistency in avowing a veneration for rank and riches deserves praise; but I must own that I have often indignantly observed that some of the *enlightened* philosophers, who talk most vehemently of the native rights of men, borrow many noble sentiments to adorn their conversation, which have no

---

[23] Principle of responsibility – the principle, famously attacked by Burke in his Address to his Bristol Constituents, that the parliamentary representative should accept instructions from his constituents.

[24] [Wollstonecraft's footnote] *King Lear* iv, l. 36–7.

influence on their conduct. They bow down to rank, and are careful to secure property; for virtue, without this adventitious drapery, is seldom very respectable in their eyes – nor are they very quick-sighted to discern real dignity of character when no sounding name exalts the man above his fellows. – But neither open enmity nor hollow homage destroys the intrinsic value of those principles which rest on an eternal foundation, and revert for a standard to the immutable attributes of God.

FASHION before EASE;
_or,_A good Constitution sacrificed for a Fantastick Form.

Plate 3. *Fashion before Ease, or A Good Constitution sacrificed for a Fantastick Form* (James Gilray, 1793). Tom Paine, wearing a French rosette in his hat, is depicted here in his old trade as a stay-[corset-]maker, trying to force Britannia into a new corset in conformity with French fashions. His tape-measure calibrates the rights of man. His trade sign promises 'Paris modes by express'.

TOM PAINE

BIOGRAPHICAL NOTE

Paine was born at Thetford in Norfolk, to a Quaker farming family. He left school at 13, served at sea, and then became a stay (corset-)maker, at which trade he was often depicted in later cartoons. In 1766 he settled at Lewes in Sussex as an exciseman, whose bad pay he defended in his first pamphlet (1772). He also ran a tobacconist's shop. But the business, and his marriage (the second, a first wife had died in 1760) foundered. Aged 37 Paine emigrated to America with the encouragement and assistance of Benjamin Franklin whom he had met in London. In America Paine worked for a Pennsylvania publisher as editor and writer. He achieved huge celebrity in 1775 through his vastly influential pamphlet *Common Sense*, a work encouraging Americans to establish their independence from Great Britain, and for his series of *Crisis* articles rallying the rebels when it seemed the English might prevail. He returned to Europe (1787) to promote (unsuccessfully) his design for a prefabricated cast-iron bridge in both England and France.

Rights of Man (1791) was the most famous response to Burke's *Reflections . . . The Rights of Man, Part the Second* followed in 1792, despite government attempts to suppress it. Paine was arraigned for prosecution and burnt in effigy by Tory 'Church and King' mobs. In autumn that year he escaped to France before, in December, a packed jury duly found him guilty of seditious libel and outlawed him. In France the first wave of revolutionary leaders gave him the key of the Bastille to give to George Washington; he was voted honorary citizen and was elected to the Assembly for no less than four Departments. However, having defended the life of the King in the winter of 1792–3, he was imprisoned and almost guillotined himself a year later (December 1793) at the instigation of Robespierre. Released in November 1794 after Robespierre's own fall, through the intervention of the American Ambassador, James Monroe, Paine, desperately ill, was nursed at the latter's house for over a year before returning to his seat in the Convention. He continued to write. His deistic and anti-clerical *Age of Reason* (1794), denounced as irreligious, was to lessen his popularity in America. In 1795 he produced two important contributions to radical political economy, *The Decline and Fall of the English System of Finance* – which predicted that the public debt would cause the financial collapse of the English war economy within twenty years – and *Agrarian Justice*, which further developed the redistributive themes of social equality advanced in *Rights of Man, Part the Second*.

Disillusioned with the course of the revolution, his position rendered awkward by war between France and America, Paine returned to America in 1802. Befriended by Jefferson, but attacked by moderates for his Jacobinism and by the devout for his deism, he died in June 1809. In a famous postscript to his life, Paine's bones were brought back to England in 1819 by William Cobbett, newly converted to the revived radical cause.

EDITORIAL NOTE

Rights of Man: Part One was first published in January 1791. The first edition was soon abandoned by his publisher, Johnson, who was intimidated by the government's reaction. A second edition, published by J. S. Jordan, immediately sold in large numbers, being circulated by organisations such as the Society for Constitutional Information. It was translated into French by the wife of the Marquis de Condorcet. *Rights of Man, Part the Second* followed in February 1792 and also achieved huge sales. Subsequent editions combined the two parts and there were many excerpted and pirated editions. Within two years a quarter of a million copies of one version or another of the text had been printed in the UK. Although there were numerous pirated editions, the texts of those sanctioned by Paine do not vary significantly. The text here is substantially that of the Second Edition (1791). The abridged edition published by Daniel Isaac Eaton in London in 1795 and most likely prepared by Paine himself has been used to guide principles of inclusion and exclusion adopted here as well as providing sub-headings in square brackets.

Modern editions:
The Complete Writings of Thomas Paine, 2 vols., ed. Philip S. Foner (repr. New York: Citadel Press, 1969 [1948]) (the modern scholarly edition of Paine's works).
Rights of Man, ed. Eric Foner (Harmondsworth: Penguin Press, 1984).
Rights of Man, ed. Gregory Claeys (Indianapolis: Heckett, 1992).

FURTHER READING

Aldridge, A. O. *Man of Reason* (London: Cresset, 1960).
Claeys, G. *Thomas Paine, Social and Political Thought* (London: Unwin, 1989).
Keane, J. *Tom Paine: A Political Life* (London: Bloomsbury, 1996).
Kramnick, I. 'Tom Paine: Radical Liberal', in *Republicanism and Bourgeois Radicalism* (Ithaca, N.Y.: Cornell University Press, 1990).
Philp, M. *Paine* (Oxford: Oxford University Press, 1989).

Rights of Man Part The First Being An Answer To Mr. Burke's Attack On The French Revolution (1791)

Among the incivilities by which nations or individuals provoke and irritate each other, Mr. Burke's pamphlet on the French Revolution is an extraordinary instance. Neither the People of France, nor the National Assembly, were troubling themselves about the affairs of England, or the English Parliament; and that Mr. Burke should commence an unprovoked attack upon them, both in Parliament and in public, is a conduct that cannot be pardoned on the score of manners nor justified on that of policy.

. . .

Not sufficiently content with abusing the National Assembly, a great part of his work is taken up with abusing Dr. Price (one of the best-hearted men that lives) and the two societies in England known by the name of the Revolution Society and the Society for Constitutional Information.

. . . Mr. Burke, speaking of [Dr Price's] sermon, says: 'The political Divine proceeds dogmatically to assert, that by the principles of the Revolution, the people of England have acquired three fundamental rights:

1. To choose our own governors.
2. To cashier them for misconduct.
3. To frame a government for ourselves.'

. . . - Mr. Burke, on the contrary, denies that such a right exists in the nation, either in whole or in part, or that it exists anywhere; and, what is still more strange and marvellous, he says: 'that the people of England utterly disclaim such a right, and that they will resist the practical assertion of it with their lives and fortunes.' That men should take up arms and spend their lives and fortunes, *not* to maintain their rights, but to maintain they have *not* rights, is an entirely new species of discovery, and suited to the paradoxical genius of Mr. Burke.

The method which Mr. Burke takes to prove that the people of England have no such rights, and that such rights do not now exist in the nation, either in whole or in part, or anywhere at all, is of the same marvellous and monstrous kind with what he has already said; for his arguments are that the persons, or the generation of persons, in whom they did exist, are dead, and with them the right is dead also. To prove this, he quotes a declaration made by Parliament about a hundred years ago, to William and Mary, in these words: 'The Lords Spiritual and Temporal, and Commons, do, in the name of the people aforesaid' (meaning the people of England then living) 'most humbly and faithfully *submit* themselves, their *heirs* and *posterities*, for EVER.'[1] . . .

. . . I shall, *sans ceremonie*, place another system of principles in opposition to his.

The English Parliament of 1688 did a certain thing, which, for themselves and their constituents, they had a right to do, and which it appeared right should be done. But, in addition to this right, which they possessed by delegation, they set up another right by assumption, that of binding and controlling posterity to the end of time. The case, therefore, divides itself into two parts; the right which they possessed by delegation, and the right which they set up by assumption. The first is admitted; but with respect to the second, I reply –

There never did, there never will, and there never can, exist a Parliament, or any description of men, or any generation of men, in any country, possessed of the right or the power of binding and controlling posterity to the 'end of time,' or of commanding for ever how the world shall be governed, or who shall govern it; and therefore all such clauses, acts or declarations by which the makers of them attempt to do what they have neither the right nor the power to do, nor the power to execute, are in themselves null and void. Every age and generation must be as free to act for itself in all cases as the age and generations which preceded it. The vanity and presumption of governing beyond the grave is the most ridiculous and insolent of all tyrannies. Man has no property in man; neither has any generation a property in the generations which are to follow. The parliament or the people of 1688, or of any other period, had no more right to dispose of the people of the present day, or to bind or to control them in any shape whatever, than the parliament or the people of the present day have to dispose of, bind or control those who are to live a hundred or a thousand years hence. Every generation is, and must be, competent to all the purposes which its occasions require. It is the living, and not the dead, that are to be accommodated. When man ceases to be, his power and his wants cease with him; and having no longer any participation in the concerns of this world, he has no longer any authority in directing who shall be its governors, or how its government shall be organised, or how administered.

I am not contending for nor against any form of government, nor for nor against any party, here or elsewhere. That which a whole nation chooses to do it has a right to do. Mr. Burke says, No. Where, then, does the right exist? I am contending for the

---

[1] See p. 66 (not quoted in full in this selection).

rights of the living, and against their being willed away and controlled and contracted for by the manuscript assumed authority of the dead, and Mr. Burke is contending for the authority of the dead over the rights and freedom of the living. There was a time when kings disposed of their crowns by will upon their death-beds, and consigned the people, like beasts of the field, to whatever successor they appointed. This is now so exploded as scarcely to be remembered, and so monstrous as hardly to be believed. But the Parliamentary clauses upon which Mr. Burke builds his political church are of the same nature.

The laws of every country must be analogous to some common principle. In England no parent or master, nor all the authority of Parliament, omnipotent as it has called itself, can bind or control the personal freedom even of an individual beyond the age of twenty-one years. On what ground of right, then, could the Parliament of 1688, or any other Parliament, bind all posterity for ever?

Those who have quitted the world, and those who have not yet arrived at it, are as remote from each other as the utmost stretch of mortal imagination can conceive. What possible obligation, then, can exist between them – what rule or principle can be laid down that of two nonentities, the one out of existence and the other not in, and who never can meet in this world, the one should control the other to the end of time?

. . .

The circumstances of the world are continually changing, and the opinions of men change also; and as government is for the living, and not for the dead, it is the living only that has any right in it. That which may be thought right and found convenient in one age may be thought wrong and found inconvenient in another. In such cases, who is to decide, the living or the dead?

. . .

It was not against Louis XVI, but against the despotic principles of the Government, that the nation revolted. These principles had not their origin in him, but in the original establishment, many centuries back: and they were become too deeply rooted to be removed, and the Augean stables[2] of parasites and plunderers too abominably filthy to be cleansed by anything short of a complete and universal Revolution. When it becomes necessary to do anything, the whole heart and soul should go into the

---

[2] Cleaning out the Augean Stables was one of the labours the mythical Greek hero, Hercules, had to perform to atone for the murder of his wife and children. The stables of Augeas held vast numbers of cattle. Hercules cleaned them by diverting the river Alpheius.

measure, or not attempt it. That crisis was then arrived, and there remained no choice but to act with determined vigour, or not to act at all . . .

. . .

. . . When despotism has established itself for ages in a country, as in France, it is not in the person of the king only that it resides. It has the appearance of being so in show, and in nominal authority; but it is not so in practice and in fact. It has its standard everywhere. Every office and department has its despotism, founded upon custom and usage. Every place has its Bastille, and every Bastille its despot. The original hereditary despotism resident in the person of the king, divides and sub-divides itself into a thousand shapes and forms, till at last the whole of it is acted by deputation. This was the case in France; and against this species of despotism, proceeding on through an endless labyrinth of office till the source of it is scarcely perceptible, there is no mode of redress. It strengthens itself by assuming the appearance of duty, and tyrannies under the pretence of obeying.

. . .

As to the tragic paintings by which Mr. Burke has outraged his own imagination, and seeks to work upon that of his readers, they are very well calculated for theatrical representation, where facts are manufactured for the sake of show, and accommodated to produce, through the weakness of sympathy, a weeping effect. But Mr. Burke should recollect that he is writing history, and not *Plays*, and that his readers will expect truth, and not the spouting rant of high-toned exclamation.

When we see a man dramatically lamenting in a publication intended to be believed that '*The age of chivalry is gone!* that *The glory of Europe is extinguished for ever!* that *The unbought grace of life* (if anyone knows what it is), *the cheap defence of nations, the nurse of manly sentiment and heroic enterprise is gone!*' and all this because the Quixote age of chivalry nonsense is gone, what opinion can we form of his judgment, or what regard can we pay to his facts? In the rhapsody of his imagination he has discovered a world of wind-mills, and his sorrows are that there are no Quixotes to attack them.[3] . . .

. . .

Not one glance of compassion, not one commiserating reflection that I can find throughout his book, has he bestowed on those who lingered out the most wretched of lives, a life without hope in the most miserable of prisons. It is painful to behold a

[3] Cervantes' *Don Quixote* had parodied the code of chivalry through the picaresque adventures of a broken-down knight, including an episode where the Don had mistakenly joined battle with the sails of a windmill.

man employing his talents to corrupt himself. Nature has been kinder to Mr. Burke than he is to her. He is not affected by the reality of distress touching his heart, but by the showy resemblance of it striking his imagination. He pities the plumage, but forgets the dying bird. Accustomed to kiss the aristocratical hand that hath purloined him from himself, he degenerates into a composition of art, and the genuine soul of nature forsakes him. His hero or his heroine must be a tragedy-victim expiring in show, and not the real prisoner of misery, sliding into death in the silence of a dungeon.

[Paine then provides an alternative account of the events in Paris on and around 14 July – the storming of the Bastille]

. . .

I cannot consider Mr Burke's book in scarcely any other light than a dramatic performance; and he must, I think, have considered it in the same light himself, by the poetical liberties he has taken of omitting some facts, distorting others, and making the whole machinery bend to produce a stage effect. Of this kind is his account of the expedition to Versailles.

[Paine provides an alternative account of the removal of the King from Versailles to Paris.]

. . .

I have now to follow Mr. Burke through a pathless wilderness of rhapsodies, and a sort of descant upon governments, in which he asserts whatever he pleases, on the presumption of its being believed, without offering either evidence or reasons for so doing.

Before anything can be reasoned upon to a conclusion, certain facts, principles, or data, to reason from, must be established, admitted, or denied. Mr. Burke with his usual outrage, abused the *Declaration of the Rights of Man*, published by the National Assembly of France, as the basis on which the constitution of France is built. This he calls 'paltry and blurred sheets of paper about the rights of man.' Does Mr. Burke mean to deny that man has any rights? If he does, then he must mean that there are no such things as rights anywhere, and that he has none himself; for who is there in the world but man? But if Mr. Burke means to admit that man has rights, the question then will be: What are those rights, and how came man by them originally?

The error of those who reason by precedents drawn from antiquity, respecting the rights of man, is that they do not go far enough into antiquity. They do not go the whole way. They stop in some of the intermediate stages of an hundred or a thousand years, and produce what was then done, as a rule for the present day.

This is no authority at all. If we travel still farther into antiquity, we shall find a direct contrary opinion and practice prevailing; and if antiquity is to be authority, a thousand such authorities may be produced, successively contradicting each other; but if we proceed on, we shall at last come out right; we shall come to the time when man came from the hand of his Maker. What was he then? Man. Man was his high and only title, and a higher cannot be given him. - But of titles I shall speak hereafter.

We are now got at the origin of man, and at the origin of his rights. As to the manner in which the world has been governed from that day to this, it is no farther any concern of ours than to make a proper use of the errors or the improvements which the history of it presents. Those who lived an hundred or a thousand years ago, were then moderns, as we are now. They had their ancients, and those ancients had others, and we also shall be ancients in our turn. If the mere name of antiquity is to govern in the affairs of life, the people who are to live an hundred or a thousand years hence, may as well take us for a precedent, as we make a precedent of those who lived an hundred or a thousand years ago. The fact is, that portions of antiquity, by proving everything, establish nothing. It is authority against authority all the way, till we come to the divine origin of the rights of man at the creation. Here our enquiries find a resting-place, and our reason finds a home. If a dispute about the rights of man had arisen at the distance of an hundred years from the creation, it is to this source of authority they must have referred, and it is to this same source of authority that we must now refer.

Though I mean not to touch upon any sectarian principle of religion, yet it may be worth observing, that the genealogy of Christ is traced to Adam. Why then not trace the rights of man to the creation of man? I will answer the question. Because there have been upstart governments, thrusting themselves between, and presumptuously working to *un-make* man.

If any generation of men ever possessed the right of dictating the mode by which the world should be governed for ever, it was the first generation that existed; and if that generation did it not, no succeeding generation can show any authority for doing it, nor can set any up. The illuminating and divine principle of the equal rights of man (for it has its origin from the Maker of man) relates, not only to the living individuals, but to generations of men succeeding each other. Every generation is equal in rights to generations which preceded it, by the same rule that every individual is born equal in rights with his contemporary.

Every history of the creation, and every traditionary account, whether from the lettered or unlettered world, however they may vary in their opinion or belief of

certain particulars, all agree in establishing one point, the unity of man; by which
I mean that men are all of one degree, and consequently that all men are born
equal, and with equal natural right, in the same manner as if posterity had been
continued by creation instead of generation, the latter being the only mode by which
the former is carried forward; and consequently every child born into the world
must be considered as deriving its existence from God. The world is as new to him
as it was to the first man that existed, and his natural right in it is of the same
kind.

The Mosaic account of the creation, whether taken as divine authority or merely
historical, is full to this point, *the unity or equality of man.* The expression admits of
no controversy. 'And God said, Let us make man in our own image . . . In the image
of God created he him; male and female created he them.'[4] The distinction of sexes is
pointed out, but no other distinction is even implied. If this be not divine authority,
it is at least historical authority, and shows that the equality of man, so far from being
a modern doctrine, is the oldest upon record.

It is also to be observed that all the religions known in the world are founded, so
far as they relate to man, on the *unity of man,* as being all of one degree. Whether in
heaven or in hell, or in whatever state man may be supposed to exist hereafter, the
good and the bad are the only distinctions. Nay, even the laws of governments are
obliged to slide into this principle, by making degrees to consist in crimes and not
in persons.

It is one of the greatest of all truths, and of the highest advantage to cultivate. By
considering man in this light, and by instructing him to consider himself in this light,
it places him in a close connection with all his duties, whether to his Creator or to
the creation, of which he is a part; and it is only when he forgets his origin, or, to use
a more fashionable phrase, his *birth and family,* that he becomes dissolute. It is not
among the least of the evils of the present existing governments in all parts of Europe
that man, considered as man, is thrown back to a vast distance from his Maker, and
the artificial chasm filled up with a succession of barriers, or sort of turnpike gates,[5]
 through which he has to pass . . .

The duty of man is not a wilderness of turnpike gates, through which he is to pass
by tickets from one to the other. It is plain and simple, and consists but of two points.
His duty to God, which every man must feel; and with respect to his neighbour,
to do as he would be done by. If those to whom power is delegated do well, they

[4] Genesis 1, 26–7.   [5] A turnpike: a barrier on a toll road.

will be respected: if not, they will be despised; and with regard to those to whom no power is delegated, but who assume it, the rational world can know nothing of them.

[OF CIVIL RIGHTS]

Hitherto we have spoken only (and that but in part) of the natural rights of man. We have now to consider the civil rights of man, and to show how the one originates from the other. Man did not enter into society to become worse than he was before, nor to have fewer rights than he had before, but to have those rights better secured. His natural rights are the foundation of all his civil rights. But in order to pursue this distinction with more precision, it will be necessary to mark the different qualities of natural and civil rights.

... Natural rights are those which appertain to man in right of his existence. Of this kind are all the intellectual rights, or rights of the mind, and also all those rights of acting as an individual for his own comfort and happiness, which are not injurious to the natural rights of others. Civil rights are those which appertain to man in right of his being a member of society. Every civil right has for its foundation some natural right pre-existing in the individual, but to the enjoyment of which his individual power is not, in all cases, sufficiently competent. Of this kind are all those which relate to security and protection.

From this short review it will be easy to distinguish between that class of natural rights which man retains after entering into society and those which he throws into the common stock as a member of society.

The natural rights which he retains are all those in which the *power* to execute is as perfect in the individual as the right itself. Among this class, as is before mentioned, are all the intellectual rights, or rights of the mind; consequently religion is one of those rights. The natural rights which are not retained, are all those in which, though the right is perfect in the individual, the power to execute them is defective. They answer not his purpose. A man, by natural right, has a right to judge in his own cause; and so far as the right of the mind is concerned, he never surrenders it. But what availeth it him to judge, if he has not power to redress? He therefore deposits this right in the common stock of society, and takes the arm of society, of which he is a part, in preference and in addition to his own. Society *grants* him nothing. Every man is a proprietor in society, and draws on the capital as a matter of right.

From these premises two or three certain conclusions will follow:

First, That every civil right grows out of a natural right; or, in other words, is a natural right exchanged.

Secondly, That civil power properly considered as such is made up of the aggregate of that class of the natural rights of man, which becomes defective in the individual in point of power, and answers not his purpose, but when collected to a focus becomes competent to the Purpose of every one.

Thirdly, That the power produced from the aggregate of natural rights, imperfect in power in the individual, cannot be applied to invade the natural rights which are retained in the individual, and in which the power to execute is as perfect as the right itself.

We have now, in a few words, traced man from a natural individual to a member of society, and shown, or endeavoured to show, the quality of the natural rights retained, and of those which are exchanged for civil rights. Let us now apply these principles to governments.

In casting our eyes over the world, it is extremely easy to distinguish the governments which have arisen out of society, or out of the social compact, from those which have not; but to place this in a clearer light than what a single glance may afford, it will be proper to take a review of the several sources from which governments have arisen and on which they have been founded.

They may be all comprehended under three heads. First, Superstition. Secondly, Power. Thirdly, The common interest of society and the common rights of man.

The first was a government of priestcraft, the second of conquerors, and the third of reason.

When a set of artful men pretended, through the medium of oracles, to hold intercourse with the Deity, as familiarly as they now march up the back-stairs in European courts, the world was completely under the government of superstition. The oracles were consulted, and whatever they were made to say became the law; and this sort of government lasted as long as this sort of superstition lasted.

After these a race of conquerors arose, whose government, like that of William the Conqueror, was founded in power, and the sword assumed the name of a sceptre. Governments thus established last as long as the power to support them lasts; but that they might avail themselves of every engine in their favour, they united fraud to force, and set up an idol which they called *Divine Right*, and which, in imitation of the Pope, who affects to be spiritual and temporal, and in contradiction to the Founder of the Christian religion, twisted itself afterwards into an idol of another shape, called

Church and State. The key of St. Peter and the key of the Treasury became quartered[6] on one another, and the wondering cheated multitude worshipped the invention.

. . .

We have now to review the governments which arise out of society, in contradistinction to those which arose out of superstition and conquest.

It has been thought a considerable advance towards establishing the principles of Freedom to say that Government is a compact between those who govern and those who are governed; but this cannot be true, because it is putting the effect before the cause; for as man must have existed before governments existed, there necessarily was a time when governments did not exist, and consequently there could originally exist no governors to form such a compact with. The fact therefore must be that the *individuals themselves*, each in his own personal and sovereign right, *entered into a compact with each other* to produce a government: and this is the only mode in which governments have a right to arise, and the only principle on which they have a right to exist.[7]

To possess ourselves of a clear idea of what government is, or ought to be, we must trace it to its origin. In doing this we shall easily discover that governments must have arisen either *out* of the people or *over* the people. Mr. Burke has made no distinction. He investigates nothing to its source, and therefore he confounds everything; but he has signified his intention of undertaking, at some future opportunity, a comparison between the constitution of England and France. As he thus renders it a subject of controversy by throwing the gauntlet, I take him upon his own ground. It is in high challenges that high truths have the right of appearing; and I accept it with the more readiness because it affords me, at the same time, an opportunity of pursuing the subject with respect to governments arising out of society.

But it will be first necessary to define what is meant by a Constitution. It is not sufficient that we adopt the word; we must fix also a standard signification to it.

A constitution is not a thing in name only, but in fact. It has not an ideal, but a real existence; and wherever it cannot be produced in a visible form, there is none. A constitution is a thing antecedent to a government, and a government is

---

[6] The heraldic term for combining two armorial devices.
[7] Contract theorists commonly distinguished between the contract establishing Society and that establishing Government. If one of these is prior it seems to privilege the resulting entity; thus Paine's insistence that the social contract comes first implies government's authority is limited to the ends of society. Hobbes by contrast – in *Leviathan* – combines the two contracts so as to avoid limiting the Sovereign's authority.

only the creature of a constitution. The constitution of a country is not the act of its government, but of the people constituting its government. It is the body of elements, to which you can refer, and quote article by article; and which contains the principles on which the government shall be established, the manner in which it shall be organised, the powers it shall have, the mode of elections, the duration of Parliaments, or by what other name such bodies may be called; the powers which the executive part of the government shall have; and in fine, everything that relates to the complete organisation of a civil government, and the principles on which it shall act, and by which it shall be bound. A constitution, therefore, is to a government what the laws made afterwards by that government are to a court of judicature. The court of judicature does not make the laws, neither can it alter them; it only acts in conformity to the laws made: and the government is in like manner governed by the constitution.

Can, then, Mr. Burke produce the English Constitution? If he cannot, we may fairly conclude that though it has been so much talked about, no such thing as a constitution exists, or ever did exist, and consequently that the people have yet a constitution to form.

Mr. Burke will not, I presume, deny the position I have already advanced – namely, that governments arise either *out* of the people or *over* the people. The English Government is one of those which arose out of a conquest, and not out of society, and consequently it arose over the people; and though it has been much modified from the opportunity of circumstances since the time of William the Conqueror, the country has never yet regenerated itself, and is therefore without a constitution.

. . .

The present National Assembly of France is, strictly speaking, the personal social compact. – The members of it are the delegates of the nation in its *original* character; future assemblies will be delegates of the nation in its *organised* character . . . The authority of the present one is to form a constitution, the authority of future assemblies will be to legislate according to the principles and forms proscribed in that constitution; and if experience should hereafter show that alterations, amendments or additions, are necessary, the constitution will point out the mode by which such things shall be done, and not leave it to the discretionary power of the future government.

A government on the principles on which constitutional governments arising out of society are established, cannot have the right of altering itself. If it had, it would be arbitrary. It might make itself what it pleased; and wherever such a right is set up, it shows there is no constitution. The act by which the English Parliament empowered itself to sit seven years, shows there is no constitution in England. It might, by the same self-authority, have sat any great number of years, or for life. The Bill which the present Mr. Pitt brought into Parliament some years ago, to reform Parliament, was on the same erroneous principle. The right of reform is in the nation in its original character, and the constitutional method would be by a general convention elected for the purpose. There is, moreover, a paradox in the idea of vitiated bodies reforming themselves.[8]

. . .

The French constitution says, *There shall be no titles*; and, of consequence, all that class of equivocal generation which in some countries is called '*aristocracy*' and in others '*nobility*,' is done away, and the *peer* is exalted into the MAN.

Titles are but nick-names, and every nick-name is a title. The thing is perfectly harmless in itself, but it marks a sort of foppery in the human character, which degrades it. It reduces man into the diminutive of man in things which are great, and the counterfeit of women in things which are little. It talks about its fine *blue ribbon* like a girl, and shows its new *garter* like a child. A certain writer, of some antiquity, says: 'When I was a child, I thought as a child; but when I became a man, I put away childish things.'[9]

. . . The genuine mind of man, thirsting for its native home, society, contemns the gewgaws that separate him from it. Titles are like circles drawn by the magician's wand, to contract the sphere of man's felicity. He lives immured within the Bastille of a word, and surveys at a distance the envied life of man.

Is it, then, any wonder that titles should fall in France? Is it not a greater wonder that they should be kept up anywhere? What are they? What is their worth, and 'what is their amount?' . . . Through all the vocabulary of Adam there is not such an animal as a Duke or a Count; neither can we connect any certain ideas with the words. Whether they mean strength or weakness, wisdom or folly, a child or a man, or the rider or the horse, is all equivocal. What respect then can be paid to that which describes nothing, and which means nothing? Imagination has given figure

---

[8] The idea of the nation's having an identity separate from its historically acquired institutional forms was one of the most striking (and contested) claims of the Abbé Sieyes, author of the pamphlet 'What is the Third Estate' which helped provoke the breakaway of the Third Estate from the traditional Estates General, thus initiating the French Revolution.

[9] St Paul's First Letter to the Corinthians, 14, §11.

and character to centaurs, satyrs, and down to all the fairy tribe; but titles baffle even the powers of fancy, and are a chimerical nondescript.

But this is not all. – If a whole country is disposed to hold them in contempt, all their value is gone, and none will own them . . . The patriots of France have discovered in good time that rank and dignity in society must take a new ground. The old one has fallen through. It must now take the substantial ground of character, instead of the chimerical ground of titles; and they have brought their titles to the altar, and made of them a burnt-offering to Reason.

If no mischief had annexed itself to the folly of titles they would not have been worth a serious and formal destruction, such as the National Assembly have decreed them; and this makes it necessary to enquire farther into the nature and character of aristocracy.

That, then, which is called aristocracy in some countries and nobility in others arose out of the governments founded upon conquest. It was originally a military order for the purpose of supporting military government (for such were all governments founded in conquest); and to keep up a succession of this order for the purpose for which it was established, all the younger branches of those families were disinherited and the law of *primogenitureship*[10] set up.

The nature and character of aristocracy shows itself to us in this law. It is the law against every other law of nature, and Nature herself calls for its destruction. Establish family justice, and aristocracy falls. By the aristocratical law of primogenitureship, in a family of six children five are exposed. Aristocracy has never more than *one* child. The rest are begotten to be devoured. They are thrown to the cannibal for prey, and the natural parent prepares the unnatural repast.

As everything which is out of nature in man affects, more or less, the interest of society, so does this. All the children which the aristocracy disowns (which are all except the eldest) are, in general, cast like orphans on a parish, to be provided for by the public, but at a greater charge. – Unnecessary offices and places in governments and courts are created at the expense of the public to maintain them.

With what kind of parental reflections can the father or mother contemplate their younger offspring? By nature they are children, and by marriage they are heirs; but by aristocracy they are bastards and orphans. They are the flesh and blood of their parents in the one line, and nothing akin to them in the other. To restore, therefore, parents to their children, and children to their parents – relations to each other, and

---

[10] The law by which the eldest son alone inherits the parents' estate.

man to society – and to exterminate the monster aristocracy, root and branch – the French Constitution has destroyed the law of P R I M O G E N I T U R E S H I P. Here then lies the monster; and Mr. Burke, if he pleases, may write its epitaph.

Hitherto we have considered aristocracy chiefly in one point of view. We have now to consider it in another. But whether we view it before or behind, or sideways, or any way else, domestically or publicly, it is still a monster.

. . .

Because, in the first place, as is already mentioned, aristocracy is kept up by family tyranny and injustice.

Secondly, Because there is an unnatural unfitness in an aristocracy to be legislators for a nation. Their ideas of *distributive justice* are corrupted at the very source. They begin life by trampling on all their younger brothers and sisters, and relations of every kind, and are taught and educated so to do. With what ideas of justice or honour can that man enter a house of legislation, who absorbs in his own person the inheritance of a whole family of children or doles out to them some pitiful portion with the insolence of a gift?

Thirdly, Because the idea of hereditary legislators is as inconsistent as that of hereditary judges, or hereditary juries; and as absurd as an hereditary mathematician, or an hereditary wise man; and as ridiculous as an hereditary poet laureate.

Fourthly, Because a body of men, holding themselves accountable to nobody, ought not to be trusted by anybody.

Fifthly, Because it is continuing the uncivilised principle of governments founded in conquest, and the base idea of man having property in man, and governing him by personal right.

Sixthly, Because aristocracy has a tendency to deteriorate the human species. By the universal economy of nature it is known, and by the instance of the Jews it is proved, that the human species has a tendency to degenerate, in any small number of persons, when separated from the general stock of society, and inter-marrying constantly with each other. It defeats even its pretended end, and becomes in time the opposite of what is noble in man. Mr. Burke talks of nobility; let him show what it is. The greatest characters the world have known have arisen on the democratic floor. Aristocracy has not been able to keep a proportionate pace with democracy. The artificial N O B L E shrinks into a dwarf before the N O B L E of Nature . . .

The French Constitution has reformed the condition of the clergy. It has raised the income of the lower and middle classes, and taken from the higher. None are now less than twelve hundred livres (fifty pounds sterling), nor any higher than two or three thousand pounds. What will Mr. Burke place against this? Hear what he says.

He says: 'That the people of England can see without pain or grudging, an archbishop precede a duke; they can see a Bishop of Durham, or a Bishop of Winchester in possession of £10,000 a-year; and cannot see why it is in worse hands than estates to a like amount, in the hands of this earl or that squire.' And Mr. Burke offers this as an example to France.

. . .

The French Constitution hath abolished or renounced *Toleration* and *Intolerance* also, and hath established UNIVERSAL RIGHT OF CONSCIENCE.

Toleration is not the *opposite* of Intolerance, but is the *counterfeit* of it. Both are despotisms. The one assumes to itself the right of withholding Liberty of Conscience, and the other of granting it.[11] The one is the Pope armed with fire and faggot, and the other is the Pope selling or granting indulgences. The former is church and state, and the latter is church and traffic.

But Toleration may be viewed in a much stronger light. Man worships not himself, but his Maker; and the liberty of conscience which he claims is not for the service of himself, but of his God. In this case, therefore, we must necessarily have the associated idea of two things; the *mortal* who renders the worship, and the IMMORTAL BEING who is worshipped. Toleration, therefore, places itself, not between man and man, nor between church and church, nor between one denomination of religion and another, but between God and man; between the being who worships, and the BEING who is worshipped; and by the same act of assumed authority which it tolerates man to pay his worship, it presumptuously and blasphemously sets itself up to tolerate the Almighty to receive it.

Were a Bill brought into any parliament, entitled, 'AN ACT to tolerate or grant liberty to the Almighty to receive the worship of a Jew or Turk,' or 'to prohibit the Almighty from receiving it,' all men would startle and call it blasphemy. There would be an uproar. The presumption of toleration in religious matters would then present itself unmasked; but the presumption is not the less because the name of 'Man' only

---

[11] Paine is here at his most radical. The toleration which was allowed dissenters in England at the end of the seventeenth century had been praised throughout the eighteenth century – for example by Voltaire in his *Philosophical Letters* – but this toleration was what we would call non-persecution: it was consistent with their being debarred from universities, voting and public office. The situation for Catholics in Ireland was much worse.

appears to those laws, for the associated idea of the *worshipper* and the *worshipped* cannot be separated. . . .

With respect to what are called denominations of religion, if every one is left to judge of its own religion, there is no such thing as a religion that is wrong; but if they are to judge of each other's religion, there is no such thing as a religion that is right; and therefore all the world is right, or all the world is wrong. But with respect to religion itself, without regard to names, and as directing itself from the universal family of mankind to the Divine object of all adoration, *it is man bringing to his Maker the fruits of his heart*; and though those fruits may differ from each other like the fruits of the earth, the grateful tribute of every one is accepted.

. . .

All religions are in their nature kind and benign, and united with principles of morality. They could not have made proselytes at first by professing anything that was vicious, cruel, persecuting, or immoral. Like everything else, they had their beginning; and they proceeded by persuasion, exhortation, and example. How then is it that they lose their native mildness, and become morose and intolerant?

It proceeds from the connection which Mr. Burke recommends. By engendering the church with the state, a sort of mule-animal, capable only of destroying, and not of breeding up, is produced, called the *Church established by Law*. It is a stranger, even from its birth, to any parent mother, on whom it is begotten, and whom in time it kicks out and destroys.

The inquisition in Spain does not proceed from the religion originally professed, but from this mule-animal, engendered between the church and the state. The burnings in Smithfield[12] proceeded from the same heterogeneous production; and it was the regeneration of this strange animal in England afterwards, that renewed rancour and irreligion among the inhabitants, and that drove the people called Quakers and Dissenters to America. Persecution is not an original feature in any religion; but it is alway the strongly-marked feature of all law-religions, or religions established by law. Take away the law-establishment, and every religion re-assumes its original benignity. In America, a catholic priest is a good citizen,[13] a good character, and a good neighbour; an episcopalian minister is of the same description: and this proceeds independently of the men, from there being no law-establishment in America.

---

[12] The execution ground for religious heretics in the sixteenth century.
[13] One of the claims made in England by Anglicans against the emancipation of Catholics was that they could not be good citizens because they owed allegiance to a foreign prince – the Pope – who in his religious capacity had absolved them from the need to keep their oaths to Protestants.

. . . Let then Mr. Burke continue to preach his antipolitical doctrine of Church and State. It will do some good. The National Assembly will not follow his advice, but will benefit by his folly. It was by observing the ill effects of it in England, that America has been warned against it; and it is by experiencing them in France, that the National Assembly have abolished it, and, like America, have established UNIVERSAL RIGHT OF CONSCIENCE, AND UNIVERSAL RIGHT OF CITIZENSHIP.[14]

. . .

The States-General were to meet at Versailles in April 1789, but did not assemble till May. They situated themselves in three separate chambers, or rather the Clergy and Aristocracy withdrew each into a separate chamber. The majority of the Aristocracy claimed what they called the privilege of voting as a separate body, and of giving their consent or their negative in that manner; and many of the bishops and the high-beneficed clergy claimed the same privilege on the part of their Order.

The *Tiers Etat* (as they were then called) disowned any knowledge of artificial orders and artificial privileges; and they were not only resolute on this point, but somewhat disdainful. They began to consider the Aristocracy as a kind of fungus growing out of the corruption of society, that could not be admitted even as a branch of it; and from the disposition the Aristocracy had shown by upholding Lettres de Cachet, and in sundry other instances, it was manifest that no constitution could be formed by admitting men in any other character than as National Men.

After various altercations on this head, the Tiers Etat or Commons (as they were then called) declared themselves (on a motion made for that purpose by the Abbé Sieyes) 'THE REPRESENTATIVE OF THE NATION; *and that the two Orders could be considered but as deputies of corporations, and could only have a deliberate voice when they assembled in a national character with the national representatives.*' This proceeding extinguished the style of *Etats Généraux*, or States-General, and erected it into the style it now bears, that of *L'Assemble Nationale*, or National Assembly.

---

[14] [Paine's footnote (excerpted)]

The manufactures of Manchester, Birmingham, and Sheffield, are the principal manufactures in England. From whence did this arise? The principal, and the generality of the inhabitants of those places, are not of what is called England, *the church established by law*; and they, or their fathers . . . withdrew from the persecutions of the chartered towns, where the test-laws more particularly operate, and established a sort of asylum for themselves in those places. It was the only asylum then offered, for the rest of Europe was worse. But the case is now changing. France and America bid all comers welcome and initiate them into the rights of citizenship. Policy and interest therefore will, but perhaps too late, dictate in England, what justice and reason could not.

This motion was not made in a precipitate manner. It was the result of cool deliberation, and concerted between the national representatives and the patriotic members of the two chambers, who saw into the folly, mischief, and injustice of artificial privileged distinctions. It was become evident, that no constitution, worthy of being called by that name, could be established on anything less than a national ground. The Aristocracy had hitherto opposed the despotism of the Court, and affected the language of patriotism; but it opposed it as its rival (as the English Barons opposed King John) and it now opposed the nation from the same motives.

. . .

It is worth remarking that the National Assembly neither pursued those fugitive [counter-revolutionary] conspirators, nor took any notice of them, nor sought to retaliate in any shape whatever. Occupied with establishing a constitution founded on the Rights of Man and the Authority of the People, the only authority on which Government has a right to exist in any country, the National Assembly felt none of those mean passions which mark the character of impertinent governments, founding themselves on their own authority, or on the absurdity of hereditary succession. It is the faculty of the human mind to become what it contemplates, and to act in unison with its object.

The conspiracy being thus dispersed, one of the first works of the National Assembly, instead of vindictive proclamations, as has been the case with other governments, was to publish a declaration of the Rights of Man, as the basis on which the new constitution was to be built, and which is here subjoined:

[Paine here included the Declaration of the Rights of Man, reproduced on pp. 33–6 in this collection.]

CH. II OBSERVATIONS ON THE DECLARATION OF RIGHTS

The three first articles comprehend in general terms the whole of a Declaration of Rights, all the succeeding articles either originate from them or follow as elucidations. The 4th, 5th, and 6th define more particularly what is only generally expressed in the 1st, 2d, and 3d.

The 7th, 8th, 9th, 10th, and 11th articles are declaratory of *principles* upon which laws shall be constructed, conformable to *rights* already declared. But it is questioned by some very good people in France, as well as in other countries, whether the 10th article sufficiently guarantees the right it is intended to accord with; besides which it takes off from the divine dignity of religion, and weakens its operative force upon the mind, to make it a subject of human laws. It then presents itself to man like light intercepted by a cloudy medium, in which the source of it is obscured from his sight, and he sees nothing to reverence in the dusky ray.[15]

The remaining articles, beginning with the twelfth, are substantially contained in the principles of the preceding articles; but in the particular situation in which France then was, having to undo what was wrong, as well as to set up what was right, it was proper to be more particular than what in another condition of things would be necessary.

While the Declaration of Rights was before the National Assembly some of its members remarked that if a declaration of rights were published it should be accompanied by a Declaration of Duties. The observation discovered a mind that reflected, and it only erred by not reflecting far enough. A Declaration of Rights is, by reciprocity, a Declaration of Duties also. Whatever is my right as a man is also the right of another; and it becomes my duty to guarantee as well as to possess.

The three first articles are the base of Liberty, as well individual as national; nor can any country be called free whose government does not take its beginning from the principles they contain, and continue to preserve them pure; and the whole of the Declaration of Rights is of more value to the world, and will do more good, than all the laws and statutes that have yet been promulgated.

In the declaratory exordium which prefaces the Declaration of Rights we see the solemn and majestic spectacle of a nation opening its commission, under the auspices of its Creator, to establish a Government, a scene so new, and so transcendantly unequalled by anything in the European world, that the name of a Revolution is diminutive of its character, and it rises into a Regeneration of man. What are the

---

[15] [Paine's footnote:]

There is a single idea, which, if it strikes rightly upon the mind either in a legal or a religious sense, will prevent any man, or any body of men, or any government, from going wrong on the subject of Religion; which is; that before any human institutions of government were known in the world, there existed, if I may so express it a compact between God and Man, from the beginning of time; and that as the relation and condition which man in his *individual person* stands in towards his Maker, cannot be changed, or any-ways altered by any human laws of human authority . . . all laws must conform themselves to this prior existing compact, and not assume to make the compact conform to the laws, which, beside being human, are subsequent thereto.

present Governments of Europe but a scene of iniquity and oppression? What is that of England? Do not its own inhabitants say it is a market where every man has his price, and where corruption is common traffic at the expense of a deluded people? No wonder, then, that the French Revolution is traduced. Had it confined itself merely to the destruction of flagrant despotism perhaps Mr. Burke and some others had been silent. Their cry now is, 'It has gone too far' – that is, it has gone too far for them. It stares corruption in the face, and the venal tribe are all alarmed. Their fear discovers itself in their outrage, and they are but publishing the groans of a wounded vice. But from such opposition the French Revolution, instead of suffering, receives an homage. The more it is struck the more sparks it will emit; and the fear is it will not be struck enough. It has nothing to dread from attacks; truth has given it an establishment, and time will record it with a name as lasting as his own.

. . .

MISCELLANEOUS CHAPTER

To prevent interrupting the argument in the preceding part of this work, or the narrative that follows it, I reserved some observations to be thrown together in a Miscellaneous Chapter; by which variety might not be censured for confusion. Mr. Burke's book is *all* Miscellany. His intention was to make an attack on the French Revolution; but instead of proceeding with an orderly arrangement, he has stormed it with a mob of ideas tumbling over and destroying one another.

But this confusion and contradiction in Mr. Burke's Book is easily accounted for. – When a man in a wrong cause attempts to steer his course by anything else than some polar truth or principle, he is sure to be lost. It is beyond the compass of his capacity to keep all the parts of an argument together, and make them unite in one issue, by any other means than having this guide always in view. Neither memory nor invention will supply the want of it. The former fails him, and the latter betrays him.

[CH. III OF HEREDITARY RIGHT]

Notwithstanding the nonsense, for it deserves no better name, that Mr. Burke has asserted about hereditary rights, and hereditary succession, and that a Nation has not a right to form a Government of itself; it happened to fall in his way to give some account of what Government is. '*Government*', says he, '*is a contrivance of human wisdom.*'

Admitting that government is a contrivance of human *wisdom*, it must necessarily follow, that hereditary succession, and hereditary rights (as they are called), can make no part of it, because it is impossible to make wisdom hereditary; and on the other hand, *that* cannot be a wise contrivance, which in its operation may commit the government of a nation to the wisdom of an idiot. The ground which Mr. Burke now takes is fatal to every part of his cause. The argument changes from hereditary rights to hereditary wisdom; and the question is, Who is the wisest man? He must now show that every one in the line of hereditary succession was a Solomon, or his title is not good to be a king. What a stroke has Mr. Burke now made! To use a sailor's phrase, he has swabbed the deck, and scarcely left a name legible in the list of Kings; and he has mowed down and thinned the House of Peers, with a scythe as formidable as Death and Time.

But Mr. Burke appears to have been aware of this retort; and he has taken care to guard against it, by making government to be not only a *contrivance* of human wisdom, but a *monopoly* of wisdom. He puts the nation as fools on one side, and places his government of wisdom, all wise men of Gotham, on the other side; and he then proclaims, and says that '*Men have a* RIGHT *that their* WANTS *should be provided for by this wisdom.*' Having thus made proclamation, he next proceeds to explain to them what their *wants* are, and also what their *rights* are. In this he has succeeded dextrously, for he makes their wants to be a *want* of wisdom; but as this is cold comfort, he then informs them, that they have a *right* (not to any of the wisdom) but to be governed by it; and in order to impress them with a solemn reverence for this monopoly-government of wisdom, and of its vast capacity for all purposes, possible or impossible, right or wrong, he proceeds with astrological mysterious importance, to tell to them its powers in these words: 'The rights of men in government are their advantages; and these are often in balance between differences of good; and in compromises sometimes between *good* and *evil*, and sometimes between *evil* and *evil*. Political reason is a *computing principle*; adding – subtracting – multiplying – and dividing, morally and not metaphysically or mathematically, true moral demonstrations.'

As the wondering audience, whom Mr. Burke supposes himself talking to, may not understand all this learned jargon, I will undertake to be its interpreter. The meaning, then, good people, of all this, is: *That government is governed by no principle whatever;*

that it can make evil good, or good evil, just as it pleases. In short, that government is arbitrary power.

But there are some things which Mr. Burke has forgotten. *First*, he has not shown where the wisdom originally came from: and *secondly*, he has not shown by what authority it first began to act. In the manner he introduces the matter, it is either government stealing wisdom, or wisdom stealing government. It is without an origin, and its powers without authority. In short, it is usurpation.

. . .

The opinions of men with respect to government are changing fast in all countries. The Revolutions of America and France have thrown a beam of light over the world, which reaches into man. The enormous expense of governments has provoked people to think, by making them feel; and when once the veil begins to rend, it admits not of repair. Ignorance is of a peculiar nature: once dispelled, it is impossible to re-establish it. It is not originally a thing of itself, but is only the absence of knowledge; and though man may be *kept* ignorant, he cannot be *made* ignorant. The mind, in discovering truth, acts in the same manner as it acts through the eye in discovering objects; when once any object has been seen, it is impossible to put the mind back to the same condition it was in before it saw it. Those who talk of a counter-revolution in France, show how little they understand of man. There does not exist in the compass of language an arrangement of words to express so much as the means of effecting a counter-revolution. The means must be an obliteration of knowledge; and it has never yet been discovered how to make man *unknow* his knowledge, or *unthink* his thoughts.

. . .

It has hitherto been the practice of the English Parliaments to regulate what was called the succession (taking it for granted that the Nation then continued to accord to the form of annexing a monarchical branch of its government; for without this the Parliament could not have had authority to have sent either to Holland or to Hanover, or to impose a king upon the nation against its will). And this must be the utmost limit to which Parliament can go upon this case; but the right of the Nation goes to the *whole* case, because it has the right of changing its *whole* form of government. The right of a Parliament is only a right in trust, a right by delegation, and that but from a very small part of the Nation; and one of its Houses has not even this. But the right of the Nation is an original right, as universal as taxation. The nation is the paymaster of everything, and everything must conform to its general will.

. . .

As Mr. Burke sometimes speaks of England, sometimes of France, and sometimes of the world, and of government in general, it is difficult to answer his book without apparently meeting him on the same ground. Although principles of Government are general subjects, it is next to impossible, in many cases, to separate them from the idea of place and circumstance, and the more so when circumstances are put for arguments, which is frequently the case with Mr. Burke.

In the former part of his book, addressing himself to the people of France, he says: 'No experience has taught us (meaning the English), that in any other course or method than that of a *hereditary crown*, can our liberties be regularly perpetuated and preserved sacred as our *hereditary right*.' . . . But besides the folly of the declaration, it happens that the facts are all against Mr. Burke. It was by the government *being hereditary*, that the liberties of the people were endangered. Charles I. and James II. are instances of this truth; yet neither of them went so far as to hold the Nation in contempt.

. . .

Mr. Burke talks about what he calls an hereditary crown, as if it were some production of Nature; or as if, like Time, it had a power to operate, not only independently, but in spite of man; or as if it were a thing or a subject universally consented to. Alas! it has none of those properties, but is the reverse of them all. It is a thing in imagination, the propriety of which is more than doubted, and the legality of which in a few years will be denied.

But, to arrange this matter in a clearer view than what general expression can convey, it will be necessary to state the distinct heads under which (what is called) an hereditary crown, or more properly speaking, an hereditary succession to the Government of a Nation, can be considered; which are –

First, The right of a particular Family to establish itself.

Secondly, The right of a Nation to establish a particular Family.

With respect to the *first* of these heads, that of a Family establishing itself with hereditary powers on its own authority, and independent of the consent of a Nation, all men will concur in calling it despotism; and it would be trespassing on their understanding to attempt to prove it.

But the *second* head, that of a Nation establishing a particular Family with *hereditary powers*, does not present itself as despotism on the first reflection; . . .

. . .

The generation which first selects a person, and puts him at the head of its Government, either with the title of King, or any other distinction, acts on its *own choice*, be it wise or foolish, as a free agent for itself. The person so set up is not hereditary, but selected and appointed; and the generation who sets him up, does not live under a hereditary government, but under a government of its own choice and establishment. Were the generation who sets him up, and the person so set up, to live for ever, it never could become hereditary succession; and of consequence hereditary succession can only follow on the death of the first parties.

As, therefore, hereditary succession is out of the question with respect to the *first* generation, we have now to consider the character in which *that* generation acts with respect to the commencing generation, and to all succeeding ones.

It assumes a character, to which it has neither right nor title. It changes itself from a *Legislator* to a *Testator*, and effects to make its Will, which is to have operation after the demise of the makers, to bequeath the Government; and it not only attempts to bequeath, but to establish on the succeeding generation, a new and different form of Government under which itself lived. Itself, as already observed, lived not under a hereditary Government but under a Government of its own choice and establishment; and it now attempts, by virtue of a will and testament (and which it has not authority to make), to take from the commencing generation, and all future ones, the rights and free agency by which itself acted.

But, exclusive of the right which any generation has to act collectively as a testator, the objects to which it applies itself in this case, are not within the compass of any law, or of any will or testament.

The rights of men in society, are neither devisable or transferable, nor annihilable, but are descendable only, and it is not in the power of any generation to intercept finally, and cut off the descent. If the present generation, or any other, are disposed to be slaves, it does not lessen the right of the succeeding generation to be free. Wrongs cannot have a legal descent. When Mr. Burke attempts to maintain that the *English nation did at the Revolution of 1688, most solemnly renounce and abdicate their rights for themselves, and for all their posterity for ever,* he speaks a language that merits not reply, and which can only excite contempt for his prostitute principles, or pity for his ignorance.

In whatever light hereditary succession, as growing out of the will and testament of some former generation, presents itself, it is an absurdity. A cannot make a will to take from B the property of B, and give it to C; yet this is the manner in which (what is called) hereditary succession by law operates. A certain former generation made a will, to take away the rights of the commencing generation, and all future ones, and convey those rights to a third person, who afterwards comes forward, and tells them, in Mr. Burke's language, that they have *no rights*, that their rights are already bequeathed to him and that he will govern in *contempt* of them. From such principles, and such ignorance, Good Lord deliver the world!

But, after all, what is this metaphor called a crown, or rather what is monarchy? Is it a thing, or is it a name, or is it a fraud? Is it a 'contrivance of human wisdom,' or of human craft to obtain money from a nation under specious pretences? Is it a thing necessary to a nation? If it is, in what does that necessity consist, what service does it perform, what is its business, and what are its merits? Does the virtue consist in the metaphor, or in the man? Doth the goldsmith that makes the crown, make the virtue also? Doth it operate like Fortunatus's wishing-cap, or Harlequin's wooden sword? Doth it make a man a conjurer? In fine, what is it? . . .

If Government be what Mr. Burke describes it, 'a contrivance of human wisdom', I might ask him, if wisdom was at such a low ebb in England, that it was become necessary to import it from Holland and from Hanover? . . . The wisdom of every country, when properly exerted, is sufficient for all its purposes; and there could exist no more real occasion in England to have sent for a Dutch Stadtholder, or a German Elector,[16] than there was in America to have done a similar thing. If a country does not understand its own affairs, how is a foreigner to understand them, who knows neither its laws, its manners, nor its language? If there existed a man so transcendently wise above all others, that his wisdom was necessary to instruct a nation, some reason might be offered for monarchy; but when we cast our eyes about a country, and observe how every part understands its own affairs; and when we look around the world, and see that of all men in it, the race of kings are the most insignificant in capacity, our reason cannot fail to ask us – What are those men kept for?

If there is anything in monarchy which we people of America do not understand, I wish Mr. Burke would be so kind as to inform us. I see in America, a government extending over a country ten times as large as England, and conducted with regularity, for a fortieth part of the expense which Government costs in England. If I ask a man in America if he wants a King, he retorts, and asks me if I take him for an idiot? How is it that this difference happens? are we more or less wise than others? I see in America the generality of people living in a style of plenty unknown in monarchical

[16] In order to prevent Catholics – the next in line – from succeeding to the throne, Parliament had twice legislated on the succession, first in the 1689 Bill of Rights in favour of William and Mary, again in the Act of Settlement in 1701.

countries; and I see that the principle of its government, which is that of the *equal Rights of Man*, is making a rapid progress in the world.

If monarchy is a useless thing, why is it kept up anywhere? and if a necessary thing, how can it be dispensed with? That *civil government* is necessary, all civilized nations will agree; but civil government is republican government. All that part of the government of England which begins with the office of constable, and proceeds through the department of magistrate, quarter-sessions, and general assize, including trial by jury, is republican government. Nothing of monarchy appears in any part of it, except in the name which William the Conqueror imposed upon the English, that of obliging them to call him 'Their Sovereign Lord the King.'

. . .

Notwithstanding the taxes of England amount to almost seventeen millions a year, said to be for the expenses of Government, it is still evident that the sense of the Nation is left to govern itself, and does govern itself, by magistrates and juries, almost at its own charge, on republican principles, exclusive of the expense of taxes. The salaries of the judges are almost the only charge that is paid out of the revenue. Considering that all the internal government is executed by the people, the taxes of England ought to be the lightest of any nation in Europe; instead of which, they are the contrary. As this cannot be accounted for on the score of civil government, the subject necessarily extends itself to the monarchical part.

When the people of England sent for George the First[17] (and it would puzzle a wiser man than Mr. Burke to discover for what he could be wanted, or what service he could render), they ought at least to have conditioned for the abandonment of Hanover. Besides the endless German intrigues that must follow from a German Elector being King of England, there is a natural impossibility of uniting in the same person the principles of Freedom and the principles of Despotism, or as it is usually called in England, Arbitrary Power. . . .

There never was a time when it became the English to watch continental intrigues more circumspectly than at the present moment, and to distinguish the politics of the Electorate from the politics of the Nation.[18] The Revolution of France has entirely changed the ground with respect to England and France, as nations; but the German

---

[17] On the death of Queen Anne, the fifty-seven Stuart Roman Catholics with closer claims to the throne were excluded in favour of George of Hanover, son of Queen Sophia of Hanover, grand-daughter of James II.

[18] An alliance of continental powers had already initiated military action against the French Revolution. The British, despite Burke's urgings, at this point remained neutral.

despots, with Prussia at their head, are combining against liberty; and the fondness of Mr. Pitt for office, and the interest which all his family connections have obtained, do not give sufficient security against this intrigue.

. . .

CONCLUSION [CH. IV OF GOVERNMENT]

Reason and Ignorance, the opposites of each other, influence the great bulk of mankind. If either of these can be rendered sufficiently extensive in a country, the machinery of Government goes easily on. Reason obeys itself; and Ignorance submits to whatever is dictated to it.

The two modes of the Government which prevail in the world, are, *first*, Government by election and representation: *Secondly*, Government by hereditary succession. The former is generally known by the name of republic; the latter by that of monarchy and aristocracy.[19]

Those two distinct and opposite forms erect themselves on the two distinct and opposite bases of Reason and Ignorance. – As the exercise of Government requires talents and abilities, and as talents and abilities cannot have hereditary descent, it is evident that hereditary succession requires a belief from man to which his reason cannot subscribe, and which can only be established upon his ignorance; and the more ignorant any country is, the better it is fitted for this species of Government.

On the contrary, Government, in a well-constituted republic, requires no belief from man beyond what his reason can give. He sees the *rationale* of the whole system, its origin and its operation; and as it is best supported when best understood, the human faculties act with boldness, and acquire, under this form of government, a gigantic manliness.

As, therefore, each of those forms acts on a different base, the one moving freely by the aid of reason, the other by ignorance; we have next to consider, what it is that gives motion to that species of Government which is called mixed Government, or, as it is sometimes ludicrously styled, a Government of *this, that* and *t' other*.

The moving power in this species of Government is, of necessity, Corruption. However imperfect election and representation may be in mixed Governments, they

---

[19] This way of categorising government dates from the debate on the American Constitution. Previously an hereditary aristocracy was merely one variant of aristocracy, and an aristocratic republic was not, as it had become for Paine, a contradiction in terms.

still give exercise to a greater portion of reason than is convenient to the hereditary Part; and therefore it becomes necessary to buy the reason up. A mixed Government is an imperfect everything, cementing and soldering the discordant parts together by corruption, to act as a whole. Mr. Burke appears highly disgusted that France, since she had resolved on a revolution, did not adopt what he calls 'A British Constitution'; and the regretful manner in which he expresses himself on this occasion implies a suspicion that the British Constitution needed something to keep its defects in countenance.

In mixed Governments there is no responsibility: the parts cover each other till responsibility is lost; and the corruption which moves the machine, contrives at the same time its own escape. When it is laid down as a maxim, that *a King can do no wrong*, it places him in a state of similar security with that of idiots and persons insane, and responsibility is out of the question with respect to himself. It then descends upon the Minister, who shelters himself under a majority in Parliament, which, by places, pensions, and corruption, he can always command; and that majority justifies itself by the same authority with which it protects the Minister. In this rotatory motion, responsibility is thrown off from the parts, and from the whole.

When there is a Part in a Government which can do no wrong, it implies that it does nothing; and is only the machine of another power, by whose advice and direction it acts. What is supposed to be the King in the mixed Governments, is the Cabinet; and as the Cabinet is always a part of the Parliament, and the members justifying in one character what they advise and act in another, a mixed Government becomes a continual enigma; entailing upon a country by the quantity of corruption necessary to solder the parts, the expense of supporting all the forms of government at once, and finally resolving itself into a Government by Committee; in which the advisers, the actors, the approvers, the justifiers, the persons responsible, and the persons not responsible, are the same persons.

By this pantomimical contrivance, and change of scene and character, the parts help each other out in matters which neither of them singly would assume to act. When money is to be obtained, the mass of variety apparently dissolves, and a profusion of parliamentary praises passes between the parts. Each admires with astonishment, the wisdom, the liberality, the disinterestedness of the other: and all of them breathe a pitying sigh at the burdens of the Nation.

But in a well-constituted republic, nothing of this soldering, praising, and pitying, can take place; the representation being equal throughout the country, and complete in itself, however it may be arranged into legislative and executive, they have all one and the same natural source. The parts are not foreigners to each other, like democracy, aristocracy, and monarchy. As there are no discordant distinctions, there is nothing to corrupt by compromise, nor confound by contrivance. Public measures appeal of themselves to the understanding of the Nation, and, resting on their own merits, disown any flattering applications to vanity. . . .

. . .

From the Revolutions of America and France, and the symptoms that have appeared in other countries, it is evident that the opinion of the world is changing with respect to systems of Government, and that revolutions are not within the compass of political calculations. The progress of time and circumstances, which men assign to the accomplishment of great changes, is too mechanical to measure the force of the mind, and the rapidity of reflection, by which revolutions are generated: All the old governments have received a shock from those that already appear, and which were once more improbable, and are a greater subject of wonder, than a general revolution in Europe would be now.

When we survey the wretched condition of man, under the monarchical and hereditary systems of Government, dragged from his home by one power, or driven by another, and impoverished by taxes more than by enemies, it becomes evident that those systems are bad, and that a general revolution in the principle and construction of Governments is necessary.

What is government more than the management of the affairs of a Nation? It is not, and from its nature cannot be, the property of any particular man or family, but of the whole community, at whose expense it is supported; and though by force and contrivance it has been usurped into an inheritance, the usurpation cannot alter the right of things. Sovereignty, as a matter of right, appertains to the Nation only, and not to any individual; and a Nation has at all times an inherent indefeasible right to abolish any form of Government it finds inconvenient, and to establish such as accords with its interest, disposition and happiness. The romantic and barbarous distinction of men into Kings and subjects, though it may suit the condition of courtiers, cannot that of citizens; and is exploded by the principle upon which Governments are now founded. Every citizen is a member of the Sovereignty, and, as such, can acknowledge no personal subjection; and his obedience can be only to the laws.

. . .

What were formerly called Revolutions, were little more than a change of persons, or an alteration of local circumstances. They rose and fell like things of course, and had nothing in their existence or their fate that could influence beyond the spot that produced them. But what we now see in the world, from the Revolutions of America and France, are a renovation of the natural order of things, a system of principles as universal as truth and the existence of man, and combining moral with political happiness and national prosperity.

'I. *Men are born, and always continue, free and equal in respect of their rights. Civil distinctions, therefore, can be founded only on public utility.*

'II. *The end of all political associations is the preservation of the natural and impre-scriptible rights of man; and these rights are liberty, property, security, and resistance of oppression.*

'III. *The nation is essentially the source of all sovereignty; nor can any* INDIVIDUAL, *or* ANY BODY OF MEN, *be entitled to any authority which is not expressly derived from it.*'

In these principles, there is nothing to throw a Nation into confusion by inflaming ambition. They are calculated to call forth wisdom and abilities, and to exercise them for the public good, and not for the emolument or aggrandisement of particular descriptions of men or families. Monarchical sovereignty, the enemy of mankind, and the source of misery, is abolished; and the sovereignty itself is restored to its natural and original place, the Nation. Were this the case throughout Europe, the cause of wars would be taken away.

. . .

Why are not Republics plunged into war, but because the nature of their Government does not admit of an interest distinct from that of the Nation? Even Holland, though an ill-constructed Republic, and with a commerce extending over the world, existed nearly a century without war: and the instant the form of Government was changed in France, the republican principles of peace and domestic prosperity and economy arose with the new Government; and the same consequences would follow the cause in other Nations.

As war is the system of Government on the old construction, the animosity which Nations reciprocally entertain, is nothing more than what the policy of their Governments excites to keep up the spirit of the system. Each Government accuses the other of perfidy, intrigue, and ambition, as a means of heating the imagination of their respective Nations, and incensing them to hostilities. Man is not the enemy of man, but through the medium of a false system of Government. Instead, there-fore, of exclaiming against the ambition of Kings, the exclamation should be directed against the principle of such Governments; and instead of seeking to reform the individual, the wisdom of a Nation should apply itself to reform the system.

Whether the forms and maxims of Governments which are still in practice, were adapted to the condition of the world at the period they were established, is not in this case the question. The older they are, the less correspondence can they have with the present state of things. Time, and change of circumstances and opinions, have the same progressive effect in rendering modes of Government obsolete as they have upon customs and manners. – Agriculture, commerce, manufactures, and the tranquil arts, by which the prosperity of Nations is best promoted, require a different system of Government, and a different species of knowledge to direct its operations, than what might have been required in the former condition of the world.

As it is not difficult to perceive, from the enlightened state of mankind, that hereditary Governments are verging to their decline, and that Revolutions on the broad basis of national sovereignty and Government by representation, are making their way in Europe, it would be an act of wisdom to anticipate their approach, and produce Revolutions by reason and accommodation, rather than commit them to the issue of convulsions.

From what we now see, nothing of reform in the political world ought to be held improbable. It is an age of Revolutions, in which everything may be looked for. The intrigue of Courts, by which the system of war is kept up, may provoke a confederation of Nations to abolish it: and an European Congress to patronise the progress of free Government, and promote the civilization of Nations with each other, is an event nearer in probability, than once were the revolutions and alliance of France and America.

JAMES MACKINTOSH

BIOGRAPHICAL NOTE

James, later Sir James, Mackintosh was born near Inverness in 1765 to a military family with a small estate. He went to King's College, Aberdeen becoming interested in philosophical and theological issues, but then studied medicine at Edinburgh and even began to practise in London, where he lived from 1788. He enjoyed and sought out controversy, joining the Society for Constitutional Information, and practised journalism. After his father's death he began to train as a barrister, being called to the bar in 1795. As a lecturer in law at Lincoln's Inn, he delivered a course of lectures on the English Constitution, and on the Law of Nations which won the praise and endorsement of Pitt and Canning. He was then offered and accepted the post of recorder for Bombay (1803–11), for which he received a knighthood. However, despite taking a huge library to India and founding a literary society there, he found the intellectual and social life too limiting. On return he was elected a Whig MP for Nairn in north-east Scotland, and subsequently for the English seat of Knaresborough. In Parliament he supported liberal politics in both criminal law and international relations. From 1818 he was professor of law and politics at Haileybury College, and was offered, but refused, the chair of moral philosophy at Edinburgh. He contributed to the *Edinburgh Review* and the *Encyclopaedia Britannica* and died in 1832 having, the previous year, supported the first reading of the Great Reform Bill.

EDITORIAL NOTE

Vindiciae Gallicae (1791) was perhaps the most erudite of the immediate defences of the Revolution in response to Burke, aimed at a polite and educated audience. As a result Mackintosh acquired some fame and was elected secretary to the moderate reformist Society of the Friends of the People. *Vindiciae Gallicae* was said to be the only work opposing Burke which formed 'a breakwater, to the general spring-tide of Burkism' amongst that group.[1] Mackintosh's appraisal of the Revolution is not dominated by any particular theoretical

---

[1] R. J. Mackintosh, *Memoirs of the life of Sir James Mackintosh* 1, p. 69. Cited in Boulton, *The Language of Politics . . .* , p. 152.

perspective, but it persistently claims that moderate reform was not possible in French circumstances. A subsequent correspondence and meeting with Burke in the last year of his life, as well as the course of the Revolution itself, however, led him, like so many radical supporters, to renounce it.[2]

Vindiciae Gallicae was published in May 1791, second and third editions with minor corrections in 1792. A French translation followed. The text used here is taken from the *Miscellaneous Works of the Right Honourable Sir James Mackintosh* (2nd edn, London: Longman, 1851).

FURTHER READING

Boulton, James *The Language of Politics in the Age of Wilkes and Burke* (London: Routledge, 1963), ch.ıx.

Boulton, James 'Literature and Ideology: James Mackintosh: *Vindiciae Gallicae*', *Renaissance and Modern Studies* 21 (1977), pp. 106–18.

Hazlitt, William *Mackintosh*, in his *The Spirit of the Age* (London: Collins, 1969 [1825]).

McKenzie, Lionel 'The French Revolution and English Parliamentary Reform: James Mackintosh and the *Vindiciae Gallicae*', *Eighteenth-Century Studies* (1981), 14(3), pp. 264–82.

Mackintosh, R. J. *Memoirs of the Life of Sir James Mackintosh*, 2 vols. (London: Longman, Brown, Green and Longman, 1836).

O'heary, Patrick *Sir James Mackintosh, the Whig Cicero* (Aberdeen University Press, 1989)

Vindiciae Gallicae (1791)

A DEFENCE OF THE FRENCH REVOLUTION AND ITS ENGLISH ADMIRERS AGAINST THE ACCUSATIONS OF THE RIGHT HON. EDMUND BURKE . . .

. . .

. . . we have first to consider the destruction of the three great corporations, of the Nobility, the Church, and the Parliaments. These three Aristocracies were the pillars which in fact formed the government of France. The question then of forming or destroying these bodies was fundamental.

---

[2] 'I abhor, abjure, and for ever renounce the French Revolution, with its sanguinary history, its abominable principles, and forever execrable leaders', *Life* I, p. 125.

There is one general principle applicable to them all adopted by the French legislators, – that the existence of Orders is repugnant to the principles of the social union. An Order is a legal rank, a body of men combined and, endowed with privileges by law. There are two kinds of inequality: the one personal, that of talent and virtue, the source of whatever is excellent and admirable in society; the other, that of fortune, which must exist, because property alone can stimulate to labour, and labour, if it were not necessary to the existence, would be indispensable to the happiness of man. But though it be, necessary, yet in its excess it is the great malady of civil society. The accumulation of that power which is conferred by wealth in the hands of the few, is the perpetual source of oppression and neglect to the mass of mankind. The power of the wealthy is farther concentrated by their tendency to combination, from which, number, dispersion, indigence, and ignorance equally preclude the poor. The wealthy are formed into bodies by their professions, their different degrees of opulence (called 'ranks'), their knowledge, and their small number . . . Not content with the inevitable inequality of fortune, they have superadded to it honorary and political distinctions. Not content with the inevitable tendency of the wealthy to combine, they have embodied them in classes. They have fortified those conspiracies against the general interest, which they ought to have resisted, though they could not disarm. Laws, it is said, cannot equalise men; – No: but ought they, for that reason to aggravate the inequality which they cannot cure? Laws cannot inspire unmixed patriotism: but ought they for that reason to foment that *corporation spirit* which is its most fatal enemy? 'All professional combinations,' said Mr. Burke, in one of his late speeches in Parliament, 'are dangerous in a free state.' Arguing on the same principle, the National Assembly has proceeded further. They have conceived that the laws ought to create no inequality of combination, to recognise all only in their capacity of citizens, and to offer no assistance to the natural preponderance of partial over general interest.

But, besides the general source of hostility to Orders, the particular circumstances of France presented other objections, which it is necessary to consider more in detail.

It is in the first place to be remarked, that all the bodies and institutions of the kingdom participated in the spirit of the ancient government, and in that view were incapable of alliance with a free constitution. They were tainted by the despotism of which they had been either members or instruments. Absolute monarchies, like every other consistent and permanent government, assimilate every thing with which they are connected to their own genius. The Nobility, the Priesthood, the Judicial Aristocracy, were unfit to be members of a free government, because their corporate character had been formed under arbitrary establishments. To have preserved these great corporations, would be to have retained the seeds of reviving despotism in the bosom of freedom. This remark may merit the attention of Mr. Burke as illustrating an important difference between the French and English Revolutions. The Clergy, the Peerage, and Judicature of England had imbibed in some degree the sentiments inspired by a government in which freedom had been eclipsed, but not extinguished. They were therefore qualified to partake of a more stable and improved liberty. But the case of France was different. These bodies had there imbibed every sentiment, and adopted every habit under arbitrary power. Their preservation in England, and their destruction in France, may in this view be justified on similar grounds. It is absurd to regard the Orders as remnants of that free constitution which France, in common with the other Gothic nations of Europe, once enjoyed. Nothing remained of these ancient Orders but the name. The Nobility were no longer those haughty and powerful Barons, who enslaved the people, and dictated to the King. The Ecclesiastics were no longer that Priesthood before whom, in a benighted and superstitious age, all civil power was impotent and mute. They had both dwindled into dependents on the Crown. Still less do the opulent and enlightened Commons of France resemble its servile and beggared populace in the sixteenth century. Two hundred years of uninterrupted exercise had legitimatised absolute authority as much as prescription can consecrate usurpation. The ancient French Constitution was therefore no farther a model than that of any foreign nation which was to be judged of alone by its utility, and possessed in no respect the authority of establishment. It had been succeeded by another government; and if France was to recur to a period antecedent to her servitude for legislative models, she might as well ascend to the era of Clovis or of Charlemagne, as be regulated by the precedents of Henry III. or Mary of Medicis. All these forms of government existed only historically.

These observations include all the Orders. Let us consider each of them successively. The devotion of the Nobility of France to the Monarch was inspired equally by their sentiments, their interests, and their habits. 'The feudal and chivalrous spirit of fealty,' so long the prevailing passion of Europe, was still nourished in their bosoms by the military sentiments from which it first arose. The majority of them had still no profession but war, no hope but in Royal favour. The youthful and indigent filled the camps; the more opulent and mature partook the splendour and bounty of the Court: but they were equally dependents on the Crown. To the plenitude of the Royal power were attached those immense and magnificent privileges, which divided France into distinct nations; which exhibited a Nobility monopolising the rewards and offices of the State, and a people degraded to political helotism.[3] For in the latter sense the assertion would have been untrue. Men do not cordially resign such privileges, nor quickly dismiss the sentiments which they have inspired . . . They have been most justly stated to be a band of political Janissaries,[4] – far more valuable to a Sultan than mercenaries, because attached to him by unchangeable interest and indelible sentiment. Whether any reform could have extracted from this body an element which might have entered into the new Constitution is a question which we shall consider when that political system comes under our review. Their existence, as a member of the Legislature, is a question distinct from their preservation as a separate Order, or great corporation, in the State . . . The suppression of the Nobility has been in England most absurdly confounded with the prohibition of titles. The union of the Orders in one Assembly was the first step towards the destruction of a legislative Nobility: the abolition of their feudal rights, in the memorable session of the 4th of August, 1789, may be regarded as the second. They retained after these measures no distinction but what was purely nominal; and it remained to be determined what place they were to occupy in the new Constitution. That question was decided by the decree of the 22nd of December, in the same year, which enacted, that the Electoral Assemblies were to be composed without any regard to rank; and that citizens of all orders were to vote in them indiscriminately. The distinction of Orders was thus destroyed: the Nobility were to form no part of the new Constitution, and were stripped of all that they had enjoyed under the old government, but their titles.

. . . A titled Nobility is the most undisputed progeny of feudal barbarism. Titles had in all nations *denoted offices*: it was reserved for Gothic Europe to attach them to *ranks*. Yet this conduct of our remote ancestors admits explanation; for with them offices were hereditary, and hence the titles denoting them became hereditary too. But we, who have rejected hereditary office, retain an usage to which it gave rise, and which it alone could justify. So egregiously is this recent origin of a titled Nobility misconceived, that it has been even pretended to be necessary to the order and existence of society; – a narrow and arrogant mistake, which would limit all political remark to the Gothic states of Europe, or establish general principles on events

---

[3] [Mackintosh's footnote:] 'I say *political* in contradistinction to *civil*, for in the latter sense the assertion would have been untrue.' By 'helotism' he was referring to slavery, the Helots were the subject population of the Ancient Spartan warrior elite.
[4] [Mackintosh's footnote:] 'See Mr. Rous's excellent Thoughts on Government.' Janissaries were the palace guards of the Turkish Sultan, hence any military force used to protect absolutist rulers.

that occupy so short a period of history, and manners that have been adopted by so slender a portion of the human race. A titled Nobility was equally unknown to the splendid monarchies of Asia, and to the manly simplicity of the ancient commonwealths.[5] It arose from the peculiar circumstances of modern Europe; and yet its necessity is now erected on the basis of universal experience, as if these other renowned and polished states were effaced from the records of history, and banished from the society of nations. . . .

. . .

The enlightened observer of an age thus distant will contemplate with peculiar astonishment the rise, progress, decay, and downfall of spiritual power in Christian Europe.[6] . . . In a state of feebleness, [the priesthood] are dangerous to liberty: possessed of power, they are dangerous to civil government itself. But the last period of their progress will be that which will appear to have been peculiarly connected with the state of France.

There can be no protection for the opulence and even existence[7] of an European priesthood in an enlightened period, but the throne. It forms the only bulwark against the inroads of Reason: for the superstition which once formed its power is gone. Around the throne therefore they rally; and to the monarch they transfer the devotion which formerly attached them to the Church; while the fierceness of priestly[8] zeal has been succeeded by the more peaceful sentiments of a courtly and polished servility. Such is, in a greater or less degree, the present condition of the Church in every nation of Europe. . . .

In the few remarks that are here made on the Nobility and Clergy of France we confine ourselves strictly to their *political* and *collective* character: Mr. Burke, on the contrary, has grounded his eloquent apology purely on their *individual* and *moral*

---

[5] [Mackintosh's footnote:]
   Aristocratic bodies did indeed exist in the ancient world, but *titles* were unknown. Though they possessed political privileges, yet as these did not affect the *manners*, they had not the same inevitable tendency to taint the public character as titular distinctions. These bodies too being in general not open to *property*, or *office*, they are in no respect to be compared to the nobles of europe. They might affect the *forms* of a free government as much, but they did not in the same proportion injure the *spirit* of freedom.

[6] [Mackintosh's footnote:] 'Did we not dread the ridicule of political prediction, it would not seem difficult to assign its period. Church power (unless some Revolution, auspicious to statecraft, should replunge Europe into ignorance) will certainly not survive the nineteenth century.'

[7] [Mackintosh's footnote:] 'I always understand their *corporate* existence.'

[8] [Mackintosh's footnote:] '*Odium Theologicum*'.

character. The latter, however, is totally irrelevant; for we are not discussing what place they ought to occupy in society as individuals, but as a body. We are not considering the demerit of citizens whom it is fit to punish, but the spirit of a body which it is politic to dissolve.

The Judicial Aristocracy formed by the Parliaments, seems still less susceptible of union with a free government. Their spirit and claims were equally incompatible with liberty. They had imbibed a spirit congenial to the authority under which they had acted, and suitable to the arbitrary genius of the laws which they had dispensed; while they retained those ambiguous and indefinite claims to a share in the legislation, which the fluctuations of power in the kingdom had in some degree countenanced. The spirit of a corporation was from the smallness of their numbers more concentrated and vigorous in them than in the Nobles and Clergy; . . . Courts of justice, in which seats were legally purchased, had too long been endured: judges who regarded the right of dispensing justice as a marketable commodity, could neither be fit organs of equitable laws, nor suitable magistrates for a free state. . . .

The three Aristocracies – Military, Sacerdotal, and Judicial – may be considered as having formed the French Government. They have appeared, so far as we have considered them, incorrigible. All attempts to improve them would have been little better than (to use the words of Mr. Burke) 'mean reparations on mighty ruins.' They were not perverted by the accidental depravity of their members; they were not infected by any transient passion, which new circumstances would extirpate; the fault was in the essence of the institutions themselves, which were irreconcileable with a free government.

But, it is objected, these institutions might have been *gradually* reformed[9] the spirit of freedom would have silently entered; the progressive wisdom of an enlightened nation would have remedied, in process of time, their defects, without convulsion. To this argument I confidently answer, that these institutions would have destroyed Liberty, before Liberty had corrected their spirit. Power vegetates with more vigour after these gentle prunings. A slender reform amuses and lulls the people: the popular enthusiasm subsides; and the moment of effectual reform is irretrievably lost. No important political improvement was ever obtained in a period of tranquillity. The corrupt interest of the governors is so strong, and the cry of the people so feeble, that it were vain to expect it. If the effervescence of the popular mind is suffered to pass

---

[9] [Mackintosh's footnote:] Burke, pp. 248–52, [Mackintosh does not quote precisely. The passage is, in this selection, p. 93].

away without effect, it would be absurd to expect from languor what enthusiasm has not obtained. If radical reform is not, at such a moment, procured, all partial changes are evaded and defeated in the tranquillity which succeeds.[10] The gradual reform that arises from the presiding principle exhibited in the specious theory of Mr. Burke, is belied by the experience of all ages. Whatever excellence, whatever freedom is discoverable in governments, has been infused into them by the shock of a revolution: and, their subsequent progress has been only the accumulation of abuse. It is hence that the most enlightened politicians have recognised the necessity of frequently recalling their first principles; – a truth equally suggested by the penetrating intellect of Machiavel, by his experience of the Florentine democracy, and by his research into the history of ancient commonwealths. Whatever is good ought to be pursued at the moment it is attainable. The public voice, irresistible in a period of convulsion, is contemned with impunity, when spoken during the lethargy into which nations are lulled by the tranquil course of their ordinary affairs . . . The National Assembly seized the moment of eradicating the corruptions and abuses which afflicted their country. Their reform was total, that it might be commensurate with the evil: and no part of it was delayed, because to spare an abuse at such a period was to consecrate it; and as the enthusiasm which carries nations to such enterprises is short-lived, so the opportunity of reform, if once neglected, might be irrevocably fled.

. . . By what principle of reason, or of justice, were they precluded from aspiring to give France a government less imperfect than accident had formed in other states? Who will be hardy enough to assert, that a better constitution is not attainable than any which has hitherto appeared? Is the limit of human wisdom to be estimated in the science of politics alone, by the extent of its present attainments? . . .

That guilt (if it be guilt) is imputable to the National Assembly. They are accused of having rejected the guidance of experience, – of having abandoned themselves to the illusion of theory, and of having sacrificed great and attainable good to the magnificent chimeras of ideal excellence. If this accusation be just, – if they have

---

[10] [Mackintosh's footnote:] 'Ignore-t-on que c'est on attaquant, en renversant tous les abus à la fois, qu'on peut espérer de s'en voir délivré sans retour; que les réformes lentes et partielles ont toujours fini par ne rien réformer; enfin, que l'abus que l'on conserve devient l'appui et bientôt le restaurateur de tous ceux qu'on croioit avoir détruits?'
[Can it be ignored that it is in attacking and reversing abuses all at once that one can hope to see oneself delivered from them once and for all; that slow and partial reforms have always ended by reforming nothing; so that the abuse which remains becomes the resting place and soon the restorer of all those that one believed oneself to have destroyed.] Adresse aux François par l'Evêque d'Autun, 11 février, 1790).

indeed abandoned experience, the basis of human knowledge, as well as the guide of human action, – their conduct deserves no longer any serious argument: but if (as Mr. Burke more than once insinuates) their contempt of it is avowed and ostentatious, it was surely unworthy of him to have expended so much genius against so preposterous an insanity. But the explanation of *terms* will diminish our wonder. Experience may, both in the arts and in the conduct of human life, be regarded in a double view, either as furnishing *models*, or *principles*. An artist who frames his machine in exact imitation of his predecessor, is in the *first sense* said to be guided by experience. In this sense all improvements of human life have been *deviations* from experience. The first visionary innovator was the savage who built a cabin, or covered himself with a rug. If this be experience, man is degraded to the unimproveable level of the instinctive animals. But in the second acceptation, an artist is said to be guided by experience, when the inspection of a machine discovers to him principles, which teach him to improve it: or when the comparison of many, both with respect to their excellences and defects, enables him to frame one different from any he had examined, and still more perfect. In this latter sense, the National Assembly have perpetually availed themselves of experience. History is an immense collection of experiments on the nature and effect of the various parts of various governments. Some institutions are experimentally ascertained to be beneficial; some to be most indubitably destructive; a third class, which produces partial good, obviously possesses the capacity of improvement. What, on such a survey, was the dictate of enlightened experience? Not surely to follow any model in which these institutions lay indiscriminately mingled; but, like the mechanic, to compare and generalise, and, guided equally by experience, to imitate and reject, . . . an experience liberal and enlightened, which hears the testimony of ages and nations, and collects from it the general principles which regulate the mechanism of society.

Legislators are under no obligation to retain a constitution, because it has been found '*tolerably* to answer the common purposes of government.' It is absurd to *expect*, but it is not absurd to *pursue* perfection. It is absurd to acquiesce in evils, of which the remedy is obvious, because they are less grievous than those which are endured by others. To suppose that social order is not capable of improvement from the progress of the human understanding, is to betray the inconsistent absurdity of an arrogant confidence in our attainments, and an abject distrust of our powers. If, indeed, the sum of evil produced by political institutions, even in the least imperfect governments, were small, there might be some pretence for this dread of innovation, – this horror at any remedy, – which has raised such a clamour over

Europe. But, on the contrary, in an estimate of the sources of human misery, after granting that one portion is to be attributed to disease, and another to private vices, it might perhaps be found that a third equal part arose from the oppressions and corruptions of government, disguised under various forms. All the governments that now exist in the world (except that of the United States of America) have been fortuitously formed: they are not the work of art. They have been altered, impaired, improved, and destroyed by accidental circumstances, beyond the foresight or control of wisdom. Their parts thrown up against present emergencies formed no systematic whole. It was certainly not to have been presumed, that these *fortuitous products* should have surpassed the works of intellect, and precluded all nearer approaches to perfection. Their origin without doubt furnishes a strong presumption of an opposite nature. It might teach us to expect in them many discordant principles, many jarring forms, much unmixed evil, and much imperfect good, – many institutions which had long survived their motive, and many of which reason had never been the author, nor utility the object . . .

. . . It was time that the human powers, so long occupied by subordinate objects, and inferior arts, should mark the commencement of a new era in history, by giving birth to the art of improving government, and increasing the civil happiness of man. It was time, as it has been wisely and eloquently said, that – legislators, instead of that narrow and dastardly *coasting*, which never ventures to lose sight of usage and precedent, should, guided by the *polarity* of reason, hazard a bolder navigation, and discover, in unexplored regions, the treasure of public felicity.

The task of the French legislators was, however, less hazardous. The philosophers of Europe had for a century discussed all objects of public economy. The conviction of a great majority of enlightened men had, after many controversies, become on most questions of general politics, uniform. A degree of certainty, perhaps nearly equal to that which such topics will admit, had been attained. The National Assembly were, therefore, not called on to make discoveries: it was sufficient if they were not uninfluenced by the opinions, nor exempt from the spirit of their age. They were fortunate enough to live in a period when it was only necessary to affix the stamp of laws to what had been prepared by the research of philosophy. They will here, however, be attacked by a futile common-place. The most specious theory, it will be said, is often impracticable; and any attempt to transfer speculative doctrines into the practice of states is chimerical and frantic. If by 'theory' be understood vague conjecture, the objection is not worth discussion: but if by theory be meant inference from the moral nature and political state of man, then I assert, that whatever such theory pronounces to be true, must be practicable, and that whatever on the subject is impracticable, must be false. To resume the illustration from the mechanical arts:- geometry, it may be justly said, bears nearly the same relation to mechanics that abstract reasoning does to politics.[11] The moral forces which are employed in politics are the passions and interests of men, of which it is the province of metaphysics to teach the nature and calculate the strength, as mathematics do those of the mechanical powers. Now suppose it had been mathematically proved, that by a certain alteration in the structure of a machine, its effect would be increased four-fold, would an instructed mechanic hesitate about the change? Would he be deterred, because he was the first to discover it? Would he thus sacrifice his own advantage to the blindness of his predecessors, and the obstinacy of his cotemporaries? Let us suppose a whole nation, of which the artizans thus rejected theoretical improvement: mechanics might there, as a *science*, be most profoundly understood, while, as an *art*, it exhibited nothing but rudeness and barbarism. The principles of Newton and Archimedes might be taught in the schools, while the architecture of the people might not have reached beyond the cabins of New Holland, or the ship-building of the Esquimaux. In a state of political science somewhat similar has Europe continued for a great part of the eighteenth century.[12]

All the great questions of general politics had, as we have remarked, been nearly decided, and almost all the decisions had been hostile to established institutions; yet these institutions still flourished in all their vigour. The same man who cultivated liberal science in his cabinet was compelled to administer a barbarous jurisprudence on the bench. The same Montesquieu, who at Paris reasoned as a philosopher of the eighteenth, was compelled to decide at Bourdeaux as a magistrate of the fourteenth century. The apostles of toleration and the ministers of the Inquisition were contemporaries. The torture continued to be practised in the age of

[11] [Mackintosh's footnote:] 'I confess my obligation for this parallel to a learned friend, who though so justly admired in the republic of letters for his excellent writings, is still more so by his friends for the rich, original, and masculine turn of thought that animates his conversation. But the Continuator of the History of Philip III, little needs my praise.'

[12] [Mackintosh's footnote:] 'Mechanics, because no passion or interest is concerned in the perpetuity of abuse, always yield to scientific improvement: politics, for the contrary reason, always resist it. It was the remark of Hobbes, 'that if any interest or passion were concerned in disputing the theorems of geometry, different opinions would be maintained regarding them.' It has actually happened (as if to justify the remark of that great man) that under the administration of Turgot a financial reform, grounded on a mathematical demonstration, has been derided as visionary nonsense. So much for the sage preference of practice to theory.'

Beccaria[13]: the Bastile devoured its victims in the country of Turgot. The criminal code, even where it was the mildest, was oppressive and savage. The laws respecting religious opinion, even where there was a pretended toleration, outraged the most evident deductions of reason. The true principles of commercial policy, though they had been reduced to demonstration, influenced the councils of no states. Such was the fantastic spectacle presented by the European nations, who, philosophers in theory, and barbarians in practice, exhibited to the observing eye two opposite and inconsistent aspects of manners and opinions. But such a state of things carried in itself the seeds of its own destruction. Men will not long dwell in hovels, with the model of a palace before their eyes.

  Such was indeed in some measure the position of the ancient world. But the art of printing had not then provided a channel by which the opinions of the learned pass insensibly into the popular mind. A bulwark then existed between the body of mankind and the reflecting few. They were distinct nations, inhabiting the same country; and the opinions of the one (I speak comparatively with modern times) had little influence on those of the other. But that bulwark is now levelled with the ground. The convictions of philosophy insinuate themselves by a slow, but certain progress, into popular sentiment. It is vain for the arrogance of learning to condemn the people to ignorance by reprobating superficial knowledge. The people cannot be profound; but the truths which regulate the moral and political relations of man, are at no great distance from the surface. The great works in which discoveries are contained cannot be read by the people; but their substance passes through a variety of minute and circuitous channels to the shop and the hamlet. . . .

  . . . The philosophers of antiquity did not, like Archimedes, want a spot on which to fix their engines; but they wanted an engine wherewith to move the moral world. The press is that engine, and has subjected the powerful to the wise. The discussion of great truths has prepared a body of laws for the National Assembly: . . . Whatever be the ultimate fate of the French Revolutionists, the friends of freedom must ever consider them as the authors of the greatest attempt that has hitherto been made in the cause of man. They never can cease to rejoice, that in the long catalogue of calamities and crimes which blacken human annals, the year 1789 presents one spot on which the eye of humanity may with complacence dwell.

  . . .

---

[13] Cesare Beccaria, d. 1794: a legal reformer whose famous *On Crimes and Punishment* anticipates the utilitarian approach of Bentham.

A Uniform Whig

"I preserve consistency, by varying my means, to secure the unity of my end." Burkes Reflections V.354.

Plate 4. *A Uniform Whig* (James Gillray, 1791). Burke is here pictured as a politically split character. To his right is a bust of King George III, on which he leans, and he carries in his right hand a copy of *Reflections* . . . His right pockets are stuffed with money and his right foot is well shod. In his left hand he carries the cap of liberty, his left shoe is unshod, his pocket is empty and his right lapel conspicuously less ornate than his right. Behind him, in the distance, the figure of Fortuna is balanced on a windmill symbolising inconstancy.

EDMUND BURKE

Burke ignored most of the replies to his *Reflections*. He was, however concerned to win over the Whig party to his view of the Revolution. The major obstacle to this was Charles James Fox, the fast-living leader of the party in the Commons and 'out of doors', and Burke's close collaborator in reform of the East India Company's rule in India and the Royal Finances. Fox remained determined to court the support of moderate reformers; Burke insistent that reform was a Trojan horse designed to introduce French Republicanism to Britain. In a dramatic scene in the House of Commons on 6 May 1791 they had very publicly ended their career-long friendship over their differences on the danger posed by the French Revolution.

During that summer the two fought for the support of the party aristocrats. Fox spent the summer in a triumphal 'progress' round the houses of Whig grandees, studiously avoiding demotic gatherings. Advised by the antiquarian lawyer Francis Hargrave, he claimed his version of radical whiggery was completely consistent with the principles of the party derived from the Revolution of 1688. In response, Burke composed the *Appeal from the New to the Old Whigs*, to 'defend myself against the extraordinary attacks of some of my late political friends'.[1] It was to be a continuing struggle. Two years later Burke's *Observations on the Conduct of the minority* was, not altogether outrageously, subtitled in a pirated edition: *Fifty-four articles of impeachment against the Rt. Hon. C. J. Fox*! In 1794 the conservative Whigs joined Pitt's Administration and Fox and his followers forced a motion rejecting the war with France. Thus Burke's aim of persuading the Whigs to support opposition to France was realised, albeit at the cost of splitting his party.

The *Appeal*'s claim is that the views put forward in *Reflections* are simply an articulation of the principles of the constitution implemented in 1688. His method of proving this is to show that Burke's views entirely fit with the

---

[1] L. G. Mitchell, *Charles James Fox and the Disintegration of the Whig Party 1782–1794* (Oxford University Press, 1971), pp. 174–5; Burke to C. C. Smith, 22 July 1791 cited in O'Gorman, *Whig Party*, p. 74.

exposition of those principles given by the Whig prosecutors of the famous Tory priest Dr Sacheverell.

The *Appeal* gave Burke the opportunity to make clear his conception of the English constitution and English political culture, a view which in *Reflections* often remained implicit in his criticism of revolutionary France.

The *Appeal* . . . was published on 3 August 1791 and reprinted five times within the year. It was also published in Dublin and New York, and translated into French.

There is no modern scholarly edition of the *Appeal*. It is to be found in all the collected editions of Burke's *Works*. It will appear in vol. IV of the *Writings and Speeches* (Oxford University Press, forthcoming).

This text is taken from Bohn's standard library edition of *Burke's Works*, 6 vols (London, Bell, 1887) vol. III.

FURTHER READING

Mitchell, L. G. *Charles James Fox and the Disintegration of the Whig Party 1782–1794* (Oxford University Press, 1971).
O'Gorman, F. *The Whig Party and the French Revolution* (London and New York: Macmillan, 1967).

An Appeal from the New to the Old Whigs in consequence of some late discussions in Parliament, relative to the reflections on the French revolution (1791)

[Mr. Burke's] associates conceive it, though a harsh, yet a necessary office, in full parliament to declare to the present age . . . that by one book he has disgraced the whole tenour of his life . . . He is advised to retire, whilst they continue to serve the public upon wiser principles, and under better auspices.

. . .

. . . It is certainly well for Mr. Burke that there are impartial men in the world. To them I address myself, pending the appeal which on his part is made from the living to the dead, from the modern Whigs to the ancient.

. . . [In *Reflections* . . .] He proposed to convey to a foreign people, not his own ideas, but the prevalent opinions and sentiments of a nation, renowned for wisdom, and celebrated in all ages for a well-understood and well-regulated love of freedom. This was the avowed purpose of the far greater part of his work. . . .

. . .

He had undertaken to demonstrate by arguments, which he thought could not be refuted, and by documents, which he was sure could not be denied that no comparison was to be made between the British government and the French usurpation. – That they who endeavoured madly to compare them, were by no means making the comparison of one good system with another good system, which varied only in local and circumstantial differences; much less, that they were holding out to us a superior pattern of legal liberty, which we might substitute in the place of our old, and, as they described it, superannuated, constitution. He meant to demonstrate, that the French scheme was not a comparative good, but a positive evil. . . .

. . . so fundamentally wrong, as to be utterly incapable of correcting itself by any length of time, or of being formed into any mode of polity, of which a member of the House of Commons could publicly declare his approbation.

. . .

He was prepared to show the madness of their declaration of the pretended rights of man; the childish futility of some of their maxims; the gross and stupid absurdity, and the palpable falsity, of others; and the mischievous tendency of all such declarations to the well-being of men and of citizens, and to the safety and prosperity of every just commonwealth. He was prepared to show that, in their conduct, the Assembly had directly violated not only every sound principle of government, but every one, without exception, of their own false or futile maxims; and indeed every rule they had pretended to lay down for their own direction.

. . .

. . . He cannot rejoice at the destruction of a monarchy, mitigated by manners, respectful to laws and usages, and attentive, perhaps but too attentive, to public opinion, in favour of the tyranny of a licentious, ferocious, and savage multitude, without laws, manners or morals, and which so far from respecting the general sense of mankind, insolently endeavours to alter all the principles and opinions, which have hitherto guided and contained the world, and to force them into a conformity to their views and actions. . . .

. . .

The burthen of proof lies heavily on those who tear to pieces the whole frame and contexture of their country, that they could find no other way of settling a government fit to obtain its rational ends, except that which they have pursued by means unfavourable to all the present happiness of millions of people, and to the utter ruin of several hundreds of thousands. In their political arrangements, men have *no right* to put the well-being of the present generation wholly out of the question.

Perhaps the *only* moral trust with any certainty in our hands, is the care of our own time. With regard to, futurity, we are to treat it like a ward.[2] We are not so to attempt an improvement of his fortune, as to put the capital of his estate to any hazard.

It is not worth our while to discuss, like sophisters, whether, in no case, some evil, for the sake of some benefit, is to be tolerated. Nothing universal can be rationally affirmed on any moral or any political subject. Pure metaphysical abstraction does not belong to these matters. The lines of morality are not like ideal lines of mathematics. They are broad and deep as well as long. They admit of exceptions; they demand modifications. These exceptions and modifications are not made by the process of logic, but by the rules of prudence. Prudence is not only the first in rank of the virtues political and moral, but she is the director, the regulator, the standard of them all . . . Without attempting therefore to define, what never can be defined, the case of a revolution in government, this I think may be safely affirmed, that a sore and pressing evil is to be removed, and that a good, great in its amount and unequivocal in its nature, must be probable almost to certainty, before the inestimable price of our own morals, and the well-being of a number of our fellow-citizens, is paid for a revolution. If ever we ought to be economists even to parsimony, it is in voluntary production of evil. Every revolution contains in it something of evil.

. . .

The attacks on the author's consistency relative to France are (however grievous they may be to his feelings) in a great degree external to him and to us, and comparatively of little moment to the people of England. The substantial charge upon him is concerning his doctrines relative to the Revolution of 1688 . . . But he is not guilty in any sense. I maintain that in his *Reflections* he has stated the Revolution and the Settlement upon their true principles of legal reason and constitutional policy.

His authorities are the acts and declarations of parliament given in their proper words . . . but it must be proved that his construction is in perfect harmony with that of the ancient whigs, to whom, against the sentence of the modern, on his part I here appeal.

. . . It rarely happens to a party to have the opportunity of a clear authentic, recorded declaration of their political tenets upon the subject of a great constitutional event like that of the Revolution. The Whigs had that opportunity, or, to speak more

[2] Wardship is a legal position of responsibility for the person and property of an individual who is incapacitated (usually by age) from acting in their own right. Crucially, anyone exercising wardship was not entitled to put the ward's property at risk.

properly, they made it. The impeachment of Dr. Sacheverel was undertaken by a Whig ministry and a Whig House of Commons, and carried on before a prevalent and, steady majority of Whig peers. – It was carried on for the express purpose of stating the true grounds and principles of the Revolution; what the, Commons emphatically called their *foundation*.[3] . . . The new Whigs hold, that the sovereignty, whether exercised by one or many, did not only originate *from* the people, (a position not denied nor worth denying or assenting to,) but that in the people the same sovereignty constantly and unalienably resides; that the people may lawfully depose kings, not only for misconduct, but without any misconduct at all; that they may set up any new fashion of' government for themselves, or continue without any government at their pleasure; that the people are essentially their own rule and their will the measure of their conduct; . . .

    I assert, that the ancient Whigs held doctrines totally different from those I have last mentioned. I assert that the foundations laid down by the Commons on the trial of Dr. Sacheverel, for justifying the Revolution of 1688, are the very same laid down in Mr. Burke's Reflections; that is to say, – a breach of the *original contract,* implied and expressed in the constitution of this country, as a scheme of government fundamentally and inviolably fixed in King, Lords, and Commons. – That the fundamental subversion of this ancient constitution, by one of its parts, – having been attempted, and in effect accomplished, justified the Revolution. That it was justified *only* upon the necessity of the case; as the *only* means left for the recovery of that ancient constitution, formed by the original contract of the British state; as well as for the future preservation of the *same* government, These are the points to be proved.

[Burke then quotes at length from the prosecution case at the famous trial of Dr Sacheverell, who, in preaching a sermon on non-resistance, cleverly impugned the legitimacy of the post-1688 settlement, derived as it was from the parliamentary resistance to James II. The Whigs were under severe ideological pressure: they

---

[3] Dr Sacheverell, a notorious High Tory Priest, was impeached before the Lords on the grounds of having preached and published a 'seditious libel' in the form of a sermon which claimed that the 'grand security of our Government . . . is founded upon the steady belief of the subject's obligation to an Absolute and Unconditional Obedience to the Supreme Power', precisely what had provoked the Glorious Revolution. This had, however, put the Whigs in the uncomfortable position of having to prove – before the Queen herself – that the grounds of the constitution were those of *dis*obedience. See Geoffrey Holmes, *The Trial of Dr Sacheverell* (1973).

could hardly press the case for the right of resistance without appearing disloyal to Queen Anne, yet if they denied the right, they acknowledged that their overthrow of James II was illegal. The trial was thus a 'show trial' in which constitutional principles, as much as Dr Sacheverell himself, were in the dock.]

. . .

I do not wish to enter very much at large into the discussions which diverge and ramify in all ways from this productive subject. But there is one topic upon which I hope I shall be excused in going a little beyond my design. The factions, now so busy amongst us, in order to divest men of all love for their country, and to remove from their minds all duty with regard to the state, endeavour to propagate an opinion, that the *people*, informing their commonwealth, have by no means parted with their power over it. This is an impregnable citadel, to which these gentlemen retreat whenever they are pushed by the battery of laws and usages, and positive conventions. Indeed it is such and of so great force, that all they have done, in defending their outworks, is so much time and labour thrown away. Discuss any of their schemes – their answer is – It is the act of the *people*, and that is sufficient. Are we to deny to a *majority* of the people the right of altering even the whole frame of their society, if such should be their pleasure? They may change it, say they, from a monarchy to a republic to-day, and to-morrow back again from a republic to a monarchy; and so backward and forward as often as they like. They are master of the commonwealth; because in substance they are themselves the commonwealth. The French Revolution, say they, was the act of the majority of the people; and if the majority of any other people, the people of England for instance, wish to make the same change, they have the same right.

Just the same undoubtedly. That is, none at all. Neither the few nor the many have a right to act merely by their will, in any matter connected with duty, trust, engagement, or obligation. The constitution of a country being once settled upon some compact, tacit or expressed, there is no power existing of force to alter it, without the breach of the covenant, or the consent of all the parties. Such is the nature of a contract. And the votes of a majority of the people, whatever their infamous flatterers may teach in order to corrupt their minds, cannot alter the moral any more than they can alter physical essence of things. The people are not to be taught to think lightly of their engagements to their governors; else they teach governors to think lightly of their engagements towards them. In that kind of game in the end the people are sure to be losers. . . .

. . .

It is not necessary to teach men to thirst after power. But it is very expedient that by moral instruction they should be taught, and by their civil constitutions they should be compelled, to put many restrictions upon the immoderate exercise of it, and the inordinate desire. The best method of obtaining these two great points forms the important, but at the same time the difficult, problem to the statesman . . . For this reason no legislator, at any period of the world, has willingly placed the seat of active power in the hands of the multitude; because there it admits of no control, no regulation, no steady direction whatsoever. The people are the natural control on authority; but to exercise and to control together is contradictory and impossible.

As the exorbitant exercise of power cannot, under popular sway, be effectually restrained, the other great object of political arrangement, the means of abating, an excessive desire of it, is in such a state worse provided for. The democratic commonwealth is the foodful nurse of ambition. Under the other forms it meets with many restraints. Whenever, in states which have had a democratic basis, the legislators have endeavoured to put restraints upon ambition, their methods were as violent, as in the end they were ineffectual: as violent indeed as any the most jealous despotism could invent. The ostracism could not very long save itself, and much less the state which it was meant to guard, from the attempts of ambition, one of the natural, inbred, incurable distempers of a powerful democracy.

But to return from this short digression, which however is not wholly foreign to the question of the effect of the will of the majority upon the form or the existence of their society. I cannot too often recommend it to the serious consideration of all men, who think civil society to be within the province of moral jurisdiction, that if we owe to it any duty, it is not subject to our will. Duties are not voluntary. Duty and will are even contradictory terms. Now though civil society might be at first a voluntary act, (which in many cases it undoubtedly was,) its continuance is under a permanent, standing covenant, co-existing with the society; and it attaches upon every individual of that society, without any formal act of his own. This is warranted by the general practice, arising out of the general sense of mankind. Men without their choice derive benefits from that association; without their choice they are subjected to duties in consequence of these benefits; and without their choice they enter into a virtual obligation as binding as any that is actual. Look through the whole of life and the whole system of duties. Much the strongest moral obligations are such as were never the results of our option . . . We have obligations to mankind at large, which are not in consequence of any special voluntary pact. They arise from the relation of man to man and man to God, which relations are not matters of choice. On the contrary, the force of all the pacts which we enter into with any particular person, or number of persons amongst mankind, depends upon those prior obligations. In some cases the subordinate relations are voluntary, in others they are necessary – but the duties are all compulsive. When we marry, the choice is voluntary, but the duties are not matter of choice. They are dictated by the nature of the situation . . . Dark and inscrutable are the ways by which we come into the world. The instincts which give rise to this mysterious process of nature are not of our making. But out of physical causes, unknown to us, perhaps unknowable, arise moral duties, which as we are able perfectly to comprehend we are bound indispensably to perform. Parents may not be consenting to their moral relation; but consenting or not, they are bound to a long train of burthensome duties towards those with whom they have never made a covenant of any sort. Children are not consenting to their relation, but their relation, without their actual consent, binds them to its duties; or rather it implies their consent, because the presumed consent of every rational creature is in unison with the predisposed order of things. Men come in that manner into a community with the social state of their parents, endowed with all the benefits, loaded with all the duties, of their situation. If the social ties and ligaments, spun out of those physical relations which are the elements of the commonwealth, in most cases begin, and always continue, independently of our will; so, without any stipulation on our own part, are we bound by that relation called our country, which comprehends (as it has been well said) 'all the charities of all'. Nor are we left without powerful instincts to make this duty as dear and grateful to us, as it is awful and coercive. Our country is not a thing of mere physical locality. It consists, in a great measure, in the ancient order into which we are born. We may have the same geographical situation, but another country; as we may have the same country in another soil. The place that determines our duty to our country is a social, civil relation.

. . .

I admit, indeed, that in morals, as in all things else, difficulties will sometimes occur. Duties will sometimes cross one another. Then questions will arise, which of them is to be placed in subordination; which of them may be entirely superseded? These doubts give rise to that part of moral science called *casuistry*; which, though necessary to be well studied . . . there is a danger that it may totally subvert those offices which it is its object only to methodize and reconcile. Duties, at their extreme bounds, are drawn very fine, so as to become evanescent . . . But the very habit of stating these extreme cases is not very laudable or safe: because, in general it is not right to turn our duties into doubts. They are imposed to govern our conduct, not to exercise our ingenuity; and therefore, our opinions about them ought not to be in a state of fluctuation, but steady, sure, and resolved.

Amongst these nice and therefore dangerous points of casuistry, may be reckoned the question . . . – Whether, after the people have discharged themselves of their original power by an habitual delegation, no occasion can possibly occur which may justify the resumption of it? . . . it is far from difficult to foresee the perilous consequences of the resuscitation of such a power in the people. The practical consequences of any political tenet go a great way in deciding upon its value. Political problems do not primarily concern truth or falsehood. They relate to good or evil. What in the result is likely to produce evil, is politically false: that which is productive of good, politically true.

. . .

. . . When the supreme authority of the people is in question, before we attempt to extend or confine it, we ought to fix in our minds, with some degree of distinctness, an idea of what it is we mean when we say the PEOPLE.

In a state of *rude* nature there is no such thing as a people.[4] A number of men in themselves have no collective capacity. The idea of a people is the idea of a corporation. It is wholly artificial; and made, like all other legal fictions, by common agreement. What the particular nature of that agreement was, is collected from the form into which the particular society has been cast. Any other is not *their* covenant. When men, therefore, break up the original compact or agreement which gives its corporate form and capacity to a state, they are no longer a people; they have no longer a corporate existence; they have no longer a legal, coactive force to bind within, nor a claim to be recognised abroad. They are a number of vague, loose individuals, and nothing more. With them all is to begin again. Alas! they little know how many a weary step is to be taken before they can form themselves into a mass, which has a true, politic personality.

We hear much from men, who have not acquired their hardness of assertion from the profundity of their thinking about the omnipotence of a *majority*, in such a dissolution of an ancient society as hath taken place in France. But amongst men so disbanded; there can be no such thing as majority, or minority; or power in any one person to bind another. The power of acting by a majority, which the gentlemen theorists seem to assume so readily, after they have violated the contract out of which

---

[4] The following account places a very Hobbesian emphasis on the anarchical qualities of the state of nature and the highly conventional character of social institutions.

it has arisen, (if at all it existed,) must be grounded on two assumptions; first, that of an incorporation produced by unanimity; and secondly, an unanimous agreement, that the act of a mere majority (say of one) shall pass with them and with others as the act of the whole.

. . . this idea of the decision of a majority . . . is one of the most violent fictions of positive law, that ever has been or can be made on the principles of artificial incorporation. Out of civil society nature knows nothing of it; nor are men, even when arranged according to civil order, otherwise than by very long training, brought at all to submit to it. The mind is brought far more easily to acquiesce in the proceedings of one man, or a few, who act under a general procuration for the state, than in the vote of a victorious majority in councils; in which every man has his share in the deliberation: For there the beaten party are exasperated and soured by the previous contention, and mortified by the conclusive defeat. This mode of decision . . . must be the result of a very particular and special convention, confirmed afterwards by long habits of obedience, by a sort of discipline in society, and by a strong hand, vested with stationary, permanent power, to enforce this sort of constructive general will . . . The laws in many countries to condemn require more than a mere majority; less than an equal number to acquit . . . In some incorporations one man speaks for the whole; in others, a few. Until the other day; in the constitution of Poland, unanimity was required to give validity to any act of their great national council or diet.[5] This approaches much more nearly to rude nature than the institutions of any other country. Such, indeed; every commonwealth must be, without a positive law to recognise in a certain number the will of the entire body.

If men dissolve their ancient incorporation, in order to regenerate their community, in that state of things each man has a right, if he pleases, to remain an individual. Any number of individuals, who can agree upon it, have an undoubted right to form themselves into a state apart, and wholly independent. If any of these is forced into the fellowship of another, this is conquest, and not compact. On every principle, which supposes society to be in virtue of a free covenant, this compulsive incorporation must be null and void.

As a people can have no right to a corporate capacity without universal consent, so neither have they a right to hold exclusively any lands in the name and title of a corporation. On the scheme of the present rulers in our neighbouring country,

---

[5] Up until the Great Diet of 1788–92, all votes in the Polish Diet [parliament] had to achieve unanimous support in order to be carried.

regenerated as they are, they have no more right to the territory called France than I have. Who are these insolent men calling themselves the French nation, that would monopolize this fair domain of nature? Is it because they speak a certain jargon? Is it their mode of chattering, to me unintelligible, that forms their title to my land? Who, are they who claim by prescription and descent from certain gangs of banditti called Franks, and Burgundians, and Visigoths,[6] of whom I may have never heard, and ninety-nine out of an hundred of themselves certainly never have heard; whilst at the very time they tell me, that prescription and long possession form no title to property? . . . By what they call reasoning without prejudice, they leave not one stone upon another in the fabric of human society. They subvert all the authority which they hold, as well as all that which they have destroyed.

As in the abstract, it is perfectly clear, that, out of a state of civil society, majority and minority are relations which can have no existence; and that, in civil society, its own specific conventions in each corporation determine what it is that constitutes the people . . . it is equally clear, that neither in France nor in England has the original or any subsequent compact of the state, expressed or implied, constituted *a majority of men, told by the head*, to be the acting people of their several communities. To enable men to act with the weight and character of a people, and to answer the ends for which they are incorporated into that capacity, we must suppose them (by means immediate or consequential) to be in that state of habitual social discipline, in which the wiser, the more expert, and the more opulent conduct, and by conducting enlighten and protect, the weaker, the less knowing, and the less provided with the goods of fortune. When the multitude are not under this discipline, they can scarcely be said to be in civil society . . .

A true natural aristocracy is not a separate interest in the state,[7] or separable from it. It is an essential integrant part of any large body rightly constituted. It is formed out of a class of legitimate presumptions, which, taken as generalities, must be admitted for actual truths. To be bred in a place of estimation; to see nothing low and sordid from one's infancy; to be taught to respect one's self; to be habituated to the censorial inspection of the public eye; to look early to public opinion; to stand upon such elevated ground as to be enabled to take a large view of the wide-spread and infinitely diversified combinations of men and affairs in a large society; to have leisure to read, to reflect, to converse; to be enabled to draw the court and

---

[6] The names of the tribes that invaded the Western Roman Empire in the fifth century.
[7] The claim made by the Abbé Sieyes in persuading the third estate (of commoners) to withdraw from the States General and assert itself as alone the representative of the State.

attention of the wise and learned wherever they are to be found; – to be habituated in armies to command and to obey; to be taught to despise danger in the pursuit of honour and duty; to be formed to the greatest degree of vigilance, foresight, and circumspection, in a state of things in which no fault is committed with impunity, and the slightest mistakes draw on the most ruinous consequences – to be led to a guarded and regulated conduct, from a sense that you are considered as an instructor of your fellow-citizens in their highest concerns, and that you act as a reconciler between God and man – to be employed as an administrator of law and justice, and to be thereby amongst the first benefactors to mankind – to be a professor of high science, or of liberal and ingenuous art – to be amongst rich traders, who from their success are presumed to have sharp and vigorous understandings, and to possess the virtues of diligence, order, constancy, and regularity, and to have cultivated an habitual regard to commutative justice – these are the circumstances of men, that form what I should call a *natural* aristocracy, without which there is no nation.

The state of civil society, which necessarily generates this aristocracy, is a state of nature; and much more truly so than a savage and incoherent mode of life. For man is by nature reasonable; and he is never perfectly in his natural state, but when he is placed where reason may be best cultivated, and most predominates. Art is man's nature. We are as much, at least, in a state of nature in formed manhood, as in immature and helpless infancy. Men, qualified in the manner I have just described, form in nature, as she operates in the common modification of society, the leading, guiding, and governing part. It is the soul to the body . . .

When great multitudes act together, under that discipline of nature, I recognise the PEOPLE. I acknowledge something that perhaps equals, and ought always to guide, the sovereignty of convention. In all things: the voice of this grand chorus of national harmony ought to have a mighty and decisive influence. But when you disturb this harmony; when you break up this beautiful order, this array of truth and nature, as well as of habit and prejudice; when you separate the common sort of men from their proper chieftains, so as to form them into an adverse army, I no longer know that venerable object called the People in such a disbanded race of deserters and vagabonds . . . They are, as they have always been reputed, rebels, They may lawfully be fought with, and brought under, whenever an advantage offers. Those who attempt by outrage and violence to deprive men of any advantage which they hold under the laws, and to destroy the natural order of life, proclaim war against them.

. . .

The pretended *rights of man*, which have made this havoc, cannot be the rights of the people. For to be a people and to have these rights, are things incompatible. The one supposes the presence, the other the absence, of a state of civil society. . . .

. . .

. . . Before [men] listen even to moderate alterations in the government of their country, they ought to take care that principles are not propagated for that purpose, which are too big for their object. Doctrines limited in their present application, and wide in their general principles, are never meant to be confined to what they at first pretend. If I were to form a prognostic of the effect of the present machinations on the people, from their sense of any grievance they suffer under this constitution, my mind would be at ease . . . It is certain, that its power is by no means in exact proportion to its reasonableness. It must always have been discoverable by persons of reflection, but it is now obvious to the world, that a theory concerning government may become as much a cause of fanaticism as dogma in religion. There is a boundary to men's passions when they act from feeling; none when they are under the influence of imagination. Remove a grievance, and, when men act from feeling, you go a great way; towards quieting, a commotion. But . . . When a man is, from system, furious against monarchy or episcopacy, the good conduct of the monarch or the bishop has no other effect, than further to irritate the adversary. He is provoked at it as furnishing a plea for preserving the thing which he wishes to destroy. His mind will be heated as much by the sight of a sceptre, a mace, or a verge, as if he had been daily bruised and wounded by these symbols of authority. Mere spectacles, mere names, will become sufficient causes to stimulate the people to war and tumult.

. . .

. . . What security is there for stopping short at all in these wild conceits? Why, neither more nor less than this – that the moral sentiments of some few amongst them do put some check on their savage theories. But let us take care. The moral sentiments, so nearly connected with early prejudice as to be almost one and the same thing, will assuredly not live long under a discipline, which has for its basis the destruction of all prejudices, and the making the mind proof against all dread of consequences flowing from the pretended truths that are taught by their philosophy.

In this school the moral sentiments must grow weaker and weaker everyday. The more cautious of these teachers, in laying down their maxims, draw as much of the conclusion as suits, not with their premises, but with their policy. They trust the rest to the sagacity of their pupils. Others, and these are the most vaunted for their spirit, not only lay down the same premises, but boldly draw the conclusions to the destruction of our whole constitution in church and state. But are these conclusions truly drawn? Yes, most certainly. Their principles are wild and wicked. But let justice be done even to frenzy and villainy. These teachers are perfectly systematic. No man who assumes their grounds can tolerate the British constitution in church or state. These teachers profess to scorn all mediocrity; to engage for perfection; to proceed by the simplest and shortest course. They build their politics, not on convenience, but on truth; and they profess to conduct men to certain happiness by the assertion of their undoubted rights. With them there is no compromise. All other governments are usurpations, which justify and even demand resistance.

. . .

The theory contained in his book is not to furnish principles for making a new constitution, but for illustrating the principles of a constitution already made. It is a theory drawn from the *fact* of our government. They who oppose it are bound to show, that his theory militates with that fact. Otherwise, their quarrel is not with his book, but with the constitution of their country. The whole scheme of our mixed constitution is to prevent any one of its principles from being carried as far, as, taken by itself, and theoretically, it would go. Allow that to be the true policy of the British system, then most of the faults with which that system stands charged will appear to be, not imperfections into which it has inadvertently fallen, but excellencies which it has studiously sought. To avoid the perfections of extreme, all its several parts are so constituted, as not alone to answer their own several ends, but also each to limit and control the others: insomuch, that take which of the principles you please – you will find its operation checked and stopped at a certain point. The whole movement stands still rather than that any part should proceed beyond its boundary. From thence it results, that in the British constitution, there is a perpetual treaty and compromise going on, sometimes openly, sometimes with less observation. . . .

. . .

It is the result of the thoughts of many minds, in many ages. It is no simple, superficial thing, nor to be estimated by superficial understandings. . . .

. . .

. . . We ought to understand it according to measure; and to venerate it where we are not able presently to comprehend.

Such admirers were our fathers to whom we owe this splendid inheritance. Let us improve it with zeal, but with fear. Let us follow our ancestors, men, not without a rational, though without an exclusive, confidence in themselves; who, by respecting the reason of others, who, by looking backward as well as forward; by the modesty as well as by the energy of their minds, went on, insensibly drawing this constitution nearer and nearer to its perfection, by never departing from its fundamental principles, nor introducing any amendment which had not a subsisting root in the laws, constitution, and usages of the kingdom. . . .

. . .

The Whigs of this day have before them, in this Appeal, their constitutional ancestors . . . They will choose for themselves. The author of the Reflections has chosen for himself. If the new order is coming on, and all the political opinions must pass away as dreams, which our ancestors have worshipped as revelations, I say for him, that he would rather be the last (as certainly he is the least) of that race of men, than the first and greatest of those who have coined to themselves Whig principles from a French die, unknown to the impress of our fathers in the constitution.

The Tree of LIBERTY, — with, the Devil tempting John Bull.

Plate 5. *The Tree of Liberty – with the Devil tempting John Bull* (James Gillray, 1798). In the Garden of Eden the serpent (Fox) tempts a well-fed John Bull with the apple of Reform from the tree of Opposition. Its roots are Envy, Ambition and Disappointment and its main branches are the Rights of Man and Profligacy, whilst the fruits include the French Liberty Cap, Revolution, Treason, Democracy, Atheism and the Corresponding Society. In the middle distance is the tree of Justice: its roots in the King, Lords and Commons, with its main branches of Law and Religion and fruits of Freedom, Happiness and Security. John Bull, his pockets full of fine 'pippins' from the tree of Justice, refuses the bitter 'medlar' of reform.

HANNAH MORE

BIOGRAPHICAL NOTE

Hannah More was born in Gloucestershire in 1745, the daughter of a schoolmaster who educated his daughters at home. She later learned languages at her oldest sister's boarding school in Bristol. Jilted by her long-time fiancé, who settled a £200 annuity on her, she renounced marriage and pursued an independent career as a playwright.[1] Through Garrick and Burke she joined their literary set, meeting Sam Johnson, Sir Joshua Reynolds and the 'bluestockings': the Elizabeths Vesey, Montagu and Carter, Hester Chapone and Frances Boscawen.[2]

In 1784 she supposedly retired from public life to Somerset. But there, under the influence of William Wilberforce and the orthodox wing of the Evangelical movement, she subsequently opened schools for the poor in several Somerset villages. She also wrote *Thoughts on the Importance of the Manners of the Great* (1788) and *An Estimate of the Religion of the Fashionable World* (1790) both of which sought to reform polite society.

In 1792, with **Village Politics**, she turned her attention to the lower orders whom she, like many others of her class, thought were dangerously influenced by revolutionary ideas. The work was a great success and was followed by the famous counter-revolutionary series, *Cheap Repository Tracts* (1795–8). Orthodox and traditionalist as she was, Hannah More promoted the education of women and established Women's Friendly Societies in Somerset.

---

[1] *A Search after Happiness: a pastoral drama* (Bristol, 1773); *The Inflexible Captive: a tragedy* (Bristol, 1774); *Percy: a tragedy* (London, 1778); *The Fatal Falsehood: a tragedy* (1779).
[2] In praise of these ladies' company she wrote:

> Let education's moral mint
> The noblest images imprint;
> Let taste her curious touchstones hold,
> To try if standard be the gold;
> But 'tis thy commerce, Conversation,
> Must give it use by circulation;
> That noblest commerce of mankind,
> Whose precious merchandise is MIND! ('The Bas Bleu' (1786), lines 242–51)

indicating an appreciation of the conversational aspects of culture emphasised earlier in the century by Shaftesbury and Hume.

EDITORIAL NOTE

The printed text is taken from *The Works of Hannah More*, 11 vols. (London: T. Cadell, 1830), vol. III.

Modern editions are:
Cheap Repository Tracts by Hannah More (New York: Garland, 1977).
Village politics (1793), with, *The Shepherd of Salisbury Plain* (*c.* 1820), Hannah More (Oxford and New York: Woodstock Books, 1995).

FURTHER READING

Hole, Robert, 'English Sermons and Tracts as Media of Debate', in M. Philp (ed.), *The French Revolution and British Popular Politics* (Cambridge: Cambridge University Press, 1991).
Hole, Robert 'British Counter-Revolutionary Popular Propaganda in the 1790s', in Colin Jones (ed.), *Britain and Revolutionary France: Conflict, Subversion and Propaganda* (Exeter: Exeter University Press, 1983).
Selected Writings of Hannah More, ed. and intr. Robert Hole (London: William Pickering, 1996).
Pederson, Susan, 'Hannah More Meets Simple Simon: Tracts, Chapbooks, and Popular Culture in Late Eighteenth-Century England', *Journal of British Studies*, 25 (1986).

Village Politics (1792)

Village politics. A dialogue between Jack Anvil, the blacksmith, and Tom Hod, the mason.

Jack.   What's the matter, Tom? Why dost look so dismal?

Tom.   Dismal, indeed! Well enough I may.

Jack.   What! is the old mare dead? or work scarce?

Tom.   No, no, work's plenty enough, if a man had but the heart to go to it.

Jack.   What book art reading? Why dost look so like a hang dog?

Tom.   (looking on his book.) Cause enough. Why I find here that I'm very unhappy, and very miserable; which I should never have known if I had not had the good luck to meet with this book. O, 'tis a precious book!

Jack.   A good sign, though, that you can't find out you're unhappy without looking into a book for it! What is the matter?

Tom.   Matter? Why I want liberty.

Jack.   Liberty! That's bad, indeed! What! has any one fetched a warrant for thee? Come, man, cheer up, I'll be bound for thee. – Thou art an honest fellow in the main, though thou dost tipple and prate a little too much at the Rose and Crown.

Tom.   No, no, I want a new Constitution.

Jack.   Indeed! Why I thought thou hadst been a desperate healthy fellow. Send for the doctor directly.

Tom.   I'm not sick; I want Liberty and Equality, and the Rights of Man.

Jack.   O, now I understand thee. What! thou art a leveller and a republican, I warrant!

Tom.   I'm a friend to the people. I want a reform.

Jack.   Then the shortest way is to mend thyself.

Tom.   But I want a general reform.

Jack.   Then let every one mend one.

Tom.   Pooh! I want freedom and happiness, the same as they have got in France.

Jack.   What, Tom, we imitate *them!* We follow the French! Why they only began all this mischief at first in order to be just what we are already; and what a blessed land must this be, to be in actual possession of all they ever hoped to gain by all their hurly-burly. Imitate *them*, indeed! Why I'd sooner go to the Negroes to get learning, or to the Turks to get religion, than to the French for freedom and happiness.

Tom.   What do you mean by that? ar'n't the French free?

Jack.   Free, Tom! aye, free with a witness. They are all so free that there's nobody safe. They make free to rob whom they will, and kill whom they will. If they don't like a man's looks, they make free to hang him without judge or jury, and the next lamp-post serves for the gallows; so then they call themselves free, because, you see, they have no law left to condemn them, and no king to take them up and hang them for it.

Tom.   Ah, but Jack, didn't their King formerly hang people for nothing too? and, besides, were not they all Papists before the Revolution?

Jack.   Why, true enough, they had but a poor sort of religion; but bad is better than none, Tom. And so was the government bad enough too; for they could clap an innocent man into prison, and keep him there, too, as long as they would, and never say, With your leave, or By your leave, Gentlemen of the Jury. But what's all that to us?

Tom. To us! Why don't our governors put many of our poor folks in prison against their will? What are all the gaols for? Down with the gaols, I say; all men should be free.

Jack. Hark'ee, Tom, a few rogues in prison keep the rest in order, and then honest men go about their business in safety, afraid of nobody; that's the way to be free. And let me tell thee, Tom, thou and I are tried by our peers as much as a lord is. Why the *King* can't send me to prison if I do no harm; and if I do, there's reason good why I should go there. I may go to law with Sir John at the great castle yonder; and he no more dares lift his little finger against me than if I were his equal. A lord is hanged for hanging matter, as thou or I should be; and if it will be any comfort to thee, I myself remember a peer of the realm being hanged for killing his man, just the same as the man would have been for killing him.

Tom. A lord hanged! Well, that is some comfort, to be sure. But have you read the Rights of Man?

Jack. No, not I: I had rather by half read the Whole Duty of Man.[1] I have but little time for reading, and such as I should therefore only read a bit of the best.

Tom. Don't tell me of those old-fashioned notions. Why should not we have the same fine things they have got in France? I'm for a Constitution, and Organisation, and Equalisation, and Fraternisation.

Jack. Do be quiet. Now, Tom, only suppose this nonsensical equality was to take place; why it would not last while one could say Jack Robinson; or suppose it could – suppose, in the general division, our new rulers were to give us half an acre of ground apiece; we could, to be sure, raise potatoes on it for the use of our families; but as every other man would be equally busy in raising potatoes for his family, why then, you see, if thou wast to break thy spade, I, whose trade it is, should no longer be able to mend it. Neighbour Snip would have no time to make us a suit of clothes, nor the clothier to weave the cloth; for all the world would be home a digging. And as to boots and shoes, the want of some one to make them for us would be a still greater grievance than the tax on leather. If we should be sick, there would be no doctor's stuff for us; for doctor would be digging too. And if necessity did not compel, and if

---

[1] 'The Whole Duty of Man': *The Whole Duty of Man According to the Law of Nature*, a popular moral treatise by Samuel Pufendorf, translated, with notes, by Jean Barbeyrac.

equality subsisted, we could not get a chimney swept, a lamp lighted, or a load of coal from pit, for love or money.

Tom. But still I should have no one over my head.

Jack. That's a mistake: I'm stronger than thou; and Standish, the exciseman, is a better scholar: so that we should not remain equal a minute. I should out-fight thee, and he'd out-wit thee. And if such a sturdy fellow as I am was to come and break down thy hedge for a little firing, or take away the crop from thy ground, I'm not so sure that these new-fangled laws would see thee righted. I tell thee, Tom, we have a fine constitution already, and our forefathers thought so.

Tom. They were a pack of fools, and had never read the Rights of Man.

Jack. I'll tell thee a story. When Sir John married, my lady, who is a little fantastical, and likes to do every thing like the French, begged him to pull down yonder fine old castle, and build it up in her frippery way. 'No,' says Sir John; 'what! shall I pull down this noble building, raised by the wisdom of my brave ancestors; which outstood the civil wars, and only underwent a little needful repair at the Revolution; a castle which all my neighbours come to take a pattern by; – shall I pull it all down, I say, only because there may be a dark closet, or an awkward passage, or an inconvenient room or two in it?[2] Our ancestors took *time* for what they did. They understood *foundation* work; no running up your little slight lath and plaster buildings, which are up in a day, and down in a night.' – My lady mumped and grumbled; but the castle was let stand and a glorious building it is; though there may be a trifling fault or two, and though a few decays want stopping; so now and then they mend a little thin, and they'll go on mending, I dare say, as they have leisure, to the end of the chapter, if they are let alone. But no pull-me-down works. What is it you are crying out for, Tom?

Tom. Why, for a perfect government.

Jack. You might as well cry for the moon. There's nothing perfect in this world, take my word for it: though Sir John says, we come nearer to it than any country in the world ever did.

Tom. I don't see why we are to work like slaves, while others roll about in their coaches, feed on the fat of the land, and do nothing.

---

[2] The image of the constitution as an old castle had been invoked by Burke in *Reflections*; see p. 69.

Jack.   My little maid brought home a storybook from the charity-school t'other day, in which was a bit of a fable about the belly, and the limbs.[3] The hands said, I won't work any longer to feed this lazy belly, who sits in state like a lord and does nothing. Said the feet, I won't walk and tire myself to carry him about; let him shift for himself; so said all the members; just as your levellers and republicans do now. And what was the consequence? Why, the belly *was* pinched, to be sure, and grew thin upon it; but the hands and the feet, and the rest of the members, suffered so much for want of their old nourishment, which the belly had been all the time administering, while they accused him of sitting in idle state, that they all fell sick, pined away, and would have died, if they had not come to their senses just in time to save their lives, as I hope all you will do.

Tom.   But the times – but the taxes, Jack.

Jack.   Things are dear to be sure; but riot and murder is not the way to make them cheap. And taxes are high; but I am told there's a great deal of old scores paying off, and paying off by them who did not contract the debt neither, Tom. Besides, things are mending, I hope; and what little is done, is for us poor people; our candles are somewhat cheaper; and I dare say, if the honest gentleman who has the management of things is not disturbed by you levellers, things will mend every day. But bear one thing in mind: the more we riot, the more we shall have to pay: the more mischief is done, the more the repairs cost: the more time we waste in meeting to redress public wrongs, the more we shall increase our private wants. And mind, too, that 'tis working, and not murmuring, which puts bread in our children's mouths, and a new coat on our backs. Mind another thing, too, we have not the same ground of complaint: in France the poor paid all the same taxes, as I have heard 'em say, and the quality paid nothing.

Tom.   Well, I know what's what, as well as another; and I am as fit to govern.

Jack.   No, Tom, no. You are indeed as good as another man, seeing you have hands to work, and a soul to be saved. But are all men fit for all kinds of things? Solomon says, How can he be wise whose talk is of oxen?[4] Every one in his way. I am a better judge of a horse-shoe than Sir John; but he has a deal better notion of state affairs than I; and I can no more do without his employ than

---

[3] The fable is told in Livy's *History of Rome.*
[4] Cited by Burke in *Reflections* . . . (Clark, p. 206, not in this edition) from Ecclesiasticus (a book found in the Latin Vulgate but relegated to the Apocrypha by Protestants), ch. xxxviii, §25.

he can do without my farriery. Besides, few are so poor but they may get a vote for a parliament-man; and so you see the poor have as much share in the government as they well know how to manage.

Tom. But I say all men are equal. Why should one be above another?

Jack. If that's thy talk, Tom, thou dost quarrel with Providence, and not with government. For the woman is below her husband, and the children are below their mother, and the servant is below his master.

Tom. But the subject is not below the king: all kings are 'crowned ruffians' and all governments are wicked. For my part I am resolved I'll pay no more taxes to any of them.

Jack. Tom, Tom, if thou didst go oftener to church, thou wouldst know where it is said, Render unto Caesar the things that are Caesar's[5]; and also, 'Fear God, honour the king.' Your book tells you that we need obey no government but that of the people; and that we may fashion and alter the government according to our whimsies: but mine tells me, 'Let every one be subject to the higher powers, for all power is of God; the powers that be are ordained of God; whosoever therefore resisteth the power, resisteth the ordinance of God.'[6] Thou sayest, thou wilt pay no taxes to any of them. Dost thou know who it was that worked a miracle, that he might have money to pay tribute with, rather than set you and me an example of disobedience to government? an example, let me tell thee, worth an hundred precepts, and of which all the wit of man can never lessen the value. Then there's another thing worth minding; when Saint Paul was giving all those directions, in the Epistle to the Romans, for obedience and submission; what sort of a king now dost think they had? Dost think 'twas a saint which he ordered them to obey?

Tom. Why, it was a kind, merciful, charitable king, to be sure: one who put nobody to death or to prison.

Jack. You was never more out in your life. Our parson says he was a monster[7] – that he robbed the rich, and murdered the poor – set fire to his own town, as fine a place as London – fiddled to the flames, and then hanged and burnt the Christians, who were all poor, as if they had burnt the city. Yet there's not a word about rising. – Duties are fixed, Tom – laws are settled; a Christian

[5] Luke, 20, §25.   [6] Romans, 13, §1–2.
[7] 'King': here, the Roman Emperor, Nero.

can't pick and choose, whether he will obey or let it alone. But we have no such trials. We have a king the very reverse.

Tom.   I say we shall never be happy, till we do as the French have done.

Jack.   The French and we contending for liberty, Tom, is just as if thou and I were to pretend to run a race; thou to set out from the starting-post when I am in already; thou to have all the ground to travel when I have reached the end. – Why, we've got it, man! we've no race to run! We're there already! Our constitution is no more like what the French one was, than a mug of our Taunton beer is like a platter of their soup-maigre.

Tom.   I know we shall be undone, if we don't get a new constitution – that's all.

Jack.   And I know we shall be undone if we *do*. I don't know much about politics, but I can see by a little, what a great deal means. Now only to show thee the state of public credit, as I think Tim Standish calls it. There's Farmer Furrow, a few years ago he had an odd fifty pounds by him; So, to keep it out of harm's way, he put it out to use, on government security, I think he calls it; well, t'other day he married one of his daughters, so he thought he'd give her that fifty pounds, for a bit of a portion. Tom, as I'm a living man, when he went to take it out, if his fifty pounds was not almost grown to an hundred! and would have been a full hundred, they say, by this time, if the gentleman had been let alone.

Tom.   Well, still, as the old saying is – I should like to do as they do in France.

Jack.   What, shouldst like to be murdered with as little ceremony as Hackabout, the butcher, knocks down a calf? or shouldst like to get rid of thy wife for every little bit of a tiff? And as to liberty of conscience, which they brag so much about, why they have driven away their parsons, ay, and murdered many of 'em, because they would not swear as they would have them. And then they talk of liberty of the press; why, Tom, only t'other day they hanged a man for printing a book against this pretty government of theirs.

Tom.   But you said, yourself, it was sad times in France, before they pulled down the old government.

Jack.   Well, and suppose the French were as much in the right as I know them to be in the wrong, what does that argue for us? Because my neighbour Furrow, t'other day, pulled down a crazy old barn, is that reason why I must set fire to my tight[8] cottage?

---

[8] Tight: snug.

Tom.   I don't see, for all that, why one man is to ride in his coach and six, while another mends the highway for him.

Jack.   I don't see why the man in the coach is to drive over the man on foot, or hurt a hair of his head, any more than you. And as to our great folks, that you levellers have such a spite against, I don't pretend to say they are a bit better than they should be; but that's no affair of mine; let them look to that; they'll answer for that in another place. To be sure, I wish they'd set us a better example about going to church, and those things: but still *hoarding's* not the sin of the age: they don't lock up their *money* – away it goes, and every body's the better for it. They do spend too much, to be sure, in feastings and fandagoes⁹; and so far from commending them for it, if I was a parson I'd go to work with 'em, but it should be in another kind of way; but as I am only a poor tradesman, why 'tis but bringing more grist to my mill. It all comes among the people. Their very extravagance, for which, as I said before, their parsons should be at them, is a fault by which, as poor men, we are benefited; so you cry out just in the wrong, place. – Their coaches and their furniture, and their buildings and their planting, employ a power of tradesmen and labourers.¹⁰ Now in this village, what should we do without the castle? Though my lady is too ranti-polish,¹¹ and flies about all summer to hot water and cold water, and fresh water and salt water, when she ought to stay at home with Sir John: yet when she does come down, she brings such a deal of gentry, that I have more horses than I can shoe and my wife more linen than she can wash. Then all our grown children are servants in the family, and rare wages they have got. Our little boys get something every day by weeding their gardens; and the girls learn to sew and knit at Sir John's expense, who sends them all to school of a Sunday besides.

Tom.   Ay, but there's not Sir Johns in every village.

Jack.   The more's the pity. But there's other help. 'Twas but last year you broke your leg, and was nine weeks in the Bristol Infirmary, where you was taken as much care of as a lord, and your family was maintained all the while by the parish. No poor-rates in France, Tom; and here there's a matter of four millions and a half paid for the poor every year, if 'twas but a little better managed.

⁹ A Spanish dance.
¹⁰ The argument is a rehearsal of Mandeville's, that private vices make public virtues and that profligacy stimulates the economy.
¹¹ Ranti-polish: manic.

Tom. Four millions and a half!

Jack. Ay, indeed. Not translated into tenpences,[12] as your French millions are, but twenty good shillings to the pound. But, when this levelling comes about, there will be no infirmaries, no hospitals, no charity-schools, no Sunday-schools, where so many hundred thousand poor souls learn to read the word of God for nothing. For who is to pay for them? – *Equality* can't afford it; and those that may be willing won't be able.

Tom. But we shall be one as good as another, for all that.

Jack. Ay, and bad will be the best. But we must work as we do now, and with this difference, that no one will be able to pay us. Tom! I have got the use of my limbs, of my liberty, of the laws, and of my Bible. The two first I take to be my *natural* rights; the two last my *civil* and *religious* rights: these, I take it, are the *true Rights of Man*, and all the rest is nothing but nonsense, and madness, and wickedness. My cottage is my castle; I sit down in it at night in peace and thankfulness, and 'no man maketh me afraid.' Instead of indulging discontent, because another is richer than I in this world (for envy is at the bottom of your equality works), I read my Bible, go to church, and look forward to a treasure in heaven.

Tom. Ay, but the French have got it in *this* world.

Jack. 'Tis all a lie, Tom. Sir John's butler says his master gets letters which say 'tis all a lie. 'Tis all murder, and nakedness, and hunger; many of the poor soldiers fight without victuals, and march without clothes. These are your *democrats*! Tom.

Tom. What, then; dost think all the men on our side wicked?

Jack. No; not so neither. If some of the leaders are knaves, more of the followers are fools. Sir John, who is wiser than I, says the whole system is the operation of fraud upon folly. They've made fools of most of you, as I believe. I judge no man, Tom; I hate no man. Even republicans and levellers, I hope, will always enjoy the protection of our laws; though I hope they will never be our law-*makers*. There are many true Dissenters, and there are some hollow Churchmen; and a good man is a good man, whether his church has got a steeple to it or not. The newfashioned way of proving one's religion is to hate somebody. Now, though some folks pretend that a man's hating a Papist, or a Presbyterian, proves him to be a good *churchman*, it don't prove him to

---

[12] A reference to the depreciating value of the assignat.

be a good *Christian*, Tom. As much as I hate republican works, I'd scorn to live in a country where there was not liberty of conscience, and where every man might not worship God in his own way. Now that liberty they had not in France; the Bible was shut up in an unknown, heathenish tongue[13]: while here, thou and I can make as free use of ours as a bishop; can no more be sent to prison unjustly than the judge who tries us, and are as much taken care of by the laws as the parliament-man who makes them. Then, as to your thinking that the new scheme will make you happy, look among your own set, and see if any thing can be so dismal and discontented as a leveller. Look at France. These poor French fellows used to be the merriest dogs in the world: but since equality came in, I don't believe a Frenchman has ever laughed.

Tom.   What, then, dost thou take French *liberty* to be?

Jack.   To murder more men in one night than ever their poor king did in his whole life.

Tom.   And what dost thou take a *democrat* to be?

Jack.   One who likes to be governed by a thousand tyrants, and yet can't bear a king.

Tom.   What is *equality*?

Jack.   For every man to pull down every one that is above him; while, instead of raising those below him to his own level, he only makes use of them as steps to raise himself to the place of those he has tumbled down.

Tom.   What is *the new Rights of Man*?

Jack.   Battle, murder, and sudden death.

Tom.   What is it to be an *enlightened people*?

Jack.   To put out the light of the Gospel, confound right and wrong, and grope about in pitch darkness.

Tom.   What is *philosophy*, that Tim Standish talks so much about?

Jack.   To believe that there's neither God, nor devil, nor heaven, nor hell: to dig up a wicked old fellow's rotten bones, whose books, Sir John says, have been the ruin of thousands, and to set his figure up in a church and worship him.[14]

Tom.   And what is a patriot according to the new school?

Jack.   A man who loves every other country better than his own, and France best of all.

---

[13] I.e., Latin. The Catholic Church forbade the reading of the Bible in vernacular languages.

[14] During the Revolution the remains of Voltaire and Rousseau were exhumed and transferred to the Pantheon.

Tom. And what is benevolence?

Jack. Why, in the new-fangled language, it means contempt of religion, aversion to justice, overturning of law, doting on all mankind in general, and hating every body in particular.

Tom. And what mean the other hard words that Tim talks about, – organisation, and function, and civism, and incivism, and equalisation, and inviolability, and imperscriptible, and fraternisation?

Jack. Nonsense, gibberish, downright hocus-pocus. I know 'tis not English; Sir John says 'tis not Latin; and his valet de sham says 'tis not French neither.

Tom. And yet Tim says he never shall be happy till all these fine things are brought over to England.

Jack. What! into this Christian country, Tom? Why, dost know they have no Sabbath in France? Their mob parliament meets on a Sunday to do their wicked work, as naturally as we do to go to church. They have renounced God's word and God's day, and they don't even date in the year of our Lord.[15] Why dost turn pale, man? And the rogues are always making such a noise, Tom, in the midst of their parliament-house, that their speaker rings a bell, like our penny-postman, because he can't keep them in order.

Tom. And dost thou believe they are as cruel as some folks pretend?

Jack. I am sure they are, and I think I know the reason. We Christians set a high value on life, because we know that every fellow-creature has an immortal soul; a soul to be saved or lost, Tom. Whoever believes that, is a little cautious how he sends a soul unprepared to his grand account. But he who believes a man is no better than a dog will make no more scruple of killing one than the other.

Tom. And dost thou think our Rights of Man will lead to all this wickedness?

Jack. As sure as eggs are eggs.

Tom. I begin to think we're better off as we are.

Jack. I'm sure on't. This is only a scheme to make us go back in every thing. 'Tis making our selves poor when we are getting rich, and discontented when we are comfortable.

---

[15] In October–November 1793 the French National Convention issued a series of decrees establishing a new revolutionary calendar numbering the years from the first year of the new constitution (1792), and the months after their natural properties. See Documents 109–11 in John Hall Stewart, *Documentary Survey of the French Revolution* (London: Macmillan, 1951).

Tom. I begin to think I'm not so very unhappy as I had got to fancy.

Jack. Tom, I don't care for drink myself, but thou dost, and I'll argue with thee, not in the way of principle, but in thy own way: when there's all equality there will be no superfluity! when there's no wages there'll be no drink; and levelling will rob thee of thy ale more than the malt-tax does.[16]

Tom. But Standish says, if we had a good government, there would be no want of any thing.

Jack. He is like many others, who take the king's money and betray him: let him give up the profits of his place before he kicks at the hand that feeds him. Though I'm no scholar, I know that a good government is a good thing. But don't go to make me believe that any government can make a bad man good, or a discontented man happy. What art musing upon, man?

Tom. Let me sum up the evidence, as they say at 'sizes[17] – Hem! To cut every man's throat who does not think as I do, or hang him up at a lamppost! – Pretend liberty of conscience, and then banish the parsons only for being conscientious! – Cry out liberty of the press, and hang up the first man who writes his mind! – Lose our poor laws! – Lose one's wife, perhaps, upon every little tiff! – March without clothes, and fight without victuals! – No trade! – No Bible! – No Sabbath nor day of rest! – No safety, no comfort, no peace in this world – and no world to come Jack, I never knew thee tell a lie in my life.

Jack. Nor would I now, not even against the French.

Tom. And thou art very sure we are not ruined?

Jack. I'll tell thee how we are ruined. We have a king, so loving, that he would not hurt the people if he could; and so kept in that he could not hurt the people if he would. We have as much liberty as can make us happy, and more trade and riches than allow us to be good. We have the best laws in the world, if they were more strictly enforced; and the best religion in the world, if it was but better followed. While Old England is safe, I'll glory in her, and pray for her; and when she is in danger, I'll fight for her, and die for her.

Tom. And so will I too, Jack, that's what I will. (sings.)

"O the roast beef of Old England!"

Jack. Thou art an honest fellow, Tom.

---

[16] Malt-tax: an excise tax on brewing, much objected to as a regressive tax on poor consumers (J. H. Plumb, *The Growth of Political Stability in England 1675–1725* [London: Macmillan, 1967], p. 149).

[17] 'sizes, i.e. the assizes, the county law courts.

Tom.   This is Rose and Crown night, and Tim Standish is now at his mischief; but we'll go and put an end to that fellow's work, or he'll corrupt the whole club.

Jack.   Come along.

Tom.   No; first I'll stay to burn my book, and then I'll go and make a bonfire and . . .

Jack.   Hold, Tom. There is but one thing worse than a bitter enemy – and that is an imprudent friend. If thou wouldst show thy love to thy king and country, let's have no drinking, no riot, no bonfires; but put in practice this text, which our parson preached on last Sunday, 'Study to be quiet, work with your own hands, and mind your own business.'

Tom.   And so I will, Jack. – Come on.

WILLIAM GODWIN

BIOGRAPHICAL NOTE

Godwin was born into a strong background of religious dissent, his father, grandfather and uncle all being dissenting ministers. After ordination he himself became minister to a congregation at Ware in Hertfordshire, but began to lose his faith, reading widely amongst the French *Philosophes*. He resigned his congregation on 1782 to write *A Life of . . . Pitt*, finally quitting the ministry altogether in 1783 and moving to London to write reviews and essays and to practise journalism. Inspired by Paine's *Rights of Man*, but convinced of the need for a more philosophical defence of the radical case, he began his masterwork.

In 1791 he met Mary Wollstonecraft, through the publisher Johnson, but it was not until after her return from France in 1796 that they formed a relationship and subsequently (though they had both criticised the institution) married. Her tragic death followed only a year later after the birth of her daughter, Mary, the future author of *Frankenstein*. Godwin's candid *Memoirs of the Author of a Vindication of the Rights of Woman* (1798) helped precipitate a moralistic reaction linking sexual liberation with revolutionary politics in the public mind, to the disadvantage of both.

Godwin now began a long slide into obscurity. When Shelley met him in 1812 he admitted to thinking Godwin had died long ago! He remarried (twice) and continued to write. His later works include novels, a play, works on history and education, and a famous controversy with Thomas Malthus in his *Thoughts occasioned by Dr Parr's Spital Sermon* (1800) and in his *Of Population* (1820). His *History of the Commonwealth* (1824) and a late philosophical essay, *Thoughts on Man* (1831), reveal a considerable retreat – already apparent in successive editions of that work – from the uncompromising rationalist positions of *Political Justice*. Unlike other radicals – notably the poets Wordsworth, Coleridge and Southey, but also the pamphleteer opponent of Burke, Sir James Mackintosh – Godwin did not abandon the radical cause, but his arguments moderated, ascribing a lesser role to human reason; they became more subtle, if less intellectually exciting. Godwin died in 1836.

EDITORIAL NOTE

The ***Enquiry Concerning Political Justice*** (1793) was an immediate and enormous, if fleeting, success, creating for its author a stellar reputation. It was followed by a 'philosophical' novel, *Caleb Williams* (1794). The two works influenced a generation of radicals and romantics. Indeed, excerpts from *Political Justice* were still being published with political intent early last century. His central, extreme individualist position impugned all social institutions (the state, family and marriage – even collaborative enterprises such as theatrical and orchestral productions) as undermining the individual's responsibility to act at all times in accordance with the greatest happiness of the greatest number. Unsurprisingly he has subsequently been claimed as 'the founder of modern anarchism' although the modern anarchist movement ultimately derived from other sources. There were three editions in Godwin's lifetime: 1793, 1796 and 1798; they differ considerably (on the changes between the editions see Philp, *Godwin's Political Justice*, cited below, *passim*). The second represents a considerable revision of the argument of the first, changes which Godwin attributed to his abandonment of the secular remnants of his Calvinism, and his reading of Hume's *Treatise* which provided a greater role for sympathy in his moral psychology. The third edition involved fewer, if still significant, changes in the role ascribed to reason. A French translation was made by Benjamin Constant but only recently published (ed. B. R. Polin, Quebec: 1972; Tübingen: M. Niemayer, 1998); a German translation was published in Würzburg in 1803. The text here is that of the first (1793) edition.

Modern editions:

Enquiry Concerning Political Justice, ed. F. E. L. Priestley, 3 vols., (Toronto University Press 1946) contains variant readings of the three editions.

Enquiry Concerning Political Justice (3rd edn), ed. and intr. Isaac Kramnick (Harmondsworth: Penguin Books, 1976).

Political and Philosophical Writings of William Godwin, ed. Mark Philp (London: Pickering, 1993); vols. III and IV contain the *Enquiry* with variant readings.

FURTHER READING

Clark, J. P., *The Philosophical Anarchism of William Godwin* (Princeton: Princeton University Press, 1977).

Locke, D., *A Fantasy of Reason: The Life and Thought of William Godwin* (London: Routledge & Kegan Paul, 1980).

Marshall, P., *William Godwin* (Princeton: Princeton University Press, 1984).

Monroe, D. H., *Godwin's Moral Philosophy* (Oxford: Clarendon, 1953).

Philp, M., *Godwin's Political Justice* (Oxford: Duckworth, 1986).

Enquiry Concerning Political Justice and its Influence on Morals and Happiness (1793)

BOOK I

THE IMPORTANCE OF POLITICAL INSTITUTIONS

CHAPTER I

INTRODUCTION

. . . If it could be proved that a sound political institution was of all others the most powerful engine for promoting individual good, or on the other hand that an erroneous and corrupt government was the most formidable adversary to the improvement of the species, it would follow that politics was the first and most important subject of human investigation.

The opinions of mankind in this respect have been divided . . .

. . .

It may however be reasonable to consider whether the science of politics be not of somewhat greater value than any of these reasoners have been inclined to suspect . . . whether government be not still more considerable in its incidental effects, than in those intended to be produced. Vice, for example, depends for its existence upon the existence of temptation. May not a good government strongly tend to extirpate, and a bad one to increase the mass of temptation? Again, vice depends for its existence upon the existence of error. May not a good government by taking away all restraints upon the enquiring mind hasten, and a bad one by its patronage of error procrastinate the discovery and establishment of truth? Let us consider the subject in this point of view. If it can be proved that the science of politics is thus unlimited in its importance, the advocates of liberty will have gained an additional recommendation, and its admirers will be incited with the greater eagerness to the investigation of its principles.

CHAPTER II

HISTORY OF POLITICAL SOCIETY

. . .

The probability of this improvement will be sufficiently established, if we consider, FIRST, that the moral characters of men are the result of their perceptions: and, SECONDLY, that of all the modes of operating upon mind government is the most considerable. In addition to these arguments it will be found, THIRDLY, that the good and ill effects of political institution are not less conspicuous in detail than in principle; and, FOURTHLY, that perfectibility is one of the most unequivocal characteristics of the human species, so that the political, as well as the intellectual state of man, may be presumed to be in a course of progressive improvement.

CHAPTER III

THE MORAL CHARACTERS OF MEN ORIGINATE IN

THEIR PERCEPTIONS

We bring into the world with us no innate principles: consequently we are neither virtuous nor vicious as we first come into existence. No truth can be more evident than this, to any man who will yield the subject an impartial consideration. Every principle is a proposition. Every proposition consists in the connection of at least two distinct ideas, which are affirmed to agree or disagree with each other. If therefore the principles be innate, the ideas must be so too. But nothing can be more incontrovertible, than that we do not bring pre-established ideas into the world with us.[1]

. . .

Experience has by many been supposed adverse to these reasonings: but it will upon examination be found to be perfectly in harmony with them. The child at the moment of his birth is totally unprovided with ideas, except such as his mode of existence in the womb may have supplied. His first impressions are those of pleasure and pain. But he has no foresight of the tendency of any sanction to obtain either the one or the other, previously to experience.

. . .

CHAPTER IV

THREE PRINCIPAL CAUSES OF MORAL

IMPROVEMENT CONSIDERED

I LITERATURE

II EDUCATION

III POLITICAL JUSTICE

There are three principal causes by which the human mind is advanced towards a state of perfection; literature, or the diffusion of knowledge through the medium of

---

[1] Godwin here clearly identifies himself with Locke in denying the existence of innate ideas. Significantly he links this to the denial of original sin.

discussion, whether written or oral; education, or a scheme for the early impression of right principles upon the hitherto unprejudiced mind; and political justice, or the adoption of any principle of morality and truth into the practice of a community.

. . .

III POLITICAL JUSTICE

The benefits of political justice will best be understood, if we consider society in the most comprehensive view, taking into our estimate the erroneous institutions by which the human mind has been too often checked in its career, as well as those well founded opinions of public and individual interest, which perhaps need only to be clearly explained, in order to their being generally received.

. . .

Again an additional argument in favour of the efficacy of political institutions arises from the extensive influence which certain false principles, engendered by an imperfect system of society, have been found to exert . . .

. . . Injustice therefore by its own nature is little fitted for a durable existence. But government 'lays its hand upon the spring there is in society and puts a stop to its motion.'[2] It gives substance and permanence to our errors. It reverses the genuine properties of mind, and instead of suffering us to look forward, teaches us to look backward for perfection. It prompts us to seek the public welfare not in innovation and improvement, but in a timid reverence for the decisions of our ancestors as if it were the nature of the mind always to degenerate, and never to advance.

CHAPTER V
INFLUENCE OF POLITICAL INSTITUTIONS EXEMPLIFIED

The efficacy of political institutions will be rendered still more evident, if we enquire into the history of the most considerable vices at present existing in society; and if it can be shewn that they derive their inveteracy from political institution.

. . .

First then it is to be observed, that, in the most refined states of Europe, the inequality of property has arisen to an alarming height. Vast numbers of their inhabitants

---

[2] [Godwin's footnote:] Logan *Philosophy of History*, p. 69. [John Logan, *Elements of the Philosophy of History. Part the First* (Edinburgh, 1781).]

are deprived of almost every accommodation that can render life tolerable or secure. Their utmost industry scarcely suffices for their support. . . .

. . .

. . . The consequences that result are placed beyond the reach of contradiction. A perpetual struggle with the evils of poverty, if frequently ineffectual, must necessarily render many of the sufferers desperate. A painful feeling of their oppressed situation will itself deprive them of the power of surmounting it. The superiority of the rich, being thus unmercifully exercised, must inevitably expose them to reprisals; and the poor man will be induced to regard the state of society as a state of war, an unjust combination, not for protecting every man in his rights and securing him the means of existence, but for engrossing all its advantages to a few favoured individuals, and reserving for the portion of the rest want, dependence and misery.

A second source of those destructive passions by which the peace of society is interrupted, is to be found in the luxury, the pageantry and magnificence with which enormous wealth is usually accompanied. Human beings are capable of encountering with chearfulness considerable hardships, when those hardships are impartially shared with the rest of the society, and they are not insulted with the spectacle of indolence and ease in others, no way deserving of greater advantages than themselves. But it is a bitter aggravation of their own calamity, to have the privileges of others forced on their observation, and, while they are perpetually and vainly endeavouring to secure for themselves and their families the poorest conveniences, to find others revelling in the fruits of their labours . . .

A third disadvantage that is apt to connect poverty with discontent consists in the insolence and usurpation of the rich . . . He seems as if he could never be satisfied with his possessions unless he can make the spectacle of them grating to others; and that honest self-esteem, by which his inferior might otherwise arrive at apathy, is rendered the instrument of galling him with oppression and injustice. . . .

. . .

CHAPTER VI

HUMAN INVENTIONS CAPABLE OF PERPETUAL IMPROVEMENT

. . . Let us carry back our minds to man in his original state, a being capable of impressions and knowledge to an unbounded extent, but not having as yet received the one or cultivated the other; . . .

. . .

Let us [now] suppose man to have gained the two first elements of knowledge, speaking and writing; let us trace him through all his subsequent improvements, through whatever constitutes the inequality between Newton and the ploughman, and indeed much more than this, since the most ignorant ploughman in civilised society is infinitely different from what he would have been, when stripped of all the benefits he has derived from literature and the arts. Let us survey the earth covered with the labours of man, houses, enclosures, harvests, manufactures, instruments, machines, together with all the wonders of painting, poetry, eloquence and philosophy.

Such was man in his original state, and such is man as we at present behold him. Is it possible for us to contemplate what he has already done, without being impressed with a strong presentiment of the improvements he has yet to accomplish? There is no science that is not capable of additions; there is no art that may not be carried to a still higher perfection. If this be true of all other sciences, why not of morals? If this be true of all other arts, why not of social institution? The very conception of this as possible, is in the highest degree encouraging. If we can still farther demonstrate it to be a part of the natural and regular progress of mind, our confidence and our hopes will then be complete. This is the temper with which we ought to engage in the study of political truth. Let us look back, that we may profit by the experience of mankind; but let us not look back, as if the wisdom of our ancestors was such as to leave no room for future improvement.

CHAPTER VII

OF THE OBJECTION OF THESE PRINCIPLES FROM THE
INFLUENCE OF CLIMATE

PART I
OF MORAL[3] AND PHYSICAL CAUSES

. . .

. . . Upon our decision in this case it depends, whether those persons act wisely who prescribe to themselves a certain discipline and are anxious to enrich their minds with science, or whether on the contrary it be better to trust every thing to the mercy of events. . . .

---

[3] Godwin here uses 'moral' in the broad eighteenth-century sense of mental or psychological as opposed to physical causation, and not as opposed to immoral.

Out of a single sensation a great variety of reflections may be generated. Let the thing perceived be a material substance of certain regular dimensions. I perceive that it has an upper and a lower surface, I can therefore conceive of it as divided . . . of its parts . . . and hence I acquire the ideas of distance and space . . . Let the sensation be a pain in the head. I am led to reflect upon its causes, its seat, the structure of the parts in which it resides, the inconvenience it imposes, the consequences with which it may be attended, the remedies that may be applied and their effects, whether external or internal, material or intellectual.

. . . Hence it inevitably follows, that physical causes, though of some consequence in the history of man, sink into nothing when compared with the great and inexpressible operations of reflection. They are the prejudices we conceive or the judgments we form, our apprehensions of truth and falsehood, that constitute the true basis of distinction between man and man. The difference between savage and savage indeed, in the first generation of the human species and in perfect solitude, can only be ascribed to the different impressions made upon their senses. . . .

. . .

. . .[But] [i]n the case of man their efficacy is swallowed up in the superior importance of reflection and science. In animals on the contrary they are left almost alone. . . .

Such is the character of man considered as an individual. He is operated upon by exterior causes immediately, producing certain effects upon him independently of the exercise of reason; and he is operated upon by exterior causes immediately, their impressions furnishing him with materials for reflection, and assuming the form of motives to act or to refrain from acting. But the latter of these, at least so far as relates to man in a civilised state, may stand for the whole. The true instruments of moral influence, are desire and aversion, punishment and reward, the exhibition of general truth, and the development of those punishments and rewards, which wisdom and error by the very nature of the thing constantly bring along with them.

PART II

OF NATIONAL CHARACTERS

. . .

. . . it has been affirmed to be 'impossible to establish a free government in certain warm and effeminate climates.'[4] To enable us to judge of the reasonableness of this

---

[4] The idea that climate exercised a strong influence on political culture was the most important eighteenth-century version of 'material' factors affecting politics. It was popularised by Montesquieu's influential *Spirit of the Laws*.

affirmation, let us consider what process would be necessary in order to introduce a free government into any country.

. . .

Let us suppose then that the majority of a nation by however slow a progress are convinced of the desirableness, or, which amounts to the same, the practicability of freedom. The supposition would be parallel, if we were to imagine ten thousand men of sound intellect, shut up in a madhouse, and superintended by a set of three or four keepers. Hitherto they have been persuaded, for what absurdity has been too great for human intellect to entertain? that they were destitute of reason, and that the superintendence under which they were placed was necessary for their preservation. They had therefore submitted to whips and straw and bread and water, and perhaps imagined this tyranny to be a blessing. But a suspicion is at length by some means propagated among them, that all they have hitherto endured has been an imposition. The suspicion spreads, they reflect, they reason, the idea is communicated from one to another through the chinks of their cells, and at certain times when the vigilance of their keepers has not precluded them from the pleasures of mutual society. It becomes the clear perception, the settled persuasion of the majority of the persons confined.

What will be the consequence of this opinion? Will the influence of climate prevent them from embracing the obvious means of their happiness? Is there any human understanding that will not perceive a truth like this, when forcibly and repeatedly presented? Is there a mind that will conceive no indignation at so horrible a tyranny? In reality the chains fall off of themselves, when the magic of opinion is dissolved. When a great majority of any society are persuaded to secure any benefit to themselves, there is no need of tumult or violence to effect it. The effort would be to resist reason, not to obey it. The prisoners are collected in their common hall, and the keepers inform them that it is time to return to their cells. They have no longer the power to obey. They look at the impotence of their late masters, and smile at their presumption. They quietly leave the mansion where they were hitherto immured, and partake of the blessings of light and air like other men.

Let us compare this theory with the history of mankind . . .

. . .

The real enemies of liberty in any country are not the people, but those higher orders who profit by a contrary system. Infuse just views of society into a certain number of the liberally educated and reflecting members; give to the people guides and instructors, and the business is done, this however is not to be accomplished but in a gradual manner . . . The error lies not in tolerating the worst form of government for a time but in supposing a change impracticable, and not incessantly looking forward to its accomplishment.

CHAPTER VIII

OF THE OBJECTION TO THESE PRINCIPLES FROM THE
INFLUENCE OF LUXURY

There is another proposition relative to the subject, which is less to be concerned as an assertion distinct in itself, than as a particular branch of that which has just been discussed; I mean the proposition which affirms, 'that nations like individuals are subject to the phenomena of youth and old age, and that, when a people by luxury and depravation of manners have sunk into decrepitude, it is not in the power of legislation to restore them to vigour and innocence.'

This idea has partly been founded upon the romantic notions of pastoral life and the golden age. Innocence is not virtue. Virtue demands the active employment of an ardent mind in the promotion of the general good. No man can be eminently virtuous, who is not accustomed to an extensive range of reflection. . . .[5]

. . .

Men always act upon their apprehensions of preferableness. There are few errors of which they are guilty, which may not be resolved into a narrow and inadequate view of the alternative presented for their choice. Present pleasure may appear more certain and eligible than distant good. But they never choose evil as apprehended to be evil. . . .

BOOK II

PRINCIPLES OF SOCIETY

CHAPTER II

OF JUSTICE

From what has been said it appears, that the subject of the present enquiry is strictly speaking a department of the science of morals. . . .

---

[5] Godwin refers to romantic notions of an idealised primitive human sensibility such as that praised by Rousseau in his *Discourse on the Origins of Inequality*. Such views fed into the belief that uncorrupted primitive cultures could have produced the supposedly ancient poems of the Gaelic bard Ossian, which caused huge interest in the mid-century. These were in fact forgeries written by a contemporary, James Macpherson (d. 1796).

. . .

. . . Justice is a rule of conduct originating in the connection of one percipient being with another. A comprehensive maxim which has been laid down upon the subject is, 'that we should love our neighbour as ourselves'. But this maxim, though possessing considerable merit as a popular principle, is not modelled with the strictness of philosophical accuracy.

In a loose and general view I and my neighbour are both of us men; and of consequence entitled to equal attention. But in reality it is probable that one of us is a being of more worth and importance than the other. A man is of more worth than a beast; because, being possessed of higher faculties, he is capable of a more refined and genuine happiness. In the same manner the illustrious archbishop of Cambray[6] was of more worth than his chambermaid, and there are few of us that would hesitate to pronounce, if his palace were in flames, and the life of only one of them could be preserved, which of the two ought to be preferred.

But there is another ground of preference, beside the private consideration of one of them being farther removed from the state of a mere animal. We are not connected with one or two percipient beings, but with a society, a nation, and in some sense with the whole family of mankind. Of consequence that life ought to be preferred which will be most conducive to the general good. In saving the life of Fenelon, suppose at the moment when he was conceiving the project of his immortal Telemachus, I should be promoting the benefit of thousands, who have been cured by the perusal of it of some error, vice and consequent unhappiness. Nay, my benefit would extend farther than this, for every individual thus cured has become a better member of society, and has contributed in his turn to the happiness, the information and improvement of others.

Supposing I had been myself the chambermaid, I ought to have chosen to die, rather than that Fenelon should have died. The life of Fenelon was really preferable to that of the chambermaid. But understanding is the faculty that perceives the truth of this and similar propositions; and justice is the principle that regulates my conduct accordingly. It would have been just in the chambermaid to have preferred the archbishop to herself. To have done otherwise would have been a breach of justice.

Supposing the chambermaid had been my wife, my mother or my benefactor. This would not alter the truth of the proposition. The life of Fenelon would still

---

[6] Archbishop Fénelon (1651–1715), a model of good-natured Christianity. Amongst his works was a famous account of the ideal education for a prince: *Telemachus*.

be more valuable than that of the chambermaid; and justice, pure, unadulterated justice, would still have preferred that which was most valuable. Justice would have taught me to save the life of Fenelon at the expence of the other. What magic is there in the pronoun 'my', to overturn the decisions of everlasting truth? My wife or my mother may be a fool or a prostitute, malicious, lying or dishonest. If they be, of what consequence is it that they are mine?

'But my mother endured for me the pains of child bearing, and nourished me in the helplessness of infancy.' When she first subjected herself to the necessity of these cares, she was probably influenced by no particular motives of benevolence to her future offspring. Every voluntary benefit however entitles the bestower to some kindness and retribution. But why so? Because a voluntary benefit is an evidence of benevolent intention, that is, of virtue. It is the disposition of the mind, not the external action, that entitles to respect. But the merit of this disposition is equal, whether the benefit was conferred upon me or upon another. Gratitude therefore, a principle which has so often been the theme of the moralist and the poet, is no part either of justice or virtue. By gratitude I understand a sentiment, which would lead me to prefer one man to another, from some other consideration than that of his superior usefulness or worth: that is, which would make something true to me (for example this preferableness), which cannot be true to another man, and is not true in itself.

. . .

. . . I hold my person as a trust in behalf of mankind. I am bound to employ my talents, my understanding, my strength and my time for the production of the greatest quantity of general good. Such are the declarations of justice, so great is the extent of my duty.

. . .

It is therefore impossible for me to confer upon any man a favour, I can only do him a right. What deviates from the law of justice, even I will suppose in the too much done in favour of some individual or some part of the general whole, is so much subtracted from the general stock, is so much of absolute injustice.

The inference most clearly afforded by the preceding reasonings, is the competence of justice as a principle of deduction in all cases of moral enquiry. The reasonings themselves are rather of the nature of illustration and example, and any error that may be imputed to them in particulars, will not invalidate the general conclusion, the propriety of applying moral justice as a criterion in the investigation of political truth.

Society is nothing more than an aggregation of individuals. Its claims and its duties must be the aggregate of their claims and duties, the one no more precarious and arbitrary than the other. What has the society a right to require from me? The question is already answered: every thing that it is my duty to do . . . – Again, What is it that the society is bound to do for its members? Every thing that can contribute to their welfare. But the nature of their welfare is defined by the nature of the mind. That will most contribute to it, which enlarges the understanding, supplies incitements to virtue, fills us with a generous consciousness of our independence, and carefully removes whatever can impede our exertions.

. . .

CHAPTER IV

OF THE EQUALITY OF MANKIND

. . .

. . . notwithstanding the incroachments that have been made upon the equality of mankind, a great and substantial equality remains. There is no such disparity among the human race as to enable one man to hold several other men in subjection, except so far as they are willing to be subject. All government is founded in opinion. Men at present live under any particular form, because they conceive it their interests to do so . . . Destroy this opinion and the fabric which is built upon it falls to the ground. . . .

The moral equality is still less open to reasonable exception. By moral equality I understand the propriety of applying one unalterable rule of justice to every case that may arise. This cannot be questioned but upon principles that would subvert the very nature of virtue. . . .

. . .

. . . We are partakers of a common nature, and the same causes that contribute to the benefit of one contribute to the benefit of another. Our senses and faculties are of the same denomination. Our pleasures and pains will therefore be the same. We are all of us endowed with reason, able to compare, to judge and to infer. The improvement therefore which is to be desired for the one is to be desired for the other. We shall be provident for ourselves and useful to each other, in proportion as we rise above the atmosphere of prejudice. The same independence, the same freedom from any such restraint, as should prevent us from giving the reins to our own understanding, or from uttering upon all occasions whatever we think to be true, will conduce to the improvement of all. . . .

. . .

CHAPTER V

RIGHTS OF MAN

. . .

. . . Whatever is meant by the term right, for it will presently appear that the sense of the term itself has never been clearly understood, there can neither be opposite rights, nor rights and duties hostile to each other. The rights of one man cannot clash with or be destructive of the rights of another; for this, instead of rendering the subject an important branch of truth and morality, as the advocates of the rights of man certainly understand it to be, would be to reduce it to a heap of unintelligible jargon and inconsistency. If one man have a right to be free, another man cannot have a right to make him a slave; if one man have a right to inflict chastisement upon me, I cannot have a right to withdraw myself from chastisement; if my neighbour have a right to a sum of money in my possession, I cannot have a right to retain it in my pocket. It cannot be less incontrovertible, that I have no right to omit what my duty prescribes.

From hence it inevitably follows that men have no rights. By right, as the word is employed in this subject, has always been understood discretion, that is, a full and complete power of either doing a thing or omitting it, without the person's becoming liable to animadversion or censure from another, that is, in other words, without his incurring any degree of turpitude or guilt. Now in this sense I affirm that man has no rights, no discretionary power whatever.

. . .

Nor is the fallacy of this language more conspicuous than its immoral tendency. To this inaccurate and unjust use of the term right we owe it, that the miser, who accumulates to no end that which diffused would have conduced to the welfare of thousands, that the luxurious man, who wallows in indulgence and sees numerous families around him pining in beggary, never fail to tell us of their rights, and to silence animadversion and quiet the censure of their own mind by reminding us, 'that they came fairly into possession of their wealth, that they owe no debts, and that of consequence no man has authority to enquire into their private manner of disposing of that which is their own.' . . .

It is scarcely necessary to add, that, if individuals have no rights, neither has society, which possesses nothing but what individuals have brought into a common stock. The absurdity of the common opinion, as applied to this subject, is still more glaring, if possible, than in the view in which we have already considered it. According to the usual sentiment every club assembling for any civil purpose, every congregation of religionists assembling for the worship of God, has a right to establish any provisions or ceremonies, no matter how ridiculous or detestable, provided they do not interfere with the freedom of others. Reason lies prostrate under their feet. They have a right to trample upon and insult her as they please. It is in the same spirit we have been told that every nation has a right to choose its form of government. A most acute, original and inestimable author was probably misled by the vulgar phraseology on this subject, when he asserted, that, 'at a time when neither the people of France nor the national assembly were troubling themselves about the affairs of England or the English parliament, Mr. Burke's conduct was unpardonable in commencing an unprovoked attack upon them.'[7]

. . .

A[n] . . . important objection to the doctrine I am maintaining is derived from the rights as they are called of private judgment, and the liberty of the press. But it may easily be shewn, that these, no more than the articles already mentioned, are rights of discretion. The political freedom of conscience and of the press . . . ought to be unrestrained, not because men have a right to deviate from the exact line that duty prescribes, but because society, the aggregate of individuals, has no right to assume the prerogative of an infallible judge, and to undertake authoritatively to prescribe to its members in matters of pure speculation.

. . .

CHAPTER VI
OF THE EXERCISE OF PRIVATE JUDGMENT

To a rational being there can be but one rule of conduct, justice, and one mode of ascertaining that rule, the exercise of his understanding . . .

. . .

The tendency of positive institution is of two sorts, to furnish me with an additional motive to the practice of virtue or right, and to inform my understanding as to what actions are right and what actions are wrong. Much cannot be said in commendation of either of these tendencies.

---

[7] [Godwin's footnote:] *Rights of Man*, page 1. [Godwin's evident belief that he was excusing Paine from a solecism in pointing out that he must have been 'misled by the vulgar phraseology' in claiming that nations had a right to choose their form of government is mistaken since, in fact, this was the basis of his famous American pamphlet, *Common Sense*, and the whole core of his *Rights of Man*.]

First, positive institution may furnish me with an additional motive to the practice of virtue. I have an opportunity of contributing very essentially to the advantage of twenty individuals; they will be benefited, and no other persons will sustain a material injury. I ought to embrace this opportunity. Here let us suppose positive institution to interfere, and to annex some great personal reward to myself to the performance of my duty. This immediately changes the nature of the action. Before I preferred it for its intrinsic excellence. Now, so far as the positive institution operates, I prefer it, because some person has arbitrarily annexed to it a great weight of self-interest. But virtue, considered as the quality of an intelligent being, depends upon the disposition with which the action is accompanied. Under a positive institution then this very action, which is intrinsically virtuous, may, so far as relates to the agent, become vicious. . . .

Secondly, positive institution may inform my understanding as to what actions are right and what actions are wrong. Here it is proper for us to reflect upon the terms understanding and information. Understanding, particularly as it is concerned with moral subjects, is the percipient of truth. This is its proper sphere. Information, so far as it is genuine, is a portion detached from the great body of truth. You inform me, 'that Euclid asserts the three angles of a plane triangle to be equal to two right angles.' Still I am unacquainted with the truth of this proposition. 'But Euclid has demonstrated it. His demonstration has existed for two thousand years, and during that term has proved satisfactory to every man by whom it has been understood.'[8] I am nevertheless uninformed. The knowledge of truth lies in the perceived agreement or disagreement of the terms of a proposition. So long as I am unacquainted with the middle term by means of which they may be compared, so long as they are incommensurate to my understanding, you may have furnished me with a principle from which I may reason truly to farther consequences, but as to the principle itself I may strictly be said to know nothing about it.

. . . By the authority adduced I might be prevailed on to yield an irregular assent to the proposition; but I could not properly be said to perceive its truth.

. . .

If there be any truth more unquestionable than the rest, it is, that every man is bound by the exertion of his faculties in the discovery of right, and to the carrying into effect all the right with which he is acquainted . . . So that from this reasoning it

---

[8] Euclid (BC third century), a famous Greek mathematician, was a pioneer geometrician. His method of deductive proof became the model of logical reasoning, frequently imitated in other disciplines by those – such as Hobbes – who sought similar standards of certainty in proof.

ultimately appears, that no man is obliged to conform to any rule of conduct, farther than the rule is consistent with justice.

. . . The universal exercise of private judgment is a doctrine so unspeakably beautiful, that the true politician will certainly resolve to interfere with it as sparingly and in as few instances as possible. Let us consider what are the emergencies that may be thought to demand an exception. They can only be briefly stated in this place, each of them requiring to be minutely examined in the subsequent stages of the enquiry.

. . . At first it may appear to be no great infringement upon the exercise of private judgment, to put it under some degree of restraint, when it leads to the commission of atrocious crimes. There are however certain difficulties in the case which are worthy to be considered.

First, as soon as we admit the propriety of a rule such as that above stated, our next concern will be with the evidence, which shall lead to the acquittal or conviction of the person accused . . . it is no trivial evil to subject an innocent man . . . to . . . punishment . . .

Secondly, the same external action will admit of every possible shade of virtue or vice. One man shall commit murder, to remove a troublesome observer of his depraved dispositions, who will otherwise counteract and expose him to the world. A second, because he cannot bear the ingenuous sincerity with which he is told of his vices. A third, from his intolerable envy of superior merit. A fourth, because he knows his adversary meditates an act of mischief. A fifth in actual defence of his father's life or his daughter's chastity . . . Can you pretend in each instance to ascertain the exact quantity of wrong, and to invent . . . punishment or restraint equivalent to each? . . .

Thirdly, punishment is not the appropriate mode of correcting the errors of mankind. It will probably be admitted, that the only true end of punishment is correction. That question will be discussed in another part of the present enquiry. 'I have done something, which though wrong in itself, I believe to be right; or I have done something which I usually admit to be wrong; but my conviction is not so clear and forcible, as to prevent my yielding to a powerful temptation.' . . . The proper way . . . of impressing [truth] upon me . . . is by appeal to my reason. . . .

. . .

Notwithstanding all these objections . . . the arguments already adduced may be sufficient to shew that punishment is always an evil, and to persuade us never to recur to it but from the most evident necessity.

. . .

BOOK III

PRINCIPLES OF GOVERNMENT

CHAPTER I

SYSTEMS OF POLITICAL WRITERS

It has appeared in the course of our reasonings upon the nature of society, that there are occasions in which it may be necessary, to supersede private judgment for the sake of public good, and to control the acts of the individual by an act to be performed in the name of the whole. It is therefore an interesting enquiry to ascertain in what manner such acts are to be originated, or in other words to ascertain the foundation of political government.

There are three hypotheses that have been principally maintained upon this subject. First, the system of force according to which '... there can be no other criterion of that restraint, than the power of the individuals who lay claim to its exercise ...

There is a second class of reasoners who deduce the origin of all government from divine right ...

The third system is that which has been most usually maintained by the friends of equality and justice; the system according to which the individuals of any society are supposed to have entered into a contract with their governors or with each other, and which founds the rights of government in the consent of the governed.

The two first of these hypotheses may easily be dismissed. . . .

The third hypothesis demands a more careful examination. . . .

CHAPTER II

OF THE SOCIAL CONTRACT

Upon the first statement of the system of a social contract various difficulties present themselves. Who are the parties to this contract? For whom did they consent, for themselves only or for others? For how long a time is this contract to be considered as binding? If the consent of every individual be necessary, in what manner is that consent to be given? Is it to be tacit, or declared in express terms.

Little will be gained for the cause of equality and justice, if our ancestors, at the first institution of government, had a right indeed of choosing the system of regulations under which they thought proper to live, but at the same time could barter away the understandings and independence of all that came after them to the latest posterity. But, if the contract must be renewed in each successive generation, what periods must be fixed on for that purpose? And if I be obliged to submit to the established government till my turn comes to assent to it, upon what principle is that obligation founded? Surely not upon the contract into which my father entered before I was born?

Secondly, what is the nature of the consent, in consequence of which I am to be reckoned the subject of any particular government? It is usually said, 'that acquiescence is sufficient; and that this acquiescence is to be inferred from my living quietly under the protection of the laws.' . . . Upon this hypothesis every government that is quietly submitted to is a lawful government, whether it be the usurpation of Cromwell or the tyranny of Caligula.[9] Acquiescence is frequently nothing more than a choice on the part of the individual of what he deems the least evil . . . [it] can scarcely be construed into consent, while the individuals concerned are wholly unapprised of the authority intended to be rested upon it.[10]

A third objection to the social contract will suggest itself . . . Allowing that I am called upon, at the period of my coming of age for example, to declare my assent or dissent to any system of opinions or any code of practical institutes; for how long a period does this declaration bind me? Am I precluded from better information for the whole course of my life? And, if not for my whole life, why for a year, a week or even an hour? If my deliberate judgment or my real sentiment be of no avail in the case, in what sense can it be affirmed that all lawful government is founded in my consent?

. . .

No consent of ours can divest us of our moral capacity. This is a species of property which we can neither barter nor resign; and of consequence it is impossible for any government to derive its authority from an original contract.

CHAPTER III

OF PROMISES

The whole principle of an original contract proceeds upon the obligation under which we are placed to observe our promises. The reasoning upon which it is founded is, 'that we have promised obedience to government, and therefore are bound to obey.' . . .

. . .

---

[9] Oliver Cromwell (1599–1658), Parliamentarian Leader in the English Civil War and eventually 'Lord Protector' in the interregnum government. Gaius Germanicus 'Caligula', Roman Emperor from 37 AD became the personification of tyranny owing to his short but brutal and casually violent reign.

[10] [Godwin's footnote:] See Hume's Essays. Part II, Essay xii ('Of the Original Contract'), [David Hume, *Essays, Moral, Political and Literary*, ed. Eugene F. Miller (Indianapolis: Liberty Fund, 1985), esp. 47ff.]

What is it then to which the obligation of a promise applies? What I have promised is either right, or wrong, or indifferent . . . A promise can make no alteration in the case. I ought to be guided by the intrinsic merit of the objects, and not by any external and foreign consideration. No engagements of mine can change their intrinsic claims.

. . .

It is undoubtedly upon this hypothesis a part of our duty to make as few promises or declarations exciting appropriate expectations as possible. He who lightly gives another the idea that he will govern himself in his future conduct, not by the view that shall be present in his mind when the conduct shall become determined on, but by the view he shall be able to take of it at some preceding period, is vicious in so doing. But the obligation he is under respecting his future conduct is, to act justly, and not, because he has committed one error, for that reason to become guilty of a second.[11]

CHAPTER IV

OF POLITICAL AUTHORITY

. . .

Government then being introduced for the reasons already assigned, the first and most important principle that can be imagined relative to its form and structure, seems to be this; that, as government is a transaction in the name and for the benefit of the whole, every member of the community ought to have some share in its administration. The arguments in support of this proposition are various.

1. It has already appeared that there is no criterion perspicuously designating any one man or set of men to preside over the rest.
2. All men are partakers of the common faculty reason, and may be supposed to have some communication with the common preceptor truth. It would be wrong in an affair of such momentous concern, that any chance for additional wisdom should be rejected; nor can we tell in many cases till after the experiment how eminent any individual may one day be found in the business of guiding and deliberating for his fellows.

---

[11] This is a classic illustration of Godwin's act-utilitarianism, that is, the position that a course of action is right not because it conforms to a rule – e.g. 'keep your promises' – which rule might be justified by appeal to the greatest happiness principle, but rather it is right if, taken on its own, of the available alternatives it produces the greatest happiness.

3. Government is a contrivance instituted for the security of individuals; and it seems both reasonable that each man should have a share in providing for his own security, and probable that partiality and cabal should by this means be most effectually excluded.

4. Lastly, to give each man a voice in the public concerns comes nearest to that admirable idea of which we should never lose sight, the uncontrolled exercise of private judgment. Each man would thus be inspired with a consciousness of his own importance, and the slavish feelings that shrink up the soul in the presence of an imagined superior would be unknown.

. . .

It may perhaps by some persons be imagined, that the doctrine here delivered . . . is nearly coincident with that other doctrine which teaches that all lawful government derives its authority from a social contract. Let us consider what is the true difference between them.

In the first place, the doctrine of common deliberation is of a prospective, and not a retrospective nature. Is the question respecting some future measure to be adopted in behalf of the community? Here the obligation to deliberate in common presents itself, as eminently to be preferred to every other mode of deciding upon the interests of the whole. Is the question whether I shall yield obedience to any measure already promulgated? Here I have nothing to do with the consideration of how the measure originated; . . .

Exclusively of this consideration, no measure is to be resisted on account of the irregularity of its derivation. If it be just, it is entitled both to my chearful submission and my zealous support. So far as it is deficient in justice, I am bound to resist. My situation in this respect is in no degree different from what it was previously to all organised government. . . .

Secondly . . . recollect what has been said upon the nature and validity of promises. If promise be in all cases a fallacious mode of binding a man to a specific mode of action, then must the argument be in all cases impertinent, that I consented to such a decision, and am therefore bound to regulate myself accordingly. It is impossible to imagine a principle of more injurious tendency, than that which shall teach me to disarm my future wisdom by my past folly. . . .

. . .

Too much stress has undoubtedly been laid upon the idea, as of a grand and magnificent spectacle, of a nation deciding for itself upon some great public principle, and of the highest magistracy yielding its claims when the general voice has pronounced. The value of the whole must at last depend upon the quality of their decision. Truth cannot be made more true by the number of its votaries. . . .

CHAPTER V
OF LEGISLATION

. . . Who is it that has the authority to make laws? What are the characteristics by which that man or body of men is to be known, in whom the faculty is vested of legislating for the rest [?].

To these questions the answer is exceedingly simple: Legislation, as it has been usually understood, is not an affair of human competence. Reason is the only legislator, and her decrees are irrevocable and uniform. . . .

. . .

. . . All political power is strictly speaking executive. It has appeared to be necessary, with respect to men as we at present find them, that force should sometimes be employed in repressing injustice; and for the same reasons it appears that this force should as far as possible be vested in the community . . . But no sooner does it wander in the smallest degree from the great line of justice, than its authority is at an end. . . .

BOOK IV
MISCELLANEOUS PRINCIPLES

CHAPTER I
OF RESISTANCE

It has appeared in the course of our reasonings upon political authority, that every man is bound to resist every unjust proceeding on the part of the community . . . He is obliged to consult his own private judgment in this case, for the same reason that obliges him to consult it in every other article of his conduct.

'But is not this position necessarily subversive of all government? . . .

. . .

The modes according to which an individual may oppose any measure which his judgment disapproves are of two sorts, action and speech. Shall he upon every occasion have recourse to the former? This it is absurd so much as to suppose. . . .

. . .

But, since force is scarcely under any circumstances to be employed . . . The resistance I am bound to employ is that of uttering the truth, of censuring in the most explicit manner every proceeding that I perceive to be adverse to the true interests of mankind. I am bound to disseminate without reserve all the principles with which I am acquainted, and which it may be of importance to mankind to know; and this duty it behoves me to practise upon every occasion and with the most persevering constancy. . . .

CHAPTER II

OF REVOLUTIONS

SECTION I

DUTIES OF A CITIZEN

. . .

. . . Gratitude to the constitution, an abstract idea, an imaginary existence, is altogether unintelligible. Affection to my countrymen will be much better proved, by my exertions to procure them a substantial benefit, than by my supporting a system which I believe to be fraught with injurious consequences.

He who calls upon me to support the constitution must found his requisition upon one of two principles. It has a claim upon my support either because it is good, or because it is British.

Against the requisition in the first sense there is nothing to object. All that is necessary is to prove the goodness which is ascribed to it. . . .

As to the demand upon me for support to the English constitution, because it is English, there is little plausibility in this argument. It is of the same nature as the demand upon me to be a Christian, because I am a Briton, or a Mahometan, because I am a native of Turkey. Instead of being an expression of respect, it argues contempt of all government, religion and virtue, and every thing that is sacred among men. If there be such a thing as truth, it must be better than error. If there be such a faculty as reason, it ought to be exerted. . . .

SECTION II

MODE OF EFFECTING REVOLUTION

. . . The revolutions of states, which a philanthropist would desire to witness, or in which he would willingly co-operate, consist principally in a change of sentiments and dispositions in the members of those states. The true instruments for changing the opinions of men are argument and persuasion. The best security for an advantageous issue is free and unrestricted discussion. In that field truth must always prove the successful champion. If then we would improve the social institutions of mankind, we must write, we must argue, we must converse. To this business there is no close; in this pursuit there should be no pause. Every method should be employed, – not so much positively to allure the attention of mankind, or persuasively to invite them to the adoption of our opinions, – as to remove every restraint upon thought, and to throw open the temple of science and the field of enquiry to all the world.

. . .

. . . Indignation, resentment and fury are to be deprecated; and all we should ask is sober thought, clear discernment and intrepid discussion. . . .

. . .

SECTION III
OF POLITICAL ASSOCIATIONS

A question naturally suggests itself in this place respecting the propriety of associations among the people at large, for the purpose of effecting a change in their political institutions. . . .

. . .

In the first place revolutions less originate in the energies of the people at large than in the conceptions of persons of some degree of study and reflection . . .

The studious and reflecting only can be expected to see deeply into future events. To conceive an order of society totally different from that which is now before our eyes, and to judge of the advantages that would accrue from its institution, are the prerogatives only of a few favoured minds . . . they cannot yet for some time be expected to be understood by the multitude . . . He, that begins with an appeal to the people, may be suspected to understand little of the true character of mind. A sinister design may gain by precipitation; but true wisdom is best adapted to a slow, unvarying, incessant progress.

. . .

. . . Discussion perhaps never exists with so much vigour and utility as in the conversation of two persons. It may be carried on with advantage in small and friendly societies. Does the fewness of their numbers imply the rarity of their existence? Far otherwise: the time perhaps will come when such institutions will be universal. Shew to mankind by a few examples the advantages of political discussion undebauched by political enmity and vehemence, and the beauty of the spectacle will soon render the example contagious. Every man will commune with his neighbour. Every man will be eager to tell and to hear what the interest of all requires them to know . . . Knowledge will be accessible to all. . . .

But these consequences are the property only of independent and impartial discussion. If once the unambitious and candid circles of enquiring men be swallowed up in the insatiate gulf of noisy assemblies, the opportunity of improvement is instantly annihilated. The happy varieties of sentiment which so eminently contribute to intellectual acuteness are lost. Activity of thought is shackled by the fear that our associates should disclaim us. A fallacious uniformity of opinion is produced, which no man espouses from conviction, but which carries all men along with a resistless tide. Clubs, in the old English sense, that is, the periodical meeting of small and independent circles, may be admitted to fall within the line of these principles. But they cease to be admissible, when united with the tremendous apparatus of articles of confederacy and committees of correspondence.[12]. . .

. . .

BOOK V
OF LEGISLATIVE AND EXECUTIVE POWER

CHAPTER XVI
OF THE CAUSES OF WAR

. . .

Accurately considered, there can probably be but two justifiable causes of war . . . these are the defence of our own liberty and the liberty of others. The well known objection to the latter these cases is 'that one nation ought not to interfere in the internal transactions of another;' and we can only wonder that so absurd an objection should have been admitted for so long . . . It may . . . be an unjustifiable undertaking

---

[12] Godwin here states his opposition to bodies such as the London Corresponding Society, which was to culminate in his attack on his intellectual protégé, John Thelwall. Although Godwin defended Thelwall in the treason trials of 1794, a year later, when the Government published its infamous 'Two Acts' banning political assembly and extending the definition of sedition, Godwin supported the government as maintaining an order and security that was threatened by the radicals. See I. Kramnick, 'On Anarchism and the Real World: William Godwin and Radical England', *American Political Science Review* 66 (1) (1972), pp. 114–28.

to force a nation to be free. But, when the people themselves desire it, it is virtue and duty to assist them in the acquisition. This principle is . . . the very same argument that should induce me to exert myself for the liberties of my own country . . . the morality that should govern the conduct of individuals and of nations is in all cases the same.[13]

CHAPTER XXI

OF THE COMPOSITION OF THE GOVERNMENT

One of the articles which has been most eagerly insisted on by the advocates of complexity in political institutions, is that of 'checks, by which a rash proceeding may be prevented, and the provisions under which mankind have hitherto lived with tranquillity, may not be reversed without mature deliberation.' We will suppose that the evils of monarchy and aristocracy are by this time too notorious to incline the speculative enquirer to seek for a remedy in either of these. 'Yet it is possible, without the institution of privileged orders, to find means that may answer a similar purpose in this respect. The representatives of the people may be distributed for example into two assemblies; they may be chosen with this particular view to constitute an upper and a lower house, and may be distinguished from each other, either by various qualifications of age or fortune, or by being chosen by a greater or smaller number of electors, or for a shorter or longer term.'[14]

. . .

The institution of two houses of assembly is the direct method to divide a nation against itself. One of these houses will in a greater or less degree be the asylum of usurpation, monopoly and privilege. Parties would expire as soon as they were born, in a country where opposition of sentiments and a struggle of interests were not allowed to assume the formalities of distinct institution.

Meanwhile a species of check perfectly simple, and which appears sufficiently adequate to the purpose, suggests itself in the idea of a slow and deliberate proceeding

---

[13] Godwin correctly paraphrases conventional international law of the time on this topic (see Emmerich de Vatell, *Les Lois des Gens* (1758), Classics of International Law (Washington, 1916), II, iv, §56).

[14] *Ancien Régime*: European parliaments had divided legislatures because they had nobilities, of distinct legal status – 'estates' – which had to be represented separately. With the abolition of nobility that reason for a second chamber disappeared. Both the American and the French revolutions wrestled with the problem of a non-privileged basis for a second chamber, a problem still unresolved in twenty-first-century Britain!

which the representative assembly should prescribe to itself. Perhaps no proceeding of this assembly should have the force of a general regulation till it had undergone five or six successive discussions in the assembly, or till the expiration of one month from the period of its being proposed. Something like this is the order of the English house of commons, nor does it appear to be by any means among the worst features of our constitution.[15] A system like this would be sufficiently analogous to the proceedings of a wise individual, who certainly would not wish to determine upon the most important concerns of his life without a severe examination, and still less would omit this examination, if his decision were destined to be a rule for the conduct and a criterion to determine upon the rectitude of other men.

. . .

Scarcely any plausible argument can be adduced in favour of what has been denominated by political writers a division of powers.[16] . . . The distinction of legislative and executive powers, however intelligible in theory, will by no means authorise their separation in practice.

. . .

CHAPTER XXII

OF THE FUTURE HISTORY OF POLITICAL SOCIETIES

. . .

Government can have no more than two legitimate purposes, the suppression of injustice against individuals within the community, and the common defence against external invasion . . . The principal object of punishment is restraint upon a dangerous member of the community; and the end of this restraint would be answered, by the general inspection that is exercised by the members of a limited circle over the conduct of each other, and by the gravity and good sense that

[15] Parliamentary bills required an initial motion to introduce them, a 'second reading' at which substantive debate would take place, and yet a third reading at which amendment could be made. Bills then had to pass through the other House – a procedure which Godwin rejects.
[16] The doctrine of division of powers seems to have been derived, in a confused way, from the idea of the Mixed Constitution in Britain through the fact that different powers were to be found in elements of that Mixed Constitution, executive in the Crown, legislative in the Commons, and judicial ultimately in the Lords. See Locke, *Two Treatises of Government*, ii, xi, xii. The ideal grew in strength throughout the eighteenth century and was foundational in the American Constitution. See James Madison, *Federalist*, no. 47.

would characterise the censures of men, from whom all mystery and empiricism[17] were banished. No individual would be hardy enough in the cause of vice, to defy the general consent of sober judgment that would surround him. It would carry despair to his mind, or, which is better, it would carry conviction. He would be obliged, by a force not less irresistible than whips and chains, to reform his conduct.

In this sketch is contained the rude outline of political government. Controversies between parish and parish would be in an eminent degree unreasonable, since, if any question arose, about limits for example, justice would presently teach us that the individual who cultivates any portion of land, is the properest person to decide to which district he would belong. No association of men, so long as they adhered to the principles of reason, could possibly have any interest in extending their territory. If we would produce attachment in our associates, we can adopt no surer method than that of practising the dictates of equity and moderation; and, if this failed in any instance, it could only fail with him who, to whatever society he belonged, would prove an unworthy member. The duty of any society to punish offenders is not dependent upon the hypothetical consent of the offender to be punished, but upon the duty of necessary defence.

. . .

CHAPTER XXIII

OF NATIONAL ASSEMBLIES

In the first place the existence of a national assembly introduces the evils of a fictitious unanimity. The public, guided by such an assembly, acts with concert, or else the assembly is a nugatory excrescence. But it is impossible that this unanimity can really exist. The individuals who constitute a nation, cannot take into consideration a variety of important questions, without forming different sentiments respecting them. In reality all matters that are brought before such an assembly are decided by a majority of votes, and the minority, after having exposed with all the power of eloquence and force of reasoning of which they are capable the injustice and folly of the measures adopted, are obliged in a certain sense to assist in carrying them into execution. Nothing can more directly contribute to the depravation of the human understanding and character. . . .

[17] Here, curiously to modern readers, in its original sense of crude and *un*scientific.

Secondly, the existence of national councils produces a certain species of real unanimity, unnatural in its character, and pernicious in its effects. The genuine and wholesome state of mind is, to be unloosed from shackles, and to expand every fibre of its frame according to the independent and individual impressions of truth upon that mind . . . But the unanimity, that results from men's having a visible standard by which to adjust their sentiments, is deceitful and pernicious.

In numerous assemblies a thousand motives influence our judgments, independently of reason and evidence. Every man looks forward to the effects which the opinions he avows will produce on his success. Every man connects himself with some sect or party. The activity of his thought is shackled at every turn by the fear that his associates may disclaim him. . . .

Thirdly, the debates of a national assembly are distorted from their reasonable tenour by the necessity of their being uniformly terminated by a vote. Debate and discussion are in their own nature highly conducive to intellectual improvement; but they lose this salutary character the moment they are subjected to this unfortunate condition. What can be more unreasonable, than to demand, that argument, the usual quality of which is gradually and imperceptibly to enlighten the mind, should declare its effect in the close of a single conversation? . . .

. . .

. . . All government corresponds in a certain degree to what the Greeks denominated a tyranny. The difference is, that in despotic countries mind is depressed by a uniform usurpation; while in republics it preserves a greater portion of its activity, and the usurpation more easily conforms itself to the fluctuations of opinion.

. . .

From these reasonings we are sufficiently authorised to conclude, that national assemblies, or in other words assemblies instituted for the joint purpose of adjusting the differences between district and district, and of consulting respecting the best mode of repelling foreign invasion, however necessary to be had recourse to upon certain occasions, ought to be employed as sparingly as the nature of the case will admit. They should either never be elected but upon extraordinary emergencies, like the dictator of the ancient Romans,[18] or else sit periodically, one day for example in

[18] 'Dictator' was an emergency office (with extraordinary but nevertheless defined and limited powers) provided for under the Roman Republican Constitution. It did not yet have the overtones of permanently unlimited rule which it later acquired in the first half of the twentieth century as a result of the opposition between the Europe of 'the Democracies' and 'the Dictatorships' – Spain, Italy and Germany.

a year, with a power of continuing their sessions within a certain limit; to hear the complaints and representations of their constituents. The former of these modes is greatly to be preferred. . . .

 . . .

CHAPTER XXIV

OF THE DISSOLUTION OF GOVERNMENT

It remains for us to consider what is the degree of authority necessary to be vested in such a modified species of national assembly as we have admitted into our system. Are they to issue their commands to the different members of the confederacy? Or is it sufficient that they should invite them to co-operate for the common advantage, and by arguments and addresses convince them of the reasonableness of the measures they propose? The former of these would at first be necessary. The latter would afterwards become sufficient: The Amphictyonic council of Greece[19] possessed no authority but that which derived from its personal character. In proportion as the spirit of party was extirpated, as the restlessness of public commotion subsided, and as the political machine be came simple, the voice of reason would be secure to be heard. An appeal by the assembly to the several districts would not fail to obtain the approbation of all reasonable men, unless it contained in it something so evidently questionable, as to make it perhaps desirable that it should prove abortive.

This remark leads us one step farther. Why should not the same distinction between commands and invitations, which we have just made in the case of national assemblies, be applied to the particular assemblies or juries of the several districts? . . . It will then be sufficient for juries to recommend a certain mode of adjusting controversies, without assuming the prerogative of dictating that adjustment. . . .

The reader has probably anticipated me in the ultimate conclusion, from these remarks. If juries might at length cease to decide and be contented to invite, if force might gradually be withdrawn and reason trusted alone, shall we not one day find that juries themselves and every other species of public institution, may be laid aside as unnecessary? Will not the reasonings of one wise man be as effectual as those of twelve? Will not the competence of one individual to instruct his neighbours be a matter of

[19] *Amphyctionies* were loose associations of states in Ancient Greece which shared in the administration of common religious shrines and ceremonies; to be contrasted with the more centralised and ultimately authoritarian military leagues such as the Peleponnesian, Boetian and Athenian.

sufficient notoriety, without the formality of an election? Will there be many vices to correct and much obstinacy to conquer? This is one of the most memorable stages of human improvement. With what delight must every well informed friend of mankind look forward to the auspicious period, the dissolution of political government, of that brute engine, which has been the only perennial cause of the vices of mankind, and which, as has abundantly appeared in the progress of the present work, has mischiefs of various sorts incorporated with its substance, and no otherwise to be removed than by its utter annihilation![20]

BOOK VI

OF OPINION CONSIDERED AS A SUBJECT OF POLITICAL INSTITUTION

CHAPTER I

GENERAL EFFECTS OF THE POLITICAL SUPERINTENDANCE OF OPINION

A principle, which has entered deeply into the systems of the writers on political law, is that of the duty of governments to watch over the manners of the people.[21] . . .

. . . Nothing can be more unquestionable than that the manners and opinions of mankind are of the utmost consequence to the general welfare. But it does not follow that government is the instrument by which they are to be fashioned.

. . .

---

[20] It is for these views that Godwin has subsequently been seen as a founder of modern anarchism. However, this is a reconstructed tradition; there is little demonstrable continuity between his thought and the anarchisms of the late nineteenth century which ultimately had other intellectual roots.

[21] Godwin's observation is clearly correct. By manners was meant the predispositions and beliefs that people brought to politics. They were closely related to 'opinion'. With the expansion of the political public, something like a public opinion had begun to emerge. It was a commonplace amongst mid-century writers to observe, with Hume, that 'government was founded on opinion'. Historians have recently been much preoccupied with these issues. (L. Klein, 'Liberty Manners and Politeness in Early Modern England', *Historical Journal* 32, (1989); N. Phillipson, Politeness and Politics in the Reigns of Anne and the Early Hanoverians', in J. G. A. Pocock and Gordon Schochet, *Varieties of British Political Thought 1500–1800* (Cambridge University Press, 1993), pp. 583–605. Iain Hampsher-Monk, 'From Virtue to Politeness', in Martin van Gelderen and Quentin Skinner (eds.), *Republicanism: A Shared European Heritage*, 2 vols. (Cambridge: Cambridge University Press, 2002) vol. II, pp. 85–105.

Nothing can be more unreasonable than the attempt to retain men in one common opinion by the dictate of authority. The opinion thus obtruded upon the minds of the public is not their real opinion; it is only a project by which they are rendered incapable of forming an opinion. Whenever government assumes to deliver us from the trouble of thinking for ourselves, the only consequences it produces are those of torpor and imbecility. . . . He that in any degree consigns to another the task of dictating his opinions and his conduct, will cease to enquire for himself, or his enquiries will be languid and inanimate.

. . .

The just conclusion from the above reasonings . . . incites us to look for the moral improvement of the species, not in the multiplying of regulations, but in their repeal. It teaches us that truth and virtue, like commerce, will then flourish most, when least subjected to the mistaken guardianship of authority and laws. . . .

CHAPTER II

ON RELIGIOUS ESTABLISHMENTS

One of the most striking instances of the injurious effects of the political patronage of opinion, as it at present exists in the world, is to be found in the system of religious conformity. Let us take our example from the church of England, by the constitution of which subscription is required from its clergy to thirty-nine articles of precise and dogmatical assertion upon almost every subject of moral and metaphysical enquiry.[22] Here then we have to consider the whole honours and revenues of the church . . . is there one man through this numerous hierarchy that is at liberty to think for himself? Is there one man among them that can lay his hand upon his heart, and, declare, upon his honour and conscience, that his emoluments have no effect in influencing his judgment? The declaration is literally impossible. The most that an honest man under such circumstances can say is, 'I hope not; I endeavour to be impartial.'

First, the system of religious conformity is a system of blind submission. In every country possessing a religious establishment, the state, from a benevolent care it may

---

[22] The Thirty-Nine Articles (originally forty-two) were drawn up by Archbishop Cranmer under Edward VI. They defined the theological tenets of the Church of England to which all Anglican ministers had to swear belief. In 1772 Anglican ministers who, like Godwin, rejected trinitarianism had petitioned Parliament to be excused from having to subscribe to the Articles. On being refused, a number of these ministers, most famously Theophilus Lindsey, had left the Church and founded or joined Unitarian congregations.

be for the manners and opinions of its subjects, publicly encourages a numerous class of men to the study of morality and virtue. What institution, we might naturally be led to enquire, can be more favourable to public happiness? . . . But unfortunately these very men are fettered in the outset by having a code of propositions put into their hands, in a conformity to which all their enquiries must terminate.[23] . . .

Secondly, the tendency of a code of religious conformity is to make men hypocrites. To understand this it may be useful to recollect the various subterfuges that have been invented by ingenious men to apologise for the subscription of the English clergy. It is observable by the way the articles of the church are founded upon the creed of the Calvinists, though for one hundred and fifty years past it has been accounted disreputable among the clergy to be of any other than the opposite, or Arminian tenets.[24] . . . Lastly, there are many who have treated these articles as articles of peace, and inferred that, though you did not believe, you might allow yourself in the disingenuity of subscribing them, provided you added to it the further guilt of constantly refraining to oppose what you considered as an adulteration of divine truth.

. . .

These arguments do not apply to any particular articles and creeds, but to the very notion of ecclesiastical establishments in general. Wherever the state sets apart a certain revenue for the support of religion, it will infallibly be given to the adherents of some particular opinions, and will operate in the manner of prizes to induce men at all events to embrace and profess those opinions. . . .

CHAPTER III

OF THE SUPPRESSION OF ERRONEOUS OPINION IN

RELIGION AND GOVERNMENT

. . .

The same reasonings that are here employed against the forcible suppression of religious heresy, will be found equally valid with respect to political. The

---

[23] Godwin is referring to the fact that taking communion in the Anglican Church was a condition of office-holding, admission to university and the professions.

[24] The theology of the articles and original *Book of Common Prayer* followed Calvin in his belief that salvation was predestined and available only to a few – the 'elect'. In the seventeenth century, the Church under Archbishop Laud moved to support the theology of the Dutch anti-Calvinist Remonstrants, led by Jacobus Arminius (b. 1560), who had held that salvation was available to all.

first circumstance that will not fail to suggest itself to every reflecting mind, is, What sort of constitution must that be which must never be examined? Whose excellencies must be the constant topic of eulogium, but respecting which we must never permit ourselves to enquire in what they consist? Can it be the interest of society to proscribe all investigation respecting the wisdom of its regulations? . . .

'But will not demagogues and declaimers lead to the subversion of all order, and introduce the most dreadful calamities?' What is the state they will introduce? Monarchy and aristocracy are some of the most extensive and lasting mischiefs that have yet afflicted mankind. Will these demagogues persuade their hearers to institute a new dynasty of hereditary despots to oppress them? Will they persuade them to create out of their own body a set of feudal chiefs to hold their brethren in the most barbarous slavery. . . . Excesses are never the offspring of reason, are never the offspring of misrepresentation only, but of power endeavouring to stifle reason and traverse the common sense of mankind.

CHAPTER VI

OF LIBELS

. . .

Laws for the suppression of private libel are properly speaking laws to restrain men from the practice of sincerity . . . [They] by perpetually menacing me with the scourge of punishment, undertake to render me habitually a coward, continually governed by the basest and most unprincipled of motives.

. . .

There is one thing more that is of importance to be observed upon this subject of libel, which is, the good effects that would spring from every man's being accustomed to encounter falshood with its only proper antidote, truth. . . . He that was conscious of his rectitude, and undebauched by ill systems of government, would say to his adversary, 'Publish what you please against me, I have truth on my side, and will confound your misrepresentations.' . . . A man, urged by indignation and impatience, may, commence a prosecution against his accuser; but he may be assured, the world, that is a disinterested spectator, feels no cordiality for his proceedings. The language of their sentiments upon such occasions is, 'What! he dares not even let us hear what can be said against him.'

. . .

CHAPTER VII

OF CONSTITUTIONS

. . . It has been said that the laws of every regular state naturally distribute themselves under two heads, fundamental and adscititious;[25] laws, the object of which is the distribution of political power and directing the permanent forms according to which public business is to be conducted; and laws, the result of the deliberations of powers already constituted. This distinction being established in the first instance, it has been inferred, that these laws are of very unequal importance, and that of consequence those of the first class ought to be originated with much greater solemnity, and to be declared much less susceptible of variation that those of the second. The French national assembly of 1789 pushed this principle to the greatest extremity, and seemed desirous of providing every imaginable security for rendering the work they had formed immortal. . . .

. . .

A celebrated objection that has been urged against the governments of modern Europe is that they have no constitutions.[26] . . .

. . . The language of permanence in this case is the greatest of all absurdities. It is to say to a nation, 'Are you convinced that something is right, perhaps immediately necessary, to be done? It shall be done ten years hence.'

The folly of this system may be further elucidated, if farther elucidation be necessary, from the following dilemma. Either a people must be governed according to their own apprehensions of justice and truth, or they must not. The last of these assertions cannot be avowed, but upon the unequivocal principles of tyranny. But, if the first be true, then it is just as absurd to say to a nation, This government, which you chose nine years ago, is the legitimate government, and the government

---

[25] Originally used to distinguish between intrinsic motion, such as that engendered by mass, from other motion, such as that which derived from external forces (Francis Bacon, *Novum Organum* (1620), xlviii, in John M. Robertson (ed.), *Philosophical Works of Francis Bacon* (London: Routledge, 1905), p. 368). Godwin is here seeking to make a distinction which was at least fuzzy in English Constitutional thinking – for which it was ridiculed by Paine – between fundamental, i.e. constitutional, and secondary law. Although the idea of 'fundamental law' is ancient, the modern idea of a written, privileged, constitutional code derives from the American states and the American Federal and French Revolutions which produced the first written national constitutions of modernity.

[26] Godwin here includes a footnote: ' Rights of Man [see this selection pp. 144–5] . . . it is to be expected that the remark would amount to an eulogium, but an eulogium to which they are certainly by no means entitled'.

which your present sentiments approve the illegitimate; as to insist upon their being governed by the dicta of their remotest ancestors, or even of the most insolent usurper.

. . .

CHAPTER X

OF THE MODES OF DECIDING A QUESTION ON

THE PART OF THE COMMUNITY

What has been here said upon the subject of qualifications, naturally leads to a few important observations upon the three principal modes of conducting election, by sortition,[27] by ballot or by vote.

The idea of sortition was first introduced by the dictates of superstition. It was supposed that, when human reason piously acknowledged its insufficiency, the Gods, pleased with so unfeigned a homage, interfered to guide the decision. This imagination is now exploded. Every man who pretends to philosophy will confess that, wherever sortition is introduced, the decision is exclusively guided by the laws of impulse and gravitation. Strictly speaking there is no such thing as contingence. . . .

. . . Men, undebauched by the lessons of superstition, would never have recourse to the decision by lot, were they not impressed with the notion of indifference, that they had a right to do any one of two or more things offered to their choice; and that of consequence, in order to rid themselves of uncertainty and doubt, it was sufficiently allowable to refer the decision of certain matters to accident. It is of great importance that this idea should be extirpated. . . . in all cases our duty is precise, and the path of justice single and direct.

. . .

---

[27] Sortition refers to any selection procedure based on chance or randomness. However bizarrely to modern sensibilities, this was identified as a democratic device by the ancient Greeks. There are arguments in favour of randomness over majoritarianism. As Hegel points out, agreeing to remove appointments or decisions from the political arena of voting or authoritative allocation renders the choice immune to criticisms of partisanship. Thus the authority of an elective Monarchy (Presidency) who owes his position to a majority (or plurality) of electors is more contentious, for that very reason, than an hereditary constitutional Monarch (who owes her position to chance – the accident of birth). See Hegel, *Philosophy of Right*, trans. with notes by T. M. Knox (Oxford: Oxford University Press, 1952), §§279, 281 and notes thereto, and more generally B. Goodwin, *Justice and the Lottery* (London: Harvester-Wheatsheaf, 1992).

· 244 ·

Ballot is a mode of decision still more censurable than sortition.[28] It is scarcely possible to conceive of a political institution that includes a more direct and explicit patronage of vice. . . . The true cure for a want of constancy and public spirit is to inspire firmness, not to inspire timidity. Truth, if communicated to the mind with perspicuity, is a sufficient basis for virtue. To tell men that it is necessary they should form their decision by ballot, is to tell them that it is necessary they should be vicious.

If sortition taught us to desert our duty, ballot teaches us to draw a veil of concealment over our performance of it. . . .

If then sortition and ballot be institutions pregnant with vice, it follows, that all social decisions should be made by open vote; that, wherever we have a function to discharge, we should reflect on the mode in which it ought to be discharged; and that, whatever conduct we are persuaded to adopt, especially in affairs of general concern, should be adopted in the face of the world.

BOOK VII

OF CRIMES AND PUNISHMENTS

CHAPTER I

LIMITATIONS OF THE DOCTRINE OF PUNISHMENT WHICH
RESULT FROM THE PRINCIPLES OF MORALITY

The subject of punishment is perhaps the most fundamental in the science of politics. . . . government, or the action of the society in its corporate capacity, can scarcely be of any utility, except so far as it is requisite for the suppression of force by force; for the prevention of the hostile attack of one member of the society upon the person or property of another, which prevention is usually called by the name of criminal justice, or punishment.

. . .

The justice of punishment therefore, in the strict import of the word, can only be a deduction from the hypothesis of free-will, and must be false, if human actions be necessary. . . . [But] Morality in a rational and designing mind is not essentially different from morality in an inanimate substance. A man of certain intellectual habits

---

[28] By ballot, Godwin means the secret casting of votes. His reasons for opposing it are similar to those later voiced by J. S. Mill in *Considerations on Representative Government* (1861), Ch. 10.

is fitted to be an assassin, a dagger of a certain form is fitted to be his instrument. . . .
The assassin cannot help the murder he commits any more than the dagger.

. . .

Thus it appears, . . . that, accurately speaking, there is no such thing as desert. It
cannot be just that we should inflict suffering on any man, except so far as it tends to
good. . . . It is right that I should inflict suffering, in every case where it can be clearly
shown that such infliction will produce an overbalance of good. But this infliction
bears no reference to the mere innocence or guilt of the person upon whom it is
made. An innocent man is the proper subject of it, if it tend to good. A guilty man
is the proper subject of it under no other point of view. . . .

. . .

CHAPTER II
GENERAL DISADVANTAGES OF COERCION

. . .

Let us reflect for a moment upon the species of argument, if argument it is to be
called, that coercion employs. It avers to its victim that he must necessarily be in the
wrong because I am more vigorous and more cunning than he. . . .

. . .

Let us consider the effect that coercion produces upon the mind of him against
whom it is employed. It cannot begin with convincing; it is no argument. . . . It
begins with violently alienating the mind from the truth with which we wish it to
be impressed. . . . If he who employs coercion against me could mould me to his
purposes by argument no doubt he would. He pretends to punish me because his
argument is important, but really he punishes me because his argument is weak.

CHAPTER VI
SCALE OF COERCION

It is time to proceed to the consideration of certain inferences that may be deduced
from the theory of coercion which has now been delivered; . . .

And, first, it evidently follows that coercion is an act of painful necessity, inconsistent with the true character and genius of mind, the practice of which is temporarily
imposed upon us by the corruption and ignorance that reign among mankind. Nothing can be more absurd than to look to it as a source of improvement. . . .

. . .

The justice of coercion is built upon this simple principle: Every man is bound to employ such means as shall suggest themselves for preventing evils subversive of general security, it being first ascertained, either by experience or reasoning, that all milder methods are inadequate to the exigence of the case. The conclusion from this principle is, that we are bound under certain urgent circumstances to deprive the offender of the liberty he has abused. Farther than this no circumstance can authorise us. . . .

. . .

. . . The person of the offender is to be restrained as long as the public safety would be endangered by his liberation. But the public safety will cease to be endangered, as soon as his propensities and dispositions have undergone a change. The connection which thus results from the nature of things, renders it necessary that, in deciding upon the species of restraint to be imposed, these two circumstances be considered jointly, how the personal liberty of the offender may be least entrenched upon, and how his reformation may be best promoted.

. . .

To conclude. . . . it might be the duty of individuals, but never of communities, to exert a certain species of political coercion; . . . founded . . . upon a consideration of . . . public security. . . . and to yield countenance to no other coercion than that which is indispensably necessary. . . . He will decline all concern in the execution of such as abuse the plea of public security to the most atrocious purposes. Every lover of justice will uniformly in this way contribute to the repeal of all laws, that wantonly usurp upon the independence of mankind, either by the multiplicity of their restrictions, or severity of their sanctions.

CHAPTER VIII
OF LAW

. . .

[Law] has been recommended as 'affording information to the different members of the community respecting the principles which will be adopted in deciding upon their actions.' It has been represented as the highest degree of iniquity, 'to try men by an *ex post facto* law, or indeed in any other manner than by the letter of a law, formally made, and sufficiently promulgated.'[29]

---

[29] For example, although Godwin does not seem to be quoting him, William Blackstone, *Commentaries on the Laws of England* (1783), vol i., ch. 2, p. 46.

How far it will be safe altogether to annihilate this principle we shall presently have occasion to enquire. It is obvious at first sight to remark, that it is of most importance in a country where the system of jurisprudence is most capricious and absurd. If it be deemed criminal in any society to wear clothes of a particular texture, or buttons of a particular composition, it is natural to exclaim, that it is high time the jurisprudence of that society should inform its members what are the fantastic rules by which they mean to proceed. But, if a society be contented with the rules of justice, and do not assume to itself the right of distorting or adding to those rules, there law is evidently a less necessary institution. The rules of justice would be more clearly and effectually taught by an actual intercourse with human society unrestrained by the fetters of prepossession, than they can be by catechisms and codes.

. . .

There is no maxim more clear than this, Every case is a rule to itself. No action of any man was ever the same as any other action, had ever the same degree of utility or injury. It should seem to be the business of justice, to distinguish the qualities of men, and not, which has hitherto been the practice, to confound them. But what has been the result of an attempt to do this in relation to law? . . .

. . . Law was made that a plain man might know what he had to depend upon, and yet the most . . . celebrated pleader in the kingdom, or the first counsel in the service of the crown, shall assure me of infallible success, five minutes before another law officer, styled the keeper of the king's conscience, by some unexpected juggle decides it against me. Would the issue have been equally uncertain, if I had had nothing to trust to but the plain unperverted sense of a jury of my neighbours, founded in the ideas they entertained of general justice? . . . Men do not quarrel about that which is evident, but that which is obscure.

. . .

The fable of Procrustes[30] presents us with a faint shadow of the perpetual effort of law. . . . There is no more real justice in endeavouring to reduce the actions of men into classes, than there was in the scheme to which we have just alluded, of reducing all men to the same stature. If on the contrary justice be a result flowing from the contemplation of all the circumstances of each individual case, if the only criterion of justice be general utility, the inevitable consequence is that, the more we have of justice, the more we shall have of truth, virtue and happiness.

---

[30] Procrustes, a mythical giant whose bed, he claimed, would fit all visitors since he either chopped or stretched them to fit it.

From all these considerations we cannot hesitate to conclude universally that law is an institution of the most pernicious tendency.

. . .

BOOK VIII

OF PROPERTY

CHAPTER I

GENUINE SYSTEM OF PROPERTY DELINEATED

The subject of property is the keystone that completes the fabric of political justice. According as our ideas respecting it are crude or correct, they will enlighten us as to the consequences of a *simple form of society without government*, and remove the prejudices that attach us to complexity. . . .

. . . it shall be the business of what remains of this work to consider, not any particular abuses which have incidentally risen out of the administration of property, but those general principles by which it has in almost all cases been directed, and which, if erroneous, must not only be regarded as the source of the abuses above enumerated, but of others of innumerable kinds, too multifarious and subtle to enter into so brief a catalogue.

What is the criterion that must determine whether this or that substance, capable of contributing to the benefit of a human being, ought to be considered as your property or mine? To this question there can be but one answer – Justice. Let us then recur to the principles of justice.

To whom does any article of property, suppose a loaf of bread, justly belong? To him who most wants it, or to whom the possession of it will be most beneficial . . .

. . .

. . . If justice have any meaning, nothing can be more iniquitous, than for one man to possess superfluities, while there is a human being in existence that is not adequately supplied with these.

Justice does not stop here. Every man is entitled, so far as the general stock will suffice, not only to the means of being, but of well being . . . It is unjust, if one man be deprived of leisure to cultivate his rational powers, while another man contributes not a single effort to add to the common stock . . . Justice directs that each man, unless perhaps he be employed more beneficially to the public, should contribute to the cultivation of the common harvest, of which man consumes a share. This reciprocity indeed, as was observed when that subject was the matter of separate consideration, is of the very essence of justice. . . .

. . .

But it has been alleged, 'that we find among different men very different degrees of labour and industry, and that it is not just they should receive an equal reward. . . .

. . . let us consider the nature of the reward which is thus proposed to industry. If you be industrious, you shall have an hundred times more food than you can eat, and an hundred times more clothes than you can wear. Where is the justice of this? . . . With this superfluity I can purchase nothing but gaudy ostentation and envy, nothing but the pitiful pleasure of returning to the poor under the name of generosity that to which reason gives them an irresistible claim, nothing but prejudice, error and vice.

. . .

Does any man doubt the truth of these assertions? Does any man doubt that, when I employ a sum of money small or great in the purchase of an absolute luxury for myself, I am guilty of vice? . . .

But, while religion inculcated on mankind the impartial nature of justice, its teachers have been too apt to treat the practice of justice, not as a debt, which it ought to be considered, but as an affair of spontaneous generosity and bounty. . . .

CHAPTER II

BENEFITS ARISING FROM THE GENUINE SYSTEM OF PROPERTY

Having seen the justice of an equal distribution of property, let us next consider the benefits with which it would be attended. . . .

. . . property brings home a servile and truckling spirit by no circuitous method to every house in the nation. Observe the pauper fawning with abject vileness upon his rich benefactor, . . . Observe the servants that follow in a rich man's train, watchful of his looks, anticipating his commands, not daring to reply to his insolence, . . . Observe the tradesman, how he studies the passions of his customers, not to correct, but to pamper them, the vileness of his flattery and the systematical constancy with which he exaggerates the merit of his commodities. Observe the practices of a popular election, where the great mass are purchased by obsequiousness, by intemperance and bribery, or driven by unmanly threats of poverty and persecution. Indeed 'the age of chivalry is' not 'gone!'³¹ The feudal spirit still survives, that reduced the great mass of mankind to the rank of slaves and cattle for the service of a few.

. . .

A second evil that arises out of the established system of property is the perpetual spectacle of injustice it exhibits. This consists partly in luxury and partly in caprice. There is nothing more pernicious to the human mind than luxury. . . . Wealth, by the sentiments of servility and dependence it produces, makes the rich man stand forward as the only object of general esteem and deference. . . . To acquire wealth and to display it, is therefore the universal passion. The whole structure of human society is made a system of the narrowest selfishness. . . .

. . .

This leads us to observe, thirdly, that the established system of property, is the true levelling system with respect to the human species, . . . Accumulated property treads the powers of thought in the dust, extinguishes the sparks of genius, and reduces the great mass of mankind to be immersed in sordid cares; beside depriving the rich, as we have already said, of the most salubrious and effectual motives to activity. If superfluity were banished, the necessity for the greater part of the manual industry of mankind would be superseded; and the rest, being amicably shared among all the active a [*sic*] vigorous members of the community, would be burthensome to none. Every man would have a frugal, yet wholesome diet; every man would go forth to that moderate exercise of his corporal functions that would give hilarity to the spirits; none would be made torpid with fatigue, but all would have leisure to cultivate the kindly and philanthropical affections of the soul, and to let loose his faculties in search of intellectual improvement. . . .

. . .

The spirit of oppression, the spirit of servility, and the spirit of fraud, these are the immediate growth of the established system of property. These are alike hostile to intellectual and moral improvement. The other vices of envy, malice and revenge are their inseparable companions. In a state of society where men lived in the midst of plenty, and where all shared alike the bounties of nature, these sentiments would inevitably expire. The narrow principle of selfishness would vanish. . . Mind would

---

³¹ A reference to Burke's lament in *Reflections*... that with the French Revolution the 'age of chivalry', and its delicate sentiments had gone, and been replaced by an age of calculating 'economists' (p. 79 in this edition). Note that whilst Burke opposed the chivalrous manners of Feudalism to the selfish calculation of the modern commercial economy, for Godwin they share a conception of private property opposed to justice.

be delivered from her perpetual anxiety about corporal support, and free to expatiate in the field of thought which is congenial to her. Each man would assist the enquiries of all.

. . .

CHAPTER III

OF THE OBJECTION TO THIS SYSTEM FROM THE ADMIRABLE
EFFECTS OF LUXURY

. . .

There is one objection that has chiefly been cultivated on English ground, and to which we will give the priority of examination. It has been affirmed 'that private vices are public benefits.' But this principle, thus coarsely stated by one of its original advocates,[32] was remodelled by his more elegant successors.[33] They observed, 'that the true measure of virtue and vice was utility, and consequently that it was an unreasonable calumny to state luxury as a vice. Luxury,' they said, 'whatever might be the prejudices that cynics and ascetics had excited against it, was the rich and generous soil that brought to perfection the true prosperity of mankind. Without luxury men must always have remained solitary savages. It is luxury by which palaces are built and cities peopled. How could there have been high population in any country, without the various arts in which the swarms of its inhabitants are busied? The true benefactor of mankind is not the scrupulous devotee who by his charities encourages insensibility and sloth; is not the surly philosopher who reads them lectures of barren morality; but the elegant voluptuary who employs thousands in sober and healthful industry to procure dainties for his table, who unites distant

---

[32] [Godwin's footnote:] Mandeville, Fable of the Bees ['Private vices public benefits' was the subtitle of Mandeville's famous *Fable of the Bees* (London, 1714), which caused great scandal by pointing out that many individual qualities thought of as vices – such as the greed and vanity which prompted luxurious and conspicuous consumption – were productive of public goods through stimulating trade and providing employment.]

[33] [Godwin's footnote:] Coventry, in a treatise entitled Philemon to Hydaspes: Hume; Essays, Part II, Essay II. [Henry Coventry's treatise is now virtually forgotten. David Hume, including the one cited here 'Of Refinement in the Arts' (first printed in the 1752 edition)) directly confronted the classical republican claims that luxury brought about the downfall of societies. Godwin did not read Hume's philosophy until after writing the first edition of *Political Justice* but he had already read the famous *Essays*. Adam Smith systematised Mandeville's insights into a theory – and defence – of a commercial society in *The Wealth of Nations* (1776), which Godwin had also read. See footnote 36 below.]

nations in commerce to supply him with furniture, and who encourages the fine arts
and all the sublimities of invention to furnish decorations for his residence.'

I have brought forward this objection, rather that nothing material might appear
to be omitted, than because it requires a separate answer. The true answer has been
anticipated . . . If land were perpetually open to him who was willing to cultivate it,
it is not to be believed but that it would be cultivated in proportion to the wants of
the community, nor by the same reason would there be any effectual check to the
increase of population.[34]

. . .

CHAPTER IV

OF THE OBJECTIONS TO THIS SYSTEM FROM THE
ALLUREMENTS OF SLOTH

Another objection which has been urged against the system which counteracts the
accumulation of property, is, 'that it would put an end to industry. We behold in
commercial countries the miracles that are operated by the love of gain. . . . If each
man found that, without being compelled to exert his own industry, he might lay
claim to the superfluity of his neighbour, indolence would perpetually usurp his
faculties, and such a society must either starve, or be obliged in its own defence to
return to that system of injustice and sordid interest, which theoretical reasoners will
for ever arraign to no purpose.'

. . . In reply, it may be observed in the first place, that the equality for which we are
pleading is an equality that would succeed to a state of great intellectual improvement.
So bold a revolution cannot take place in human affairs, till the general mind has
been highly cultivated. The present age of mankind is greatly enlightened; but it is
to be feared is not yet enlightened enough. Hasty and undigested tumults may take
place under the idea of an equalisation of property; but it is only a calm and clear

---

[34] Godwin's economic argument here is distinctly archaic and at variance with most economic
thinking since Locke. Locke claimed that private ownership of land, beyond what could be worked
by one individual, although it required hired labour, but was both more productive and therefore
supported greater populations at a higher standard of living than subsistence agriculture. Thus,
even if there were unclaimed land available, population growth would be maximised by increasing
the intensity of cultivation rather than increasing the extent of it on a peasant–proprietor basis. This
claim was endorsed by Smith and other more advanced economic thinkers, who argued that, given
free trade, the productivity of the agricultural sector placed no medium-term limits on population
growth.

conviction of justice, of justice mutually to be rendered and received, of happiness to be produced by the desertion of our most rooted habits, that can introduce an invariable system of this sort. Attempts without this preparation will be productive only of confusion. Their effect will be momentary, and a new and more barbarous inequality will succeed. . . .

. . .

From the sketch which has been here given it seems by no means impossible, that the labour of every twentieth man in the community would be sufficient to maintain the rest in all the absolute necessaries of human life. If then this labour, instead of being performed by so small a number, were amicably divided among them all, it would occupy the twentieth part of every man's time. . . . half an hour a day, seriously employed in manual labour by every member of the community, would sufficiently supply the whole with necessaries. Who is he that would shrink from this degree of industry? . . .

. . .

Meanwhile it is sufficiently obvious, that the motives which arise from the love of distinction are by no means cut off, by a state of society incompatible with the accumulation of property . . . This passion, no longer permitted to lose itself in indirect channels and useless wanderings, will seek the noblest course, and perpetually fructify the seeds of public good. Mind, though it will perhaps at no time arrive at the termination of its possible discoveries and improvements, will nevertheless advance with a rapidity and firmness of progression of which we are at present unable to conceive the idea.

. . .

CHAPTER VI

OF THE OBJECTION TO THIS SYSTEM FROM THE INFLEXIBILITY
OF ITS RESTRICTIONS

An objection that has often been urged against a system of equal property, is, 'that it is inconsistent with personal independence. Every man according to this scheme is a passive instrument in the hands of the community. He must eat and drink, and play and sleep at the bidding of others. . . .

. . .

But the truth is, that a system of equal property requires no restrictions or superintendence whatever. There is no need of common labour; common meals or common magazines [storehouses]. These are feeble and mistaken instruments for restraining the conduct without making conquest of the judgment. If you cannot bring over the hearts of the community to your party, expect no success from brute regulations. If you can, regulation is unnecessary. . . .

. . .

From these principles it appears that every thing that is usually understood by the term co-operation, is in some degree an evil. . . .

. . .

. . . It may be a curious speculation to attend to the progressive steps by which this feature of human society may be expected to decline. For example: shall we have concerts of music? The miserable state of mechanism of the majority of the performers is so conspicuous, as to be even at this day a topic of mortification and ridicule. Will it not be practicable hereafter for one man to perform the whole? Shall we have theatrical exhibitions? This seems to include an absurd and vicious cooperation. It may be doubted whether men will hereafter come forward in any mode gravely to repeat words and ideas not their own? It may be doubted whether any musical performer will habitually exercise the compositions of others. We yield supinely to the superior merit of our predecessors, because we are accustomed to indulge the inactivity of our own faculties. All formal repetition of other men's ideas seems to be a scheme for imprisoning for so long a time the operations of our own mind. It borders perhaps in this respect upon a breach of sincerity, which requires that we should give immediate utterance to every useful and valuable idea that occurs to our thoughts.

. . .

Another article which belongs to the subject of co-operation is cohabitation.

. . . [This] is particularly interesting, as it includes in it the subject of marriage. It is absurd to expect that the inclinations of two human beings should coincide through any long period of time. To oblige them to act and live together, is to subject them to some inevitable portion of thwarting, bickering and unhappiness. This cannot be otherwise, so long as man has failed to reach the standard of absolute perfection. The supposition that I must have a companion for life, is the result of a complication of vices. It is the dictate of cowardice, and not of fortitude. It flows from the desire of being loved and esteemed for something that is not desert.

But the evil of marriage as it is practised in European countries lies deeper than this. The habit is, for a thoughtless and romantic youth of each sex to come together, to see each other for a few times and under circumstances full of delusion, and then to vow to each other eternal attachment. What is the consequence of this? In almost every instance they find themselves deceived. They are reduced to make the best of an irretrievable mistake. They are presented with the strongest imaginable temptation to become the dupes of falsehood. . . .

Add to this, that marriage is an affair of property, and the worst of all properties. So long as two human beings are forbidden by positive institution to follow the dictates of their own mind, prejudice is alive and vigorous. So long as I seek to engross one woman to myself, and to prohibit my neighbour from proving his superior desert and reaping the fruits of it, I am guilty of the most odious of all monopolies . . .

The abolition of marriage will be attended with no evils. . . .[35]

. . . I shall assiduously cultivate the intercourse of that woman whose accomplishments shall strike me in the most powerful manner. 'But it may happen that other men will feel for her the same preference that I do.' This will create no difficulty. We may all enjoy her conversation; and we shall all be wise enough to consider the sensual intercourse as a very trivial object. This, like every other affair in which two persons are concerned, must be regulated in each successive instance by the unforced consent of either party. . . .

. . .

These observations lead us to the consideration of one additional difficulty, which relates to the division of labour. Shall each man make all his tools, his furniture and accommodations? This would perhaps be a tedious operation. Every man performs the task to which he is accustomed more skilfully and in a shorter time than another. It is reasonable that you should make for me, that which perhaps I should be three or four times as long making, and should make imperfectly at last. Shall we then introduce barter and exchange? By no means. . . .

The division of labour, as it has been treated by commercial writers, is for the most part the offspring of avarice. It has been found that ten persons can make two hundred and forty times as many pins in a day as one person.[36] This refinement is the growth of luxury. The object is to see into how vast a surface the industry of the lower classes

---

[35] Despite these protestations Godwin was to marry, not only Mary Wollstonecraft, who tragically died in childbirth a year later, but on two subsequent occasions as well.

[36] [Godwin's footnote:] Smith's Wealth of Nations Book I, Chap. I. [In this famous passage Smith identifes eighteen separate operations in the making of a pin and cites a manufactory with ten members making 48,000 pins per day. If each man performed all the operations he could 'not have made twenty, perhaps not one pin in a day; that is certainly not the two hundred fortieth . . . part of what they are at present capable of performing, in consequence of a proper division and combination of their different operations'. (*Wealth of Nations*, I. i. §3)]

may be beaten, the more completely to gild over the indolent and the proud. The ingenuity of the merchant is whetted, by new improvements of this sort to transport more of the wealth of the powerful into his own coffers. The possibility of effecting a compendium of labour by this means will be greatly diminished, when men shall learn to deny themselves superfluities. The utility of such a saving of labour, where labour is so little, will scarcely balance against the evils of so extensive a cooperation. . . .

CHAPTER VII

OF THE OBJECTION TO THIS SYSTEM FROM THE
PRINCIPLE OF POPULATION

An author who has speculated widely upon subjects of government,[37] has recommended equal, or, which was rather his idea, common property, as a complete remedy, to the usurpation and distress which are at present the most powerful enemies of human kind, . . . But, after having exhibited this picture, not less true than delightful, he finds an argument that demolishes the whole, and restores him to indifference and despair, in the excessive population that would ensue.

. . .

Let us here return to the sublime conjecture of Franklin, that 'mind will one day become omnipotent over matter.'[38] If over all other matter, why not over the matter of our own bodies? . . .

. . . Mind modifies body involuntarily. Emotion excited by some unexpected word, by a letter that is delivered to us, occasions the most extraordinary revolutions in our frame, . . . These symptoms we may either encourage or check. . . . There is nothing indeed of which physicians themselves are more frequently aware, than of the power of the mind in assisting or retarding convalescence.

Why is it that a mature man soon loses that elasticity of limb, which characterises the heedless gaiety of youth? Because he desists from youthful habits. He assumes an air of dignity incompatible with the lightness of childish sallies. He is visited and vexed with all the cares that rise out of our mistaken institutions, and his heart is

---

[37] [Godwin's footnote:] Robert Wallace, *Various Prospects of Mankind, Nature and Providence* (London, 1761). [Prospect II, offered 'The model of a perfect Government'.]

[38] [Godwin's footnote:] I have no other authority to quote for this expression than the conversation of Dr Price. Upon enquiry I am happy to find it confirmed to me by Mr William Morgan, the newphew of Dr Price, who recollects to have heard it repeatedly mentioned by his uncle.

no longer satisfied and gay. Hence his limbs become stiff and unwieldy. This is the forerunner of old age and death.

The first habit favourable to corporeal vigour is cheerfulness. Every time that our mind becomes morbid, vacant and melancholy, a certain period is cut off from the length of our lives. Listlessness of thought is the brother of death. But cheerfulness gives new life to our frame and circulation to our juices. . . .

. . .

The true source of cheerfulness is benevolence. . . . novelty is a fading charm . . . Thus the aged are generally cold and indifferent; how should it be otherwise? The pursuits of mankind are commonly frigid and contemptible, and the mistake comes at last to be detected. But virtue is a charm that never fades. . . .

The application of these reasonings is simple and irresistible. If mind be now in a great degree the ruler of the system, why should it be incapable of extending its empire? If our involuntary thoughts can derange or restore the animal economy, why should we not in the process of time, in this as in other instances, subject the thoughts which are at present involuntary to the government of design? If volition now can do something why should we not in the process of time, in this as in other instances, subject the thoughts which are at present involuntary to the government of design? If volition can do something, why should it not go on to do still more and more? There is no principle of reason less liable to question than this, that, if we have in any respect a little power now, and if mind be essentially progressive, that power may, and, barring any extraordinary concussions of nature, infallibly will, extend beyond any bounds we are able to prescribe to it.

. . .

To apply these remarks to the subject of population.[39] The tendency of a cultivated and virtuous mind is to render us indifferent to the gratifications of sense. . . . The gratifications of sense please at present by their imposture. We soon learn to despise the mere animal function, which, apart from the delusions of intellect, would be nearly the same in all cases; and to value it, only as it happens to be relieved by personal charms or mental excellence. . . .

The men therefore who exist when the earth shall refuse itself to a more extended population, will cease to propagate, for they will no longer have any motive, either of error or duty, to induce them. In addition to this they will perhaps be immortal.

---

[39] Such views, later repeated in Godwin's *The Enquirer* (1787), prompted the vigorous and famously pessimistic response of Thomas Malthus in his *Essay on the Principle of Population* (1798).

The whole will be a people of men, and not of children. Generation will not succeed generation, nor truth have in a certain degree to recommence her career at the end of every thirty years. There will be no war, no crimes, no administration of justice as it is called, and no government. . . .

. . .

CHAPTER VIII

OF THE MEANS OF INTRODUCING THE

GENUINE SYSTEM OF PROPERTY

. . .

No idea has excited greater horror in the minds of a multitude of persons, than that of the mischiefs that are to ensue from the dissemination of what they call levelling principles.[40] . . .

. . .

. . . [But] here it plainly appears that mischief is by no means inseperable from the progress. In the mere circumstances of our acquiring knowledge and accumulating one truth after another there is no direct tendency to disorder. Evil can only spring from the clash of mind with mind . . . becoming impatient of the opposition they have to encounter.

In this interesting period, in which mind shall arrive as it were at the true crisis of its story, there are high duties incumbent upon every branch of the community. First, upon those cultivated and powerful minds, that are fitted to be precursors to the rest in the discovery of truth. They are bound to be active, indefatigable and disinterested. It is incumbent upon them to abstain from inflammatory language, from all expressions of acrimony and resentment. It is absurd in any government to erect itself into a court of criticism in this respect, and to establish a criterion of liberality and decorum; but for that very reason it is doubly incumbent on those who communicate their thoughts to the public, to exercise a rigid censure over themselves . . .

Nor is it less necessary that they should be urged to tell the whole truth without disguise. No maxim can be more pernicious than that which would teach us to consult the temper of the times, and to tell only so much as we imagine our contemporaries

---

[40] The 'Levellers', a radical movement during the English Civil War, were charged (incorrectly) with seeking to introduce equality of property. Subsequently any disliked radical ideas were liable to be denounced as 'levelling'.

will be able to bear. This practice is at present almost universal, and it is the mark of a very painful degree of depravity. We retail and mangle truth. We impart it to our fellows, not with the liberal measure with which we have received it, but with such parsimony as our own miserable prudence may chance to prescribe. We pretend that truths fit to be practised in one country, nay, truths which we confess to be eternally right, are not fit to be practised in another. That we may deceive others with a tranquil conscience, we begin deceiving ourselves. We put shackles on our minds, and dare not trust ourselves at large in the pursuit of truth. . . . What I should desire is, not by violence to change its institutions, but by reason to change its ideas. I have no business with factions or intrigue; but simply to promulgate the truth, and to wait the tranquil progress of conviction. . . .

. . .

. . . If man be endowed with a rational nature, then whatever is clearly demonstrated to his understanding to have the most powerful recommendations, so long as that clearness is present to his mind, will inevitably engage his choice. . . . This is confirmed to us, if a truth of this universal nature can derive confirmation from partial experiments, by the regular advances of the human mind from century to century, since the invention of printing.

. . .

It will not be right to pass over a question that will inevitably suggest itself to the mind of the reader. 'If an equalisation of property be to take place, not by law, regulation or public institution, but only through the private conviction of individuals, in what manner shall it begin? . . .

. . .

Let us reflect for a moment on the gradual consequences of this revolution of opinion. Liberality of dealing will be among its earliest results, and of consequence accumulation will become less frequent and less enormous. Men will not be disposed, as now, to take advantage of each other's distresses, and to demand a price for their aid, not measured by a general standard, but by the wants of an individual. They will not consider how much they can extort, but how much it is reasonable to require. The master tradesman who employs labourers under him, will be disposed to give a more ample reward to their industry; which he is at present enabled to tax chiefly by the neutral circumstance of having provided a capital. Liberality on the part of his employer will complete in the mind of the artisan, what ideas of political justice will probably have begun. He will no longer spend the little surplus of his earnings in that dissipation, which is at present one of the principal causes that subject him to the arbitrary pleasure of a superior. . . .

. . .

One remark will suggest itself upon these considerations. 'If the inevitable progress of improvement insensibly lead towards an equalisation of property, what need was there of proposing it as a specific object to men's consideration?' The answer to this objection is easy. The improvement in question consists in a knowledge of truth. . . . Whatever be the object towards which mind spontaneously advances, it is of no mean importance to us to have a distinct view of that object. Our advances will thus become accelerated. It is a well known principle of morality, that he who proposes perfection to himself, though he will inevitably fall short of what he pursues, will make a more rapid progress, than he who is content to aim only at what is imperfect. The benefits to be derived in the interval from a view of equalisation, as one of the great objects towards which we are tending, are exceedingly conspicuous. Such a view will strongly conduce to make us disinterested now. It will teach us to look with contempt upon mercantile speculations, commercial prosperity, and the cares of gain. It will impress us with a just apprehension of what it is of which man is capable and in which his perfection consists; and will fix our ambition and activity upon the worthiest objects. Mind cannot arrive at any great and illustrious attainment, however much the nature of mind may carry us towards it, without feeling some presages of its approach; and it is reasonable to believe that, the earlier these presages are introduced, and the more distinct they are made, the more auspicious will be the event.

Plate 6. *Copenhagen House* (James Gillray, 1795). A depiction of the famous open-air meeting with John Thelwall haranguing the crowd on the nearest rostrum whilst his assistants hold up the resolutions of the London Corresponding Society. In the foreground some kind of gambling is being conducted in relation to the Seditious Practices Bill, signatures for a petition are being collected from slaves wearing 'Thelwall' caps and 'Thelwall's real Democratic Gin' is being dispensed. (Notoriously alcohol was provided as a bribe at elections where there were wide – 'democratic' – franchises.)

THE LONDON CORRESPONDING
SOCIETY

HISTORICAL NOTE

The London Corresponding Society was formed in January 1792 by nine men
most famously including Thomas Hardy, a tailor turned radical politician who
later wrote a history of the Society. Its purpose was parliamentary reform –
specifically, and at the outset, to gain a vote for those 'who were not house-
keepers, but had arrived at the years of maturity, and had an inherent right to
a vote but were unconstitutionally deprived of it.'[1] The majority were artisans:
shoemakers and tailors, small craftsmen and traders, but there were some who
were more educated, amongst them Maurice Margarot, a graduate who had
studied in Geneva, and Joseph Gerrald, a lawyer.[2] Its membership grew rapidly
and it was soon forced to establish separate divisions, each of up to forty-six
members. At its height in 1795 the LCS counted 3,576 members each paying a
penny a week, and at a famous meeting the same year, near the Copenhagen
House Inn at Islington just outside London, 100,000 people attended to hear
speeches from John Thelwall and others, which were relayed to three separate rostrums spaced out across the field. Their success prompted government
concern. Publicans who allowed meetings on their premises were threatened
with the loss of their licence and spies were recruited to infiltrate the Society.
Treason trials of those involved in that summer's 'National Convention' held
in Edinburgh produced, under heavy direction from the judge, sentences of
life transportation for Margarot and Gerrald (who died on the journey) and
for the Scots radicals William Skirving, Thomas Muir and the Rev. Thomas
Fyshe Palmer. They were followed, in November 1794, by the trials in London of
Thomas Hardy, John Horne Tooke and John Thelwall for high treason. The jury
there proved less impressionable. All were acquitted and proceedings against
a further nine abandoned. The following year, despite Thelwall's appeal at the
Copenhagen House meeting for action to remain peaceful, the King's coach was

---

[1] Thomas Hardy, *Account of the origin of the London Corresponding Society* (1799) in Mary Thrale,
Selections from the Papers of the London Corresponding Society 1792–1799 (Cambridge: Cambridge
University Press, 1983), p. 5.
[2] Thrale, *Selections*, p. xix gives a list.

attacked on his way to open Parliament. The Ministry responded by introducing the Treasonable Practices and Seditious Meetings Bills, which made effective public political protest impossible.[3] The society was proscribed by name in 1799.

The LCS was by no means the only non-parliamentary political organisation. Its founders benefited from advice from long-standing gentlemen radicals such as the republican Thomas Brand Hollis, and John Horne Tooke of the more middle-class Society for Constitutional Information and the Society of the Friends of the People. Moreover, once established, the LCS discovered or encouraged the emergence of similar societies in Sheffield, Edinburgh, Manchester and across the river at Borough. Correspondence took place with these and other groups in Paisley, Stockport, Norwich, Bath, Glasgow, Durham, Banff, Dundee, Leeds, Hertford, etc.

Over a period of seven years the LCS produced not only broadsides and 'Declarations', they published a barrage of minutes of meetings and letters of solidarity with other British (and French) societies. In their appeals to fellow citizens they articulated specific political claims to political rights beyond anything heard since the 1640s, and in systematically publishing these 'proceedings' they sought to display themselves to the world as quite the equals in organisational propriety and etiquette of their social betters. Such proceedings, however, were also provocative in their ostentatious use of egalitarian republican forms of address, particularly the ubiquitous 'citizen', and in the ostentatiously published 'communication' with societies in other cities and in France. The style and form of the Society's output demonstrates as much about the power of the new forms of politics as does its content. As one of the contributors to the Society's magazine put it: 'the doctrine of Association is one of the grandest attainments of the present age'.[4]

EDITORIAL NOTE

The ***Two Addresses*** reproduced here date from 1793 and 1794. The first, drawn up by Thomas Hardy and Maurice Margarot, follows the Government's rejection

---

[3] The Bills, introduced on 6 and 10 November, passed rapidly and received the Royal Assent on 18 December 1795. They made public meetings of 50 or more people illegal and expanded the definition of treason to include speaking or writing in such a way as to incite hatred or contempt of the King or established government or to seek to make him change his measures or ministers or to intimidate or overawe either of the Houses of Parliament. Albert Goodwin, *The Friends of Liberty*, pp. 384–8.

[4] *The Moral and Political Magazine of the LCS*, May 1797, in Michael T. Davis, ed., *LCS 1792–1799*, vol. IV, p. 219.

of French offers of peace, the rejection of reform petitions to Parliament and the defeat of Grey's motion to introduce a Bill for Parliamentary Reform. The second (confusingly one of two such *Addresses* with this date) is by Thelwall and was written in the aftermath of the Scottish Treason trials at which Margarot and Gerrald (the LCS delegates to the National Convention) had been sentenced to transportation for life. The final piece is from a handbill issued as part of the campaign against the Bills increasing the definition of sedition and banning public meetings. It reveals very clearly the equivocation the LCS felt about how far action should – or could – remain peaceful. By 1797, when peaceful meetings were being successfully disbanded, a militant breakaway group had formed – the United Englishmen, modelled on the United Irishmen. I have retained the original typesetting, which reveals some sense of the increasing urgency and desperation felt by the Society as the government sought to repress the reform movement.

Modern editions:

London Corresponding Society 1792–1799, 6 vols., ed. and introd. Michael T. Davies (London: Pickering and Chatto, 2002).

Selections from the Papers of the London Corresponding Society 1792–1799, ed. with introd. Mary Thale (Cambridge: Cambridge University Press, 1983).

FURTHER READING

Barrell, J. *Imagining the King's Death: Figurative Treason, Fantasies of Regicide, 1793–1796* (Oxford University Press, 2000).

Black, E. *The Association: British Extra-Parliamentary Political Organisation 1763–1793* (Cambridge, Mass.: Harvard University Press, 1963).

Collins, H. 'The London Corresponding Society' in J. Saville (ed.), *Democracy and the Labour Movement* (London: Lawrence and Wishart, 1954).

Emsley, C. 'The Pop-Gun Plot 1794' in M. Davis (ed.), *Radicalism and Revolution in Britain, 1775–1848* (Basingstoke: Macmillan, 2000).

Goodwin, A. *The Friends of Liberty* (London: Hutchinson, 1979).

Philp, M. (ed.) *The French Revolution and British Popular Politics* (Cambridge University Press, 1991).

Thale, M. 'London Debating Societies in the 1790s', *Historical Journal* 32 (98) (1989).

Two Addresses (1793 and 1794)

ADDRESS TO THE NATION, FROM THE
LONDON CORRESPONDING SOCIETY[1]

FRIENDS AND FELLOW COUNTRYMEN

GLOOMY as is the prospect now before us, and unpleasing as is the task to bring forth into open day the calamitous situation of our Country: We conceive it necessary to direct the public eye, to the ease of our misfortunes, and to awaken the sleeping reason of our Countrymen, to the pursuit of the only remedy, which can ever prove effectual, namely; – *A thorough Reform in Parliament, by the adoption of an equal Representation obtained by Annual Elections and Universal Suffrage.* We do not address you in the confidence of personal importance. – We do not presume upon the splendor of exalted situation; but as Members of the same Society, as Individuals, zealously labouring for the welfare of the Community; we think ourselves entitled to a share of your attention.

At a time when many of the now accumulated Evils, although not unforeseen, were yet at a distance, The *London Corresponding Society* united, and called upon their Fellow Citizens to join with them in reclaiming a Right stolen by Treachery, and with-held by Oppression. – Ignorance, the most strenuous supporter of Despotism, We laboured to destroy; the Rights of the People to an equal Representation We publicly supported, and proved the restoration of those Rights, to be the only permanent remedy to the then existing grievances! Grievances which for want of that remedy, have in the short space of Eighteen months been increased ten-fold on this credulous, supine, and unsuspecting Nation.

Success attended the endeavours of our Society; but a success no ways adequate to the importance of our Cause! Deep rooted Prejudices adopted by ignorance, cherished by interest, and confirmed, by apathy, very much impeded the progress that might have been made upon the understanding of a Nation, which boasts itself to be the most enlightened in Europe. Experience has however, proved that the public mind is too generally enervated by luxury, or borne down by misery and oppression.

Here it is proper to remind you, of the false and calumnious Aspersions which have been so industriously circulated since November last: At that time of general

---

[1] 8 July 1793.

Consternation, when the cry of danger to the Constitution was raised and extensively propagated; when the alarm of *Riots* and *Insurrections*, was founded by Royal Proclamations and re-echoed by Parish Associations; Reform, was branded by the name of Innovation, and whoever dared to affirm, that the House of Commons ought to be restored to that State of Independence in which it was settled at the Revolution; and that unnecessary Places and Pensions ought to be abolished, was stigmatised as a Leveller, and an enemy to his King and Country.[2]

Even the dependants of Ministry, have in Parliament acknowledged; that those reports of Riots and Insurrections were groundless; but that acknowledgement though evincing the criminality of those *trumped up false-hoods* has not lessened their effect on this deluded nation.

Yet, no *ways* discouraged by these alarms, by the fulsome effusions of what was falsely called loyalty,[3] nor by that torrent of prejudice which for a while, set reason and reflection equally at defiance; we pursued with firmness the course prescribed by the Constitution, for obtaining a redress of Grievances, -and disregarding the; visionary alarms of Sedition, our Constitutional Rights proved our shield against the most dangerous Combination of Interest and Prejudice, that ever threatened the Liberties of a Free Country.

Our Petition to parliament was received – read – and ordered to lay on the Table – the principle contained therein: 'That no man shall be taxed, but by the consent of himself, or his Representative freely chosen by himself.' Neither was, nor could be denied to be a *Principle* of our Constitution; but its effects *could* at that time be

[2] In May 1792 the Government had issued a Royal Proclamation, calling on loyal subjects to resist attempts to subvert the constitution. The decision to prosecute Paine followed. In November counter-radical activity was greatly increased: John Reeves had founded, with government assistance, a Loyalist Association: The Association for the Preservation of Liberty and Property against Republicans and Levellers; Home Secretary Dundas had circulated local officials to recruit 'merchants and lawyers' in the towns and 'farmers and yeomen' in the countryside in support of the constitution; lawyers were recruited for the prosecution of 'seditious literature' in all the major towns. Local 'church and king' mobs were encouraged sometimes by local magistrates – to attack radicals' meeting places, newspapers and houses (Goodwin, *Friends of Liberty*, pp. 215, 264).
[3] [*Address* footnote:] *Loyalty*, is derived from the old French word *Loyalté*, and strictly signifies an attachment to the laws; but by the fraudulent practices of Courtiers, exercised with too much success on vulgar ignorance, the term is often perverted to signify, an attachment to Kings, and their measures, even when evidently in opposition to law, and the Constitution of the Country. [The derivation is right and interestingly the *OED* gives some support for this view of the development of its meaning. The primary meaning is 'faithful adherence to one's promise' whilst 'enthusiastic reverence for the person and family of the sovereign' is a 'recent use'.]

evaded by those whose interests it was to perpetuate abuses at the expense of the Public.

The protraction of Reform, however, has not been the only evil which has arisen from the credit so rashly given to reports of Riots and insurrections. To that credulity, and to the want of circumspection, naturally attendant on the fears so artfully raised, we, may justly attribute the present Ruinous and Disgraceful War overlooking the aggrandizement of Russia, and disregarding the cruel dismemberment of Poland; under the flimsy excuse of assisting *those who apparently did not care to fight for themselves, our Allies the Dutch*; the National Honour has been staked; the minister has been armed with new and unexampled powers, and the troops of Britain, have been sent to co-operate with the most detestable of Despots.

British gold now subsidises armies of Continental Slaves, and the blood of half Europe is pledged for the destruction of France![4] supplies of every kind are sent from hence! Commerce is nearly stopped! Failures innumerable take place! Manufacturers are ruined! Artisans are starving! Provisions rise in price! the Revenue decreases, and fresh Taxes are wanting! For fresh supplies of blood, the Liberties of our Country are invaded! the Seaman is forcibly torn from his family! the Peasant is kidnapped from the plough! and the starving Labourer is compelled to sell his Life and his Liberty for Bread: – If such, O much oppressed Britons! are the effects of a Four months' War, what are you to expect when it shall have lasted as many years?

Still farther to increase our private calamities; and to augment our national disgrace; we have seen offers of Peace spurned with contempt, and the breach between the two countries widened by the rejection of Reconciliation; thus are we doomed to a continuance of National misery, and to an addition of National dishonour from a War commenced with injustice, prosecuted with inquisitorial obstinacy; and likely, to end in eternal infamy.

To palliate the injustice of the War, France is reproached with Anarchy: while Despots and their Ministers, boast their diabolical skill in promoting it. To soothe the public grievances, the agents of Corruption have ever since the commencement

---

[4] The British government had maintained an official policy of neutrality towards the Revolution, although increasingly anxious about the fate of the Netherlands which would give France command of the whole channel coastline. Over the summer of 1791 Prussia and Austria had formed an alliance with the aim of restoring the French monarchy, and they invaded France in July 1792. Britian had hired Honoverian mercenaries to defend the Netherlands in January 1793, and the French declared war on Britain in February. In order to keep Prussia and Austria on side, Britain was prepared to agree to the dismemberment of Poland and other territorial deals on continental Europe.

of the War, predicted that the distracted State of France, must in a few weeks put a period to it. Predictions so repeatedly falsified must be attributed either to fraud or folly.

Conscious as we are, that the trading and commercial interests of this Country, are neither *satisfied* of the policy of the War, nor *duped* by any delusive prospect of success, we cannot attribute the little resistance which has hitherto been made to it; to any thing else than the depraved Rate of the Representation, for had they that weight in Parliament, which the spirit of the Constitution evidently intended, and which was confirmed by the Revolution in 1688, We doubt not their open declarations against a War, so hostile to their Interests, and to the cause of Humanity, would ere now have refuted the fictitious idea of its being popular, necessary, or just.

To obtain a compleat Representation is our only aim – contemning all party distinctions, we seek no advantage which every individual, of, the community will not enjoy equally with ourselves – We are not engaged in Speculative and Theoretical schemes; the motive of our present conduct is the actual sense of injury and oppression; We feel the weight of innumerable abuses, to which the invasion of our rights has given birth, and which their restoration can alone remove.

But sensible that our efforts, if not seconded, by the Nation at large, must prove ineffectual, and only needlessly expose us to the malevolence of the public plunderers; we conjure you, by the love you bear your country, by your attachment to freedom, and by your anxious care for the welfare of your posterity, to suffer yourselves no longer to be deluded by artful speeches, and by interested men; but to sanction with your approbation, our constitutional endeavours, and pursue with union and firmness the track we have pointed out: Thus countenanced by our country, we pledge ourselves, as you will perceive, by the following, resolutions, never to recede, or slacken, but on every occasion to redouble our zealous, exertions, in the cause of Constitutional Freedom.

RESOLVED UNANIMOUSLY

I. That nothing but a fair, adequate and annually renovated Representation in Parliament, can ensure the freedom of this country.

II. That we are fully convinced, a thorough Parliamentary Reform, would remove every grievance under which we labour.

III. That we will never give, up the pursuit of such Parliamentary Reform.

IV. That if it be a part of the power of the king to declare war when and against whom he pleases, we are convinced that such power must have been granted to him under the condition, that it should ever be subservient to the national advantage.

V. That the present war against France, and the existing alliance with the Germanic Powers, so far as it relates to the prosecution of that war, has hitherto produced, and is likely to produce nothing but national calamity, if not utter ruin.

VI. That it appears to Us that the wars in which Great Britain has engaged, within the last hundred years, have cost her upwards of *Three Hundred and Seventy Millions!* not to mention the private misery occasioned thereby, or the lives sacrificed; therefore it is a dreadful speculation for the people of this country to look up to; That the Cabinet have engaged in a treaty with a foreign Prince, to be supplied with troops for a long period of years, and for a purpose unknown to the people of England.

VII. That we are persuaded the majority, if not the whole of those wars, originated in Cabinet intrigue, rather than in absolute necessity.

VIII. That every nation has an unalienable right to choose the mode to which it will be governed, and that it is an act of Tyranny and Oppression in any other nation to interfere with, or attempt to control their choice.

IX. That peace being the greatest of blessings, ought to be sought most diligently by every wise government, to be most joyfully accepted when reasonably proffered, and to be concluded most speedily when the object, of the war is accomplished.

X. That we do exhort every well wisher to his country, not to delay in improving himself in constitutional knowledge.

XI. That those men who were the first to be seized with a panic, should be the last whom prudence would entrust with the management of a war.

XII. That Great Britain is not Hanover!

XIII. That regarding union as indispensably necessary to ensure success, we will endeavour to the utmost of our power, to unite more closely with every political Society in the nation, associated upon the same principles with ourselves.

XIV. That the next general Meeting of this Society, be held on the first Monday in September, unless the Committee of Delegates shall find it necessary to call such meeting sooner:

XV. That the foregoing Address and Resolutions be signed by the Chairman and by the Secretary, and that *Twenty Thousand Copies* of them be printed, published and distributed [gratis.]

    MAURICE MARGAROT, CHAIRMAN.
    THOMAS HARDY, SECRETARY.

Monday, July 8, 1793,
Crown and Anchor Tavern,
Strand.

The Chairman having left the Chair, it was unanimously Resolved That the thanks of this Society be given to Citizen MARGAROT, for the great attention which he has given to the interests of this Society, and particularly, for his impartiality and proper conduct at this meeting.

It was likewise unanimously Resolved, That, the Thanks of this Society be given to Citizen HARDY, for his unremitting perseverance and exertions in the Cause of Freedom.

ADDRESS of the LONDON CORRESPONDING SOCIETY, united for the Purpose of obtaining Universal Suffrage and Annual Parliaments; to the various PATRIOTIC SOCIETIES of GREAT BRITAIN.
CITIZENS![5]

IT is with equal surprise and indignation that this Society have beheld the late rapid encroachments made by some of the constituted powers in this country upon the freedom of Britons – the attacks (hitherto unparalleled, since the *disastrous days of* CHARLES *the First*, and JAMES *the Second*) that have been successively made upon

---

[5] 1794.

the constitutional and natural rights of the subject; the flagrant attempts on the *personal security of individuals,* by an infamous inquisitorial system of SPIES and INFORMERS, and *formal processes of* PERSECUTION FOR OPINION, and the unqualified attempt to *annihilate the intellectual progress of man* by the suppression of what has hitherto been held as our *birthright* and *peculiar prerogative* – the free and peaceable enquiry into the PRINCIPLES OF LEGISLATION, and the practices of EXECUTIVE GOVERNMENT.

CITIZENS!

We are well assured of your sympathy in the feelings which these alarming, and (since the REVOLUTION THAT PLACED THE PRESENT FAMILY UPON THE THRONE) unprecedented stretches of Prerogative have excited in our bosoms; and more especially in the *horror and execration* with which we cannot cease to contemplate the *conduct of certain* MAGISTRATES, particularly in the TOWN and COUNTY of EDINBURGH; where, *in direct* VIOLATION, *not only of the* GENERAL PRINCIPLES *but of the* EXPLICIT *and* AVOWED MAXIMS *both of the* COMMON AND STATUTE LAW *of the Country,* unprecedented *affronts,* and even PERSONAL VIOLENCE (to the scandal of FREEDOM and JUSTICE) have been exerted to interrupt and disperse a *legal, peaceable,* and *enlightened assembly* of PATRIOTS, whose constitutional exertions for *reforming the abuses of our* PARLIAMENTARY REPRESENTATION, and *redressing thereby,* the GRIEVANCES *under which we labour,* demand, instead of *prosecutions, fines, imprisonments, and* TRANSPORTATION, *Civic Crowns from their Country,* and the *Applauses and admiration of Mankind.*[6]

CITIZENS!

Though we are of no *party,* and behold with perfect indifference, the struggles and contentions of *interested factions,* we believe there can be, at this time, but one opinion (among *placemen pensioners,* and *expectants* alone excepted) concerning the conduct and principles of the PRESENT ADMINISTRATION – An *Administration* which has not only advanced with unparalleled boldness in its repeated *attacks upon our* CONSTITUTIONAL LIBERTY; but has plunged also, in *hitherto unheard of* INFAMY, the *once* awful name of *Britain* – an *Administration* which, not content with overwhelming in WANT and MISERY the PEOPLE for whose prosperity it was

[6] The first two meetings of the Edinburgh reform Convention in December 1792 and April 1793, although mild in substance, had provocatively adopted French Revolutionary terminology. As a result Thomas Muir and Rev. Thomas Palmer had been tried for sedition and sentenced to transportation.

their duty to provide, and *endangering* the CONSTITUTION which they pretended so servilely to adore, by *precipitating the nation into an* UNJUST and RUINOUS WAR, has conducted that war, *not upon the open and magnanimous principles* upon which this country had formerly used to pride itself, but upon a *new fangled* and extravagant system of CORRUPTION and TREACHERY, and, by the *peculiar absurdity*, as well as the *meanness* of its measures has brought a STAIN upon the NATIONAL CHARACTER of BRITAIN, which nothing but the *attested disapprobation of the people* can obliterate from the memory of Europe An *administration* which, not content with these *external stains* with which it has blotched the *once fair character of the country*, has introduced, also ACCUMULATED DISEASES and CORRUPTIONS *into its very vitals* – under the deceitful and insinuating title of *Associations for the protection of liberty and property*, has publickly patron-ised a new species of STAR CHAMBER INQUISITION[7] (an institution so justly execrated in the TYRANNICAL REIGNS *of the* Stewarts);-and has either flagitiously authorised or supinely suffered the inferior magistracy to trample on the sacred boundaries meant to secure the liberties of the people, to exceed the consti-tutional limits of their authority and to make the civil arm an engine of violence and depredation.

CITIZENS,

We wish to be candid in the midst of all the censures which injustice forces from our lips; and it is therefore that we make it a matter of doubt (it not having yet been proved) whether the illegal insult we have received, and the deep wound that has been given to the yet remaining liberties of Britain, in the treatment of the several Delegates of the British Convention, whose persons and papers have so unlawfully been seized and made the subjects of unprecedented prosecutions, were committed or not by the express orders of his Majesty's Ministers. To us, however, it appears that a violation so open and flagitious of every natural and constitutional right, would not have been ventured upon by these inferior engines of authority, without the encouragement and assured protection of higher powers.

CITIZENS! it is necessary that these circumstances should be boldly and severely investigated – it is necessary for the promotion of this investigation, that the Friends

---

[7] Star Chamber: a special court set up, probably under Henry VII, comprising selected members of the King's Council, to hear a range of offences against public order and misconduct of public officers; outside the normal structure of courts, and hence of access to a jury, it was much complained of as an infringement on the liberties of subjects. It became a symbol of the King's aspiration to rule outside the law and was abolished by the Long Parliament in 1641.

of Liberty should act with unanimity and concert; and it is therefore that we thus, in a body, address your respective Societies.

By what means shall this concert be effected? Though in Scotland all law and liberty have been violated to crush association and enquiry, remember that, if we have the *will*, we have yet the *power*, in this or any other part of *England* to assemble, by a still more general delegation (and we recommend it to you to hold yourselves in preparation for such a measure, should it be found necessary) to co-operate in the constitutional measures of our Committee of Convention yet assembled. Exigencies may arise in which we ought not to trust to the slow, the precarious, and imperfect intercourse of epistolary correspondence; and the friends of liberty ought to be, and we trust they are rather *animated* than *intimidated* by the opposition they have met with and the treatment of their glorious and enlightened champions.

But independent of the specific *mode* of co-operation (upon which we anxiously expect your sentiments) there is a particular measure, which with your approbation and concurrence, we wish to adopt, namely, a *Remonstrance* to each of the three branches of the Legislature against the dangerous innovations which prerogative and ministerial artifice are making upon the *valuable parts* of our Laws and Constitution the system of spies and persecutions[8] – the usurpations of inferior magistrates and particularly the alarming transactions of the police and courts of law in Scotland, where all shadow of Liberty seems annihilated by the rod of power – that invincible spirit alone excepted that reigns in the hearts of a brave and enlightened people.

CITIZENS, we wish in this remonstrance, to demand an immediate enquiry into the nature of our constitutional rights; the instructions (if any) which the Judges and Magistrates have received, relative to their alarming conduct, the authority by which such instructions (if real) have been given, and just and constitutional vengeance upon the heads of those who shall be found to have been the real violators of such laws as were meant for the protection of liberty, and the happiness and prosperity of the people.

Such, Fellow Citizens, is the measure relative to which we call upon you for your immediate opinion. If in such a measure you will co-operate with us, let us know,

---

[8] The government was using a network of spies and paid informers from amongst the members of the Corresponding Societies to gather intelligence about their activities.

without delay, the proposed means of your co-operation. Should any other appear more advisable, we shall be happy to have your sentiments without delay.

In the mean time we remain,

in all the zeal and ardour of the love of liberty,

Yours,

THE LONDON CORRESPONDING SOCIETY

Resolved at a General Meeting of the said Society, held on Monday the 20th of January 1794, that a printed Copy of the above Letter be sent, without Delay, to the Secretaries and Chairmen of – the respective patriotic Societies in Great Britain and Ireland.

RESOLVED, that during the ensuing Session of Parliament, the General Committee of this Society do meet daily, for the purpose of watching the proceedings of the Parliament, and of the Administration of the Government of this Country. And that upon the first introduction of any bill or motion inimical to the liberties of the people such as for LANDING FOREIGN TROOPS IN GREAT BRITAIN or IRELAND, for SUSPENDING THE HABEAS CORPUS ACT, for PROCLAIMING MARTIAL LAW, or for PREVENTING THE PEOPLE FROM MEETING IN SOCIETIES FOR CONSTITUTIONAL INFORMATION, or any OTHER INNOVATION of a similar nature, that, on any of these emergencies the General Committee shall issue summonses to the Delegates of each division, and also to the Secretaries of the different Societies affiliated and corresponding with this Society, forthwith to call a GENERAL CONVENTION OF THE PEOPLE, to be held at such place, and in such a manner as shall be specified in the summons for the purpose of taking such measures into their consideration.

J. MARTIN Chairman,

T. HARDY, Secretary.

THOMAS SPENCE

BIOGRAPHICAL NOTE

Spence was born in Newcastle to working-class parents on 21 June 1750. He was taught to read the Bible at home – his parents were Glassites, a communitarian Christian sect – and he subsequently read widely. Influenced by a local radical Presbyterian minister, the Rev. James Murray and the emergent urban radicalism of the Wilkes years, Spence became involved in local political agitation against land enclosure and became a founder member of the Newcastle Philosophical Society in 1775. In November of that year he delivered a controversial lecture to the Society denouncing private ownership of land, and advocating instead its control by democratic parish councils, a form of elementary municipal agrarian socialism. He referred to this political and economic utopia variously as 'Spensonia' or 'Crusonia' – cleverly recruiting the popularity of Defoe's novel for his cause. Spence was expelled from the society for his political views but published his lecture and repeated his ideas in *The Poor Man's Advocate* (1779) and *A Supplement to the History of Robinson Crusoe* (1782): from this time also dates Spence's other life-long campaign – for the phoneticisation of English spelling as a way of broadening education. *The Grand Repository of the English Language* (1775) and *Real Reading Made Easy* (1782) were part of a self-consciously political campaign to empower the poor and deprived by 'free[ing] the poor and the stranger, the industrious and the innocent, from vecsatious, tedious and ridiculous absurdities'. He occasionally combined his political and his phonetic campaigns, as in *A S'upl'im'int too thi Histire ov Robinson Kruzo being TH'I H'IST'IRE ov KRUZO'Z IL'IND down too the prezint Tim* (Nuk'as'il 1782)!

In 1792 Spence moved to London where he subsequently reprinted his lecture as **The Real Rights of Man** (1793) and sold it and other pamphlets from a stall. From 1793 to 1795 he edited an important radical weekly *Pig's Meat* – the title drawing on Burke's reference to the poor as the 'swinish multitude'. This was a hotch-potch of radical and republican sound-bites, ancient and modern, and probably an important source for many uneducated radicals seeking authority and justifications for their position in the inherited political culture of the time.

He also published many versions of his plan for constitutional and economic reform. He was arrested several times between December 1792 and December 1794 but, although spending some months in prison, was either released without charge or formally acquitted. Clearly a target of the authorities he was finally convicted of sedition in 1801 and imprisoned for a year. Indefatigably, on his release, he immediately republished the works for which he had been convicted. He died in 1814.

There was a macabre postscript to his life of essentially non-violent campaigning. A group of followers formed the Society of Spencean Philanthropists from which emerged the more violent, if somewhat pathetic, insurrectionists of the Cato Street Conspiracy (1820).

EDITORIAL NOTE

Spence's lecture was originally printed close to the time of its original delivery in Newcastle, in 1775, but no version of it from that period survives. The original title was probably *Property in Land Every Man's Right*. Spence reprinted it many times in various versions. The title *The Real Rights of Man* was probably not used until after Paine's work was published in order to distinguish his own more radical position. The text used here dates from 1793.

Modern editions:

The Political Works of Thomas Spence, ed. H. T. Dickinson (Newcastle upon Tyne: Avro, 1982).

Pig's Meat: Selected Writings of Thomas Spence, Radical and Pioneer Land Reformer, ed. G. I. Gallop (Nottingham: Spokesman, 1982).

FURTHER READING

Ashraf, P. M. *The Life and Times of Thomas Spence* (Newcastle upon Tyne: Frank Graham, 1983).

Chase, M. *The People's Farm: English Agrarian Radicalism 1775–1840* (Oxford: Clarendon Press, 1988).

McCalman, I. *Radical Underworld, Prophets, Revolutionaries and Pornographers in London 1795–1840* (Cambridge University Press, 1988; Oxford University Press, 1993).

Rudkin, O. *Thomas Spence and his Connections* (London: Allen & Unwin, 1927).

The Real Rights of Man (1793)

A LECTURE READ AT THE PHILOSOPHICAL SOCIETY IN NEWCASTLE ON NOVEMBER 8TH, 1775, FOR PRINTING OF WHICH THE SOCIETY DID THE AUTHOR THE HONOUR TO EXPEL HIM[1]

Mr President, It being my turn to lecture, I beg to give some thoughts on this important question, viz. – Whether mankind in society reap all the advantages from their natural and equal rights of property in land and liberty, which in that state they possibly may and ought to expect? And as I hope you, Mr President and the good company here, are sincere friends to truth, I am under no apprehensions of giving offence by defending her cause with freedom. That property in land and liberty among men in a state of nature ought to be equal, few, one would be fain to hope, would be foolish enough to deny. Therefore, taking this to be granted, the country of any people, in a native state, is properly their common, in which each of them has an equal property, with free liberty to sustain himself and family with the animals, fruits and other products thereof. Thus such a people reap jointly the whole advantages of their country, or neighbourhood, without having their right in so doing called in question by any, not even the most selfish and corrupt. For upon what must they live if not upon the productions of the country in which they reside? Surely to deny them that right is in effect denying them a right to live. Well, methinks some are now ready to say, but is it lawful, reasonable and just, for this people to sell, or make a present even, of the whole of their country, or common, to whom they will, to be held by them and their heirs for ever?

To this I answer, if their posterity require no grosser materials to live and move upon than air, it would certainly be very ill-natured to dispute their right of parting, for what of their own, their posterity would never have occasion for; but if their posterity cannot live but as grossly as they do, the same gross materials must be left them to live upon. For the right to deprive anything of the means of living, supposes a right to deprive it of life; and this right ancestors are not supposed to have over their posterity.

---

[1] Spence had joined the club at its foundation in 1775 and printed and sold his lecture without permission, and propagated his views at other clubs too. He reprinted the work many times, often with additional dialogues such as the one reproduced here, and he continued to do so after his move to London in 1792, first as *The Real Rights of Man* (1793), a title designed to draw attention to his critique of what he regarded as Paine's inadequate radicalism.

Hence it is plain that the land or earth, in any country or neighbourhood, with everything in or on the same, or pertaining thereto, belongs at all times to the living inhabitants of the said country or neighbourhood in an equal manner. For, as I said before, there is no living but on land and its productions, consequently, what we cannot live without we have the same property in as our lives.

Now as society ought properly to be nothing but a mutual agreement among the inhabitants of a country to maintain the natural rights and privileges of one another against all opposers, whether foreign or domestic, it would lead one to expect to find those rights and privileges no further infringed upon among men pretending to be in that state, than necessity absolutely required. I say again, it would lead one to think so. But I am afraid whoever does will be mightily mistaken. However, as the truth here is of much importance to be known, let it be boldly fought out; in order to which it may not be improper to trace the present method of holding land among men in society from its original.

If we look back to the origin of the present nations, we shall see that the land, with all its appurtenances, was claimed by a few, and divided among themselves, in as assured a manner as if they had manufactured it and it had been the work of their own hands; and by being unquestioned, or not called to an account for such usurpations and unjust claims, they fell into a habit of thinking, or, which is the same thing to the rest of mankind, of acting as if the earth was made for or by them, and did not scruple to call it their own property, which they might dispose of without regard to any other living creature in the universe. Accordingly they did so; and no man, more than any other creature, could claim a right to so much as a blade of grass, or a nut or an acorn, a fish or a fowl, or any natural production whatever, though to save his life, without the permission of the pretended proprietor; and not a foot of land, water, rock or heath but was claimed by one or other of those lords; so that all things, men as well as other creatures who lived, were obliged to owe their lives to some or other's property; consequently they like the creatures were claimed, and, certainly as properly as the wood herbs, etc., that were nourished by the soil. And so we find, that whether they lived, multiplied, worked or fought, it was all for their respective lords; and they, God bless them, most graciously accepted of all as their due. For by granting the means of life, they granted the life itself; and of course, they thought they had a right to all the services and advantages that the life or death of the creatures they gave life to could yield.

Thus the title of gods seems suitable enough to such great beings; nor is it to be wondered at that no services could be thought too great by poor dependent needy wretches to such mighty and all-sufficient lords, in whom they seemed to live and move and have their being. Thus were the first land-holders usurpers and tyrants; and all who have since possessed their lands, have done so by right of inheritance, purchase, etc., from them; and the present proprietors, like their predecessors, are proud to own it; and like them, too, they exclude all others from the least pretence to their respective properties. And any one of them still can, by laws of their own making, oblige every living creature to remove off his property (which, to the great distress of mankind, is too often put in execution); so of consequence were all the landholders to be of one mind, and determined to take their properties into their own hands, all the rest of mankind might go to heaven if they would, for there would be no place found for them here. Thus men may not live in any part of this world, not even where they are born, but as strangers, and by the permission of the pretender to the property thereof; which permission is, for the most part, paid extravagantly for, though many people are so straitened to pay the present demands, that it is believed if they hold on, there will be few to grant the favour to. And those landmakers, as we shall call them, justify all this by the practice of other manufacturers, who take all they can get for the products of their hands; and because that everyone ought to live by his business as well as he can, and consequently so ought the land-makers. Now, having before supposed it both proved and allowed, that mankind have as equal and just a property in land as they have in liberty, air, or the light and heat of the sun, and having also considered upon what hard conditions they enjoy those common gifts of nature, it is plain they are far from reaping all the advantages from them which they may and ought to expect.

But lest it should be said that a system whereby they may reap more advantages consistent with the nature of society cannot be proposed, I will attempt to show the outlines of such a plan.

Let it be supposed, then, that the whole people in some country, after much reasoning and deliberation, should conclude that every man has an equal property in the land in the neighbourhood where he resides. They therefore resolve that if they live in society together, it shall only be with a view that everyone may reap all the benefits from their natural rights and privileges possible.

Therefore a day appointed on which the inhabitants of each parish meet, in their respective parishes, to take their long-lost rights into possession, and to form themselves into corporations. So then each parish becomes a corporation, and all men who are inhabitants become members or burghers. The land, with all that appertains to it, is in every parish made the property of the corporation or parish, with as ample power to let, repair, or alter all or any part thereof as a lord of the manor enjoys over his lands, houses, etc.; but the power of alienating the least morsel, in any manner, from the parish either at this or any time hereafter is denied. For it is solemnly agreed to by the whole nation that a parish that shall either sell or give away any part of its landed property, shall be looked upon with as much horror and detestation, and used by them as if they had sold all their children to be slaves, or massacred them with their own hands. Thus are there no more nor other lands in the whole country than the parishes; and each of them is sovereign lord of its own territories.

Then you may behold the rent which the people have paid into the parish treasuries, employed by each parish in paying the Government its share of the sum which the Parliament or National Congress at any time grants; in maintaining and relieving its own poor, and people out of work; in paying the necessary officers their salaries; in building, repairing, and adorning its houses, bridges, and other structures; in making and maintaining convenient and delightful streets, highways, and passages both for foot and carriages; in making and maintaining canals and other conveniences for trade and navigation; in planting and taking in waste grounds; in providing and keeping up a magazine of ammunition, and all sorts of arms sufficient for all its inhabitants in case of danger from enemies; in premiums for the encouragement of agriculture, or anything else thought worthy of encouragement; and, in a word, in doing whatever the people think proper; and not, as formerly, to support and spread luxury, pride, and all manner of vice. As for corruption in elections, it has now no being or effect among them; all affairs to be determined by voting, either in a full meeting of a parish, its committees, or in the house of representatives, are done by balloting, so that votings or elections among them occasion no animosities, for none need to let another know for which side he votes; all that can be done, therefore, in order to gain a majority of votes for anything, is to make it appear in the best light possibly by speaking or writing. Among them Government does not meddle in every trifle; but on the contrary, allows each parish the power of putting the laws in force in all cases, and does not interfere but when they act manifestly to the prejudice of society and the rights and liberties of mankind, as established in their glorious constitution and laws. For the judgment of a parish may be as much depended upon as that of a House of Lords, because they have as little to fear from speaking or voting according to truth as they.

A certain number of neighbouring parishes, as those in a town or county, have each an equal vote in the election of persons to represent them in Parliament, Senate, or Congress; and each of them pays equally towards their maintenance. They are chosen thus: all the candidates are proposed in every parish on the same day, when the election by balloting immediately proceeds in all the parishes at once, to prevent too great a concourse at one place; and they who are found to have a majority, on a proper survey of the several poll-books, are acknowledged to be their representatives.

A man by dwelling a whole year in any parish, becomes a parishioner or member of its corporation; and retains that privilege till he lives a full year in some other, when he becomes a member in that parish, and immediately loses all his right to the former for ever, unless he choose to go back and recover it by dwelling again a full year there. Thus none can be a member of two parishes at once, and yet a man is always member of one though he move ever so oft.

If in any parish should be dwelling strangers from foreign nations, or people from distant countries who by sickness or other casualties should become so necessitous as to require relief before they have acquired a settlement by dwelling a full year therein; then this parish, as if it were their proper settlement, immediately takes them under its humane protection, and the expenses thus incurred by any parish in providing those not properly their own poor being taken account of, is discounted by the Exchequer out of the first payment made to the State. Thus poor strangers, being the poor of the State, are not looked upon with an envious eye lest they should become burthensome, – neither are the poor harassed about in the extremity of distress, and perhaps in a dying condition, to justify the litigiousness of the parishes.

All the men in every parish, at times of their own choosing, repair together to a field for that purpose, with their officers, arms, banners, and all sorts of martial music, in order to learn or retain the complete art of war; there they become soldiers. Yet not to molest their neighbours unprovoked, but to be able to defend what none have a right to dispute their title to the enjoyment of; and woe be to them who occasion them to do this, they would use them worse than highwaymen or pirates if they got them in their power.

There is no army kept in pay among them in times of peace, as all have property alike to defend, they are alike ready to run to arms when their country is in danger; and when an army is to be sent abroad, it is soon raised, of ready trained soldiers, either as volunteers or by casting lots in each parish for so many men.

Besides, as each man has a vote in all the affairs of his parish, and for his own sake must wish well to the public, the land is let in very small farms, which makes employment for a greater number of hands, and makes more victualling of all kinds be raised.

There are no tolls or taxes of any kind paid among them by native or foreigner, but the aforesaid rent which every person pays to the parish, according to the quantity, quality, and conveniences of the land, housing, etc., which he occupies in it. The government, poor, roads, etc. etc., as said before, are all maintained by the parishes with the rent; on which account all wares, manufactures, allowable trade employments or actions are entirely duty free. Freedom to do anything whatever cannot there be bought; a thing is either entirely prohibited, as theft or murder; or entirely free to everyone without tax or price, and the rents are still not so high, notwithstanding all that is done with them, as they were formerly for only the maintenance of a few haughty, unthankful landlords. For the government, which may be said to be the greatest mouth, having neither excisemen, customhouse men, collectors, army, pensioners, bribery, nor such like ruination vermin to maintain, is soon satisfied, and moreover there are no more persons employed in offices, either about the government or parishes, than are absolutely necessary; and their salaries are but just sufficient to maintain them suitably to their offices. And, as to the other charges, they are but trifles, and might be increased or diminished at pleasure.

But though the rent, which includes all public burdens, were obliged to be somewhat raised, what then? All nations have a devouring landed interest to support besides those necessary expenses of the public; and they might be raised very high indeed before their burden would be as heavy as that of their neighbours, who pay rent and taxes too. And it surely would be the same for a person in any country to pay for instance an increase of rent if required, as to pay the same sum by little and little on everything he gets. It would certainly save him a great deal of trouble and inconvenience, and Government much expense.

But what makes this prospect yet more glowing is that after this empire of right and reason is thus established, it will stand for ever. Force and corruption attempting its downfall shall equally be baffled, and all other nations, struck with wonder and admiration at its happiness and stability, shall follow the example; and thus the whole earth shall at last be happy and live like brethren.

AN INTERESTING CONVERSATION, BETWEEN A GENTLEMAN AND THE AUTHOR,
ON THE SUBJECT OF THE FOREGOING LECTURE

Gent. So I understand you are the Author of this strange Lecture?

Auth. Yes, Sir.

Gent. Well, though I am a friend to the Reformation of the world, I did not expect any one's ideas would have been carried to such extravagant lengths on the subject as your's.

Auth. And I am as strangely puzzled to conceive how any one, not afraid of the freedom of his own thoughts, could stop any thing short of the system there laid down.

Gent. Indeed! But who, pray, among all the Revolutionists in either America, France, or England, or any where else, ever disputed or attempted to invalidate the rights of the landed interest? Or, does Paine, whose publications seem to satisfy the wishes of the most sanguine Reformers, glance in the least on their rights? This is taking too great liberties.

Auth. I cannot help it. I would sooner not think at all, than check my thoughts on a subject so important. – I hate patching and cobling. Let us have a perfect system that will keep itself right, and let us have done; for what is radically wrong must be a continual plague.

But, Sir, why all this anxiety and concern for the interests of landlords? Those who can reward as they can will never want advocates to defend their cause, whether it be good or bad. 'Will you plead for Baal? If Baal be a god, let him plead for himself'.

The Reformers, of whom you say you are one, indulge establishments as old and as defensible as the monopoly of land, and think they are only using the Rights of Men: allow me therefore, to take the same liberty with what I think amiss; and let Baal, as I say, plead for himself. So, Sir, your servant, you may dislike my free manner of defending doctrines, which I think of such magnitude.

Gent. Nay, stop a little Sir, you must excuse me. I was only acting in character; you must allow Baal, as you say, to plead for himself, for I being a landlord cannot be expected to lose an estate without some defence; therefore, indulge me with the solution of such difficulties as appear to me in the principles and execution of your plan, that if I am a loser I may be satisfied that the public good absolutely requires it.

You build your system, I observe, on the supposition that men have the same right to property of land as they have to liberty, and the light and heat of the sun, which I grant is a very just position, respecting men in a natural, or in their primeval state; but this antient and universal right is so set aside and disused, that it seems quite forgot and expunged from the catalogue of the Rights of Men; besides, there was nobody found murmuring at the want of it.

Auth. It is, indeed, very amazing, that people should never think more seriously of such an essential and inestimable privilege, considering the many express declarations to that purpose, to be met with both in the scriptures and in the best of prophane authors. Permit me, then, to produce two or three of the most remarkable passages: and first, from Leviticus, Chap. 25th.

> 'And thou shalt number seven sabbaths of years unto thee, seven times seven years; and the space of the seven sabbaths of years shall be unto thee forty and nine years. Then shalt thou cause the trumpet of the Jubilee to sound, on the tenth day of the seventh month, in the day of atonement shall ye make the trumpet sound throughout all your land. And ye shall hallow the fiftieth year, and proclaim liberty throughout all the land, unto all the inhabitants thereof: It shall be a Jubilee unto you; and ye shall return every man unto his possession, and ye shall return every man unto his family.'

And again in the same chapter, it is said,

> 'The land shall not be sold for ever; for the land is mine; for ye are strangers and sojuurners [*sic*] with me.'

Thus you see God Almighty himself is a very notorious leveller, and certainly meant to stir up the people every fiftieth year, to insist upon liberty and equality, or the repossession of their just rights, whether their masters or creditors were agreeable or not, or whether they might deem it seditious or no; and we may suppose that such of the latter as were covetous ungodly men would behave very frowardly, and quit their hold with much reluctance, and would be far from promoting such a revolution.

Then we may be certain that as often as such periodical revolutions happened in favour of the Rights of Man, they must arise from, and were procured by the irresistable importunities of the slaves and landless men.

Thus we find personal liberty and landed property very properly linked together by our all-wise creator, nor is the one of much consequence without the other. Indeed, I think all our landless people had better live in slavery, under humane masters, that would provide them with the necessaries of life, than be turned out of their rights as outcasts upon the face of that earth whereon they must neither feed nor rest.

Well, we have heard what God has said on the subject, let us next hear what man says. Locke, in his treatise of government writes thus:

'Whether we consider natural reason, which tells us, that men, being once born, have a right to their preservation, and consequently to meat and drink, and such other things as nature affords for their subsistence. Or, revelation, which gives us an account of those grants God made of the world to Adam, and to Noah and his sons; it is very clear that God, as King David says, Psalm 115, 16, has given the earth to the children of men, given it to mankind in common.'[2]

Here we find this great man concurring in the same fundamental principles, as we shall likewise Puffendorf, in his Whole Duty of Man, according to the law of nature, where he observes, that

'As those are the best members of a community, who without any difficulty allow the same things to their neighbour, that themselves require of him, so those are altogether incapable of society, who, setting a high rate on themselves in regard to others, will take upon them to act in any thing towards their neighbour, and expect greater deference, and more respect than the rest of mankind; and, in their intolerant manner, demanding a greater portion unto themselves of those things, to which all men having a common right, they can in reason claim no larger a share than other men: whence this also is an universal duty of the law natural, That no man, who has not a peculiar right, ought to arrogate more to himself than he is ready to allow to his fellows, but that he permit other men to enjoy equal privileges with himself.'[3]

Such declarations being frequent in all the best Authors, one would think they would rouse the most supine to consider their contemptible and degraded situation, who, from being the rightful lords of the creation, and only a little lower than the angels, and crowned by their maker, with glory and honour, tamely prostrate themselves to the earth, to a state worse than a reptile, for any one that will be insolent enough to pass over.

But, Sir, people never thought it was practicable to enjoy an equal property in land. For the mechanics thought they could not themselves cultivate land if they were possessed of it, and that therefore thousands would be selling their portions to others, which would soon reduce things to the same situation as at present. And besides, they could not be at the trouble, nor put themselves so much out of temper, so as like the Jews, to demand a restitution of the land and an abolition of debts every fiftieth year. No, they would rather sit down contently on their dunghills, under all

[2] Locke, *Two Treatises of Government*, II, v, §25.
[3] S. Puffendorf, *On The Whole Duty of Man and Citizen according to Natural Law* [1673], ed. James Tully, trs. Michael Silverthorn (Cambridge University Press, 1991), Bk I, 7, §.3.

their affronts, with their wives and children starving about them than give offence to their masters by seditiously claiming their rights as men.

But, by giving the land to the parishes, they will be eased at once of all those troublesome apprehensions; one hearty revolution and one jubilee will do the business for ever: for we find societie once possessed of land do not easily give it up, but are very tenacious of their property of which we have many instances, there hardly being a corporation but what has landed property, and have retained the same for many ages.

So here is a simple, easy, practicable scheme, which people may see realised in every corporate body; wherefore, as people will now think themselves qualified to manage their own estates by the agency of their parish officers, for their own advantage, they must of course think landlords of no more use, and will grow weary of them. The payment of rent to a landlord, will be like-giving [*sic*] money to a highwayman, and they will pant to be rid of their insupportable burdens all at once. In short, Sir, when the public machine is thus set a going on nature's principles, like nature itself, it will never err to any great degree, but on the least aberrition immediately rebound back to its just equilibrium.

Gent. But, Sir, I am not so partial to corporation government, but I can see many things amiss in them. There is often much party work, and I am afraid the people at large would reap small benefit from their landed property, as is too much the case in most of the corporations already in being.

Auth. The corporations now in being were established in times of ignorance, when very few were qualified to take cognizance of public affairs, wherefore the mass of the burghers were never suffered in their own persons to make choice of their magistrates or agents, but every company or trade chose an elector, and these were to make a kind of sham choice of magistrates and officers, for all this was settled in reality before in the common council; and the same practice to the great ease and content of the sluggish people, is still continued, which I hope you do not think I approve of; for I see no reason why a candidate for a magistracy or other office may not, after proper examination in respect to abilities, be proposed in every distinct company or trade at the same hour, and then in their own persons proceed to election. Candidates would not find it so easy to make a party among the burghers at large, as they do now among a few deputies, electors, or liverymen; but I hope if the people were but once put right (for they never have been so yet) they would be wise enough never to relapse into insignificance again, and find it worth their while to act in person as much as they could, by admitting of no electors or deputies between them and the person or thing to be voted for; for if a parish were found to be too populous to vote conveniently and expeditiously in one place, they would surely have the sense to divide the parish into such a sufficiency of districts or departments as should render business speedy and generally satisfactory.

I should likewise expect that they would have the sense to cause the parish accounts to be minutely stated and printed, at least every quarter; and the national accounts to be in the same manner printed, at least every year. And I should likewise with that the rents or rates might be collected monthly, as the poor rate is now, which, when once paid, would be in full of all demands, both for rent and taxes.

In short, Sir, if I thought the people at large would ever become so despicably destitute of common sense, as to be incapable of conducting such simple transactions with any little accidental variations after being thus fairly put right – I say, instead of exciting my pity as they now do, I would, like their tyrants, hold them in the most sovereign contempt and derision; nay, I would rejoice in seeing them all delivered over to cruel task-masters, planters, negro-drivers, landlords, and all the devils on earth. Moreover, I would endeavour to get into some infernal office myself, and make my thong the most terrible of the terrible.

But I am far from apprehending this will ever be the case, for it is impossible for the world to become generally ignorant again, as it was before the art of printing. Knowledge has been constantly increasing ever since that happy invention, and will infallibly continue to do so while the world endures.

Is it not astonishing, Sir, that republicans who long to put the affairs of a nation into the hands of commissioners or delegates, should despair of managing the rents or revenues of a parish in the same popular way? Is national democracy easier than parochial? Or are the pure rights of a man less defensible against landlords, than the rights of society against kings? The landlords are, and always were, the first infringers on the rights of man, and pave the sure way to regal tyranny. If the earth would remain barren and uncultivated, and if men, like brutes, would live in caves rather than build houses, etc., by means of their own agents or commissioners, then by all means let them have landlords. But then I, for my part, as much despair of the management of a nation by delegation, as others do of a parish, and therefore to me, kings seem to be to the full as necessary to a state, as landlords to a parish. Wherefore in the name of common sense, let us either quietly submit to matters of every description, or manfully aspire after perfect freedom from every imposition. For why should we despair of managing small affairs as well as great.

Gent. But I am at a great loss to conceive what will become of all the landed people, gentlemen of the law, gentlemens' [*sic*] servants, many artisans and tradesmen, entirely dependent on the nobility and gentry, and also the soldiers, for you intend all your citizens to be soldiers.

Auth. You will observe, Sir, that I am proceeding in this affair entirely in confidence of the people having common sense, and that they will, when once put right, put their senses forth to use on all occasions; and, I likewise, suppose they may have as much compassion on those affected by the change of affairs, as justice and necessity will admit of. So, in all probability, on that memorable day, that grand jubilee, when every parish, in some country shall take into its possession its indubitable rights, I mean the land with all its appurtenances, as structures, buildings, and fixtures, and mines, woods, waters, etc., contained within itself: I say, though according to right and system they must seize upon these, I expect they would leave every person in possession of his money and moveable effects to dispose of at his pleasure. The quondam landlords might therefore be reasonably expected to subsist comfortably upon these effects, all their lives with economy, I am sure few of the rest of the people would have as much at that day to their share; and as to their children, they would doubtless suit their education to their prospects, which would be no other than to live as sober, industrious citizens, maintained by their own industry. And what should hinder them by trading or farming to increase their effects under so mild and cherishing a government, as well as others? The same may be said of gentlemen of the law, and other eminent artists or tradesmen, who might suffer by the change; as for the private soldiers and subalterns, I would wish them to be sent every man to his own parish, there to receive his pay for life, and be employed in training his fellow-parishioners; and the general officers, I hope, the government would provide for in like ample manner. And with respect to other individuals, whether servants, mechanics, or revenue officers, who, having no effects accumulated, and might be reduced by any cause whatever, either at this or any future period to require assistance, I hope their respective parishes would prove generous, and sympathizing benefit societies for support of them all, until they could again provide for themselves; and the parishes, no doubt, would contrive to make such persons contribute, if in health, towards the public good by their labours and to this they surely would not object.

Gent. But, friend, what do you expect by all this? Though your scheme should succeed, you cannot expect an estate for your trouble, and both you and your posterity for ever must be content to herd with the common mass, without any hopes of flattering distinction: but if your plan should not succeed, then you must expect a spiteful and powerful opposition in all you go about, from those you are seeking to overthrow.

Mr Paine acts more cautiously, and does not hurt the feelings of any gentleman that is unconnected with government, and so, of course, may retain their good will, notwithstanding all the lengths he goes; and may, even with a good grace, consistent with his reform, enjoy a very handsome estate, and with all his boasted liberty and equality, may roll in his chariot on the labours of his tenants.

Auth. The contempt and ungenerous rebuffs of the opulent I have already pretty well experienced, and do yet expect; but the feelings occasioned by beholding the struggles of temperance, frugality, and industry, after an honest livelihood, which ought to be easily attainable by every one, have always been sufficiently powerful to enable me to despise them. Yes, those sympathetic feelings were impressed deep on my heart, being first excited by the many difficulties my poor parents experienced in providing for, and endeavouring to bring up their numerous family with decency and credit, which I thought very hard, as none could be more temperate, frugal, nor industrious.

I began, Sir, to look round to know the cause of this piercing grievance, and I found thousands rioting in all the abominations of luxury and dissipation, as if there had been no being in heaven or earth but themselves, and as if they had been created for the sole purpose of destroying the fruits of the earth; and again, I beheld myriads in a much worse condition than my own family. Then I began to read, and I found the savages in Greenland, America, and at the Cape of Good Hope, could all by their hunting and fishing procure subsistence for their families. Then I enquired whether men left the rude state of a savage voluntarily for greater comforts in a state of civilisation, or whether they were conquered, and compelled into it for the benefit of their conquerors. My experience compelled me to conclude the latter, for I could observe nothing like the effects of a social compact; wherefore, I concluded that all our boasted civilisation is founded alone on conquest; nor will any men leave their rude state to be treated with contempt, pay rents and taxes, and starve among us. Savages may sometimes suffer want though that is but rare, but the poor tamed wretch drags on a despicable, miserable, and toilsome existence, from generation to generation. This surely looks exceeding bad, that among men in such high refinement and so capable of rendering each other happy, by being reciprocally useful to each other: thousands should nevertheless be in so wretched a state, that savages would not change conditions with them.

Such studies, Sir, as these, were what stirred me up with an irresistible enthusiasm, to lay before the world a plan of society, so consonant to the Rights of Man, that even savages should envy, and wish to become members thereof.

Plate 7. *The Prophet of the Hebrews – the Prince of Peace Conducting the Jews to the Promised Land* (James Gillray, 1795). The cartoon links the religious enthusiast Richard Brothers with Fox and other supporters of Revolutionary ideas whom he is carrying on his back. Brothers is being followed by poor people with hopes of 'everlasting life'. Holding his 'Revelations' in his hand he treads royalty and nobility underfoot as he makes his way towards a distant hill which is topped by a gallows (c.f. Burke's remark that 'at the end of every visto you see the gallows'.) To Brothers's right an earthquake-stricken London is in flames and to his left there are disasters at sea. Above him flies an ironic owl, the symbol of wisdom, whilst to the right devils dance around the moon, a symbol of inconstancy.

RICHARD BROTHERS

BIOGRAPHICAL NOTE

Richard Brothers, a mild, gentlemanly and not at all 'enthusiastic' man, was born in Placentia, Newfoundland in 1757, emigrated to London as a boy and served in the Navy. After his discharge in 1783 he continued to travel widely. In 1786 he married, but was subsequently deserted by his wife. Returning to London in 1787 he lived on his Navy pension and worshipped at a Baptist church. From 1789 he refused to take the oath which was a condition of receiving his pension, and in 1791 was admitted to the workhouse. From this time too, he began to experience divine visions in which he became convinced that he was the Nephew of God and the leader whose role it was to lead the Jews back to Israel – one of the events that, according to Biblical prophecy, preceded Christ's second coming. London was identified with the emblematic Babylon of *Revelations* 17 the destruction of which would also precede the last judgement. In 1792 Brothers identified the French Revolution itself as a judgement of God, and he wrote warning prominent politicians not to oppose it. Convinced of the depravity of the English Monarchy and Empire he prophesied its destruction at the hands of the French – the instruments of God's judgement – and the destruction of London by an earthquake.

Millenarian language was not so far from the mainstream in the eighteenth century. Sects such as the Muggletonians and followers of Jacob Boehme persisted underground and their ideas occasionally surfaced strikingly, as in the writings of William Blake. As Burke discerned, there was more than a hint of millenarianisms at the end of Price's sermon (text 2), and rationalist dissenters such as Priestley were not immune to its appeal. Indeed the Rev. Joseph Towers, a politically radical Unitarian, published his own *Illustrations of Prophecy* (1796). What distinguished Brothers from other 'prophets' of his century was the strength of his following and the disciples he found amongst the 'respectable classes'. A wealthy Captain Hanchett took up his cause and paid for a printing of Brothers's revelations. John Finlayson, a Scots lawyer, and several Anglican clergymen as well as many lesser figures joined his supporters. Most influential of all, an MP, Nathaniel Brassey Halhed, an East India Company official and a translator and scholar of Persian, took up Brothers's cause, publishing a vindication of his prophecies and defended him in the Commons after Brothers's arrest and imprisonment in an insane asylum. Brothers became a *cause célèbre* discussed in all the literary reviews. There were many publications in support of him and letters discussed his authenticity in the newspapers. He was depicted in popular cartoons (see Plate 7). Further collections of prophetic writings were published. Some diarists and commentators reported, in the summer of 1795, a real feeling of impending disaster and numbers of people left London in expectation of its destruction. Modern readers should note that in all the discussion of Brothers the issue was whether he was a false or a true prophet, and not whether prophecy was a real or an unreal category.

EDITORIAL NOTE

A Revealed Knowledge of the Prophecies and Times, Book the First, Wrote under the direction of the LORD GOD, And published by his sacred command went through four London editions and another in Dublin. There were seventeen editions in America and French and German translations. The text used here is taken from a copy of the first, London edition, in the Betjeman Collection of the Exeter University Library, see also:

Halhed, Nathaniel Brassey, *The Whole of the Testimony to the Authenticity of the Prophecies and Mission of Richard Brothers* (London, 1795)

FURTHER READING

Garrett, Clark *Respectable Folly Millenarians and the French Revolution in France and England* (Baltimore and London: Johns Hopkins University Press, 1975).
Harrison, J. F. C. *The Second Coming, Popular Millenarianism 1780–1850* (London: Routledge, 1979).

A Revealed Knowledge of the Prophecies and Times (1794)

A

REVEALED KNOWLEDGE

OF THE

PROPHECIES AND TIMES

- - - - - - -

BOOK THE FIRST

- - - - - - -

WROTE UNDER THE DIRECTION OF THE

LORD GOD

AND PUBLISHED BY HIS SACRED COMMAND

IT BEING THE

FIRST SIGN OF WARNING

FOR *THE BENEFIT OF ALL NATIONS*

CONTAINING, WITH OTHER

GREAT AND REMARKABLE THINGS

NOT REVEALED TO ANY OTHER PERSON ON EARTH

THE

RESTORATION OF THE HEBREWS

TO JERUSALEM, BY THE YEAR OF 1798

UNDER THEIR REVEALED

PRINCE AND PROPHET,

RICHARD BROTHERS

. . .

THE JUDGEMENT OF GOD

The very loud and unusual kind of thunder that was heard in the beginning of January, 1791, was the voice of the angel mentioned in the eighteenth chapter of the revelation, proclaiming the judgment of God and the fall of Babylon the Great: it was the loudest that ever was heard since man was created, and shook the whole earth every time the angel spoke; it roared through the streets of, and made a noise over London like the falling of mountains of stones.

Many buildings were damaged at the time of this thunder, and many persons were frightened by it; the great flashes of lightening proceeded also from the angel, and was, according [to] the first verse, reflected from the brightness of his glory.

. . .

The Lord God was so exceeding angry at that time of the loud thunder . . . that he determined to . . . burn her immediately with fire from heaven; soon afterwards I was informed by revelation of what the thunder meant, and was commanded to go from London a distance of eighteen miles. I had *similar to the prophet Daniel at Babylon*, an attending angel to explain all the visions and support me under the grief I was loaded with for its approaching fall.

. . .

In addition to all that God had promised and repeated by his angel . . . he was now pleased to give me another proof of his unalterable regard, and convince me by it, that, *although he could not in justice to his recorded judgements, spare London*, yet, for my sake he would show mercy to some; and take care by sickness and other causes to remove the persons I desired should be saved to a sufficient distance . . .

Among those I mentioned was William Pultney, William Pitt, Gilbert Elliot, Charles Grey, the Earl of Buckinghamshire, the Marquis of Lansdown, the Earl of Chatham, Maitland now called Earl of Lauderdale; Henry Phipp . . . John Dalrymple, John Griffin Griffin, Alderman Picket . . .

. . .

Again I was in a vision and saw London a scene of confusion; it was effected on a sudden; all of the people were armed and appeared quite furious; I was carried through the city in the Spirit of God to see all things that were designed should come to pass, and be informed how quick they should be accomplished.

After this I was in a vision and saw a large river run through London coloured with human blood . . .

. . .

. . . I prayed and entreated the Lord God to give me one more instance of his mighty regard, *by sparing London and the great multitude in it.* I said I acknowledge O Lord my God, that the people do very wrong, but it is through compulsion and for want of knowing better.

The Lord God was so highly displeased, that I should, after all his former kindness, strain his affection and entreat him to annul his *recorded judgement*, as to stop me . . . in a voice of great sharpness and anger . . .

In ten days after the three I was in a vision, and being carried up to heaven, the Lord God spoke to me from the middle of a large white cloud, and said in a strong clear voice – All, All. I pardon London and all the people in it, for your sake: there is no other man on earth that could stand before me to ask for so great a thing.

. . .

That all men of wisdom and discernment may understand, on reading the revelation, that there are two cities mentioned in it spiritually, under the names of Babylon the Great, I will assist them by clearly marking out the distinction.

Rome, the spiritual Babylon, mentioned in the seventeenth chapter, is described, in the third vierse, *to be away into the wilderness*; meaning, by the words, into the wilderness, that is that the city is situated *inland*.

But London, the spiritual Babylon, also mentioned in the eighteenth chapter, is described by St. John, *as the greatest sea-port* for ships, wealth and commerce, in the world.

. . .

Read attentively the eighteenth chapter; and you will perceive described in it, the prodigious wealth, grandeur, and commerce of London: then remember, that the very great thunder and lightening I have mentioned was in the depth of winter, *an unusual time of year for the like*; but they were as St. John exactly describes them, in the first and second verses. Meditate apon these things, weigh them attentively in your mind, and all that I have wrote besides and the spirit of God, if you love wisdom, will enlighten your understanding to see, and will also strike you with a conviction of their truth.

VERSE XVII

And I saw an angel standing in the sun; and he cried with a loud voice, (meaning the thunder,) saying to all the fowls that fly in the midst of heaven, Come, and gather yourselves together to the supper of the great God;

That ye may eat the flesh of kings, and the flesh of captains, and the flesh of mighty men, and the flesh of horses, and of them that sit on them; and the flesh of all men, both free and bond, both small and great.

The dead will increase so fast, and be in such prodigious numbers, when this judgment takes place, that the living will not be sufficient to bury them, but will leave the bodies exposed to the fowls of heaven for meat.

. . .

The 15th of August 1793, was the time appointed by the Lord God to fulfil the parts of the Revelation I have mentioned, and punish the world with desolation; but from his great mercy- and regard for me, that I may be esteemed in this country, and by all others, when I am revealed, suspended his judgment for a time – it hangs however over all nations.

Look at the age of the world; read attentively the chapters I have mentioned,[1] with what I have wrote besides; and you will discover in your own breast a light, to see and believe by. That *light, I mean*, which is often called *a certain something*, an *internal monitor*, that applauds man for courting wisdom, for being just, and doing good; but that never fails to reproach him for embracing folly, and doing evil: it is indeed no other than the Spirit of the living God. All the prophecies, given in visions from God, are concealed from the knowledge of man by mysterious allusions, until the proper time, and the appointed person for them to be revealed to. For it is not in the cunning of any one man, even assisted by the wisdom of all the rest on earth, to search out the deep secrets of God, or with truth to unfold the meaning of his visions; They are wonderful; they cannot be discovered until God himself pleases to remove the covering of secrecy; and, through an appointed person, blesses the world with a knowledge of their true meaning.

The fulfilling of the judgments of God, however destructively they may prove to the governments and nations which they are directed against, are not allowed to affect my personal safety, nor operate in the least to my prejudice: for the certainty of any elevation, to the greatest *principality* that ever will be in the world, cannot be prevented by the rise or fall of any human power on earth; because it is the repeated covenant of God to my forefathers, and his sacred promise now by Revelation to my self.

The obscurity of David was no objection, with a discerning God, to make him the monarch of Israel, and afterwards promise the succession to his family for ever; neither is mine now to his fulfilling that promise, and holding me up to the world, as the visible governor of the Jews . . .

I am the prophet that will be revealed to the Jews, to order their departure from all nations, to go to the land of Israel, their own country, in a similar manner to Moses in Egypt, but with additional power.

. . .

---

[1] Brothers began the pamphlet with a recalculation of the age of the earth which he used to predict the date of the Last Judgement as 19 November 1795.

It is fifteen hundred years since my family was separated from the Jews, and lost all knowledge of its origin; the last on record, in the Scripture, is James: xiii chap. 55 ver. Of St. Matthew. Told me by revelation,

The government of the Jewish nation will, *under the Lord God*, be committed to me, that the everlasting covenant from him to David may be manifested in the visible Prince and Governor of the Jews.

. . .

A Knowledge of the Scriptures, the prophecies I have mentioned, and all that I have wrote besides, have been communicated to me through visions and revelations from the Lord God: the prophet Daniel, and St. John the Apostle, were instructed, in the same manner, to write what they have.

It is by the saving of multitudes; by revealing, not only a true interpretation of the prophecies, but also a knowledge of the times, and those secret parts of the Scripture which are not made known to any other man under heaven, that the Lord God begins with announcing to the world a knowledge of his mighty judgments, *the return of his former mercy to the Hebrews,* their speedy restoration to Jerusalem, and the rise of a favourite family.

RICHARD BROTHERS,

London, No. 57, Paddington Street, 3d of the month called January,

1794.

Promis'd Horrors of the French INVASION, — or — Forcible Reasons for negociating a Regicide PEACE. Vide. The Authority of Edmund Burke.

Plate 8. *Promised Horrors of the French Invasion or Forcible reasons for negociating a Regicide Peace. Vide the authority of Edmund Burke* (James Gillray, 1796). The French army of invasion marches amidst carnage from the King's burning Palace of St James's past White's, the Tory Club which is being sacked by the invaders. Opposite, Brookes's, the Whig club, has set up a guillotine on the balcony. Next to it, Priestley brandishes a 'new code of laws' and a burning copy of *Magna Carta* over a tray of severed heads. In the centre of the street Pitt, lashed to a pole topped by the red cap of liberty, is being flogged by Fox. To the right of them Thelwall spurs on the Bull of (Duke of) Bedford, which has tossed Burke who has let fall his *Letters on a Regicide Peace* and his *Letter to a Noble Lord.* Behind him Sheridan creeps off into the club cellars with the remains of the British Treasury. In the foreground, Acts of Parliament and the Bill of Rights are bundled up with other statutes labelled 'waste paper' and in the corner a basket with a head and a pair of bagpipes (a peasant instrument) has a delivery label 'to the care of Mr Horne Tooke', Tooke being one of the defendants in the Treason Trials.

EDMUND BURKE

EDITORIAL NOTE

The **Two Letters on a Regicide Peace** (1796) were amongst the last things Burke wrote, and his last word on the French Revolution. Their history is complex. Three years into the war with France, and following the fall of Robespierre, Pitt's ministry was exploring the possibility of peace negotiations with the regime. In 1795 Lord Auckland had published a pamphlet: *Some Remarks on the Apparent Circumstances of the War* . . . suggesting the possibility and advisability of peace with France. Burke, who had long been seeking to persuade the government to pursue an interventionist war to restore the monarchy in France, immediately began to write a reply in the form of a letter to Lord Fitzwilliam, the leader of the Yorkshire Whigs (where Burke now had his parliamentary seat). This was put aside in 1796 whilst he wrote what later became the first two letters – of which an excerpt from the first is printed here. These were published by Burke as *Two Letters Addressed to a member of the present Parliament on the proposals for Peace with the Regicide Directory of France By the Right Hon. Edmund Burke* in October 1796. Burke then began to revise the original letter to Fitzwilliam as well as composing *A Third Letter* . . . which was unfinished at Burke's death in 1797. The *Third Letter* was completed and published separately by his literary executors in 1797. When, in 1812, the first edition of Burke's complete *Works* was published, the editors printed a completed version of the Fitzwilliam letter as the *Fourth Letter on a Regicide Peace*, presenting the four as a complete and integral set.

Modern editions:
Writings and Speeches vol. XI, ed. R. B. McDowell (Oxford: Clarendon, 1991).
Full texts, *Empire and Community, Edmund Burke's Writings and Speeches on International Relations*, ed. David Fidler and Jennifer M. Welsh (Boulder, Co.: Westview, 1999) [excerpts from Letter I, with a substantial introduction].

FURTHER READING

Armitage, David 'Edmund Burke and Reason of State' *Journal of the History of Ideas*, 61 (4) (Oct. 2000), pp. 617–34.

Boucher, D. 'The Character of the History of the Philosophy of International Relations and the Case of Edmund Burke', *Review of International Studies* 17 (1990), 127.

Davidson, J. 'Natural Law and International Law in Burke', *Review of Politics* 21 (1959), 485.

Hampsher-Monk, Iain, 'Burke's Changing Justification for Intervention', *Historical Journal* 48 (1) (2005), 65–100.

Harle, V. 'Burke the International Theorist – or the War of the Sons of Light and the Sons of Darkness', *European Values in International Relations*, ed. V. Harle (Oxford: Clarendon, 1990).

Vincent, R. J. 'Edmund Burke and the Commonwealth of Europe: The Cultural Bases of International Order', *Classical Theories of International Relations*, ed. I. Clarke and I. B. Neumann (Basingstoke: Macmillan Press, 1996).

Welsh, J. M. *Edmund Burke and International Relations the Commonwealth of Europe and the Crusade against the French Revolution* (Basingstoke and New York: Macmillan and St Martin's Press).

First Letter on a Regicide Peace (from *Two Letters . . . on the proposals for Peace with the Regicide Directory of France*) (1796)

. . .

A Government of the nature of that set up at our very door, has never been hitherto seen, or even imagined, in Europe. What our relation to it will be cannot be judged by other relations. It is a serious thing to have a connexion with a people, who live only under positive, arbitrary, and changeable institutions; and those not perfected nor supplied, nor explained, by any common acknowledged rule of moral science. I remember that in one of my last conversations with the late Lord Camden, we were struck much in the same manner with the abolition in France of the law, as a science of methodized and artificial equity. France, since her Revolution, is under the sway of a sect, whose leaders have deliberately, at one stroke, demolished the whole body of that jurisprudence which France had pretty nearly in common with other civilized countries. In that jurisprudence were contained the elements and principles of the law of nations,[1] the great ligament of mankind. With the law they

[1] The Law of Nations was that part of Roman law which claimed to codify those legal practices common to different political communities in their relations with each other. Another notion, ultimately a Stoic one, was that *any* recognisably human society would have to adhere to broadly the same rules – natural law – which could be arrived at by a process of philosophical reflection. Inter-state applications of the theory of Natural Law, pioneered by Grotius, were easily assimilated to this older, Roman law tradition.

have of course destroyed all seminaries in which jurisprudence was taught, as well as all the corporations established for its conservation.[2] I have not heard of any country, whether in Europe or Asia, or even in Africa on this side of Mount Atlas, which is wholly without some such colleges and such corporations, except France. No man, in a publick or private concern, can divine by what rule or principle her judgments are to be directed; nor is there to be found a professor in any University, or a practitioner in any Court, who will hazard an opinion of what is or is not law in France, in any case whatever. They have not only annulled all their old treaties, but they have renounced the law of nations from whence treaties have their force. With a fixed design, they have outlawed themselves, and, to their power, outlawed all other nations.

Instead of the religion and the law by which they were in a great politic communion with the Christian world, they have constructed their Republic on three bases, all fundamentally opposite to those on which the communities of Europe are built. Its foundation is laid in Regicide; in Jacobinism; and in Atheism; and it has joined to those principles, a body of systematic manners which secures their operation.

If I am asked how I would be understood in the use of these terms, Regicide, Jacobinism, Atheism, and a system of correspondent manners and their establishment, I will tell you.

I call a commonwealth *Regicide*, which lays it down as a fixed law of nature, and a fundamental right of man, that all government, not being a democracy, is an usurpation; that all Kings, as such, are usurpers, and for being Kings, may and ought to be put to death, with their wives, families, and adherents. The commonwealth which acts uniformly upon those principles; and which after abolishing every festival of religion, chooses the most flagrant act of a murderous Regicide treason for a feast of eternal commemoration, and which forces all her people to observe it – this I call *Regicide by establishment*.

Jacobinism is the revolt of the enterprising talents of a country against its property. When private men form themselves into associations for the purpose of destroying the pre-existing laws and institutions of their country; when they secure to themselves an army by dividing amongst the people of no property, the estates of the ancient and lawful proprietors; when a state recognizes those acts; when it does not make confiscations for crimes, but makes crimes for confiscations; when it has it's principal strength, and all it's resources in such a violation of property; when it stands chiefly

---

[2] As well as revoking all the customary and Feudal law and *ancien régime* court structure, the Revolutionary regime in 1793 closed the law schools and abolished the profession of advocate.

upon such a violation; massacring by judgments, or otherwise, those who make any struggle for their old legal government, and their legal, hereditary, or acquired possessions – I call this *Jacobinism by Establishment.*

I call it *Atheism by Establishment*, when any State, as such, shall not acknowledge the existence of God as a moral Governor of the World; when it shall offer to Him no religious or moral worship: when it shall abolish the Christian religion by a regular decree; when it shall persecute with a cold, unrelenting, steady cruelty, by every mode of confiscation, imprisonment, exile, and death, all it's ministers; when it shall generally shut up, or pull down, churches; when the few buildings which remain of this kind shall be opened only for the purpose of making a profane apotheosis of monsters whose vices and crimes have no parallel amongst men, and whom all other men consider as objects of general detestation, and the severest animadversion of law.[3] When, in the place of that religion of social benevolence, and of individual self-denial, in mockery of all religion, they institute impious, blasphemous, indecent theatric rites, in honour of their vitiated, perverted reason, and erect altars to the personification of their own corrupted and bloody Republick; when schools and seminaries are founded at public expence to poison mankind, from generation to generation, with the horrible maxims of this impiety; when wearied out with incessant martyrdom, and the cries of a people hungering and thirsting for religion, they permit it, only as a tolerated evil – I call this *Atheism by Establishment.*

When to these establishments of Regicide, of Jacobinism, and of Atheism, you add the *correspondent system of manners*, no doubt can be left on the mind of a thinking man, concerning their determined hostility to the human race. Manners are of more importance than laws. Upon them, in a great measure, the laws depend. The law touches us but here and there, and now and then. Manners are what vex or sooth, corrupt or purify, exalt or debase, barbarize or refine us, by a constant, steady, uniform, insensible operation, like that of the air we breathe in. They give their whole form and colour to our lives. According to their quality, they aid morals, they supply them, or they totally destroy them. Of this the new French Legislators were aware; therefore, with the same method, and under the same authority, they settled a system of manners, the most licentious, prostitute, and abandoned that ever has been known, and at the same time the most coarse, rude, savage, and ferocious. Nothing in the Revolution, no, not to a phrase or a gesture, not to the fashion of a hat

---

[3] In 1791, the Church of Ste Geneviève in Paris had been converted into a Pantheon in imitation of the Classical Roman shrine to 'all the gods', and the remains of revolutionary heroes Voltaire, Rousseau and Marat were re-interred there.

or a shoe, was left to accident. All has been the result of design; all has been matter of institution. No mechanical means could be devised in favour of this incredible system of wickedness and vice, that has not been employed. The noblest passions, the love of glory, the love of country, have been debauched into means of it's preservation and it's propagation. All sorts of shews and exhibitions calculated to inflame and vitiate the imagination, and pervert the moral sense, have been contrived. They have sometimes brought forth five or six hundred drunken women, calling at the bar of the Assembly for the blood of their own children, as being royalists or constitutionalists. Sometimes they have got a body of wretches, calling themselves fathers, to demand the murder of their sons; boasting that Rome had but one Brutus, but that they could shew five hundred.[4] There were instances in which they inverted and retaliated the impiety, and produced sons, who called for the execution of their parents. The foundation of their Republic is laid in moral paradoxes. Their patriotism is always prodigy. All those instances to be found in history, whether real or fabulous, of a doubtful public spirit, at which morality is perplexed, reason is staggered, and from which affrighted nature recoils, are their chosen, and almost sole examples for the instruction of their youth.

The whole drift of their institution is contrary to that of the wise Legislators of all countries, who aimed at improving instincts into morals, and at grafting the virtues on the stock of the natural affections. They, on the contrary, have omitted no pains to eradicate every benevolent and noble propensity in the mind of men. In their culture it is a rule always to graft virtues on vices. They think everything unworthy of the name of public virtue, unless it indicates violence on the private. All their new institutions, (and with them every thing is new) strike at the root of our social nature. Other Legislators, knowing that marriage is the origin of all relations, and consequently the first element of all duties, have endeavored, by every art, to make it sacred. The Christian Religion, by confining it to the pairs, and by rendering that relation indissoluble, has, by these two things, done more towards the peace, happiness, settlement, and civilization of the world, than by any other part in this whole scheme of Divine Wisdom. The direct contrary course has been taken in the Synagogue of Antichrist, I mean in that forge and manufactory of all evil, the sect which predominated in the Constituent Assembly of 1789. Those monsters employed the same, or greater industry, to desecrate and degrade that State, which

[4] Lucius Junius Brutus (d. BC, 509), the Roman Patrician who overthrew Tarquin the Proud and established the republic, famously showed his virtue and commitment to liberty by sentencing his own sons to death for plotting to restore the monarchy.

other Legislators have used to render it holy and honourable. By a strange, uncalled-for declaration, they pronounced, that marriage was no better than a common civil contract.[5] It was one of their ordinary tricks, to put their sentiments into the mouths of certain personated characters, which they theatrically exhibited at the bar of what ought to be a serious Assembly. One of these was brought out in the figure of a prostitute, whom they called by the affected name of 'a mother without being a wife.' This creature they made to call for a repeal of the incapacities, which in civilized States are put upon bastards. The prostitutes of the Assembly gave to this their puppet the sanction of their greater impudence. In consequence of the principles laid down, and the manners authorised, bastards were not long after put on the footing of the issue of lawful unions. Proceeding in the spirit of the first authors of their constitution, succeeding assemblies went the full length of the principle, and gave a licence to divorce at the mere pleasure of either party, and at a month's notice. With them the matrimonial connexion is brought into so degraded a state of concubinage, that, I believe, none of the wretches in London, who keep warehouses of infamy, would give out one of their victims to private custody on so short and insolent a tenure. There was indeed a kind of profligate equity in thus giving to women the same licentious power. The reason they assigned was as infamous as the act; declaring that women had been too long under the tyranny of parents and of husbands. It is not necessary to observe upon the horrible consequences of taking one half of the species wholly out of the guardianship and protection of the other.

The practice of divorce, though in some countries permitted, has been discouraged in all. In the East polygamy and divorce are in discredit; and the manners correct the laws. In Rome, whilst Rome was in it's integrity, the few causes allowed for divorce amounted in effect to a prohibition.[6] They were only three. The arbitrary was totally excluded; and accordingly some hundreds of years passed, without a single example

---

[5] The Constitution of 1791 Title II, §7 declared marriage to be only a civil contract; the Decree of 20 September 1792 transferred to the state responsibility for the recording of the major life-events – birth, marriage and death – as well as prescribing a purely secular form of marriage. It was accompanied by a specific decree regulating divorce through the request of either party on grounds of incompatibility, or a range of more serious grounds. See John Hall Stewart, *A Documentary Survey of the French Revolution* (London and New York: Macmillan, 1951), pp. 234, 322, 333.

[6] It is unclear which period Burke refers to here. The oldest laws (under the Kings) allowed divorce by husbands (but not by wives) only for poisoning their children, copying their keys or adultery; all other separations prescribed half of the property should go to the wife. By the end of the Republican period one writer regarded divorce as the commonest way of ending a marriage. See Lewis and Reinhold, *Roman Civilisation Sourcebook I: The Republic* (New York: Harper and Rew, 1966), pp. 60, 485.

of that kind. When manners were corrupted, the laws were relaxed; as the latter always follow the former, when they are not able to regulate them, or to vanquish them. Of this circumstance the Legislators of vice and crime were pleased to take notice, as an inducement to adopt their regulation: holding out an hope, that the permission would as rarely be made use of. They knew the contrary to be true; and they had taken good care, that the laws should be well seconded by the manners. Their law of divorce, like all their laws, had not for it's object the relief of domestic uneasiness, but the total corruption of all morals, the total disconnection of social life.

It is a matter of curiosity to observe the operation of this encouragement to disorder. I have before me the Paris paper, correspondent to the usual register of births, marriages, and deaths.[7] Divorce, happily, is no regular head of registry among civilized nations. With the Jacobins it is remarkable, that divorce is not only a regular head, but it has the post of honor. It occupies the first place in the list. In the three first months of the year 1793, the number of divorces in that city amounted to 562. The marriages were 1785; so that the proportion of divorces to marriages was not much less than one to three; a thing unexampled, I believe, among mankind. I caused an enquiry to be made at Doctor's Commons,[8] concerning the number of divorces; and found, that all the divorces, (which, except by special Act of Parliament, are separations, and not proper divorces) did not amount in all those Courts, and in a hundred years, to much more than one fifth of those that passed, in the single city of Paris, in three months. I followed up the enquiry relative to that city through several of the subsequent months until I was tired, and found the proportions still the same. Since then I have heard that they have declared for a revisal of these laws: but I know of nothing done. It appears as if the contract that renovates the world was under no law at all. From this we may take our estimate of the havoc that has been made through all the relations of life. With the Jacobins of France, vague intercourse is without reproach; marriage is reduced to the vilest concubinage; children are encouraged to cut the throats of their parents; mothers are taught that tenderness is no part of their character; and to demonstrate their attachment to their party, that they ought to make no scruple to rake with their bloody hands in the bowels of those who came from their own.

---

[7] The paper Burke refers to is the Parisian *Moniteur*, 4 March 1793.
[8] Doctors' Commons: the London law college where Roman law was taught. Law relating to divorce, deriving as it did from Canon (Church) law, itself derived from Roman law, was taught at Doctors' Commons, rather than in the Inns of Court, where English Common law was taught.

To all this let us join the practice of *cannibalism*, with which, in the proper terms, and with the greatest truth, their several factions accuse each other. By cannibalism, I mean their devouring, as a nutriment of their ferocity, some part of the bodies of those they have murdered; their drinking the blood of their victims, and forcing the victims themselves to drink the blood of their kindred slaughtered before their faces. By cannibalism, I mean also to signify all their nameless, unmanly, and abominable insults on the bodies of those they slaughter.

As to those whom they suffer to die a natural death, they do not permit them to enjoy the last consolations of mankind, or those rights of sepulture, which indicate hope, and which mere nature has taught to mankind in all countries, to soothe the afflictions, and to cover the infirmity of mortal condition. They disgrace men in the entry into life; they vitiate and enslave them through the whole course of it; and they deprive them of all comfort at the conclusion of their dishonoured and depraved existence. Endeavoring to persuade the people that they are no better than beasts, the whole body of their institution tends to make them beasts of prey, furious and savage. For this purpose the active part of them is disciplined into a ferocity which has no parallel. To this ferocity there is joined not one of the rude, unfashioned virtues, which accompany the vices, where the whole are left to grow up together in the rankness of uncultivated nature. But nothing is left to nature in their systems.

The same discipline which hardens their hearts relaxes their morals. Whilst courts of justice were thrust out by revolutionary tribunals, and silent churches were only the funeral monuments of departed religion, there were no fewer than nineteen or twenty theatres, great and small, most of them kept open at the public expense, and all of them crowded every night. Among the gaunt, haggard forms of famine and nakedness, amidst the yells of murder, the tears of affliction, and the cries of despair, the song, the dance, the mimic scene, the buffoon laughter, went on as regularly as in the gay hour of festive peace. I have it from good authority, that under the scaffold of judicial murder, and the gaping planks that poured down blood on the spectators, the space was hired out for a show of dancing dogs.[9] I think, without concert, we have made the very same remark on reading some of their pieces, which, being written for other purposes, let us into a view of their social life. It struck us that the habits of Paris had no resemblance to the finished virtues, or to the polished vice, and elegant, though not blameless luxury, of the capital of a great empire. Their

---

[9] Public executions were commonly occasions of entertainment in eighteenth-century France and England.

society was more like that of a den of outlaws upon a doubtful frontier; of a lewd tavern for the revels and debauches of banditti, assassins, bravos, smugglers, and their more desperate paramours, mixed with bombastick players, the refuse and rejected offal of strolling theatres, puffing out ill-sorted verses about virtue, mixed with the licentious and blasphemous songs, proper to the brutal and hardened course of life belonging to that sort of wretches. This system of manners in itself is at war with all orderly and moral society, and is in it's neighbourhood unsafe. If great bodies of that kind were anywhere established in a bordering territory, we should have a right to demand of their Governments the suppression of such a nuisance. What are we to do if the Government and the whole community is of the same description? Yet that Government has thought proper to invite ours to lay by its unjust hatred, and to listen to the voice of humanity as taught by their example.

The operation of dangerous and delusive first principles obliges us to have recourse to the true ones. In the intercourse between nations, we are apt to rely too much on the instrumental part. We lay too much weight upon the formality of treaties and compacts. We do not act much more wisely when we trust to the interests of men as guarantees of their engagements. The interests frequently tear to pieces the engagements; and the passions trample upon both. Entirely to trust to either, is to disregard our own safety, or not to know mankind. Men are not tied to one another by papers and seals. They are led to associate by resemblances, by conformities, by sympathies. It is with nations as with individuals. Nothing is so strong a tie of amity between nation and nation as correspondence in laws, customs, manners, and habits of life. They have more than the force of treaties in themselves. They are obligations written in the heart. They approximate men to men, without their knowledge, and sometimes against their intentions. The secret, unseen, but irrefragable bond of habitual intercourse, holds them together, even when their perverse and litigious nature sets them to equivocate, scuffle, and fight about the terms of their written obligations.

As to war, if it be the means of wrong and violence, it is the sole means of justice amongst nations. Nothing can banish it from the world. They who say otherwise, intending to impose upon us, do not impose upon themselves. But it is one of the greatest objects of human wisdom to mitigate those evils which we are unable to remove. The conformity and analogy of which I speak, incapable, like every thing else, of preserving perfect trust and tranquillity among men, has a strong tendency to facilitate accommodation, and to produce a generous oblivion of the rancour of their quarrels. With this similitude, peace is more of peace, and war is less of war.

I will go further. There have been periods of time in which communities, apparently in peace with each other, have been more perfectly separated than, in later times, many nations in Europe have been in the course of long and bloody wars. The cause must be sought in the similitude throughout Europe of religion, laws, and manners. At bottom, these are all the same. The writers on public law have often called this aggregate of nations a Commonwealth. They had reason. It is virtually one great state having the same basis of general law; with some diversity of provincial customs and local establishments. The nations of Europe have had the very same Christian religion, agreeing in the fundamental parts, varying a little in the ceremonies and in the subordinate doctrines. The whole of the polity and economy of every country in Europe has been derived from the same sources. It was drawn from the old Germanic or Gothic custumary[10]; from the feudal institutions which must be considered as an emanation from that custumary; and the whole has been improved and digested into system and discipline by the Roman law. From hence arose the several orders, with or without a Monarch, which are called States, in every European country; the strong traces of which, where Monarchy predominated, were never wholly extinguished or merged in despotism. In the few places where Monarchy was cast off, the spirit of European Monarchy was still left. Those countries still continued countries of States; that is, of classes, orders, and distinctions, such as had before subsisted, or nearly so. Indeed the force and form of the institution called States, continued in greater perfection in those republican communities than under Monarchies.[11] From all those sources arose a system of manners and of education which was nearly similar in all this quarter of the globe; and which softened, blended, and harmonized the colours of the whole. There was little difference in the form of the Universities for the education of their youth, whether with regard to faculties, to sciences, or to the more liberal and elegant kinds of erudition. From this resemblance in the modes of intercourse, and in the whole form and fashion of life, no citizen of Europe could be altogether an exile in any part of it. There was nothing more than a pleasing variety to recreate and instruct the mind, to enrich the imagination, and to meliorate the heart. When a man travelled or resided for health, pleasure, business or necessity, from his own country, he never felt himself quite abroad.

---

[10] Custumary: a written collection of legal customs, hence the customary law of a particular people.
[11] States: Burke identifies the European state with the (e)states or legal orders of which it is composed. The contrast was with those monarchies which lacked 'intermediate orders' and were hence despotic. The distinction is elaborated by Montesquieu and was a commonplace of eighteenth-century political thought.

The whole body of this new scheme of manners, in support of the new scheme of politics, I consider as a strong and decisive proof of determined ambition and systematic hostility. I defy the most refining ingenuity to invent any other cause for the total departure of the Jacobin Republic from every one of the ideas and usages, religious, legal, moral, or social, of this civilized world, and for her tearing herself from its communion with such studied violence, but from a formed resolution of keeping no terms with that world. It has not been, as has been falsely and insidiously represented, that these miscreants had only broke with their old Government. They made a schism with the whole universe; and that schism extended to almost every thing great and small. For one, I wish, since it is gone thus far, that the breach had been so complete, as to make all intercourse impracticable; but, partly by accident, partly by design, partly from the resistance of the matter, enough is left to preserve intercourse, whilst amity is destroyed or corrupted in its principle.

This violent breach of the community of Europe we must conclude to have been made, (even if they had not expressly declared it over and over again) either to force mankind into an adoption of their system, or to live in perpetual enmity with a community the most potent we have ever known. Can any person imagine, that in offering to mankind this desperate alternative, there is no indication of a hostile mind, because men in possession of the ruling authority are supposed to have a right to act without coercion in their own territories? As to the right of men to act any where according to their pleasure, without any moral tie, no such right exists. Men are never in a state of *total* independence of each other. It is not the condition of our nature: nor is it conceivable how any man can pursue a considerable course of action without it's having some effect upon others; or, of course, without producing some degree of responsibility for his conduct. The *situations* in which men relatively stand produce the rules and principles of that responsibility, and afford directions to prudence in exacting it.

Distance of place does not extinguish the duties or the rights of men; but it often renders their exercise impracticable. The same circumstance of distance renders the noxious effects of an evil system in any community less pernicious. But there are situations where this difficulty does not occur; and in which, therefore, these duties are obligatory, and these rights are to be asserted. It has ever been the method of publick jurists, to draw a great part of the analogies on which they form the law of nations from the principles of law which prevail in civil community. Civil laws are not all of them merely positive. Those which are rather conclusions of legal reason, than matters of statutable provision, belong to universal equity, and are universally applicable. Almost the whole praetorian law is such.[12] There is a *Law of Neighbourhood* which does not leave a man perfect master on his own ground. When a neighbour sees a *new erection,* in the nature of a nuisance, set up at his door, he has a right to represent it to the judge; who, on his part, has a right to order the work to be staid; or if established, to be removed. On this head, the parent law is express and clear; and has made many wise provisions, which, without destroying, regulate and restrain the right of *ownership,* by the right of *vicinage.* No *innovation* is permitted that may redound, even secondarily, to the prejudice of a neighbour. The whole doctrine of that important head of praetorian law, '*De novi operis nunciatione,*'[13] is founded on the principle, that no *new* use should be made of a man's private liberty of operating upon his private property, from whence a detriment may be justly apprehended by his neighbour. This law of denunciation is prospective. It is to anticipate what is called *damnum infectum,* or *damnum nondum factum,* that is a damage justly apprehended but not actually done.[14] Even before it is clearly known whether the innovation be damageable or not, the judge is competent to issue a prohibition to innovate, until the point can be determined. This prompt interference is grounded on principles favourable to both parties. It is preventive of mischief difficult to be repaired, and of ill blood difficult to be softened. The rule of law, therefore, which comes before the evil, is amongst the very best parts of equity, and justifies the promptness of the remedy; because, as it is well observed, *Res damni infecti celeritatem desiderat et periculosa est dilatio.*[15] This right of denunciation does not hold, when things continue, however inconveniently to the neighbourhood, according to the *antient* mode. For there is a sort of presumption against novelty, drawn out of a deep consideration of human

[12] Praetorian Law: Praetors administered the Law, two held 'royal' power, i.e. powers to intervene by prerogative.

[13] 'On the notice to be given concerning new works', Title 39 in *The Digest* of Roman law, of Justinian (d. 565 AD).

[14] Burke refers to two actions available in Roman law: the *Missio in possessionem Damni Infectum,* and the *Praetorian Stipulatio.* The first is a claim that a neighbour's property was in such a state of dilapidation as to threaten damage to one's own. The other remedy, the Praetorian Stipulation, resulted from a petition to a senior magistrate that works about to be done to a neighbour's property were prejudicial to one's own. If successful the petition resulted in the magistrate requiring the other party to make a promise, backed by some surety, that the offender would not proceed with the threatened works, or offer indemnity in the event of any damage resulting. Peter Stein, *A Textbook of Roman Law* 3rd edn (Cambridge: Cambridge University Press, 1963), pp. 724–8; and R. W. League, *Roman Private Law,* 2nd edn, ed. C. H. Ziegler (London: Macmillan, 1930), p. 306.

[15] 'Issues, or matters detrimental to other parties must be swiftly dealt with and delay is dangerous.'

nature and human affairs; and the maxim of jurisprudence is well laid down, *Vetustas pro lege semper habetur.*[16]

Such is the law of civil vicinity. Now where there is no constituted judge, as between independent states there is not, the vicinage itself is the natural judge. It is, preventively, the assertor of its own rights; or remedially, their avenger. Neighbours are presumed to take cognizance of each other's acts. *Vicini vicinorum facta praesumuntur scire.*[17] This principle, which, like the rest, is as true of nations as of individual men, has bestowed on the grand vicinage of Europe a duty to know, and a right to prevent, any capital innovation which may amount to the erection of a dangerous nuisance. Of the importance of that innovation, and the mischief of that nuisance, they are, to be sure, bound to judge not litigiously; but it is in their competence to judge. They have uniformly acted on this right. What in civil society is a ground of action, in politick society is a ground of war. But the exercise of that competent jurisdiction is a matter of moral prudence. As suits in civil society, so war in the political, must ever be a matter of great deliberation. It is not this or that particular proceeding, picked out here or there, as a subject of quarrel, that will do. There must be an aggregate of mischief. There must be marks of deliberation; there must be traces of design; there must be indications of malice; there must be tokens of ambition. There must be force in the body where they exist; there must be energy in the mind.[18] When all these circumstances combine, or the important parts of them, the duty of the vicinity calls for the exercise of it's competence; and the rules of prudence do not restrain, but demand it.

In describing the nuisance erected by so pestilential a manufactory, by the construction of so infamous a brothel, by digging a night-cellar for such thieves, murderers, and house-breakers, as never infested the world, I am so far from aggravating, that I have fallen infinitely short of the evil. No man who has attended to the particulars of what has been done in France, and combined them with the principles there asserted, can possibly doubt it. When I compare with this great cause of nations, the trifling

---

[16] 'Antiquity always has the force of law.'
[17] 'Local residents are presumed to know the facts about the neighbourhood', a legal maxim from the *Institutes* of Sir Edward Coke.
[18] Burke's writing here loosely recalls Locke's account of the justification for resistance: 'Revolutions happen not upon every little mismanagement in publick affairs . . . But if a long train of Abuses, Prevarications, and Artifices, all tending the same way, make the design visible to the People, and they cannot but feel what they lie under, and see, whether they are going . . . (*Two Treatises*, ii, §225).

points of honour, the still more contemptible points of interest, the light ceremonies, the undefinable punctilios, the disputes about precedency, the lowering or the hoisting of a sail, the dealing in a hundred or two of wild-cat skins on the other side of the globe, which have often kindled up the flames of war between nations, I stand astonished at those persons who do not feel a resentment, not more natural than politic, at the atrocious insults that this monstrous compound offers to the dignity of every nation, and who are not alarmed with what it threatens to their safety.

I have therefore been decidedly of opinion, with our declaration at Whitehall, in the beginning of this war, that the vicinage of Europe had not only a right, but an indispensable duty, and an exigent interest, to denunciate this new work before it had produced the danger we have so sorely felt, and which we shall long feel.[19] The example of what is done by France is too important not to have a vast and extensive influence; and that example, backed with it's power, must bear with great force on those who are near it; especially on those who shall recognize the pretended Republic on the principle upon which it now stands. It is not an old structure which you have found as it is, and are not to dispute of the original end and design with which it had been so fashioned. It is a recent wrong, and can plead no prescription. It violates the rights upon which not only the community of France, but all communities, are founded. The principles on which they proceed are *general* principles, and are as true in England as in any other country. They who (though with the purest intentions) recognize the authority of these Regicides and robbers upon principle, justify their acts, and establish them as precedents. It is a question not between France and England. It is a question between property and force. The property claims; and its claim has been allowed. The property of the nation is the nation. They who massacre, plunder, and expel the body of the proprietary, are murderers and robbers. The State, in its essence, must be moral and just: and it may be so, though a tyrant or usurper should be accidentally at the head of it. This is a thing to be lamented: but this notwithstanding, the body of the commonwealth may remain in all it's integrity and be perfectly sound in it's composition. The present case is different. It is not a revolution in government. It is not the victory of party over party. It is a destruction and decomposition of the whole society; which never can be made of right by any faction, however powerful, nor without terrible consequences to all about it, both in

---

[19] Burke wishfully misrepresents the Government's position which was limited to countering French aggression, and remained firmly opposed to the imposition of a full restoration or a counter-revolutionary government on France. Jennifer Mori, *William Pitt and the French Revolution* (Edinburgh: University of Keele Press, 1977), p. 149–50.

the act and in the example. This pretended Republic is founded in crimes, and exists by wrong and robbery; and wrong and robbery, far from a title to any thing, is war with mankind. To be at peace with robbery is to be an accomplice with it.

Mere locality does not constitute a body politick. Had Cade[20] and his gang got possession of London, they would not have been the Lord-Mayor, Aldermen, and Common Council. The body politick of France existed in the majesty of it's throne; in the dignity of it's nobility; in the honour of it's gentry; in the sanctity of it's clergy; in the reverence of it's magistracy; in the weight and consideration due to it's landed property in the several bailliages[21]; in the respect due to it's moveable substance represented by the corporations of the kingdom. All these particular *moleculae* united, form the great mass of what is truly the body politick, in all countries. They are so many deposits and receptacles of justice; because they can only exist by justice. Nation is a moral essence, not a geographical arrangement, or a denomination of the nomenclator. France, though out of her territorial possession, exists; because the sole possible claimant, I mean the proprietary, and the Government to which the proprietary adheres, exists and claims. God forbid, that if you were expelled from your house by ruffians and assassins, that I should call the material walls, doors and windows of –, the ancient and honourable family of –. Am I to transfer to the intruders, who not content to turn you out naked to the world, would rob you of your very name, all the esteem and respect I owe to you? The Regicides in France are not France. France is out of her bounds, but the kingdom is the same.

. . .

[20] John 'Jack' Cade, led a rebellion from Kent in 1450 and briefly threatened the capital.
[21] Bailliage: an (area of) jurisdiction.

JOHN THELWALL

BIOGRAPHICAL NOTE

John Thelwall was born on 27 July 1764 in Covent Garden, London. His father, a silk merchant, died when he was nine and the family business struggled to survive. A studious child, he received a wide but erratic education with the help of various friends and his own efforts, studying law at the Middle Temple, Latin with a friend and medicine at Guy's and St Thomas's. He wrote poetry (a continuing interest), biography (of John Howard the prison reformer) and edited *The Biographical and Imperial Magazine*.

An initial Toryism was overwhelmed in his mid-twenties by his always strong sense of social justice and indignation at the slave trade But it was, he later claimed, fury at Burke's attack on the aspirations of the French Revolutionaries 'that made me so zealous a reformer . . .'[1] Despite a slight speech impediment, Thelwall had always been an active debater, and took to active politics under the wing of John Horne Tooke, a seasoned campaigner. Thelwall joined the moderate reform group, the Society for Friends of the People in 1792, and in 1794 the larger, more radical and artisan London Corresponding Society, rapidly gaining a reputation as an orator speaking regularly to larger and larger audiences in halls and outside. On one famous occasion in October 1795 he drew what was probably up to that time the largest political audience ever of over 150,000 people in Copenhagen Fields. As a proportion of London's population (then one million) this was equivalent today to a crowd of over a million and a half.

In 1794 Thelwall, together with eleven others including Horne Tooke, and Thomas Hardy, secretary of the LCS, was arrested and charged with high treason. He had prepared to conduct his own defence (which he later published as *The Natural and Constitutional Rights of Britons*) but was told by Thomas Erskine, his distinguished defence lawyer, that he would be hanged if he did! His acquittal was met with huge street celebrations and added to the popularity of his lectures. But the right of free speech – the subject of his next public lecture – had clearly not been established, and in December 1795 the infamous 'Two Acts'

---

[1] John Thelwall, *The Tribune*, 3 (1796), p. 95.

were passed, suppressing public meetings, political association and criticism of the government. For a while Thelwall tried to evade the proscription by offering lectures on Roman history – a thinly veiled attack on tyranny. But everywhere he was followed by government spies and informers. He fell out with William Godwin, who, though more radical in his aims than Thelwall, rejected all means other than 'calm and reasoned argument' and explicitly criticised 'the system of political lecturing' in his *Considerations on Lord Grenville's and Mr Pitt's Bills* (1795).

Despite attracting the praise and friendship of Coleridge, other supporters and backers, both financial and intellectual, drifted away. A national tour of lectures met with both large and appreciative audiences and attacks by loyalist mobs. In 1797 he withdrew from political activity altogether to a smallholding in Brecon but returned to London in 1801 to start a school of elocution and rejoined radical politics when they revived cautiously in 1818. He died in 1834.

EDITORIAL NOTE

The Rights of Nature was, like Paine's *Agrarian Justice*, written in the winter of 1795, a time of serious food shortage. Both works argued a case for redistribution deriving, in Thelwall's case, from an extension of aboriginal Lockean land rights into the advanced exchange economy, and showing an increasing accommodation to modern proto-industrial conditions. Thelwall pitches this against what he calls the feudal system of which he takes Burke's *Regicide Peace* to be a defence. This was to be Thelwall's last major political work.

Modern edition:
The Politics of English Jacobinism, the writings of *John Thelwall*, ed. and intr. G. Claeys (Pennsylvania: Pennsylvania State University Press, 1995).

FURTHER READING

Cestre, C. *John Thelwall, a Pioneer of Democracy and Social Reform in England during the French Revolution* (London: Swann Sonneschein, 1906).
Gallop, G. 'Ideology and the English Jacobins: The Case of John Thelwall', *Enlightenment and Dissent*, 5 (1986), pp. 3–20.
Hampsher-Monk, I. 'John Thelwall and the Eighteenth-Century Radical Response to Political Economy', *Historical Journal* 34 (1991), pp. 1–20.
Scrivener, M. 'John Thelwall's Political Ambivalence', in Michael Davis (ed.), *Radicalism and Revolution in Britain, 1775–1848: Essays in Honour of Malcom I. Thomas* (New York: St Martin's Press, 1999), pp. 69–83.
Scrivener, M. *Seditious Allegories: John Thelwall and Jacobin Writing* (Pennsylvania State University Press, 2001).

The Rights of Nature Against the Usurpations of Establishments (1796)

LETTER II
FIRST PRINCIPLES: OR, ELEMENTS OF
NATURAL AND SOCIAL RIGHTS

I. 'The operation of dangerous and delusive first principles', says Mr. B. 'obliges us to have recourse to the true ones.' Let us see, then, how far his own principles are dangerous and delusive, and refer to the great code of Reason and Nature, to discover what are the true. It is not, indeed, very easy to extract Mr. B.'s principles. His mode of writing is at once declamatory and dogmatical in the highest degree. Assertion and metaphor mingle in such splendid confusion; and facts without proofs, and conclusions without arguments, are so accumulated and involved, that it is almost impossible to decide what is to be regarded as premises, and what is illustration. The following, however, appear to be the principles upon which he rests his arguments.

1. That 'Men are neither tied to one another by treaties and compacts', nor by 'interests'; but 'are led to associate by resemblances, by conformities, by sympathies.'
2. That 'War is the sole means of justice among nations': and that nothing can banish it from the world.'
3. That 'the cause of why many nations in Europe have been less separated, in later times, in the course of long and bloody wars, than communities, apparently at peace in other periods, must be sought in the similitude throughout Europe of religion, laws, and manners.'
4. That the sources of this similitude are 'the feudal institutions emanating from the old Germanic or Gothic custumary, improved and digested into system and discipline by the Roman law.'
5. That 'the several orders (which are called States) arising from this system, may, if they choose, *cast off* Monarchy'; because the force and form of the 'institutions called states, have continued in greater perfection in Republican communities, than under Monarchies.' But,
6. That for any nation to form 'a new scheme of manners, in support of a new scheme of politics', is an outrage against 'the *aggregate* commonwealth of Europe.' (Hence

he concludes that – 'those miscreants', the French Republicans, have 'made a schism with the whole universe.')

7. That 'the analogies which form the law of nations, are to be drawn from the principles which prevail in the civil community.'

8. That 'the *Law of Neighbourhood* does not leave a man perfect master of his own ground':-as in the case of *nuisances;* which the neighbours 'have a right *to represent to the* JUDGE, *who,* on his part, has a right to order the work to be staid; or, if established, to be removed.'

9. That 'this right of denunciation does not hold when things continue, *however inconveniently* to the neighbourhood, according to the *ancient mode.*'

10. That 'where *there is no constituted Judge,* as between independent states there is not, the vicinity itself is the natural judge.'

11. That 'what in civil society is a ground of action, in politic society is a ground of war.'

From these premises, Mr. B. deduces, *generally,* 'a right and duty', in the grand vicinage of Europe, to 'prevent any capital innovation which may amount (in the judgment of that vicinage) 'to the erection of a dangerous nuisance'; and, *particularly,* to persevere, by process of fire and sword, by pillage, murder, and desolation, to the abatement of that grand innovation, the French Revolution, and the restoration of the *ancient* (and therefore unimpeachable) nuisance of which, heretofore, we so unreasonably complained. – And this, I am told, is considered as the strong part of Mr. B.'s pamphlet. It may be so: but, to me, at least, its strength, like that of Sampson,[2] is wrapped in mystery. It must lie in the hair, or some other ornamental part; for, in the limbs and portions of the argument, I see it not.

In the first place, the premises are too many, and too unconnected to serve as a basis of just reasoning. First principles are, in their very nature, few and simple; and though the result of them, when demonstrated, may in their turns, be used as premises, yet they must grow out of some common data, like branches from the parent stock, in all the simplicity of induction. It is the trick of sophists to overburden the memory with a crowd of intricate propositions, which dazzle where they should elucidate, and confound where they should convince.

---

[2] According to the Old Testament, after Sampson's prodigious strength had enabled him to free the Jews from the Philistines, he was persuaded by Delilah, whom he loved, to reveal that the secret of his strength lay in his uncut hair. She had it cut off whilst he was asleep so the Philistines were able to capture him. Judges 15–16.

I.2

With respect to the propositions themselves, the first and second, instead of simple *data*, or self-evident, elementary truths, are complex dogmas, which, at least, require much argument to establish them; and which, if established, would not answer the purpose for which they are advanced . . . Thus, although it should be admitted (as, 'where there is no constituted tribunal' to enforce the compact, we must admit) that 'papers and seals' cannot, and perhaps ought not to 'tie men to one another', that, 'the interests frequently tear to pieces the engagements, and the passions trample on both', yet the other branch of this proposition is by no means a concomitant truth. 'Resemblances, conformities, and sympathies', have, it is granted, much to do with *individual associations*; but (torn and trampled upon by our unruly passions, as, in common with many nobler parts of our nature, they too frequently are) 'the interests' have still more: and, even independent of all these, there are a thousand accidents or necessities, imperious in their nature, by which passions, interests, and sympathies are all, in innumerable instances, alike controlled. This, so true with respect to individuals, is still more so of *national intercourse*. 'Distance of place', though it 'does not extinguish the duties or the rights of men', not only alters their reciprocal claims and obligations, but weakens their sympathies, restrains their passions, and resigns them more completely to the influence of those interests, those necessities, and that habitual routine, the powerful operation of which, even in the closest intimacies of social life, cannot be rationally disputed.

I deny, then, in the main, the argument of sympathies and resemblances, as chief causes of confederacy, or intercourse among nations: Trusting – or, at least (to speak with more modesty) *hoping*, that there is not much resemblance, not much conformity, no very strong and intimate sympathy (however close may be the alliance) between the Governors of this country and those German and Russian despots, whose sanguinary ambition tore, with cannibal ferocity, the bowels of dismembered Poland, and strewed the streets of Warsaw with unexampled massacre.[3] . . .

. . .

The real cause of the phenomenon is to be sought in the commercial system; which, while it furnishes the pretences and means of war, still keeps up a circuitous and clandestine, if not direct and open intercourse between contending nations.

[3] Britain connived in two partitions of Poland (1792 and 1795) (the second following the suppression of a liberationist uprising) in order to secure the support of continental powers in the war against France.

This, also, it is which, not only more than treaties and compacts, but more than resemblances, conformities, sympathies – more than *vicinity* itself, binds together the aggregate of nations into what Mr B. calls the community of Europe.

4.5.6. From what remains, it appears – that, according to the *true first principles* of Aristocratic logic, all palatable and wholesome knowledge must be derived from the maxims and institutions of those polite and erudite constitution-mongers, the Goths and Vandals of the fifth century; hashed up (or, as Mr. B. has it, 'improved and digested') 'with the decrees of despots and praefects of the Eastern and Western Empire, into a sort of politico-salmagundy[4] of superstition, barbarism, incongruous tyranny, and mock morality; sauced, seasoned, and garnished to the true taste of royal and aristocratical epicureanism, by those scientific cooks, the jurists and publicists of the Roman and Germanic schools. In other words, 'the old Germanic or Gothic custumary, disciplined and systematised by the Roman law', is the great repository of all elementary truths, whether of politics, of morals, or of manners! – the source of all wisdom and all *civilization*! – the quarry from which are to be hewn the pillars of our freedom, and 'the Corinthian capitals of polished society'!

By the said Custumary is also to be decided what revolutions may, and what may not be made; and under what particular circumstances, and for what particular purposes, monarchs may be killed off: – 'Cast off', I believe, he calls it: – but it is much the same – 'the states, or privileged classes, orders, and distinctions' (of ancient, or of modern times) in whose behalf this revolutionary right is admitted, seldom demurring much between casting and killing off, either monarchs or people, as best suited their ambitious purposes. In this country, in particular, they have generally preferred the latter: though instances of each abound. The *History of England*, from the Conquest, is little else than a chronicle of usurpations, and revolutions, and regicides. . . .

. . .

To proceed – In the first place, I deny that the Germanic or Gothic custumary is, or that any custumary or establishment can be, in point of right, the authoritative repository of first principles: and for this reason – Either that custumary or establishment must have been eternal, or it must have had an origin. This claim of eternity no European establishment has the modesty to prefer. They must have *originated*, therefore, in *chance*, in *usurpation*, or in *right*. If in chance, they can be

---

[4] Salmagundy: a mixed dish comprising meat, eggs anchovies, and spices, hence any heterogenous mixture.

no authorities; and we must look in them, not for elements, but for incongruities; not for first principles, but a chaotic mass: – If in usurpation, they are only precedents of wrong; and precedents of wrong cannot be authoritative sources of the principles of right. Right principles may, it is true, become incorporated with them – good fruit engrafted upon a bad stock: but you are not, therefore, authorised to pronounce, by mere reference to the trunk, that whatever it produces is good. If they originated in right, then had they *a right to originate*; and the very existence is a precedent sanctifying that principle of innovation they are so frequently quoted to bar.

Deny me this; and you deny to man, in one age and period of the world, that free, or moral agency, which, in another, you are obliged to admit: In other words – You unhinge the great system of the universe, and substitute in its place, a chaos of your own creation; in which man is no longer man – no longer an organised being of a distinct and regular species, propagating, from race to race, his particular kind; but an anomalous deformity, owing his existence to a sort of equivocal generation; neither deriving nor imparting a specific nature, nor holding a fixed station in the ranks of being.

. . .

7. As for 'the analogies which form the law of nations', – I deny, in the first place, that any such thing as a law of Nations, does, in fact, exist. While that republic of princes, the Germanic constitution, was any thing more than an expensive mockery, there was, indeed, a sort of public law in Germany – or, more correctly, perhaps, a pact of conspiracy against the rest of Europe; as, in the ancient world, during the existence of the Amphictyonic league,[5] there was also, a public law of Greece: but as for a law of nations, in any accurate, or extensive sense, this is one of the sublime speculations of modern Jacobinism – a germ of *universal peace and fraternity* – a mere philosophical embrion, crude, as yet, and uncounted in the world of being; though so impregnated, I believe, with the quickening seeds of truth, that it cannot fail of an eventual birth. At least, I am one of those *incorrigibles* who expect to behold something more than the cradle of its infancy; and who expiate in the alluring hope of bequeathing to posterity the tranquil security and ever-growing blessings which the maturity of such an institution might dispense. At present, however, no such terrestrial Providence exists. The moral agency of governments is reduced to no fixed

---

[5] Amphyctionic League: an association of states in Ancient Greece devoted to the care of common religious sites. It was commonly regarded during this period as a proto-typical confederation of states.

principle; and while individuals, in their particular communities, are condemned to the cells, and fetters, and strait waist-coats of oppressive and superfluous laws, the great community of nations remains in a state of anarchy; and madmen and ruffians pillage, murder, and destroy at pleasure.

Grotius and Puffendorf may be quoted to eternity, and their teamed dust thrown, upon *every occasion*, in the eyes of an ignorant multitude: but the governments, who quote them, laugh at their own juggle. These equivocal appeals are used by statesmen for no better purpose than to blind the people when they would lead them into war: as horses are muffled that they may be tied to the mill; or as the Spaniard, at his bull-fight, shakes his robe at the boisterous victim, and dazzles him while he strikes the blow.

8. The analogy, then, is deficient in an essential member. The *vicinage* can appeal to no common law, declaring what is *nuisance* and what is not. It can plead no compact, no delegation or convention, real or *virtual*, in any period of the world, assenting to the establishment of such law: no impartial arbitrator – no constituted organ by which the decisions of such law could be pronounced. Mr. B.'s *vicinage is* a jury in its own cause. It is, indeed, upon a large and tremendous scale, a *self-constituted Revolutionary Tribunal* fulminating the barbarous decisions dictated by its own blind passions and perverted interests, and alternately carrying them into execution, by military violence, or yielding its own neck to the triumphant victims it had wantonly and impotently condemned.

9. 10. 11. The very admission, in the tenth proposition, that 'betweeen the independent states there is no constituted judge', before whom 'the denunciation' can be brought, would, therefore, be sufficient to bar the analogy. But the objection rests upon still stronger grounds. The *reason* of the law of civil vicinity, does not apply to the vicinage of nations: and Mr. B. is too scientific a lawyer to deny in *theory*, though he may be too professional a lawyer, having taken so good a fee, to admit in *practice*, that the *reason of the law* is its noblest and most essential part.

Neighbours in a civil community, have their *common*, as well as their *individual rights*; the former derived from nature, and secured (or meant to be secured) by the specific compact under which the community exists; the latter, generally speaking, created by the compact; and growing out of its specific provisions; and, therefore, fit objects of superintendance and restriction to the authority under which they exist. (Nations have, also, their common as well as individual rights: but neither the one nor the other originate in compacts of vicinage – for between the community of nations no such compact exists. *They* are bottomed, all, in nature; and by the principles of nature they must be tried.) It is the duty then of every civil community to take care, that the *subordinate rights of compact* do not encroach too far upon the *common rights of nature*, as, 'if a man were left perfect master of his own ground', might be the case. Hence the right of denunciation in the respective neighbourhoods; and tribunals for the abatement of nuisance. But this nuisance, I repeat it, must consist in the particular invasion of some common right: The law, in this respect, being a sort of assertion of the original equality of man; who, though he has yielded much to compact and individual appropriation, yet retains a sort of quitrent,[6] as an evidence of his title, and a vestige of his common right. Thus, for example, *Man has naturally an equal claim to the elements of nature*; and although earth has been appropriated, by expediency and compact [for the basis of which appropriation see the following Letter] light, air, and water (with some exceptions) still continue to be claimed in common.

The light which illumines my premises, belongs equally to my neighbour as to me: it is therefore a nuisance to block it out. The air I breathe must be breathed, also, by him; and the stream that flows through my garden waters his: If I stop the one with a dam, or poison the other by 'a pestilential manufactory', I make my individual right of compact a mean of usurpation upon the common and superior rights of nature: in other words, I commit a nuisance; and it must be abated.

In these, and like instances, the innovation, and rightly, constitutes the nuisance; and you cannot abate what is 'according to the ancient mode': for property is, upon both sides, concerned; and all property, except the actual produce of individual labour, comes by compact: you must take it, therefore, as the compact gives it. With respect to 'brothels and night-cellars for thieves, murderers, and house-breakers', the case is different. The common rights of the immediate neighbourhood may be, in some degree, annoyed; but the principal nuisance is to the community at large, and consists in the danger to the morals and security of society; over which the laws, made, or pretended to be made, by and for the whole, have 'a right, and a duty, to preside.' The proprietors, therefore, of these seminaries, the other parts of the denunciation being clearly sustained, would not, I conceive, be at liberty to plead 'that they were *old creations*.' Neither, I presume, would the plea of 'old creation' answer the purpose of a proprietor indicted for not taking down a tumbling house: and even Mr. Justice Reeves[7] (whose duty it is, in this district, to preside over such

---

[6] Quitrent: a rent paid in lieu of services attached to a property-right.
[7] Justice Reeves: founder of the government-backed, anti-radical Association for the preservation of property against Republicans and Levellers.

presentations) would be obliged to acknowledge, that buildings may become nuisances by being too old, as well as by being too new. – But how does this reasoning apply to nations?

Mr. B. tells us (and he gives abundance of hard words for proofs) that the *new erection*, in France, is a pestilential nuisance. Some French declaimer may, perhaps, as dogmatically affirm, that the old erection, in England, is a tumbling nuisance: that, partly by the ravages of time, and still more by the sapping and mining arts of its pretended guardians, the beams are disjointed and the foundations gone. But what of all this? – If their innovation is so pestilential a nuisance, so much the worse for them: for they must live in the stench. If our *old edifice is* a tumbling nuisance, so much the worse for us: for our houses will be endangered by the fall. But the pillars of our constitution will not tumble upon their heads: nor will their pestilential manufactory poison our air. Let them build, and brew, and innovate, in what manner they please; but the light will still shine as bright as ever – the air still refresh us with its wonted purity – the dews of heaven fatten our land, as heretofore, and the sea flow on, regardless of their dykes and mill-dams. As for the contents of their night-cellars, they would scarcely have come so far as to rifle *our* travellers, and break *our* houses; or, if they had, we have police officers enough to bring them to justice – as soon as they would *fetch their weight.*

In short – Hostility there may be between nation and nation, and injustice there may be in a thousand shapes; but there can be no such thing as nuisance. All that Mr. B. declaims about – all the arguments of ministers, and all the proclamations, declarations, manifestoes, &c. of all the allies, amount to no more than this – that France has *set* an *example* which the old governments of Europe (and I do not wonder at them) are not disposed to approve. But in what part of 'the praetorian law' does Mr. B. meet with *the nuisance of example?*

If my neighbour upholds doctrines I do not approve – if he is addicted to practices which I consider as immoral – if he keeps a swarm of concubines, or, what I regard as still more vicious, swears at his servants and whips his children – if he makes his drawing-room his kitchen, entertains his guests in a cellar, stirs his fire with a silver spoon, and sleeps in the cock-loft, or the gutter, I may pity him as a madman, or renounce his acquaintance; but do I indict him for a nuisance, with an ass's plea, that I am in danger of being seduced by his example? – It is a most impolitic concession made by the old governments, when they so vehemently proclaim, that if their swords do not overthrow the French Republic, the example of the French Republic will overthrow them!

11. Having swept away the rubbish of the Gothic custumary, and proved Mr. B.'s first principles to be no principles at all, I proceed to examine the question upon the broad grounds of reason and moral justice: for though I deny, altogether, the right of foreign interference, and consider no war as justifiable, but a war of simple and absolute self-defence, war or peace, under existing circumstances, is an inferior consideration; and the present contest must be regarded with diminished abhorrence, if the principles of reason and justice will not vindicate the Revolution against which it has been directed.

Jacobinism then (like all other systems) is to be tried by reference to the first principles of nature. If it is constituted of these elements, then is it limbed in adamant[8]; and in vain shall the puny lance of sophistry assail 'its colossal form.' If these elements enter not into the composition, then is it, indeed, 'a vast, tremendous, unformed spectre', and 'the overpowered imagination' cannot be too soon relieved from the delusion. Let the light of reason be the test; and we are willing to abide the issue. If Jacobinism be a spectre, before that light it will most assuredly flee. If it abides the searching rays of enquiry, I, for one, will lean against it, with confidence, as the bulwark of my integrity, and the rock of my strength.

Let us enquire, then, *what* JACOBINISM *really is?* – not what it is represented by Mr. B. – *What the* OLD GOVERNMENTS *of* EUROPE *really are?* – not what their advocates would wish us to believe them.

Properly to decide these questions, we must travel a great way back, out of our present habits and modes of thinking: We must consider, *What man is by nature?* and *What society has made him? What are his powers and his faculties, and* (if I may so express myself) *his capabilities?* and, *What is his actual condition?*

The whole argument of the enemy – the soul that animates the splendid eloquence of Burke, and the vapour that inflates the mediocrity of Pitt, emanate from the hypothesis that in the old systems every thing is right: at least as right as the nature of man admits. If this be true, and I can be shewn the truth, *Be they immortal!* shall be my dying words. We, on the contrary, affirm, that there is, in these systems, much that is corrupt and oppressive; much that is injurious to the comfort and morals of mankind, repugnant to his nature, and hostile to his very existence. Nay, some there are, who consider the whole frame of society as radically vicious; founded upon false principles, and supported by systematic oppression.

[8] Adamant: a legendary exceptionally hard and unbreakable mineral.

In differences so important, to what authority shall we appeal? To the tribunals of our opponents? – to the fields of slaughter? No: Nature – the great frame and deducible principles of the universe, must decide the question. When I talk, however, of nature, and *the natural condition of man*, I do not refer to any supposed era of perfect happiness, or poetical vision of a golden age: neither do I mean to argue upon any theological or philosophical hypothesis of origin or creation. The fact is, that the world is known to us only as a populous world; and man as a gregarious animal. How he originated, and what was his solitary condition (if solitary it ever was) are questions that may amuse our fancy, or exercise our faith; but with political enquiry they have nothing to do.

Little more concern have we with narratives, or fables, of the origin of civil institution. This is a subject more profitable in speculation than as a matter of history. It is of little consequence what circumstances produced, or what motives influenced the first formation of political societies: for precedents of wrong cannot alter the nature of right. It is more important to discover what the objects of association ought to be, than to be informed what they actually have been. Fortunately, the most important is, also, the most practicable enquiry. History, obscure with respect to the early transactions of particular states, is, of necessity, silent as to the beginnings of constituted society. But politics has its romance, as well as natural philosophy; and the former, as the latter, can produce its Burnets and its Buffons,[9] to fill up the vacuum of authentic record with Histories of Unknown Ages, and Chronicles of suppositious Facts. Even the sage Polybius,[10] like the eccentric Burke, has indulged his fancy with discoveries in this *terra incognita* of human history; shewing us how government was first instituted, and wherefore it first began. Such whimsies amuse, but they cannot instruct us. The fact is, we are not only unacquainted with solitary man, but with society uninfluenced by political compact. Even the savages in the recently discovered islands, have their forms of settled institution, and have made *some* progress in the arts of government: and a 'Society founded in natural appetites and instincts, and not in any positive institution'[11] is to be sought only in the pages of sophists and visionaries.

---

[9] Burnet: Bishop Gilbert Burnet, d. 1715, author of a noted *History of the Reformation*, and *A History of his own Times*. Bouffon: Georges Louis Leclerc, Comte de Buffon, d. 1788, French naturalist, author of *Histoire Naturell* (1749).
[10] Polybius, fl. BC second century. Greek historian.
[11] [Thelwall's footnote:] Burke, *A Vindication of Natural Society, Works*, [Bohn (ed.), vol. I, p. 7].

The only apparent exceptions (and they are exceptions big with instruction) are in the instances of *founding new states;* either by emigration (as in the case of Rome, and some of the American provinces); or by the breaking up of old governments (as in France and Holland.) To neither of these instances, however, can we look for examples of simple origin. They are only *great changes* in political society: and though, in the former, men seek new territories, to try new experiments, yet 'communities' (as B. rightly expresses it) 'do not consist in geographical arrangement, or a denomination of a nomenclator'; and, although, in the latter, they should utterly destroy the very basis of former tyrannies, yet they necessarily retain the ideas, passions, habits and experience, derived from the state of political society, under which they have lived: they are, therefore, in both instances, innovators, rather than founders. As far, however, as these habits and passions would permit, men have always, under such circumstances, appealed to first principles. The vague and floating ideas of equal and common rights, which no state of society can entirely eradicate, embody themselves on such occasions, and extort reverence even from the profligate, and homage from the ambitious.

Thus . . . the promiscuous throng of emigrants and refugees who founded the Roman state, not only elected their government, and chose their governors by UNIVERSAL SUFFRAGE – from the king and the senators to the pettyest annual officer . . . but, taking possession of an uninhabited, and unappropriated spot, they divided the land also among them, in equal portions. . . .

But though neither history nor observation furnish any examples either of unassociated man, or of society without some sort of political institution, yet is it not difficult to form a distinct idea of what may be called the natural condition of man: that is, to distinguish, in our minds, between what the individual has derived from nature, and what has been conferred, or abrogated, by civil society. When I talk, therefore, of *man in his natural state,* I mean to consider him *simply as an individual, stripped of all the relationships of Society, independent of its compacts, and uninfluenced by its reciprocations.* This abstraction is absolutely necessary for the impartial examination of the subject: for the rights of man must grow out of the nature of man; and the excellence of all social institution must consist in its conformity to that nature, and the security of those rights. But how shall we know what those rights and that nature are, till we have properly distinguished between the qualities of the individual and the sophistications of society.

The rights of man, thus considered, are simple in their elements. They are determined by his wants, and his faculties; and the means presented by the general system of nature (that is to say, by the frame and elements of the material universe) for the gratification of the former, and the improvement of the latter. . . .

This basis may be laid in the following axiom – *Man, from the very circumstance of his existence, has an inheritance in the elements and powers of nature, and a right to exercise his faculties upon those powers and elements, so as to render them subservient to his wants, and conducive to his enjoyments.* In other words – Man is the sovereign; the material universe is the subject; his faculties are the powers by which he enforces his authority; and expediency is his rule of right. He is a despot, to the limit of his power, over the physical universe; and he has a right to be so. But this very right precludes him from despotising over his species: for the argument that applies to one, is of force for all, and to know the natural rights of others, it is only necessary to know our own.

. . .

III. That in a society where no compact, or regular association existed (supposing such state of society practicable) these rights would equally belong to every individual, is evident. It is demonstrable by reason. It is palpable to sympathy. The only question is – *Whether this equality of rights is surrendered – or rather, whether, in reason and justice, it ought to be surrendered, by civil compact, or political association?*

To answer this question properly, we must consider several others. – 1. *What is the rational object of civil association?* Is it not the general good? – 2. *In what does the general good consist?* Is it not in the security of the rights (and, what necessarily depends upon those rights, the happiness) of the whole? – 3. By what means can civil association best secure those rights? I answer – *first*, by generalizing and ascertaining them; and, *secondly*, by establishing a universal reciprocation; and thus involving the particular good in the good of the whole, and securing the good of the whole by particular interests.

Herein consists, then, the main *distinction between natural* (that is to say, *individual) and social* (or *political) right*. Natural, or original right, is (if I may so express myself) merely *physical*: that is to say, it consists in the mere powers and means of the individual; in the direction and exercise of which he is himself sole umpire. (Hence the impossibility of such a state of society; for judgments will differ, even where judgments are consulted; animal strength and cunning will differ; desires will clash; and the anarchic *Tyranny of Physical Force* must inevitably follow: at least, such will be the case while man continues either what he is, or what he has hitherto been. – I mean not to bar the flight of speculative philosophy. I admit – I uphold the eternal improvability of man. What he may sometime be, if governments do not check his course, it were presumption to determine. What he may not be, bigotry will alone pronounce.) Civil Society, by creating a common interest, establishing reciproca-tions, and binding the respective individuals by mutual pledges, adds to the physical a *moral right*. In other words, it creates Duties commensurate with the Rights; and makes the former the guarantee of the latter. It proceeds, or ought to proceed, upon the inculcation of the maxim – *What I have a* RIGHT *to demand for myself, it is my* DUTY *to secure to others*. Thus, then, the superadded, or artificial rights do not destroy the original. Nature is still paramount: but it is nature *en masse*, instead of individual nature. It is the aggregate of individuals securing its parts, and judging for the whole; instead of leaving those parts to contend, and destroy each other. Its business is not to abrogate rights, but secure them; not to restrict our faculties and enjoyments, but to improve both the one and the other.

. . .

Thus, then, the just and rational object of civil institution is, not to retrench, but to equalize and secure the natural rights of man, by substituting moral arbitration for physical force: that is to say, by instituting tribunals for the regulation of indi-vidual conduct; that whenever supposed rights (that is to say, particular interests) clash, violence may be prevented, and personal differences be decided by aggregate reason. Of this aggregate reason, Law ought to be the epitome, and Magistracy the organ.

It is upon these principles only, that a multitude of individuals can be melted and organized into one harmonious mass. Thus only can they really become a com-munity, or body politic: for where one part tramples, with rude and brutal inso-lence upon another, it is not a body politic, but a state of unequal war. When the arbitrary will of a few, wallowing in wealth and luxury, decides upon the fate, the feelings, the existence of a starving multitude, it is not a compact of civil associa-tion, but a wicked and lawless anarchy, where Violence and Conspiracy usurp the chair of Government, and the caprice of domineering pride is substituted for settled principle.

Under such systems, it is impossible that the general intellect should properly expand, the heart be meliorated, or the condition of the mass improved. Better for man were the rudest barbarism of nature, than such a state of political communion! – better were savage nakedness, and the dowerless freedom of his woods and caves, than the wretched mockery of such a state of civilization and refinement. To such a state of society, however, though but too prevalent, no body of men, no individual, ever voluntarily submitted: and if they had, such submission, instead of being binding upon their posterity, would have been an act of insanity, equally inconsistent with their duties and their rights; and therefore not obligatory upon themselves.

To conclude – It appears to me, fellow-citizens, that the rational object of political society is the promotion of the welfare and happiness of the whole; that the welfare and happiness of the whole depend upon the secure enjoyment of their natural rights; and that, consequently, society ought to protect and preserve those rights entire. It ought to do something more. It ought not merely to *protect*, but to improve the physical, the moral, and intellectual enjoyments, not of a few only, but of the whole population of the state. It ought to expand the faculties, encrease the sympathies, harmonize the passions, and promote the general welfare of mankind. This were national prosperity indeed! – national grandeur, and national glory. All that has hitherto assumed those names, is mockery and cruel insult.

When these principles are invaded, it follows of course, that the injured have a right to demonstrate and seek redress: when they are obstinately and systematically violated, 'obedience becomes a question of prudence, not of morality'; and the people (all gentler means having been found ineffectual) have a right – a firm, inalienable right, to renounce the broken compact, and dissolve the system.

END OF THE SECOND LETTER

LETTER III
ORIGIN AND DISTRIBUTION OF PROPERTY

I. Having contrasted, in the preceding Letter, the principles of Mr. B. and the principles of jacobinism; or, in other words, the principles of the Gothic Custumary and those of Nature, let us trace them through their respective systems, and illustrate their respective operations upon the condition, the morals, and the happiness of man.

'The property of the nation is the nation', says the feudalist; and the principle results from his premises. '*The population of the nation is the nation!*' replies the exulting jacobin; and assenting Nature ratifies the proposition. But in order that we may properly understand the maxim of Mr. B. and all the important conse-quences that would follow, it is necessary to enquire What property, in reality, is? and how that which is called property originated and exists? for property, as it is generally understood, is certainly neither coeval with man, nor an immediate or inevitable consequence of political Society: though, under proper regulations, it is an advantage to which the compacts of society alone could have given birth. In

· 331 ·

this research, unlike the essential subject of the former letter, history affords much light. . . .

. . . for History, though never to be admitted as the *mistress*, is an important *handmaid* of political science. In other words, history is to be consulted, not for *precedents* that must be followed, but for *examples* that should be weighed: not for dogmas to restrain, but for circumstances to illustrate, our speculations: and, as far as they extend, for land-marks to direct our course. In short, it is a mere repertory of facts, of all descriptions – the good, the bad, and the equivocal; . . .

II. Having premised this much, on the uses of history in political discussion, I shall proceed with a brief and general review of the progress of society, with reference to the origin and distribution of property, and its influence on the general liberty and happiness of the human race.

1. The simplest condition of man we are acquainted with, and that, in all probability, out of which every other state has arisen, by a series of progressive *innovations*, is *the Savage State*.[12] In this first stage of Society, an almost absolute equality prevails. The earth uncultivated, or nearly so, is of course regarded as the common mother, rather than the private property, of the tribe that wanders over its surface; and the wild animals it feeds, and the spontaneous produce it affords, are the unquestioned right of the individual whose fortune, or whose assiduity, secures the first possession. Distinctions of power, under such circumstances, could only rise from inequalities of strength or intellect; and these must, of necessity, be small. . . .

These rude tribes, have their assemblies, their orators, their legislators, to whom they look with reverence in cases of public exigency; and whose power encreases in proportion as common dangers call for united exertions. The authority of the chief may, in some instances, become almost absolute, in times of war: but it leads to no permanent distinctions of wealth or influence; and the ideas of property are scarcely extended beyond the right of the individual to the trophies he may gain in the field, and the temporary affluence resulting from the fortune of the chase.

---

[12] Philosophical historians of the eighteenth century commonly distinguished four stages in the evolution of humankind, roughly distinguished by the mode of economic subsistence, and yielding appropriate different conceptions of property. They were hunting and fishing, pastoral agriculture (herding), arable agriculture (farming), and commerce. See Adam Smith, *Lectures on Jurisprudence*, ed. R. L. Meek, D. D. Raphael and P. G. Stein (Oxford University Press, 1978) *(1762–3 cycle)*, §27. Some writers further distinguished savages (hunters), who do not recognise property, from barbarians (shepherds), who do, but still lacked a literary culture and an ability to perpetuate a civilisation. See, e.g. Chris Berry, *The Social Theory of the Scottish Enlightenment* (Edinburgh University Press, 1997), pp. 93ff.

2. Passing from the savage to *the Pastoral State*, we make a stride of some importance in the progress of government, of civilization, and property. Man having tamed a useful animal, led it to pasture, protected it from beasts of prey, and contributed to the multiplication of its species and the rearing of its feeble young, acquires the same property in his flock, and upon the same principle, that the savage acquired in the game he had ensnared or killed. Still, however, the property extends only to the animal. The earth, and its vegetation, continue the common inheritance of all: and for this, for reasons which, growing out of the nature of things, operate upon the rude minds that could not explain them. He who tames and protects a stock or herd, of whatever description, claims, by appropriation, only the profit of his own industry; and, generally speaking, does but grasp the exclusive benefit of that which, but for his assiduity, would not have, *beneficially*, existed. But in the earth, which he has not laboured – in the vegetation he has not cultivated, he can have no exclusive property. The former is a common element, upon which every individual has a common right to employ his faculties; – the latter, the spontaneous gift of Nature to all her children, in which all have a common inheritance.

Even in flocks and herds, the property of the individual, in *such a state*, may extend to usurpation: for if it were possible for one man to *reclaim* (as it is called) and monopolize the whole race of useful animals running wild in a particular district, he could have no moral right to do so: because he would, thereby, preclude all others from their common right of exerting their faculties, for their own advantage, upon an important part of gifts of nature. – It cannot be too often repeated, that *Property is the fruit of useful industry; but the means of being usefully industrious are the common right of all.*

Property, in this state, it is obvious, though grounded in the same principle (possession, resulting from the exertion of individual faculty upon the common gifts of nature) differs, in some essential characters, from property in the state before described. Among savage tribes, there is, indeed, scarcely any thing which, in the general sense, can be regarded as property at all: in a nation of shepherds, it assumes a sort of permanency, and a capacity for accumulation. It becomes, accordingly, a temptation to violence, on the one hand; and an object of jealous protection, on the other. Hence the necessity of more intimate association, and firmer compact. . . .

But whatever may be the advantages of these rude states of society, in point of liberty and independence, they are little calculated for permanent establishment. While the earth remains uncultivated, the subsistence of man, even in the most genial climates, is scanty and precarious; the social passions are languid and joyless; the faculties are sluggish; the intellect slumbers,[13] as it were; and all the nobler and finer feelings of our nature, lie benumbed in the oblivious bog of indolence: the endearing inter-courses of friendship are scarcely known; the reciprocations of relationship are but a sad chain of domestic tyranny and servitude; and even the dearest and sweetest of those connections which give an interest, and a zest, to civilized life, exhibits, in the hut of the savage or the barbarian, a disgusting picture, that paints, beyond the force of words, the melancholy conviction, that *liberty, without moral and intellectual improvement, is only a privilege of the strong to tyrannise over the feeble* . . . Yet so imperfectly does . . . the soil administer to their simple wants, that an enlargement of territory is fought for with as much sanguinary ferocity, for the poor privilege of hunting and fishing, as by more civilized barbarians, for fame, and glory, and power and increased revenue. – In short the savage and pastoral states, are states of almost incessant war; . . .

3. Such, my fellow-citizens! are the miserable and degrading circumstances atten-dant upon these rude conditions of society. From these circumstances, nothing can redeem mankind but the steady cultivation of the earth. The earth is cultivated; and the face of society is changed, and nature itself subdued and altered. But is the condition of the mass improved? Are their real enjoyments increased? – their actual sufferings diminished? Are there no circumstances attendant upon the partial pros-perity which cultivation has ultimately produced, more bitter in their consequences, to the laborious multitude, than all the miseries of penurious equality? Certainly, at least, it is, that agriculture, from the very first, if it brought its blessings upon the world, brought, with them, its mischiefs, also.

. . .

Not to dwell upon partial evils, let us examine the general operation of the agricul-tural system: admitting, in the outset, that its advantages are positive and inherent, and the evils it has produced, generally speaking, adventitious only; and, therefore, capable of correction.

III. An immediate, or, at least, a necessary consequence of the agricultural state, is the appropriation of land: an appropriation which, duly understood, and under proper restrictions, rests upon the joint foundations of general expediency, and of individual right. The basis of property has already been defined, as *the right of the*

[13] Many writers, most famously Hume particularly in the *Essay* 'Of Refinement in the Arts', argued that the human intellect developed as a result of the stimulation provided by the social environment. One of the advantages of the emergence of a commercial society was that it stimulated the intellect to make calculations, seek advantages, make innovations, refine taste, etc.

individual to the advantages resulting from his own industry and faculties, employed upon the common elements of nature. By the same right, therefore, that the savage appropriates the game transfixed with his dart, and the shepherd challenges the stock he has reclaimed and pastured, the cultivator, also, claims, as his own, the produce of the land he has cultivated: for the earth is a common element, in which he had a common inheritance; and the fruit it produces, under his cultivation, is the creation of his industry. Still, however, the earth itself was the common element: and the property, in this state, consisted, not in the land, but in the produce. For the foundation of what is called Landed Property, we must appeal, not to physical or abstract right, but to moral and political expediency.

In some particular cases, indeed, if we may rely upon the authorities that record the fact, agriculture has been the joint concern of the whole state; and the common territory has been cultivated by common labour. In all instances, the perfect appropriation of the land must have been gradually effected: for it is difficult for man, in any state, to dispossess himself of the idea of a right of common inheritance in the earth which he inhabits. The Germans, in the days of Tacitus, had made, in their rude way, considerable progress in the arts of government. Society was separated into casts and classes; and four distinct orders accurately defined the degrees of honour and of servitude among those fierce barbarians[14]: yet we learn, that 'in cultivating the soil, they did not settle on one particular spot. The lands were taken possession of, in turns, by the whole community, according to the number of cultivators; and were divided among them, according to their respective ranks. . . . The arable lands were changed every year; and the pastures remained uncultivated: . . .'[15]

. . . But wherever the agricultural system preponderated, and the product of cultivation became a principal object, it is scarcely possible that experience should not soon suggest the general expediency of permanent possession in the individual who was to cultivate: for man is a selfish animal; and earth, that it may be abundant in

---

[14] Some of those Scots writers who had theorised about the stages of social development had seen the differentiation of social ranks or classes as an integral part of the process. Notably John Millar, *The Origin of the Distinction of Ranks* (London, 1779), and Adam Smith, *Theory of the Moral Sentiments* (London, 1759). On this see Berry, *Social Theory*, p. 99ff.

[15] Thelwall's account draws on Julius Ceasar's observations on the Germans in his *The Gallic Wars* and on the Roman historian Tacitus' *Germania* written at the end of the first century AD. This is the classic source used by early modern social historians who wanted to know about the world outside Rome. Tacitus himself writes about the warlike and free Germans acutely conscious of the loss of Republican liberty at that time in Rome itself.

production, requires, not only the plough and the seed, that prepare the particular harvest, but the manuring toil that improves it from generation to generation.

But though *production*, of necessity, became a principal object, *distribution*, in the early stages of agricultural society, would not be neglected. The ideas of primitive equality were not obliterated; and the temptations to monopoly were few: and the probability is, that every wandering tribe first taking possession of a district, with a view to cultivation, would, like the original founders of the Roman state, canton out the territory in equal portions: and, thus, would the equality of distribution, reconcile general expediency with the particular interests of the individual, and the principle of common right.

Every thing, indeed, in the rude stages of society, had a tendency to support this equal distribution. Population was thin; and the abundant territory offered to every cultivator more than he could occupy: and even when population increases (as in the agricultural state it naturally will) the case is not materially altered. The degree of knowledge (or rather of ignorance) is nearly uniform. The feebleness of political institution, and the laxity of civil compact, encourage habitual independence. Legislation has not yet become the property of the few: and above all, the inequalities of physical force are not, in these rude beginnings of society, rendered more disproportionate by the exclusive appropriation of arms, the establishment of magazines, for instruments of destruction, to enable the few to plunder and overawe the many; and the employment of selected bands of ruffians, hired first, like mercenaries, and afterwards compelled, like slaves, to perpetrate the robberies, and protect the usurpations of despotic rulers.

Under such circumstances, it is true, the acquisitions of the father would, in the natural course of things, descend to the children: but they would descend under such restrictions as would render permanent property least inconsistent with the common claims of mankind. While any portion of waste land remained, they would feel and act upon the just and natural principle, that territorial property consisted, accurately speaking, in the cultivation – not in the earth; and that, of course, *land uncultivated is still inheritance in common*, and cannot, till labour makes it so, be the peculiar property of any individual. If, therefore, the cultivator had more children than one, the eldest, when he arrived at man's estate, would take possession of a fresh farm; in which example he would be followed by other of his brethren, till it came to the youngest; who, in all probability, the father growing old and feeble, would remain with him, as an assistant, till his death; and would succeed, of course, to the paternal farm. Some relics of this state of society, as judge Blackstone observes, still remain in this country, in the sort of tenure, once prevalent among the Northern nations, and among us, called *Borough-English*; by which the landed property, or 'burgage tenement', descends to the *youngest son.*[16]

When the whole district inhabited by any community, had become appropriated by cultivation, except what was still thought necessary to preserve in common, for the purposes of pasturage [a thing, of course, to be decided, by actual or implied compact, by the whole community]; a different mode of descent arose, by necessity, out of the new circumstances; and domestic migration being no longer practicable, the whole family remained *in a state of dependence* upon the father, and divided the estate at his demise. . . .

IV. From the necessities arising out of these new circumstances, it is evident, that a great and important change must be progressively induced in the condition of the human race. – From this time, we must bid a sad farewell to that equality of landed possession, which, if philosophy did not forbid me to hope, and humanity prohibit me from propagating, philanthropy would impel me to wish. I say, my fellow-citizens! and I call upon you to engrave the maxim on your hearts! that Philosophy and Humanity forbid the propagation of this levelling doctrine. Philosophy forbids it, because the ideas, the habits, the necessities of the present state of social progress – nay, the very circumstances naturally growing out of the system of cultivation, when carried to any high and advantageous extent, render such equality totally impracticable: – Humanity forbids it, because the vain attempt to execute so wild a scheme, must plunge the world into yet unheard-of horrors; must send forth the pretended reformer, armed with the dagger in one hand, and the iron crow in the other, to pillage, murder and destroy; and, after all, to no better end, than to transfer all property from the proud and the polished, the debauched, effeminate and luxurious, to the brutal, the ignorant, and the ferocious; and to constitute, from the vulgar band of plunderers and assassins, a new 'Gothic Custumary' – a new order of proprietors and nobility. But though we ought not – must not sweep down all property in a torrent of blood, let us not 'shrink from the *critical but salutary duty*' of examining the foundations on which it stands, and discriminating clearly between property and plunder – between right and usurpation. Nor let the high and affluent – for there are some among them whose hearts are warm and benevolent, and whose alarms are honest – and to such I address myself – Let not them shrink from

---

[16] [Thelwall's footnote:] William Blackstone's *Commentaries [on the Laws of England]*, Bk II, §6, p. 83. He calls it, indeed, a relick of the pastoral state. But, in the mere pastoral state, no such thing as property is acknowledged.

the well-meant enquiry, nor impoliticly deem the friend of man their foe. If they are just, they have nothing to dread from investigation; and property, like morals, will stand more firm upon the solid foundations of reason and expediency, than upon the 'arbitrary' and mysterious bases of authority and superstition.

. . .

From that state of society, then, and those circumstances of distribution, the contemplation of which led me into this digression, necessarily arose the distinction intended to be marked by the vulgar application of the word Property – that is to say, the distinction between the large proprietor and the small. And this, I conceive, to be the distinction Mr. B. intends to mark by the extravagant exclamation – 'The property of the country is the country'! Indeed, it is impossible he should mean any thing else – for as all mankind (as will be presently shewn) have property – essential property, in the genuine sense of the word, the exclamation would, upon any other interpretation, be totally without meaning. And thus is the political existence or non-existence of man, to be decided by the cube rule that measures his paternal acres, or the arithmetic that strikes a balance in his ledger.

V. But these circumstances were also fraught, in their progress, with still more important consequences. From the inequalities inevitably produced, and the means soon discovered of increasing them; and from the indolence, prodigality, and disasters of some, and the peculiar fortune of others, arose, in process of time, the *distinction of* PROPRIETOR *and* LABOURER. The cultivator, whose farm was too small for the support of himself and family, or who had been obliged to supply some temporary want by bartering away his penurious inheritance, was necessitated, for subsistence, to become the hireling labourer of him whose possessions had increased beyond the limits of individual culture. In this distinction (however natural, and therefore, justifiable in itself), are laid the first foundation of what may be called the *Tyranny of Property*: that is to say – *the power and disposition of the wealthy few, to oppress and plunder the indigent and unprotected many.*

At first, indeed, this unhappy distinction would not be productive of any serious oppression. The proprietors must be too many, and the labourers too few, to give the former any very extensive power of taking advantage of the dependent state of the latter. Their contract would, therefore, be comparatively fair, and grounded in mutual advantage: the workman deriving a full subsistence from his labour; and the employer (himself a labourer also) deriving but little more. Of such a state of reciprocation (growing out of the very nature of things) it would be scarcely reasonable to complain: but when we look upon the consequences which have arisen out of the distinction, and trace the progress of its abuses to their present enormous height, I cannot but repeat the enquiry – *Is the condition of the multitude improved?*

The whole condition of the universe has been materially altered by cultivation. That cultivation has been conducted by the labour and diligence of the mass of mankind. Is it right, then, that a few should monopolize all the advantages of this new state of man, and leave to the toiling multitude only a dark vicissitude of woes – only a sad transition from penurious indolence to laborious wretchedness? It is not right. There is no argument to be devised by all the pensioners in the universe, that can justify such oppression; and the territorial monopolist, who thus grinds and tramples upon the laborious cultivator, without whose toil his vaunted estate would be a barren wilderness, alters the very nature of his tenure, and turns his property into usurpation and plunder.

Let the proprietor reflect upon the nature of his possession – let him reflect upon the genuine basis of property. What is it, after all, but human labour? And who is the proprietor of that labour? – Who, but the individual who labours? As for landed property, I repeat it – it has not its foundations in natural or physical right; but in moral and political expediency. But moral and political expediency refer not to the individual, but to the whole society. That which is expedient for the whole, is politically expedient. The expediency of individual interest, is the expediency of the swindler, and the housebreaker. If monopoly is not encouraged – if the possession of the land is left to flow and descend in its own natural channels, the laws of the country rather restraining than encouraging accumulation; and above all, if labour has its adequate reward, I maintain that the permanent possession of land is morally and politically expedient; because it assists production, without preventing distribution; and thereby benefits the whole human race. But if all this social order is inverted – if accumulation is not only encouraged, but enforced, and if the labourer, the *real cultivator, is* insulted with such wages as are totally insufficient for the decent and comfortable subsistence of himself and family, then (I repeat it and I will abide by the text in all the courts of law to which I can possibly be summoned) that which is miscalled landed property, is the worst of usurpation and plunder.

We have heard much of the Rights of Property, and the Rights of Nations. (Of the Rights of Man, also, we have heard some things, well worthy of serious consideration.) Much also we have heard of the Rights of the Peerage, the Rights of Parliaments, and the Rights of the Crown; let us, for once, enquire a little into the RIGHTS OF LABOURERS: for rights, as labourers, they most undoubtedly have, grounded on the triple basis of *nature*, of *implied compact*, and *the principles of civil association*.

1. As for his *natural* rights – it will be admitted, I suppose, in terms, however it may be denied in practice, that the labourer is a man. As man he is joint heir to the common bounties of nature; and, in all physical and moral justice, is the proprietor, also, of whatever his labour and faculties add to the common stock. Were he still the rude inhabitant of such a state, where the blessings, and the drudgery of cultivation were unknown – the indolent wanderer of the woods and mountains, he would have, as I have shewn, some rights, some inheritance, some means of solace and support; and the imperious land-holder, the great funded proprietor, the prodigal statesman, yea, the sceptered sovereign of the most refined and polished state, who now, from the profits of his toil, banquets in luxury, and lolls on down, would have wandered, in savage nakedness, like himself; would have slept on the same cold earth, and shared in all his penury, and all his hardships.

Whatever were the worth of these rude gifts and accommodations, the very frame and constitution of society has robbed him of them. He comes from the hand of Nature into a state of cultivation; and finds the world of nature destroyed by the world of art. His inheritance is alienated, and his common right appropriated, even before his birth. He appeals to Nature and how does this common parent of us all reply? She answers (through that organ of reason that dwells in every breast) *Society is responsible, in the first place, for an equivalent for that which society has taken away. For the rest, you have still a right to employ your faculties for your own advantage; and, in the reciprocations of society, to receive as much from the toil and faculties of others, as your own toil and faculties threw into the common stock. You have a right to the gratification of the common appetites of Man; and to the enjoyment of your rational faculties. The intercourse of the sexes, and the endearment of relative connection, are your right inalienable. They are the bases of existence; and nothing in existence – no, not even your own direct assent, can, justly, take them away.*

2. Does the employer reject this decision of nature? Does he plead some recent compact between himself and the labourer? *I agreed with you for so much; and I pay you what I agreed!* I answer, that an unjust agreement, extorted by the power of an oppressor, is, morally, and politically, void. Yet such, in a variety of instances, are the compacts between the labourer and the employer. The territorial monopolist dictates the terms upon which he will condescend to employ the disfranchised labourer, from morn to night, in the cultivation of his fields, and the repair of his hedges and ditches. Does the latter demur about the price – *Fellow! there are many labourers and few employers. If you do not choose to drudge through the whole day for half a meal, go home to your family, and starve there altogether. If* you *will not work for half a loaf,*

there are others that will: and if you CONSPIRE *together to get a whole one, we will send you to the house of correction!!!* Is this a compact, or a tyrannous usurpation?

But there is a compact – a sacred compact, implied in the very distinction of labourer and employer: And the terms of this compact are to be decided, not by the power of the one, and the wretchedness of the other, but by the reason of the thing, and the rules of moral justice. This reason, and these rules, call upon us to appreciate, with impartiality, the comparative value of capital and of labour; since the former, without the latter, could *never* be productive; and the latter, without the former, in the present state of society, cannot have the means of production. Such an estimate, fairly made, would place the labourer in a very different condition from that to which he has generally been condemned. Such an estimate would teach us, that the labourer has a right to a share of the produce, not merely equal to his support, but, proportionate to the profits of the employer.

3. This argument of implied compact is, also, supported by the very principles upon which all civil association rests. Mankind, when they abandon their woods and savage independence, abandon them for a common, not for a particular, advantage. They do not consent, that thenceforward the many shall be more wretched; that the few may be better accommodated. No: the object is, to promote the accommodation of the whole. When they give up their common interest in the spontaneous produce of the earth, and yield it to appropriated culture; they mean to increase the comforts and abundance of all, not the luxury and wantonness of a faction. . . .

To conclude – From the whole of this argument, and from all the principles laid down in this and the preceding letter, it results, that the landed proprietor is only a trustee for the community; and although he has a right to compensation for the due management of the deposit, if he monopolizes the advantages, in which all are concerned, and for which all labour, he is guilty of robberies – robbery of [committed by the] rich and powerful upon the defenceless poor.

I have not time – I have not space, to illustrate every principle, as I could desire – else could I call a blush upon the cheek of those who boast the advantages of civilized society – else could I call to view the comparative condition of the naked savage of America, who 'sees his humble lot, the lot of all', and that of the poor, wretched, o'er-toiled, half-starved, ill-clad, and worse-lodged labourer of Britain; who, in the midst of surrounding luxury, splendour, and refinement, rears his half-naked children in savage ignorance, and hears them cry for bread, when bread is not his to give them. The naked savage of America! ! ! – I declare in the very bitterness of sympathy, that to me, the condition of the naked savage appears, by far, more tolerable than that of a large portion, at least, of the laborious classes in this happy, flourishing, cultivated island: blessed as it is with all the salutary institutions, drawn from the old Germanic or Gothic custumary! . . .[17]

What then, it will be said, would you lead us back to savage barbarism? Would you strip Nature of all the embellishments and refinements of civilization, and turn her, wild and naked, again into her woods? – No: I answer, no. I would extend civilization: I would encrease refinement. I would improve the real dignity of Nature. I would clothe her, completely, – magnificently clothe her: but I would not load her with absurd decorations, nor disguise her genuine proportions. I would have her decent, and, if possible, elegant, in every part. . . . It is Mr. B. and his college, who would drive us back into the woods, to learn the arts of civilization and government from the half-naked barbarism of the Goths and Germans. It is Sir W. Blackstone, and the fraternity of Lincoln's Inn, that would refer us, for 'the element and principles of laws, to the custom of the Britons and Germans in the times of Caesar and of Tacitus.' – *Black. Com.* vol. i p. 36.[18] The crime of the Jacobin is, that he looks forward to a state of society more extensive in its refinements – more perfect, and more general in its improvements, than any which has yet been known.

. . .

---

[17] A reference to Locke's famous claim, justifying the private ownership of land, that, as a result of the absence of private property amongst the American Indians, their king 'feeds, lodges and is clad worse than a day Labourer in *England*' (John Locke, *Two Treatises of Government* [1689], Second Treatise, §41).

[18] Blackstone, *Commentaries* Bk I, §1, p. 35.

INDEX

Washington, George, 133
Waterloo, 22
Wedgwood, Josiah, 18
Wesley, Charles, 44
Wesley, John, 44
What is the Third Estate?, 5
Whig Party, 7, 8, 12, 13, 20, 22, 179–80, 182–4, 193
    Yorkshire Whigs, 301
Whitfield, John, 44
Wilkes, John, 51, 276
William the Conqueror, 13, 143, 145, 160
William of Orange, King, 65, 135
Wollstonecraft, Mary, 14, 18, 20, 24, 60, 104–31,
    209, 256
    *Historical and Moral View of the Origin and
        Progress of the French Revolution and
        the Effect it has Produced on Europe*
        (1794), 104
    *Letters written in . . . Sweden, Norway and
        Denmark*, 104
    Mary (1788), 104
    Thoughts on the Education of Daughters
        (1786), 104
    Vindication of the Rights of Men, A (1790),
        104–31
    Vindication of the Rights of Woman (1792),
        105
    Wrongs of Woman, or Maria, 104
    on barbarism, 109
    on beauty, 124–5
    on Burke's depiction of the French
        Revolution, 115–16
    on charity, 108
    on chivalry, 116
    on custom, 107, 110, 111
    on dignity, 110, 123, 131
    on education, 105, 122
    on enthusiasm, 123
    on Europe, 125
    on filial affection, 107
    on friendship, 108
    on liberty, 106–7, 125–6
    on luxury, 115
    on manners, 107
    on marriage, 114
    on men, 122
    on middle class, 114–15
    on morality, 120, 125, 126
    on privileges, 113
    on property, 107, 109, 113–15
        on private interest, 120
    on reason, 107, 126, 130
    on rights, 106–7, 110, 119
    on romance, 116
    on sensibility, 117
    on servility, 115
    on slavery, 109, 129
    on superstition, 108
    on truth, 111
    on virtue, 118, 119
    on women, 114, 115, 124–5
Wooler, T. J., 23
Wordsworth, William, 23, 209
Working classes, 19, 23

Yorke, Henry Redhead, 20